The Democratic Party
AND THE
Politics of Sectionalism,
1941–1948

The Democratic Party

AND THE

Politics of Sectionalism,

1941–1948

ROBERT A. GARSON

Louisiana State University Press
BATON ROUGE

*London School of Economics
and Political Science*

ISBN 0–8071–0070–6
Library of Congress Catalog Card Number 73–93121
Copyright © 1974 by Louisiana State University Press
All rights reserved
Manufactured in the United States of America

Designed by Dwight Agner. Set in 11/13 Linotype Caledonia,
and printed and bound by The Colonial Press Inc.,
Clinton, Massachusetts.

For my mother and father

Contents

Preface

THE METAMORPHOSIS of the Democratic party during the 1920s from a largely rural to a predominantly urban organization was often a painful and baffling experience for white southerners, who had constituted the backbone of the party since Reconstruction. Nevertheless, the vast majority of Dixie Democrats rapidly reconciled themselves to this transformation during the Great Depression of the following decade. Dire economic adversity, with its consequential social dislocation, prompted southerners to discard their preoccupations with Prohibition and fundamentalist religion. After 1933 they resolved to assist Franklin D. Roosevelt revitalize the party and to concentrate on overcoming the suffering and misery that enveloped every community in the nation.

The majority of southerners, who were understandably and correctly concerned about the immediate problems of unemployment and declining prices, did not fully realize that they were irrevocably submerging their own special authority and preoccupations for the greater interest of the party. They were content to sacrifice many of their cherished credos and interests in the attempt to cope with the new emergency. This sense of nationwide partisan cohesion gave both the president and his party a sense of confidence and ideological commitment that had not been apparent since the early days of Woodrow Wilson's presidency. Indeed, by 1936 the party could boast so much of its unity of purpose that the Democratic convention readily abrogated its once hallowed two-thirds rule for the nomination on the grounds that the party "is no longer a sectional party; it has become a great national party."

Yet only twelve years later, when the nation had survived without serious political scars a depression and a cataclysmic world war, southerners no longer expressed adulation for their historic party. During the war, but more particularly afterward, they had attempted to halt and possibly even reverse the thrust of the economic and social reforms initiated by Roosevelt and his successor, Harry S. Truman. The New Deal, they argued, had been a necessary weapon in the battle against the slump. They maintained, however, that it was unnecessary and even prodigal to continue to increase the powers of the federal government when the nation's economy was healthy and prosperous. But it was not social reform per se that was anathema to many old-line Dixie Democrats. Far more traumatic was that the Democratic party had become a political association in which labor unions, industrial workers, liberal intellectuals, and, above all, dispossessed Negroes had come to predominate, while, apparently, white southerners, the onetime nucleus of the party, were playing an increasingly subordinate role. Furthermore, under the leadership of President Truman the party had resolved to sponsor a civil rights program that threatened to subvert the South's racial system. It was clear by 1948 that southerners could never expect to revive the authority which they had enjoyed in the early part of the century. Indeed, this change can be illustrated well by contrasting the euphoria of the 1936 Democratic National Convention with the bitter divisiveness of the same assembly twelve years later. At the 1948 convention two delegations from Dixie walked out, while nearly all the remaining delegates refused to support the incumbent president. Southerners had only harsh words for the party leadership. According to one veteran politician, southerners had "been buffeted around long enough and they are not going to stand for it any longer."

This book attempts to examine how and why the Democratic party transformed itself from a great national party in 1936 to a sectional party just over a decade later. It is confined to those domestic questions that affected the South directly. Its focus is largely on political events in Washington, their repercussions in Dixie, and the way in which these processes influenced the style and content of southern politics. It will be shown that as Democratic presidents intensified their calls for social reform, southern conservatives subtly but discernibly resorted to the use of sectional rhetoric, rather than substantive argument, to combat the growth of government paternalism. The South became increasingly self-conscious of its peculiar political status within the nation. Even the younger politicians, some of whom had associated themselves with the growth of an indigenous liberalism during the war, were wary of continuing to support the party that appeared hostile to Dixie's historic posture toward the Negro. This new particularism, however, only served to convince party professionals from the North that Dixie was politically dispensable. They prevailed upon Truman to base his political strategies on the needs of the urban coalition and, concomitantly, to ignore any possible political consequences below the Potomac. These tactics finally convinced those southerners anxious to preserve their own brand of *Herrenvolk* democracy that they should either form a new, regionally based party or align themselves with those onetime bêtes noires of the South, the Republicans. Whatever courses southerners subsequently took, the Democratic party was never again upheld as the embodiment of race, country, God, and southern womanhood.

There are two language usages in this book that should be mentioned here. First, I have defined the South in this study as the eleven states which composed the Confederacy from 1861 to 1865: Alabama, Arkansas, Florida, Georgia, Louisiana, Mississippi, North Carolina, South Carolina, Tennessee, Texas, and Virginia. Occasionally when other states have been included, particularly in statistical data, I have drawn appropriate attention. Conversely, all the other states are conveniently grouped together as the North, although, as will be apparent, the North often will denote the metropolitan states. Furthermore, I usually have not mentioned the party affiliation of southerners, since all of them discussed here were Democrats. Second, I have been ruthlessly subjective in my use of the words *liberal* and *conservative*. Basically, for the purpose of this study I have defined a liberal as a person who broadly accepted the precepts of Franklin Roosevelt's New Deal and, later, his so-called economic bill of rights. Conservatives, for all intents and purposes, opposed these programs for social reform. I hope that the more subtle distinctions will emerge in the text.

This book could not have been written without the aid and encouragement of a number of persons and organizations. I am particularly indebted to the Department of History at Louisiana State University, which provided me with both a base and sustenance during my year in the South. I was particularly fortunate to come under the tutelage of Professor T. Harry Williams, who shared with me both his insights into and his enthusiasm for southern history. I should also like to thank the staff of the Harry S. Truman Library who made my month's stay at Independence both rewarding and enjoyable and the Harry S. Truman Library Institute for National and International Affairs which provided a generous research grant-in-aid. The Social Science Research Council and the United States–United Kingdom Education Commission also provided financial aid for my travels in the United States. The staffs of the libraries mentioned in my bibliography of manuscript sources all provided invaluable help. Jonathan Daniels and Senator J. Strom Thurmond permitted me to examine their private papers, and Mrs. Olin Johnston allowed me access to those of her late husband. The staff of the University of Kentucky Library kindly microfilmed relevant portions of the Alben W. Barkley collection which I was unable to examine in person. I would also like to acknowledge the diligent editing of Marie Carmichael of the Louisiana State University Press.

This book emerged from a doctoral dissertation written under the scrupulous supervision of Dr. William Letwin at the London School of Economics. His stimulating teaching has left a lasting impression. My colleagues in the Department of American Studies at the University of Keele have provided a felicitous ambiance in which to work, and Richard Maidment, perhaps unknowingly, contributed some valuable ideas. Finally, I have been extremely fortunate to have had the support of Yvonne, my wife, who always helped me maintain a detached and even humorous perspective. Her sensitivity was even more valuable than her considerable labors at the typewriter and at innumerable libraries.

CHAPTER ONE

From the Grand Coalition
to the Fragile Coalition,
1933–1942

Iᴛ ᴍᴀʏ not have been solely the cold, biting wind that sent shivers down the spines of those southerners who were fortunate enough to attend Franklin Delano Roosevelt's inauguration on March 4, 1933. The last Democrat to take that solemn oath sixteen years earlier had been Woodrow Wilson, a president who probably had done more to rehabilitate the South politically and socially than any other person since the Civil War. It seemed that the new president might follow in those illustrious footsteps. He, like Wilson, had smashed the Republicans' electoral hegemony and seemed to possess those qualities that befitted a chief executive and party leader. Roosevelt was certainly a welcome contrast to Al Smith, the previous Democratic nominee for president. Smith had left his party practically in ruins by dint of his openly flouted Catholicism, his penchant for alcohol, and a cockney East Side accent that advertised his humble tenement upbringing. On the other hand, Roosevelt, the country squire from upstate New York, seemed to have that essential ambiance of aloofness and propriety, combined with a sense of political dedication, that old-line southern politicians reputedly so admired. These were certainly the very qualities that Woodrow Wilson, who was something of a folk hero south of the Potomac, had himself possessed. And, for those who liked to stretch their imaginations a little—and the economic crisis would surely permit some inventive license—it could be said that FDR resembled Wilson in his facial characteristics too.[1]

Nevertheless, the early euphoria soon altered its character, perhaps even declined somewhat. Dixie Democrats soon realized that they would not enjoy the same relationship with the new president that they had experienced under Woodrow Wilson. Even before his inauguration Roosevelt had indicated preference for the advice of intellectuals and professional social workers over that of southern stalwarts. There was no *eminence grise* in the White House who hailed from Dixie. Clearly his close advisers and cabinet members did not come from the same mold as Wilson's entourage. The new cabinet included only three southerners, none of whom was particularly influential in framing domestic policies. And his brain trust was dominated by northern academics, most of whom advocated a vast extension in the powers of the federal government. Nevertheless, southerners still exercised a preeminent influence in Congress and were destined to play a strategic role on Capitol Hill such as they and their forebears had done in the early days of the New Freedom.

Although the legislation of the first hundred days did not bear the stamp of traditional southern ideas on economic individualism and governmental circumscription, most southerners welcomed the establishment of those agencies that sought to alleviate the worst scars of the depression and to rationalize industry and agriculture. Dixie Democrats, like other Americans, were prepared to abandon many long cherished credos in return for a massive mobilization of the nation's resources against widespread unemployment and hunger. They recognized that their constituents, who had so often in the past

1 David Burner, *The Politics of Provincialism: The Democratic Party in Transition, 1918–1932* (New York, 1968), 206–16; James MacGregor Burns, *Roosevelt: The Lion and the Fox* (New York, 1956), 3–46, 163–64; Frank Freidel, *F.D.R. and the South* (Baton Rouge, 1965), chap. 1.

viewed the centralization of economic and political power with suspicion, were clamoring for relief and that neglecting demands of this kind might well result in repudiation at the polls. There was an added incentive for their warm embrace of the early New Deal. Numerous jobs were being created within the new relief agencies. As members of Congress generally recommended personnel for these posts, they were able through their powers of patronage to form a substantial and loyal political following in their constituencies.[2]

Even though the early New Deal was unquestionably popular in the South, certain elements criticized it in its embryonic stages.[3] Opposition came from a variety of sources and for a number of reasons. There were some politicians, particularly in Congress, who were unwilling to shed their allegiance to Wilsonian policies of economic decentralization. Foremost in this category were Senators Harry F. Byrd and Carter Glass of Virginia and Josiah W. Bailey of North Carolina. They believed that the remedy to the depression lay not in price supports and guaranteed minimum wages, but in a restoration of free competition, unencumbered by either governmental authority or monopolies. Senator Bailey echoed the view of this group when he stated that "the accepted doctrine for one hundred and fifty years is that fundamental economic laws are natural laws, having the same source as physical laws." Thus, former Wilsonian Progressives and their political descendants condemned the new administration for embarking upon programs that were

2 Arthur M. Schlesinger, Jr., *The Age of Roosevelt, II: The Coming of the New Deal* (Boston, 1959), 554–55; James T. Patterson, *Congressional Conservatism and the New Deal* (Lexington, 1967), 4–11; Jack B. Key, "Henry B. Steagall: The Conservative as Reformer," *Alabama Review*, XVII (July, 1964), 198–209; Walter J. Heacock, "William B. Bankhead and the New Deal," *Journal of Southern History*, XXI (August, 1955), 347–59.

3 For the New Deal's general popularity among farmers and workers see: John Dean Minton, "The New Deal in Tennessee, 1932–1938" (Ph.D. dissertation, Vanderbilt University, 1959), 178, 210–14; Lionel V. Patenaude, "The New Deal and Texas" (Ph.D. dissertation, University of Texas, 1953), 239; George B. Tindall, *The Emergence of the New South, 1913–1945* (Baton Rouge, 1967), 505–12.

apparently without precedent and that introduced policies to hamper the operations of a free market.[4]

There were southerners, however, whose preoccupation with laissez faire was less altruistic. Some businessmen and office-holders, who were sympathetic with local business interests, condemned such agencies as the National Recovery Admin-istration (NRA) and, later, the National Labor Relations Board on the grounds that they deprived southern industry and com-merce of essential economies. Manufacturers claimed that the provisions in the NRA establishing minimum wages and pro-tecting the right of workers to form unions deprived them of the edge they enjoyed over their competitors in the North, where wages were higher and unionism was more widespread. Indeed, this uneasiness resulted in the formation of special business associations dedicated to combating New Deal re-forms. Perhaps the most important of these associations was the Southern States Industrial Council, founded in 1934. This or-ganization, with headquarters in Nashville, Tennessee, con-cerned itself with preserving the peculiar interests of southern industry and business. It grew rapidly in membership, volume of disapprobation, and scope of criticism. While in its early years the council confined itself to economic matters, it would soon be a focal organization in the defense of an emergent southernism.[5]

A third source of opposition to the Roosevelt administration came from a small group of southerners who felt that the New Deal, irrespective of its short-term economic rewards, was threatening to disturb the entire fabric of their region's social structure. The Democratic administration, these southerners be-lieved, was unduly sympathetic to labor unionism, reform of the sharecropping system, and, worst of all, the aspirations of

4 Otis L. Graham, *An Encore for Reform: The Old Progressives and the New Deal* (New York, 1967), 68; John R. Moore, *Senator Josiah William Bailey of North Carolina* (Durham, 1968), 91.
5 Minton, "The New Deal in Tennessee," 134–36; Raymond Wolters, *Negroes and the Great Depression: The Problem of Economic Recovery* (Westport, Conn., 1970), 98–103.

the southern Negro. This distinctively southern group, which was poorly organized, was distinguished by two qualities. First, its attacks on the New Deal were particularly emotional and demagogic, and, second, unlike those who opposed the New Deal on economic grounds, it invoked continually symbols of southernism and sectionalism in attacks on the administration. Thus, while conservatives, such as Josiah Bailey and Carter Glass, railed against the New Deal for flouting economic and constitutional precepts, these professional southerners condemned the president for his insensitivity, indeed, even his betrayal, of the South's historical legacies.

The critics who raised the race issue and other symbols of southern solidarity were a motley assortment. They included John H. Kirby, a Houston oil and lumber millionaire, who formed the Southern Committee to Uphold the Constitution, and Governor Eugene Talmadge of Georgia, who was as famous for his red suspenders as he was for his confinement of striking textile workers into "concentration camps."[6] They were tacitly supported by people who resented the participation of Negroes in relief programs and by a minority of white tenants and landlords who believed that the Agricultural Adjustment Administration (AAA) was responsible for the formation of the Southern Tenant Farmers' Union, which for a short time challenged sharecropping, the South's antipathy to unionism, and Jim Crow itself.[7] However, white supremacy was their main springboard. For example, at a convention held in Macon, Georgia, in January, 1936, to unify these forces, the race issue was emphasized by the distribution of scurrilous photographs

6 Sarah M. Lemmon, "Governor Eugene Talmadge and the New Deal," *James Sprunt Studies in History and Political Science,* XXXIX (Chapel Hill, 1957), 153–62; Reinhard H. Luthin, *American Demagogues: Twentieth Century* (Boston, 1954), 191–95; Herman Talmadge, interview with author, September, 1969.

7 On the AAA and the Southern Tenant Farmers' Union, see David E. Conrad, *The Forgotten Farmers: The Story of the Sharecroppers in the New Deal* (Urbana, 1965); Donald H. Grubbs, *Cry from the Cotton: The Southern Tenant Farmers' Union and the New Deal* (Chapel Hill, 1971).

of Eleanor Roosevelt, the president's wife, linked arm in arm with two Negroes.[8]

Although opposition to the New Deal in the South was vocal and, in certain sections of the community, even widespread, it is important to recognize that the vast majority of southerners did not share the views of either the orthodox fiscal conservatives or of the race-baiters. They recognized that the federal government was daily breaking new paths in its attempts to soften the hardship in country and town. Moreover, the administration did not seem, at least in the earlier years of the depression, to tread in areas of southern sensitivity. Roosevelt was a partisan Democrat, who deliberately consulted with congressional leaders and wielded his powers of patronage judiciously, yet harshly. He had given in to southerners in the Cotton Section of the AAA in his purge of counselors who had wanted to reform Dixie's agricultural system. And, above all, he had made only symbolic gestures to black leaders, who wanted the president to acknowledge their special difficulties by appointing Negroes to senior positions in the various agencies. Most white southerners recognized that segregation remained unscarred and that Negroes still depended largely on the goodwill of whites in the various agencies. In short, the vast majority of white southerners were more impressed by the benefits of Roosevelt's policies than they were disturbed by their assumed shortcomings.[9]

The widespread acceptance of the New Deal below the Potomac was firmly underlined in the election campaign of 1936.

8 New York *Times*, January 5, 30, 1936; Lemmon, "Governor Eugene Talmadge and the New Deal," 164–65; George Wolfskill, *The Revolt of the Conservatives: A History of the American Liberty League, 1934–1940* (Boston, 1962), chap. 7; Patenaude, "The New Deal and Texas," 154–63.
9 Allen F. Kifer, "The Negro under the New Deal, 1933–1941" (Ph.D. dissertation, University of Wisconsin, 1961), *passim*; Leslie H. Fishel, "The Negro in the New Deal Era," *Wisconsin Magazine of History*, XLVIII (Winter, 1964–65), 111–21; Wolters, *Negroes and the Great Depression, passim*; Arthur M. Schlesinger, Jr., *The Age of Roosevelt, III: The Politics of Upheaval* (Boston, 1960), 421; Walter White, *A Man Called White* (New York, 1948), 169–70.

In Georgia Eugene Talmadge was resoundingly defeated at the polls in his race for the Senate against Richard B. Russell, a loyal New Dealer.[10] At the Democratic National Convention later that year nearly all southern delegates agreed to the abolition of the two-thirds rule. It was this rule, of course, that had in the past guaranteed southerners a veto in the nominating process—and had been responsible for defeating Al Smith at the 1924 Democratic convention. However, in 1936 southerners felt that Roosevelt had destroyed the last vestiges of sectionalism and had united the party beyond all dreams. The Democratic party, they agreed, was now a cohesive, unified movement and cumbersome rules had consequently been rendered superfluous. Senator Bennett Champ Clark of Missouri, chairman of the Committee on Rules at the convention, could proudly boast that "the Democratic Party is no longer a sectional party; it has become a great national party."[11]

Senator Clark's confident proclamation was borne out by the results of the 1936 election. In his resounding victory Roosevelt had managed to rally the mass of urban workers and southern Democrats behind him. Indeed, the Wilson coalition of 1916 paled beside the new Roosevelt coalition. It seemed to contemporaries that the schism between northern urban and rural southern wings of the party during the twenties had been relegated to the dusty pages of history. The party, despite whispers of discontent from certain quarters, had at last found unity and meaning in the person of Franklin Roosevelt.

Southern Democrats soon realized, however, that the president's massive victory could augur ill. Roosevelt would have won without a single electoral vote from Dixie. In the big cities

---

10 New York *Times*, March 5, 12, 1936; Joseph L. Bernd, *Grass Roots Politics in Georgia* (Atlanta, 1960), 7–8.
11 Democratic National Committee, *Official Report of the Proceedings of the Democratic National Convention, 1936*, p. 191; Myron G. Blalock to Oveta C. Hobby, April 17, 1948, in Box 117, Tom Connally Papers, Manuscripts Division, Library of Congress, Washington, D.C.; Tom Connally and Alfred Steinberg, *My Name Is Tom Connally* (New York, 1954), chap. 22; Schlesinger, *The Politics of Upheaval*, 580–81.

blue-collar workers and Negroes turned out in large numbers to vote for the president. Until 1936 southern Democrats had constituted the mainstay of the Democratic party. They had provided large sums of money for campaigns and had influenced, even determined, the making of the party platform. No Democratic candidate had ever planned election strategies without the full and expected support of the South. But Roosevelt's overwhelming victory suggested that a Democratic candidate could thenceforth make political calculations based on expectations of support from cities, and not necessarily from the courthouses below the Mason-Dixon Line. Moreover, labor unions contributed substantially to the campaign chest, while subventions from business interests slumped drastically. And, portentously for the South, Negroes, despite misgivings about Roosevelt's caution on civil rights issues, abandoned their ties with the Republican party and flocked to the Democrats. It seemed, therefore, that workers and Negroes would play an increasingly influential role within the party. Thus, the grand coalition of urban workers and southerners marked also the beginning of the political emancipation of the national Democratic party from the grip of southerners.[12]

Both the president and leading conservatives within the party recognized that they were no longer politically interdependent. Roosevelt believed that his mandate in 1936 would enable him to press harder for reform legislation and to remove

12 Samuel Lubell, *The Future of American Politics* (London, 1952), 54–63; Samuel J. Eldersveld, "The Influence of Metropolitan Party Pluralities in Presidential Elections since 1920: A Study of Twelve Key Cities," *American Political Science Review*, XLIII (December, 1949), 1189–206; Carl Degler, "American Political Parties and the Rise of the City: An Interpretation," *Journal of American History*, LI (June, 1964), 41–59; James A. Harrell, "Negro Leadership in the Election Year 1936," *Journal of Southern History*, XXXIV (November, 1968), 546–84; Schlesinger, *The Politics of Upheaval*, 598–600; Louise Overacker, "Labor's Political Contributions," *Political Science Quarterly*, LIV (March, 1939), 58–63; Louise Overacker, "Campaign Funds in the Presidential Election of 1936," *American Political Science Review*, XXXI (June, 1937), 473–98; William H. Riker, "The CIO in Politics, 1936–1946" (Ph.D. dissertation, Harvard University, 1948), 96–97, 284–86.

all possible obstacles to his designs. Thus, in 1937 he urged Congress to pass legislation that would enable him to "pack" the Supreme Court and to rationalize policy making within executive agencies by the creation of the executive office of the president. He also called for the establishment of national labor standards.

These proposals disturbed several Democratic leaders, including such formerly loyal southerners as Senator Tom Connally of Texas and Vice President John Nance Garner. They felt that Roosevelt's recommendations, particularly on the Supreme Court, marked an end to the president's conviction that agreement between the various sections of his party should be maintained. Roosevelt, they supposed, either expected members of his party to concur with him in all circumstances or felt that the support of certain members was dispensable. In fact, this latter suspicion was confirmed in 1938 when Roosevelt personally undertook to secure the defeat of Senators Walter F. George of Georgia, Ellison D. Smith of South Carolina, and Millard E. Tydings of Maryland in their respective primary races. The president, it seemed, was seeking not only to extend the New Deal but to remold the Democratic party into a cohesive, disciplined party. While he still welcomed the support of the South, he would no longer bow to its interests or to its political spokesmen for the sake of party harmony.[13]

Southern congressmen responded to these developments by asserting their independence in the division lobbies. They suc-

13 Patterson, *Congressional Conservatism and the New Deal*, 86–94; Burns, *Roosevelt: The Lion and the Fox*, 291–315; Connally and Steinberg, *My Name Is Tom Connally*, 189; William E. Leuchtenburg, *Franklin D. Roosevelt and the New Deal* (New York, 1963), 232–39; Samuel I. Rosenman (comp.), *The Public Papers and Addresses of Franklin D. Roosevelt* (New York, 1941), VII, 391–400; A. Blair Crownover, "Franklin D. Roosevelt and the Primary Campaigns of the 1938 Congressional Election" (Senior thesis, Princeton University, 1955), 69–132; Bernard F. Donahoe, *Private Plans and Public Dangers: The Story of FDR's Third Nomination* (Notre Dame, 1965), 74–86; Luther H. Zeigler, "Senator Walter George's 1938 Campaign," *Georgia Historical Quarterly*, XLIII (December, 1959), 333–52; Tindall, *The Emergence of the New South*, 628; Virginius Dabney, *Below the Potomac* (New York, 1942), chap. 2.

cessfully delayed passage of the fair labor standards and executive reorganization bills and became more outspoken in their criticisms of the administration. But it is important to notice that the style and language of their criticism was that used by most other conservatives. They argued that the president was usurping his powers and that his policies were slowly destroying free competition. They did not, at this date, condemn Roosevelt for threatening to disturb the traditions and life-styles of the South. Admittedly, sectional rhetoric was occasionally used, particularly during debates on the fair labor standards bill, which affected Dixie more than any other region. But generally the references to the South were more reminiscent of the southern chambers of commerce than of the committed Dixie rebel. Moreover, there was no discernible southern position on all these issues.[14]

An interesting episode in the winter of 1937 illustrates the generally nonsectional orientation of most southern senators. In December Senator Bailey drew up plans to produce a document, styled as a conservative manifesto, that would serve as an ideological yardstick for congressional conservatives. Together with nine other Senate Democrats from both North and South and two Republicans, Bailey hoped to create a bipartisan coalition to scrutinize all the administration's proposals. The promulgators of the manifesto demanded that all future legislation should recognize the need for tax reductions, a balanced budget, and a viable profits system. It is important to notice, however, that this first formal attempt to thwart the New Deal transcended regional lines and avoided sectional references. The declaration of principles, drafted mainly by Bailey and Republican Senators Arthur H. Vandenberg of Michigan and Warren Austin of Vermont, was given the catholic title of "An Address to the People of the United States." Democratic dissidents from Dixie identified themselves in this document as conservatives, not as southerners. So, although by the time

14 Patterson, *Congressional Conservatism and the New Deal*, 86–94, 149–54, 182–83, 193–98.

Roosevelt sought to purge his party there was indeed a high proportion of disaffected southerners within the Democratic ranks, there was nothing exclusively southern about this group. The manifesto sought to unite critics across class, regional, and party lines. Criticism was not based, as it would be in later years, on the grounds that the South's peculiar civilization had been endangered by the New Deal.[15]

This avoidance of sectional issues generally characterized the efforts of those southern Democrats who hoped to prevent Roosevelt's nomination for a third term. Anti–New Dealers focused their critical energies on the lack of precedence for a third term and defended their quest for a new nominee in the name of tradition. There is no indication in studies of the third-term campaign that Roosevelt's southern opponents argued that his renomination would in any way undermine their region's traditions. Despite their expressed fears of the welfare state, there was no real appraisal of Dixie's allegiance to the Democratic party. Indeed, Roosevelt's failure to purge the party in 1938 may have given dissidents a renewed confidence in their ability to influence policy making. Thus, the third-term controversy was a comparatively mild affair. Roosevelt's opponents, who rallied around Vice President Garner and James Farley, Democratic national chairman, were not prepared to break with the party.[16] As the *Texas Weekly*, an anti–New Deal journal, commented: "The South has no choice, of course, but to continue to support the Democratic party." [17]

Indeed, Roosevelt's critics knew that their views were not shared by the mass of southerners. Democratic officials at the state and county level, with the exception of those in the Byrd organization in Virginia, ignored the advice of their elder states-

---

15 John R. Moore, "Senator Josiah W. Bailey and the 'Conservative Manifesto' of 1937," *Journal of Southern History*, XXXI (February, 1965), 21–39.
16 Donahoe, *Private Plans and Public Dangers*, 96–99; Hugh Ross, "The Third Term Campaign of 1940" (Ph.D. dissertation, Stanford University, 1959), 50–59, 80; Olin D. Johnston to FDR, July 24, 1940, in PPF 2361, Franklin D. Roosevelt Papers, Franklin D. Roosevelt Library, Hyde Park, N.Y.; assorted correspondence, in Box 108, Connally Papers.
17 *Texas Weekly*, February 3, 1940.

men to send uninstructed delegates to the national convention. They recognized that Roosevelt's popularity in Dixie was undiminished.[18] He was, as John Temple Graves remarked, "the Democratic party, the rebel yell, Woodrow Wilson and Robert E. Lee rolled into one," and to defy Roosevelt would be tantamount to repudiating the South's political heritage.[19]

Thus, in 1940 dissident southerners were unable to muster support for their plans to prevent a third-term nomination. Anyway, there was scarcely any reason for southerners to challenge the Democratic president. He had shown unrivaled concern for those who had suffered in the depression and had personalized the office of the president in a way that was probably unprecedented. Above all, he had done nothing in the realm of race relations to offend southern voters. There was, therefore, no apparent cause to surrender their allegiance to the party of their forefathers. The Democratic party in Dixie seemed as secure as ever, and, despite the strength of the urban coalition, FDR had resisted growing demands from that quarter to support protective legislation for Negroes. Southern opposition to the president remained diffuse and unorganized. Anti–New Deal business organizations found themselves out of favor with "little New Deal" administrations in various southern states, and habitual race-baiters could not attract sustained support. Even stalwarts such as Josiah Bailey and Carter Glass remained curious political luxuries in a section that saw no contradiction between supporting these conservative Wilsonians and voting for Roosevelt. Furthermore, these congressional critics attacked the New Deal primarily for its unnecessary emphasis on government paternalism and its growing authority over the economy. And by 1940 they hoped that with the emergence of full employment as a result of the defense crisis the era of political experimentation was drawing to a

18 Ross, "The Third Term Campaign of 1940," 60–63; Josiah W. Bailey to Clyde R. Hoey, April 17, 1940, and Bailey to James Farley, May 15, 1940, in Josiah W. Bailey Papers, Duke University Library, Durham, N.C.; Donahoe, *Private Plans and Public Dangers*, 151–53.

19 John Temple Graves, *The Fighting South* (New York, 1943), 114.

close. Their hallmark was conservatism, not southernism. They argued in economic and constitutional, not sectional, terms. It seemed, therefore, that as long as Roosevelt remained clear of growing pressures from labor and Negro leaders to align himself with the aspirations of the civil rights advocates, then his personal authority, as well as the supremacy of the Democratic party, would remain unchallenged below the Potomac.

The election of 1940 was, of course, overshadowed by the defense crisis. The rapid increase in demand for arms, particularly after the passage of Lend-Lease, reduced dramatically the unemployment rate. Hitler's armies had apparently succeeded where eight years of Roosevelt's New Deal had failed. Pleas of downcast men and women for work in a Works Projects Administration (WPA) project were now replaced by urgent cries from manufacturers for labor. The mood in Washington also changed. The president no longer seemed so preoccupied with finding humane solutions to the problems of unemployment and security. He now emphasized efficiency in government. "Here in Washington, we are thinking in terms of speed and speed now," he told the nation.[20]

The administration's determination to secure the full utilization of manpower and resources was reflected in the growth of ad hoc defense agencies. In 1941 the Office of Production Management (OPM) replaced the old National Defense Advisory Commission as the overseer of industrial production. It was headed by William S. Knudsen, formerly of General Motors, and Sidney Hillman, the principled but nevertheless flexible president of the Amalgamated Clothing Workers (CIO). In March, 1941, Roosevelt also set up the National Defense Mediation Board (NDMB), consisting of representatives of labor, management, and the public, to keep the peace on the factory floor.

The new mood in Washington was cautiously welcomed by

20 James MacGregor Burns, *Roosevelt: The Soldier of Freedom, 1940–1945* (New York, 1970), 51.

anti–New Deal Democrats. It appeared, for a short time at least, that the crusading spirit of the New Deal was at its ebb. The president was preoccupied with foreign affairs, and former reform missionaries, such as Rexford Tugwell and Henry Wallace, who was now vice president, seemed to have disappeared into the political twilight. Hardheaded businessmen, such as Donald Nelson of Sears, Roebuck and William Knudsen, now colored government policy. Although they were discomfited by the extension of executive powers, the anti–New Dealers could console themselves in the knowledge that these agencies sought a rapid normalization of business activity.[21]

Nevertheless, anti–New Deal congressmen realized that the president and the agency heads solely determined the policies. Should the administration decide to alter course and achieve social reform through the instrumentality of the agencies, then they would be almost impotent in preventing such action. Moreover, since they had no control whatsoever over individual decisions, they recognized that concentrated vigilance was necessary to deter the administration from pursuing social reform.

Southern Democrats were particularly wary about the administration's labor policies. They recognized that labor had played a decisive role in the president's reelection and suspected that union leaders would seek political rewards for their contributions. The appointment of Sidney Hillman to the OPM, together with appointments of other union officials to lesser government posts, seemed to confirm their qualms that labor would share, if not determine, government policy. Although they craved harmony in labor-management relations, they feared that the government would make irreversible concessions to labor in return for industrial peace. This might result not only in the rapid unionization of southern workers and the possible erosion of Dixie's competitive advantages, but also

---

21 Herman M. Somers, *Presidential Agency: OWMR, The Office of War Mobilization and Reconversion* (Cambridge, 1950), chap. 1; Matthew Josephson, *Sidney Hillman: Statesman of American Labor* (New York, 1952), 480–518; Joel Seidman, *American Labor from Defense to Reconversion* (Chicago, 1953), 26–28.

would cement further the alliance between labor and the Democratic party—a phenomenon that was presumed to be antipodal to the interests of the South.

Concerned southerners thus sought to restrain labor's power and to apprise the administration of their misgivings. They were reinforced in their determination by the victories of the United Mine Workers in the South. The miners, led by blustering John L. Lewis, had triumphed twice in 1941 when they successfully persuaded the NDMB to eliminate the pay differential in northern and southern coal fields and when union shops were formed in a number of southern pits after prolonged strikes.[22] Led by Congressman Howard W. Smith of Virginia, southerners sought to pass legislation that would prohibit strikes for a closed shop and would provide for a cooling-off period. They received widespread support from various state legislatures, farm organizations, and business journals. The *Texas Digest* even suggested "the interests of workers and collective bargaining must be suspended for the time being."[23] Congressman Sam Hobbs of Alabama tried to persuade members of Roosevelt's cabinet to recommend antistrike legislation themselves but grudgefully reported that complacency and fear of retribution prevented them from resisting the unions. It seemed to Hobbs that the administration had abdicated to labor leaders who were only interested in securing recognition of the closed shop and higher wages. However, it would be at least another two years until a majority of southern Democrats were sufficiently aroused to challenge the president's policies.[24]

22 F. Ray Marshall, *Labor in the South* (Cambridge, 1967), 150–51; Seidman, *American Labor from Defense to Reconversion*, 45–46, 61.

23 Willis Robertson to FDR, October 8, 1941, in 1941 File, Sam Rayburn Papers, Sam Rayburn Library, Bonham, Texas; Walter Sillers to Will Whittington, November 18, 1941, and Committee Representing Lowndes County (Miss.) Farmers to Bilbo, January 13, 1942, in Theodore G. Bilbo Papers, University of Southern Mississippi Library, Hattiesburg; *Texas Digest,* June 7, 1941.

24 Samuel F. Hobbs to Guy Hood, November 27, 1941, and Hobbs to Edgar Sheffield, November 6, 1941, in Samuel F. Hobbs Papers, University of Alabama Library, Tuscaloosa.

The outbreak of war after the attack on Pearl Harbor only exacerbated the dilemma of anti–New Deal Democrats. They wanted to give the president full and unfettered support in his battle for production and price stabilization, but at the same time were wary of abdicating their already declining authority to the executive branch. Roosevelt, as will be seen, had already used his emergency powers in an unprecedented manner in an attempt to guarantee against racial discrimination in employment. So, although southern Democrats joined fellow members of Congress in delegating more powers to the president, they must have done so with some foreboding. Nevertheless, after Pearl Harbor they overwhelmingly voted for the first and second war powers acts which authorized the president "to make such redistribution of functions as he may deem necessary . . . [and] in such manner as in his judgment shall seem best fitted to carry out the purposes of this title." [25]

Thus, although conservatives acquiesced in the establishment of such new war boards as the War Production Board, the War Labor Board, and the Office of Price Administration (OPA), they made it clear that they saw these as necessary, albeit distasteful, measures to guarantee a stable and productive economy.[26] They were determined, however, to undo the remaining vestiges of the reformist New Deal. Harry Byrd and "his gang of anti–New Dealers," according to Senator William B. Bankhead of Alabama, planned to eliminate the Farm Security Administration, the Civilian Conservation Corps, and the National Youth Administration.[27] The advocates of retrenchment argued that the booming economic prosperity had eliminated any need for these recovery agencies and that there were no

25 Nathan Grundstein, *Presidential Delegation of Authority in Wartime* (Pittsburgh, 1961), 50–51.
26 Seidman, *American Labor from Defense to Reconversion,* chap. 5; Somers, *Presidential Agency,* 20–28; Roland Young, *Congressional Politics in the Second World War* (New York, 1956), chap. 4; Harvey C. Mansfield *et al., A Short History of OPA* (Washington, D.C., 1947), 18–24.
27 Memo, Edwin M. Watson to FDR, January 5, 1942, in President's Secretary's File, U.S. Senate Folder, Roosevelt Papers.

longer even any political justifications for them. Senator Bailey informed Ed Flynn, chairman of the Democratic National Committee, that he would be unflinching in his support of the war effort, but that "the necessity of the war will require a great reduction in non-defense expenditures." [28] Governor J. Melville Broughton of North Carolina was equally emphatic. "We should be diligent," he warned, "to guard against social and economic experiments that are unsound and subject to condemnation, but which are being 'trotted out' in this emergency period." [29]

Concern over the use of the new war powers was also voiced by influential businessmen and community leaders. The uproar over price stabilization and the eagerness of the War Labor Board to recognize unions was, of course, nationwide and not confined to the South. Nevertheless, since southern politicians were generally less susceptible than representatives of metropolitan states to multiple constituency pressures, they may have been more receptive to complaints from the business quarter. Moreover, there were fewer counterpressures from the mass of southerners whose enthusiasm for the administration was less intense now that the New Deal had lost its vitality. Manufacturers especially resented the tendency of the War Labor Board to reduce the regional wage differential, particularly in the economically volatile textile industry. They were frustrated by stringent price controls and complained that they were unable to compensate for rising wage costs with price increases.[30] And

---

28 Bailey to Ed Flynn, August 8, 1942, and Bailey to J. Paul Leonard, February 11, 1942, in Bailey Papers.
29 *Textile Bulletin,* September 1, 1942; also, B. S. Womble to Robert L. Doughton, December 7, 1942, in Robert L. Doughton Papers, Southern Historical Collection, University of North Carolina, Chapel Hill.
30 Union membership increased by over 65 percent between 1940 and 1945. In 1940 27.2 percent of all workers in nonagricultural establishments were organized, while in 1945 this proportion had risen to 35.8 percent. See U.S. Bureau of the Census, *Historical Statistics of the United States from Colonial Times to 1957* (Washington, D.C., 1960), 98. The figures, though not the trends, vary somewhat in Seidman, *American Labor from Defense to Reconversion,* 104–108. See also, Marshall, *Labor in the South,* 228; Mansfield *et al., A Short History of OPA,* 42–43; Ben B. Gossett to O. Max Gardner, May 27, 1942, in Bailey Papers.

they objected to the flood of reports and questionnaires that they were required to fill in for the OPA. "It will not be long until you will be filling out a questionnaire," griped C. A. Cannon, the North Carolina textile magnate, to Robert Doughton, chairman of the House Committee on Ways and Means.[31]

The anxiety of southern Democrats about the powers of the war agencies was unquestionably heightened by Roosevelt's acquiescence to the creation of the Fair Employment Practices Committee (FEPC) in June, 1941. This first open commitment to a policy of racial equality in employment practices demonstrated that the president would not be constrained by precedent or legislative prescription in his use of executive powers. The federal bureaucracy, as congressmen rapidly learned, was often more susceptible to lobbying and pressure than was Congress. Pressure groups, after all, had to convert a large number of senators and representatives to secure favorable legislation. In the executive branch, on the other hand, often only one or two key administrators—or the president himself—had to be contacted to effect change. It thus seemed that a counter-strategy might have to be formulated to reduce the exposure of the executive branch to pressures from groups that were committed to wide-sweeping social reforms.

Southern Democrats were anguished particularly about one pressure group, the civil rights organizations, for Negro leaders had finally managed to prevail upon the president in 1941 to reverse his policy of benign neglect toward the Negro. Southerners remembered that during the depression Roosevelt had not challenged the South's (or the nation's) racial practices. He had refused to support antilynching legislation and did not use the full authority of his office to secure fair treatment for Negroes in the New Deal welfare programs. Roosevelt's reticence had been largely due to the political indispensability of southern Democrats—at least in the period 1933–1936—and to the

31 C. A. Cannon to Doughton, December 4, 1942, in Folder 1064, Doughton Papers.

corollary weak and politically ineffective civil rights organizations.[32] Now, during the defense crisis, it seemed that this situation had reversed itself. The president was now prepared to respond to the demands of the increasingly articulate Negro at the expense of that pedestal of the Democratic party, the South.

The defense crisis and the election of 1940 had been largely responsible for the growing effectiveness of civil rights leaders. Negroes were tantalized by the hopes of lucrative employment in the burgeoning defense industries and by the promise of various nondiscrimination directives. However, the economic lot of the Negro did not improve. In October, 1940, only 5.4 percent of all United States Employment Service placements in twenty selected defense industries were nonwhite, and even this figure fell to 2.5 percent in April, 1941. Similarly, Negroes were excluded from skilled jobs and training programs in the armed services.[33] Negro leaders were well aware that they constituted a potentially rich source of much-needed skilled manpower. They had little difficulty in demonstrating, to the embarrassment of the president, that the widely publicized shortage of manpower was an illusion, since there were millions of underemployed Negroes anxious to acquire new skills. The administration also found it more difficult to ignore the Negro for political reasons. Roosevelt himself had calculated that the Negro vote in the North was essential to a Democratic victory in 1940. Consequently, he had preached equality of opportunity in his campaign speeches as a counter to the Republicans' promise of a "square deal" for Negroes. He had conferred with civil rights leaders about discrimination in the armed services and defense industries; and he had appointed William H.

32 Wolters, *Negroes and the Great Depression,* xi–xiii; White, *A Man Called White,* 169–70.
33 Gunnar Myrdal, *An American Dilemma: The Negro Problem and Modern Democracy* (New York: McGraw-Hill, 1964), ccix, 20n, 412; Josephson, *Sidney Hillman,* 520; Richard M. Dalfiume, "Desegregation of the United States Armed Forces, 1939–1953" (Ph.D. dissertation, University of Missouri, 1966), 31–36.

Hastie, a prominent Negro lawyer, as assistant on Negro affairs in the War Department.[34]

Civil rights leaders, however, were not satisfied with these modest crumbs. They recognized that their electoral power and their growing importance in a booming economy should enable them to extract a more positive commitment from the administration. It was time, they felt, for the president to cease his ambivalence on the race question.[35] A New York Negro informed Roosevelt that blacks "feel their votes were among that large balance of power which swung you into office for two successive terms. They feel you have never come out openly on the question of the Negro and that your language has always been so vague and general as to protect your prestige with the Southern bloc."[36] Negroes pointed to a recent White House statement in defense of segregation in the armed services and to declining employment prospects for nonwhites as evidence that the president was prepared to make only symbolic concessions to minority groups. Instead, they demanded a forthright and specific executive order that would prohibit discrimination in all federally supported defense industries.[37]

The instigator of this new militancy was the energetic president of the Brotherhood of Sleeping Car Porters, A. Philip Randolph. Together with Walter White, executive secretary of the National Association for the Advancement of Colored People (NAACP), and Lester Granger, executive director of the Urban League, Randolph proposed that a march on Washing-

34 Dalfiume, "Desegregation of the United States Armed Forces," 42, 53–54; memo, Stephen T. Early to General Edwin Watson, September 19, 1940, in OF 2538, Roosevelt Papers.
35 See, for example, Walter White to Colonel Chesley W. Jurney, February 7, 1941, in Box 263/3, Files of the National Association for the Advancement of Colored People, Manuscripts Division, Library of Congress, Washington, D.C. (hereafter cited as NAACP Files); Walter White to Jacob Billikopf, October 9, 1940, in OF 2538, Roosevelt Papers.
36 Pauli Murray to FDR, July 23, 1942, in OF 93, Roosevelt Papers.
37 Herbert Garfinkel, When Negroes March: The March on Washington Movement in the Organizational Politics for FEPC (Glencoe, Ill., 1959), 23–34; Dalfiume, "Desegregation of the United States Armed Forces," 49–50.

ton be staged to demand stronger action against discrimination. The leaders hastily organized the March on Washington Committee, the first, national, all-Negro attempt to apply pressure by mass demonstration for immediate government action. Randolph was confident that he could lead 100,000 Negroes to the Washington Monument on July 1, 1941.[38]

Roosevelt watched these plans apprehensively. He feared that Randolph would destroy the image of national unity he was so carefully nursing. He endeavored, therefore, to appease the marchers. In the spring of 1941 Sidney Hillman of OPM urged all employers who held defense contracts with the federal government to abandon their discriminatory practices. This gesture, however, was ineffective, since William Knudsen, Hillman's colleague, refused to sign the directive. In June, Eleanor Roosevelt, Aubrey Williams, head of the National Youth Administration, and Mayor Fiorello La Guardia used their good offices in an attempt to persuade Randolph to call off the march. But Randolph would not budge. The president finally gave in. He preferred to concede to the civil rights movement and risk a breach with the South than to face an embarrassing demonstration at the doorstep of the arsenal of democracy.[39]

The ensuing executive order declared that it was the "duty" of employers and labor unions "to provide for the full and equitable participation of all workers in defense industries, without discrimination, because of race, creed, color, or national origin." All defense contracts were required to include a provision obliging the contractor not to discriminate against any employee. The Fair Employment Practices Committee, appointed by the president, was set up in OPM. The committee was instructed to investigate complaints, "to redress valid grievances, and to rec-

38 Garfinkel, *When Negroes March,* 39–57.
39 For accounts of the maneuvers that culminated in the creation of the FEPC, see *ibid.,* chap. 2; Louis Ruchames, *Race, Jobs, and Politics: The Story of FEPC* (New York, 1957), chap. 1; Charles S. Johnson, *Patterns of Negro Segregation* (New York, 1943), chap. 5.

ommend to government agencies and to the President measures required to implement the order." [40]

The executive order was, as James MacGregor Burns has remarked, "a pontifical document with very small teeth." [41] It had only eighty thousand dollars to spend in the first year of operation, and its effectiveness was sharply limited by the lack of any enforcement powers. Despite these limitations, the order was clearly a break with the past. For the first time since Reconstruction, a president had made open cause with civil rights groups, and this time he was a Democrat. Gunnar Myrdal wrote in 1944 that the order represented "the most definite break in the tradition of federal unconcernedness about racial discrimination" that had ever occurred.[42] The federal government now was authorized to cancel contracts in order to force firms to employ and upgrade Negroes and other minority groups. But it was not only this changed attitude toward the Negro that was new. A Democratic president had risked a possible break with Dixie by treading upon the very issue that had made the South "solid" in the first place. Presumably, Roosevelt calculated either that southerners would turn a blind eye or that the support of the Negro in the metropolitan states was ultimately more crucial than that of the South.

At first, it seemed that most southerners would ignore the FEPC in the hope that an absence of publicity would cause the committee to fade into oblivion. Southerners realized that the committee possessed little real power. They also feared the possible cancellation of valuable defense contracts and so were wary of defying the FEPC prematurely. And, above all, Mark Ethridge, its first chairman and a phlegmatic Mississippian, seemed anxious to mollify southern whites. He reassured critics that "Executive Order 8802 is a war order, and not a so-

40 U.S. Fair Employment Practices Committee, *First Report* (Washington, D.C., 1945), 104–105.
41 Burns, *Roosevelt: The Soldier of Freedom*, 124.
42 Myrdal, *An American Dilemma*, 416.

cial document" and disavowed all intentions of interfering with racial segregation. He argued that its abandonment would be "against the general peace and welfare." [43]

Nevertheless, although southerners recognized the limitations of the FEPC, they were aware that their racial practices were now no longer a private matter. The FEPC publicized the incidence of discrimination in employment and was a concrete reminder that Washington could ultimately determine employment patterns in the South. In June, 1942, for example, the FEPC held public investigations in Birmingham, Alabama, for three days. A number of Negroes and labor leaders openly testified that several local firms had refused to hire Negroes on principle. A typical firm was the Gulf Shipbuilding Corporation of Chickasaw, Alabama, which had hired no Negroes except as office porters—despite the fact that blacks made up over one third of the local population. The committee ordered the shipyard to cease this practice and recommended a training program for minority groups.[44]

A storm of hostility followed the hearings in Birmingham. Newspaper editors, influential politicians, and leading businessmen condemned the hearings as an unwarranted interference. *Alabama,* a racist business weekly, assailed the "3 Day Carnival of Reform" and asked: "If the apostles of New Dealism will send their sleuths, their prosecutors, and their judges into the very heart of the South to stir up the delicate issue of the equality of the races, to what further point on the long road towards despotic and absolute regimentation will they have the effrontery to go?" [45] The governor of Alabama, Frank M. Dixon, was less virulent but no less concerned. He understood that the FEPC hear-

---

43 Ruchames, *Race, Jobs, and Politics,* 28.
44 Summary of the Hearings of the President's Committee on Fair Employment Practices, held in Birmingham, Alabama, June 19, 1942, and Findings and Directions Against Gulf Shipbuilding Corporation, Chickasaw, Alabama, in RG 228-71, Office Files of Malcolm Ross, Records of the Committee on Fair Employment Practices, National Archives, Washington, D.C.
45 Quoted in Ruchames, *Race, Jobs, and Politics,* 43.

ings signaled a new preoccupation with social leveling, despite
the dominant concern in Washington with industrial mobilization. He feared that, despite Ethridge's reassurances, the committee would soon interfere with Jim Crow and warned of "bitterness and passion among our people." [46]

This growing apprehensiveness in Dixie over the race issue
was reinforced and magnified in 1942 when the House of Representatives passed a federal anti-poll tax bill. For over two years
members of Congress, under the leadership of Democratic Congressman Lee E. Geyer of California, who had introduced the
first anti-poll tax bill in 1939, had been planning to remove this
restriction on the suffrage. Negro organizations had been campaigning busily for its elimination and had concentrated their
lobbying activities on congressmen from the metropolitan states
in the North. They believed that federal prohibition against the
payment of a poll tax in the eight states below the Mason-Dixon
Line, where the tax was still operative, would open up the voting
booths to Negroes.[47] They also recognized that, irrespective of
its final effect on the suffrage, its abolition at Washington's behest would be an embarrassing blow to the proponents of *Herrenvolk* democracy, whose predecessors had introduced the tax at
the turn of the century to reduce the level of voter participation
and exorcise corruption. For this reason southern politicians vehemently opposed the anti-poll tax campaign. Although some of
them were prepared to remove the restriction by amendment to
the state constitutions, they would not tolerate any move, backed

---

46 Frank M. Dixon to Hobbs, November 24, 1942, in Hobbs Papers; Graves,
   The Fighting South, 121–24, 135.
47 The poll tax also disfranchised a number of whites who were either unable
   or unwilling to pay. However, studies have shown that the poll tax was
   only a contributory factor to the low level of voter participation. Negroes
   were excluded from the polls by such other means as the literacy test, the
   white primary, social custom, and intimidation. Indeed, there was no
   significant increase in voter turnout when the poll tax was abolished in
   three southern states in 1920, 1934, and 1937. The eight states that still
   retained the poll tax in 1942 were Alabama, Arkansas, Georgia, Mississippi,
   South Carolina, Tennessee, Texas, and Virginia. See Frederic D. Ogden,
   The Poll Tax in the South (University, Ala., 1958), chap. 5; V. O. Key,
   Southern Politics in State and Nation (New York, 1949), chap. 28.

by civil rights groups, to abolish the tax by federal legislation.[48]
So, when the anti-poll tax bill reached the Senate, southern senators, with the notable exception of Claude Pepper of Florida, closed rank.[49] They felt that the bill was being pushed unscrupulously by their Democratic colleagues from the North who were afraid of the political consequences of ignoring the campaigns of civil rights and electoral reform organizations. They believed that their assault on the bill was fully justified, despite their earlier assurances that divisive political tactics would be postponed for the duration of the war. It was not the South, they argued, that had opened up old wounds but certain groups in the North who were planning to use the war emergency to further social reform. Thus, the successful filibuster against the bill had wider political and sectional undertones. "Why bring about any further disunity by pushing such legislation at a time when the efforts of every American should be directed towards winning the war?" wondered Governor Richard M. Jefferies of South Carolina.[50] Some southern whites thought they knew the auspicious answer. For, after the passage in September, 1942, of the soldiers' voting act, which exempted members of the armed services from payment of the poll tax, southerners grew increasingly convinced that the Democratic leadership would risk the possible sacrifice of southern support in return for votes from the urban coalition. "The South is being sold down the river," prophesied one of Robert Doughton's correspondents, and "it thus

48 For further discussion of the political and constitutional foundations of southern opposition to anti-poll tax legislation, see: Ogden, *The Poll Tax in the South*, 79–81, 95; Key, *Southern Politics*, 594–96; Janice E. Christensen, "The Constitutionality of National Anti-Poll Tax Bills," *Minnesota Law Review*, XXXIII (February, 1949), 217–54; Joseph E. Kallenbach, "Constitutional Aspects of Federal Anti-Poll Tax Legislation," *Michigan Law Review*, XLV (April, 1947), 717–32. Also, Allen E. Ellender, interview with author, September, 1969.

49 Alexander Rudolph Stoesen, "The Senatorial Career of Claude D. Pepper" (Ph.D. dissertation, University of North Carolina, 1965), 177–78.

50 Telegram, Richard M. Jefferies to Joseph C. O'Mahoney, September 22, 1942, in Box 13, Richard M. Jefferies Papers, South Caroliniana Library, Columbia, S.C.; also, Heber Ladner to Bilbo, October 21, 1942, in Bilbo Papers.

appears that the soldiers and sailors are being used as a door through which Negro politics may march." [51]

This embryonic sense of sectional identity and frustration revealed itself in the midterm election campaigns of 1942. Although one must take care not to exaggerate the degree of disaffection from the administration at this stage, there were clear signs of growing restlessness. In Dixie a number of aspirants to office emphasized distinctly sectional themes rather than the traditional anti–New Deal sentiments. Conservatism was beginning, but only beginning, to assume a southern tinge. The electorate as a whole seemed disinterested in economic issues. Therefore, several contestants for political office sought to arouse the voters' alleged complacency by warning of the dangers to the caste system.[52] The race issue was raised in at least five primary campaigns in the South. Governor Dixon of Alabama publicized his refusal to sign a prisoners' contract as the result of the creation of the FEPC.[53] In neighboring Georgia Eugene Talmadge, campaigning against Ellis G. Arnall, declared that "we love the Negro in his place, but his place is at the back door." [54] Similar sentiments were echoed in South Carolina and Mississippi. "In all cases," commented Jessie Daniel Ames, a leading member of the interracial movement in the South, "accusations are against institutions, organizations, and individuals outside the South. Sectionalism is being revived." [55]

Perhaps the most serious warning of a rift in the national Democratic party came from Alabama. A month before the No-

---

51 George W. Williams to Doughton, 1942 (undated, probably September, 1942), in Folder 1069, Doughton Papers; also U.S. House of Representatives, Committee on the Election of the President, Vice-President, and Representatives in Congress, *Hearings to Amend the Soldiers' Voting Act,* 78th Cong., 1st Sess., 9–12.
52 FDR to Elmer Davis, October 12, 1942, in OF 1113, Roosevelt Papers; Bailey to M. M. Redden, September 7, 1942, in Bailey Papers.
53 Graves, *The Fighting South,* 135.
54 Quoted in Thomas Elkin Taylor, "A Political Biography of Ellis Arnall" (M.A. thesis, Emory University, 1959), 82.
55 Commission on Interracial Cooperation Clip Sheet, Ser. 1, No. 3, August 17, 1942, in Jessie Daniel Ames Papers, Southern Historical Collection, University of North Carolina, Chapel Hill.

vember elections Gessner T. McCorvey, chairman of Alabama's Democratic state executive committee and a leader of the conservative, Black Belt wing of the party, filed a number of complaints with E. Ray Scott, treasurer of the Democratic National Committee.[56] Scott had been in the South to raise funds for the forthcoming elections. When he returned to Washington, McCorvey warned him that Alabama Democrats would be reluctant to contribute to the campaign chests until they had "some definite assurance from National Headquarters that our party was going to turn over a new leaf insofar as the handling of the negro situation in the South was concerned." McCorvey remonstrated that a "rising tide of indignation . . . is sweeping over the South as a result of the orders and regulations coming out of Washington dealing with the negro question down here. We are going to have white supremacy in the South regardless of what happens in other sections of the country." He appreciated that the national Democratic hierarchy was solicitous of the votes of northern Negroes, but countered that "those of us down here are entitled to far more consideration at the hands of the National Committee of our Party than we have received." He warned that attempts either to compel the races to work side by side with one another or to abolish the poll tax would be resisted. McCorvey concluded that "President Roosevelt and his wife have done more towards upsetting and disturbing the friendly relations heretofore existing between the white people and the colored people of the South than all the other presidents and their wives who have occupied the White House during the time I have been old enough to take notice of such matters." [57]

Although antipathy toward the administration was rising unmistakably in the South, the elections of 1942 seemed to indicate that Roosevelt was losing his hold over the imagination of all

56 For a discussion of the composition of Alabama's Democratic party, see Key, *Southern Politics*, 36–52.
57 Gessner T. McCorvey to E. Ray Scott, October 2, 1942, in Box 1, Records from the Democratic National Committee, Franklin D. Roosevelt Library, Hyde Park, N.Y. (Hereafter cited as DNC Files.)

Americans. Political lethargy was rampant. In the industrial cities of the North where voter turnout was markedly low—altogether, only 28,000,000 out of a potential 80,000,000 voters went to the polls—several proadministration Democrats were defeated. Even old George Norris of Nebraska, whom Roosevelt had personally endorsed, fell victim to the anti–New Deal tide. The president had suffered his greatest setback since taking office. In the new Seventy-eighth Congress the Democratic majority in the House would be only six seats and in the Senate, twenty. It seemed that southern conservatives at last could attend the requiem for the New Deal.[58]

The administration was taken by surprise at this setback. Edwin W. Pauley, secretary of the Democratic National Committee, consequently sent requests to party leaders throughout the country for their diagnoses of the election results. The responses were particularly revealing. They showed that the South had become more critical of Roosevelt than any other section. For example, 36.1 percent of all the respondents cited resentment of bureaucracy in their locale as a reason for diminished enthusiasm for the administration. But 51.5 percent of southern replies mentioned bureaucracy specifically. Similarly, 21.3 percent of the national sample expressed resentment of the administration's wartime labor policies, while 44.1 percent of southern Democrats alluded to labor in this context. And, while only 8.7 percent of all the respondents cited the general unpopularity of the New Deal, 10.3 percent of southerners warned that an overall reaction against the New Deal was responsible for the recent reverses.[59]

The criticism of respondents from below the Potomac was cutting and reproachful. Southerners were apparently skeptical of "free-wheeling–new dealing" and were "sick and tired" of its

58 Joseph Gaer, *The First Round: The Story of the CIO Political Action Committee* (New York, 1944), 56; Burns, *Roosevelt: The Soldier of Freedom,* 279–81.
59 Post-Mortem Survey of the 1942 Election Carried Out by the Democratic National Committee, in Box 37, DNC Files. The "South" in the survey included the old Confederacy, Kentucky, Missouri, Oklahoma, and West Virginia.

"socialistic tendency and bureaucratic domination." Congressman Albert Thomas of Texas thought members of Congress and other loyal Democrats had received "roughshod treatment by some of the bureaucrats"; he yearned for a restoration of the traditional Democratic leaders to party councils.[60] Southerners also complained of the administration's growing sympathy for organized labor and grudgefully felt that the unions had been "given carte blanche to do just about what it wishes to do generally," while, by implication, southerners were asked to tolerate their declining influence.[61] Rather surprisingly, the race issue was scarcely mentioned in this survey. This would suggest that at this stage party regulars were still more concerned with the wider ramifications of the president's domestic policies than with the narrower, regional facets. However, party stalwarts could not be sure that they could contain the insurgency for long.

Thus, by the end of 1942 while the administration was absorbed in the problems of increasing industrial production, southern Democrats were questioning the authority of their own party leader. They had hoped that Roosevelt would recognize southern nuances in the formulation of war production policies. They were aware that they had always constituted the mainstay of the party and that they had also been the principal contributors to party funds.[62] They felt that the president had turned his back on the South by ignoring its leaders in his decisions and in his appointments policies. He seemed more amenable to the new men of power, such as Sidney Hillman, Walter White, and other leaders of the urban coalition, than to the congressional leader-

---

60 Dan R. McGehee to Edwin Pauley, November 12, 1942, John L. McClellan to Pauley, November 11, 1942, Albert Thomas to Pauley, November 12, 1942, in Box 37, DNC Files.

61 Pete Jarman to Pauley, January 5, 1943, W. R. Poage to Pauley, November 17, 1942, in Box 37, DNC Files.

62 In the 1936 election, for example, the South (the old Confederacy plus Kentucky, Maryland, Missouri, Oklahoma, and West Virginia) had contributed $1,111,924 in donations of over $100 to Democratic party funds. This represented 37.8 percent of the total. The wealthier Northeast had contributed 28.8 percent of party funds, and the West only 6.4 percent. Overacker, "Campaign Funds in the Presidential Election of 1936," 495.

ship. He appeared more anxious to include organized labor in party councils and the war agencies than southern political stalwarts. Worse still, he had surrendered to the Negro leadership by creating the FEPC. The veteran anti–New Dealer, Josiah Bailey, aptly summed up the South's predicament to James Farley, who had been chairman of the Democratic party for eight years and had himself broken with the president in a state of disillusion. He wrote: "It is a great pity that our Party has fallen into the hands of a faction of extremists most of whom never were Democrats, and it is a great pity also that it is the Democratic Party which has destroyed States' Rights and it is the Democratic Party which has erected certain labor leaders into the position of tyrants. It is the Democratic Party that has intensified bureaucracy to such an extent that the people are in revolt." [63] In fact, the South was not yet in revolt. But it was restless.

63 Bailey to James A. Farley, December 5, 1942, in Bailey Papers.

CHAPTER TWO

Dr. New Deal versus
Dr. Win the War: Washington,
1943–1944

THE ATMOSPHERE on Capitol Hill was decidedly different when the new Congress rose in prayer. The conservative ranks had swollen, and nobody expected pioneering political surprises. Veteran New Dealers, once thought invincible, had been banished to their home towns. In their place sat political novices, many of them Republicans, who believed that the political tide had now ebbed away from the White House and was flowing toward the eager proponents of "normalcy" and efficiency. The southerners were still there, of course. Some, like Senators Claude D. Pepper of Florida and Lister Hill of Alabama, were determined to keep the New Deal alive. Others, however, saw that the time was ripe to supplant the New Deal coalition. Roosevelt was absorbed in wartime diplomacy and the production battle. Despite the broad powers of the war agencies and the occasional calls for an expansion in the social services, there was a sharp diminution in reformist rhetoric from the White House. Indeed, by the end of the year, Roosevelt would be proclaiming the demise of "Dr. New Deal." Above all, the electorate no longer seemed hypnotized by the lures of social reform. The economy was in full swing, unemployment had given way to labor shortages, and, despite complaints from the unions, Americans had more money to spend than ever before.

Advocates of retrenchment were confident that they could not only block all tendencies to increase the powers of the federal government but also undo those New Deal reforms that they had found unnecessary in the thirties. The New Deal now seemed irrelevant. There were no unemployed to swell the work forces of the CCC and WPA, and it seemed only logical to abolish these underused and allegedly overstaffed agencies. In the Senate Harry F. Byrd of Virginia reactivated his Joint Committee on Non-Essential Expenditures, while in the House Howard W. Smith, Byrd's political protégé, presided over his suggestive Special Committee to Investigate Acts of Executive Agencies Beyond the Scope of Their Authority. As their nomenclatures suggest, these committees were authorized to trim the powers and functions of federal agencies wherever possible. A growing number of Democrats no longer looked to the president for leadership and guidance, as they had done in the first hundred days of the New Deal. They believed that the recent election and the national preoccupation with the war had placed responsibility upon Congress to restrict new executive initiatives in the area of social and economic reform. Robert Doughton believed that the country wanted Congress to "cut out all unnecessary federal expenditures, retain such social reforms as are wholesome and necessary, eliminate those that are unnecessary, and do everything possible we can to win the war in the shortest time possible." [1] It was, of course, for Congress to decide upon the question of which reforms were necessary. If Congress failed to set the tone of domestic policy, then not only would it reinforce the growing power of Roosevelt's labor supporters but it could also circumscribe its own influence after the war. "Unless the Congress takes the initiative," wrote Democratic Congressman Wesley F. Disney of Oklahoma, "of course the Treasury will come forth with a program, and the doctrine that the Executive

---

[1] Doughton to James A. Meeks, November 17, 1942, in Folder 1058, Doughton Papers; Doughton to C. A. Cannon, December 5, 1942, in Folder 1064, Doughton Papers.

Department is primary and the Congress secondary will become the more accepted and relied upon." [2]

Congressional conservatives began the new session of Congress by striking at relatively minor particulars of the war program. They recognized that they were in the same quandary as Roosevelt. They were as anxious as the president to avoid open ideological division in time of war. They felt, therefore, that it was incumbent upon them to quarantine the New Deal by surreptitious or gradual means whenever possible. Democrats in particular did not want to risk a schism, particularly since Roosevelt himself had tempered his reforming zeal. His State of the Union address in January, 1943, had played down the theme of reform and had stressed the need for efficiency and unity.[3] His opponents thus hoped to force the president to continue in this vein. Congressman Hugh Peterson of Georgia hailed Roosevelt's message as "conducive to unity among all factions," and Josiah Bailey vowed, in a moment of self-delusion: "I have utterly dismissed everything like politics, so far as my course is concerned." [4]

Politics, however, did not disappear. In the opening months of 1943 the skirmishes over Roosevelt's policies continued in familiar fashion. Conservative Democrats intensified their campaign to dampen the president's war powers. For example, in February the National Resources Planning Board, which had been responsible for research on budgeting and national social needs since 1933, was terminated when the House Appropriations Committee refused to renew its funds. It had been the brainchild of the academic planners of the early New Deal, and the advocates of laissez faire thus welcomed the liquidation of the board that had promised continuation of the welfare state in times of prosper-

---

2 Wesley F. Disney to Walter George, December 11, 1942, in Folder 1066, Doughton Papers.
3 Rosenman (comp.), *The Public Papers and Addresses of Franklin D. Roosevelt*, XII, 21–34.
4 Atlanta *Constitution*, January 8, 1943; Bailey to O. Max Gardner, February 27, 1943, in Bailey Papers.

ity.[5] Southern Democrats were also instrumental in annulling a controversial component of the president's stabilization program. Four southerners on the House Committee on Ways and Means joined their fellow Republicans in February to quash the president's proposals for a statutory limitation on salaries of $25,000 a year for the duration of the war. Roosevelt's stand on salaries was primarily a gesture to the labor unions which also had been asked to exercise restraint in their wage demands. Opponents of the proposal objected to this extension of presidential authority as well as to the political ramifications of Roosevelt's motive.[6]

Roosevelt's critics did not solely confine themselves to gnawing at executive powers. Dissident Democrats were eager to foreclose the development of closer ties with the more radical elements in the party. They found one opportunity to strike at the party leadership in February, 1943, when they resolved to embarrass their national party chairman, Edward J. Flynn. Flynn had never been a popular party leader. He lacked James Farley's graceful determination and had been implicated in charges of scandal and graft. Moreover, he was held responsible for the Democratic setback in 1942. So, when Roosevelt nominated Flynn to serve as ambassador to Australia, party critics jumped at the opportunity to show their concern over Roosevelt's political predilections by uniting to quash Flynn's nomination.

Masterminding the opposition was Senator Kenneth D. McKellar of Tennessee. McKellar, a crusty septuagenarian and a protégé of Edward Crump, boss of Memphis, had been a loyal New Deal Democrat during the depression. However, he had gradually turned against the administration. But unlike some of his other southern colleagues, he was as concerned about patron-

5 Landon G. Rockwell, "The Planning Function of the National Resources Planning Board," *Journal of Politics*, VII (May, 1945), 169–78. The appropriation was not restored in conference in June and so the board's functions finally terminated on July 1.

6 New York *Times*, February 14, 1943. The chairman of the Ways and Means Committee, Robert Doughton, voted to sustain the order despite pressures from his constituency. Thomas Franks to Doughton, December 8, 1942, in Folder 1065, Doughton Papers. See also Young, *Congressional Politics in the Second World War*, 98–100.

age and constituency politics as he was about the fundamental assumptions of the New Deal. McKellar had had sharp differences with the administration over planning and personnel policy in the Tennessee Valley Authority. Indeed, the wounds had become so deep that he had wanted all appointments to federal jobs carrying a salary of over $4,500 a year to be subject to Senate confirmation. So, when the president submitted Flynn's name for confirmation by the Senate, McKellar saw his opportunity to strike at the alleged indifference of the administration to his state's technological and political needs. Other southerners, who had formerly expressed alarm over their exclusion from the policy-making councils of the party, rallied around McKellar. They first persuaded Flynn to resign as chairman of the Democratic National Committee and after a prolonged fight forced the president to withdraw the nomination.[7] Flynn's defeat was not only "a demonstration of the new independence of Congress" but also was a victory for the party critics who hoped to alter the character of the Democratic party.[8]

The anti–New Deal bloc seemed to move from victory to victory. In June, 1943, conservatives shifted their tactics from eating away at the edges of the president's power to assailing directly those agencies that had incorporated so much of the spirit of the New Deal. The Civilian Conservation Corps, the Works Progress Administration, and the National Youth Administration were all eviscerated when Congress refused to renew appropriations for them. Roosevelt had specifically urged that these agencies be continued. Their elimination, therefore, was something of a personal rebuke, especially since the president saw the CCC and NYA as training grounds for communal and democratic values.

---

7 Edward J. Flynn, *You're the Boss* (New York, 1947), 172–77; Robert Ellis Thiel, "Kenneth D. McKellar and the Politics of the Tennessee Valley Authority" (M.A. thesis, University of Virginia, 1967), 45–104; New York *Times,* February 1, 1943; Tindall, *The Emergence of the New South, 1913–1945,* 723.
8 Atlanta *Constitution,* February 3, 1943; Kenneth D. McKellar to Mrs. Berry Brooks, February 28, 1943, in Kenneth D. McKellar Papers, Memphis Public Library, Memphis, Tenn.

They were also fervently championed by labor and Negro organizations, and their liquidation was a poignant reminder that no program could be continued or enacted without the blessing of party regulars.[9]

Roosevelt was undoubtedly aware of these political configurations. Yet, although he often tempered his reputedly visionary zeal, he was determined to oversee the extension of the welfare state when the war was over. Although he tried to tone down social issues and even appeared to waver at times, he still was committed to the view that welfare legislation should be consolidated during the war so that the government would be well equipped to meet problems of unemployment and economic want in the postwar period. As early as December, 1942, he had advised Robert Doughton that "this is the time to strengthen, not to weaken the social security system" and that he would submit a comprehensive program for social reform.[10] Accordingly, on March 10, 1943, Roosevelt submitted to Congress a special message in which he urged a planned reconversion policy and a national "cradle-to-grave" insurance system against unemployment, old age, and ill health.[11]

Roosevelt's message confirmed the worst fears of his critics. Not only, it seemed, was the president determined to extend the provinces of the New Deal but he was also insensitive to public opinion and the mood of many party stalwarts, who had unambiguously indicated a desire for retrenchment in domestic policy. Walter George of Georgia, chairman of the Senate Finance Committee, announced that he would bide his time in considering the

9 Circular, Walter White to "friendly Congressmen," June, 1943, and White to John Taber, June 18, 1943, in Box 263/1, NAACP Files; Doughton to Dr. Frank P. Graham, May 26, 1943, in Folder 1113, Doughton Papers; Bailey to C. L. Shuping, February 19, 1943, in Bailey Papers; assorted letters in Aubrey Williams File, Bilbo Papers.
10 Roosevelt hoped to persuade Doughton to work for expansion of the social security system by pointing out that increased contributions would be anti-inflationary and would thus serve a dual purpose. FDR to Doughton, December 3, 1942, in Folder 1064, Doughton Papers.
11 Rosenman (comp.), *The Public Papers and Addresses of Franklin D. Roosevelt*, XII, 122–23.

president's proposals and would in no way be involved in legislation that was contrary to the nation's interest.[12] Robert Doughton dismissed the scheme as utopian and declared unequivocally that "expenditures would bankrupt the Government or the taxpayers and the moral effect upon the people would be most serious." Doughton, apparently oblivious to the irony of his own position, felt that Roosevelt's sole motive was to cement the alliance with labor and radical groups in the North. "There is some politics mixed up with the proposal," he wrote with indignation.[13] His constituents, especially in the business community, agreed. Columnists in the *Textile Bulletin,* published in North Carolina, assailed "those superior individuals, who feel that they have been previously entrusted with a mission to guide and control the economic activities of this nation," [14] and found the president's recommendations to be "100% communistic on the communistic principle." [15]

There was one fundamental, philosophical question that underscored the protracted debate on the future of the New Deal. Should the quest for political advantage or a new welfare system be undertaken when all the resources of the nation were needed to provide essential war matériel without delay or confusion? In other words, was there even a moral case, let alone a pertinent argument, for offering altruistic schemes for social welfare, while soldiers on the battlefields waited with anticipation for war supplies? Both the administration and its critics naturally insisted that they were preoccupied with winning the war. Roosevelt, however, believed that the war effort would be seriously undermined if workers and soldiers were not offered security and guarantees against possible ill fortune. His opponents, on the other hand, argued that the economy would be adversely affected and

---

12 Atlanta *Constitution,* March 11, 1943.
13 Doughton to R. M. Hanes, March 13, 1943 (folder number unknown), in Doughton Papers.
14 C. T. Revere, "Cotton and Other Problems," *Textile Bulletin,* March 15, 1943.
15 Gus W. Dyer, "National Resources Planning Board's Recommendations Are Analyzed," *Textile Bulletin,* April 15, 1943.

individual incentive destroyed if paternalistic schemes were devised. The war, they argued, should not be exploited to lay the foundations for a welfare state. War demanded self-sacrifice and was not a dress rehearsal for utopia.

These two views came into sharpest conflict on the question of labor relations. The labor unions believed that the war should be exploited to boost their economic and political power. The president recognized the need to secure the full cooperation of labor and thus was prepared to recognize the principle of union security and shared prosperity. He was also sympathetic to labor's contention that curtailment of industrial action was incongruous with the libertarianism generally associated with the war against the Axis. His critics, however, were alarmed at the president's growing predilections for labor's aspirations. They believed that labor should forego the right to bring industry to a standstill in pursuit of its goals. The needs of the country were preeminent, and it was legitimate to circumscribe certain union activities during the emergency.[16]

They thus sought to restrict the right to strike guaranteed under the Norris-La Guardia and Wagner acts. Although the incidence of strikes had diminished drastically in 1942, a number of dramatic walkouts occurred in vital industries in the opening months of 1943. The most publicized was led by John L. Lewis of the United Mine Workers. Lewis, with his usual truculence, had demanded a wage increase of two dollars a day. The case was referred to the War Labor Board, but Lewis, eager to destroy the stabilization program, contemptuously boycotted the board and refused to appear before it. When the miners struck on April 30, the president seized the mines and ordered Harold Ickes, fuel administrator, to operate them.[17]

This strike, together with walkouts in the plastics, rubber, and railroad industries, hardened the determination of Congress to prohibit wartime strikes. The battle cry against the

16 Burns, *Roosevelt: The Soldier of Freedom*, 259–65, 334–38.
17 Foster Rhea Dulles, *Labor in America: A History* (3rd ed.; New York, 1966), 337–39; U.S. Bureau of the Census, *Historical Statistics*, 99.

unions was raised by two southerners, Congressman Howard W. Smith of Virginia and Senator Tom Connally of Texas. Each sponsored a bill which provided for a thirty-day cooling-off period and authorized the president to seize any plant that was threatened by industrial action. Furthermore, labor leaders would be criminally liable for fomenting strikes during government operations. The bill also outlawed political contributions by unions. This last provision, which was hardly relevant to the fundamental problem of crippling strikes, reflected the sponsors' uneasiness at the growing partnership of the Democrats and the labor unions.[18]

Southern Democrats overwhelmingly supported the Smith-Connally bill. For years they had railed against labor's power, and it seemed that Roosevelt was unwilling to confront the unions for political reasons. The strikes were not only crippling the war effort but were paradoxically bringing union leaders and Roosevelt (in his role of industrial peacemaker) closer together. Since the president was reluctant to deal ruthlessly with the violators of the no-strike pledge, it was incumbent upon Congress to deal with the situation. Robert Doughton supported the bill because Roosevelt seemed "unable to cope with the situation, and it is doubtful if he has sufficient authority to do so."[19] Doughton undoubtedly was aware of resentment by local businessmen. One North Carolinian, an official of the Lenoir Chamber of Commerce, was "not only disgusted but completely nauseated with the pampering that has been given organized labor and its racketeer leaders by the present administration." He admonished that if Congress failed to pass anti-union legislation, "this section will not again support a democratic candidate for president be it Roosevelt or anyone else."[20]

18 U.S. House of Representatives, Committee on Military Affairs, *Hearings to Authorize Operation by the United States of Certain Plants in the Interests of National Defense*, 78th Cong., 1st Sess., *passim*.
19 Doughton to William Green, May 11, 1943, in Folder 1109, Doughton Papers; Burnet R. Maybank to Archie P. Owens, May 21, 1943, in Burnet R. Maybank Papers, South Carolina Department of Archives, Columbia.
20 J. C. Baskervill to Andrew J. May, May 16, 1943, in Folder 1110, Doughton Papers.

Only five southern Democrats in the House of Representatives voted against the bill, while eighty-one nonsouthern Democrats opposed it. In the Senate the split between northern and southern Democrats was wider still. Not one southerner voted against it.[21] Only heretics, such as Cameron Morrison of North Carolina and John W. Flannagan, an anti-Byrd Democrat from Virginia, were loath to curb labor's rights under the Wagner Act. The vast majority of southerners wanted to prevent labor from securing more political and economic gains from the war. Even Congressman Albert Gore of Tennessee, who usually was favorably disposed toward the administration, fretted: "We have permitted political organizations, under the name of organized labor, to grow to such proportions that they threaten the sovereignty of the government itself." [22]

Roosevelt did not agree with the southerners. After careful deliberation and cogent advice to sign the bill "in the interests of national unity," he decided to return the bill to Congress with a firm veto.[23] He argued that the bill was embarrassing and dishonorable since it questioned the veracity of the no-strike pledge and that certain provisions, such as the one for a secret ballot, could precipitate a strike rather than prevent one. The thirty-day cooling-off period, he objected, "might well become a boiling period instead of a cooling period," and that "far from discouraging strikes, these provisions would stimulate labor unrest." [24] Congress, however, was not persuaded. On the same day it received the message, the Senate voted to override the veto by 50 votes to 25, while the House, also without further deliberation, overrode the veto by 244 votes to 108. As might have been expected, no southern Democrat in the Senate

21 Congressional Record, 78th Cong., 1st Sess., 3993, 5392.
22 Ibid., 5228–229, 5240, 5310.
23 Telegram, Tom Connally to FDR, June 23, 1943, memo, Henry L. Stimson and Frank Knox to Harold D. Smith, June 17, 1943, unsigned and undated memo to FDR, in OF 407 B, Roosevelt Papers.
24 Rosenman (comp.), The Public Papers and Addresses of Franklin D. Roosevelt, XII, 268–71.

voted to sustain, and in the House only four supported the president's veto.[25]

Despite the virtually unequivocal hostility of southerners on Capitol Hill to the government's labor policy, the controversy over the Smith-Connally bill was not really a sectional skirmish in the historical sense of the term. The advocates of strike control did not identify their pet bill with the special needs of their local institutions. In particular, southerners did not develop arguments that revolved around apparent threats to Dixie's political culture or social harmony. The basic issue transcended sectional considerations, although Democrats did tend to divide along geographical lines on labor matters—as they did on various aspects of the president's social welfare policies. However, southerners were aware that there were wider ramifications that did impinge directly upon the South's interests. The growing rift with the administration was an unambiguous sign that Dixie's influence within the party had declined and that there had been a concomitant increase in the prestige and authority of labor leaders, social workers, and bureaucratic planners. Conservative Democrats—and most of them were from the South —believed that the war should be used to retrieve an ideology and a political balance that had eroded during the depression. This basic conviction overshadowed any resurgence in sectional self-consciousness that might have appeared. Notwithstanding the occasional use of sectional catchphrases in the debates of 1943, the president's critics still identified themselves as conservatives and proponents of laissez faire, and not as southerners.

If the future of the New Deal, the stabilization program, and labor-management relations had been the only matters of contention during the war, then sectional antagonism might never have arisen. However, as will be seen, southern Democrats, including loyal New Dealers, increasingly became aware that

25 *Congressional Record*, 78th Cong., 1st Sess., 6489, 6548.

their regional peculiarities were endangered from political forces beyond their direct control. This situation had been brought about by the radical changes in the composition of the Democratic party at large. Southerners, it appeared, had become less influential in Democratic councils, while leaders of the urban coalition, who were often union organizers and civil rights advocates, were in a strong position to press the administration and certain members of Congress from the large cities of the North to support measures to democratize the political structure of the South. This meant, in short, that the administration and its congressional supporters were now more susceptible to demands for the enfranchisement of the Negro. It was this development, together with connected issues, that transformed southern conservatism into a reinvigorated, self-conscious southernism.

There were two major items of legislation that came before the Seventy-eighth Congress which would affect directly the voting patterns and political structure of the South. One was already a familiar feature: an anti-poll tax bill. The other, to be examined shortly, was on the surface more remote from areas of southern sensitivity. This second controversial bill would provide for a federal ballot for soldiers serving away from home.

The first proposal, the anti-poll tax bill, passed the House of Representatives only after a bitter fight. Southern congressmen had tried to bottle up the bill in the Committee on the Judiciary. However, two keenly interested pressure groups, the National Association for the Advancement of Colored People and the National Committee to Abolish the Poll Tax, had persuaded sufficient congressmen from the North to sign a discharge petition to bring the bill onto the floor of the House without the assent of the Judiciary Committee.[26] The southerners were not deterred. In the ensuing debate they not only spoke against the portents of the bill but also against the political climate

26 Sylvia Beitscher to Walter White, March 19, 1943, George H. Bender to Walter White, June 4, 1943, in Box 263/4, NAACP Files.

that had been responsible for making the passage of the bill even possible. Eugene E. Cox of Georgia, a cantankerous, messianic opponent of Roosevelt, turned to his Republican colleagues and chided: "While you gave the Negro his freedom you lost him to those in the Democratic Party operating in the name of the New Deal who came along with more alluring promises and took him away from you. . . . This is a sorry bid for the Negro vote." [27] Cox's sentiments were widely shared. Most southerners suspected that the motives behind the support for the bill were at best interested and at worst sinister. James Whitten of Mississippi drew attention to the role that the labor organizations had played in securing its discharge. The labor unions, he maintained, did not want "to improve the lot of the Negro in the South, but to add to the Negro membership of their labor unions in the North and East, to appeal to the Negro vote in these sections, in other words to exploit him." Moreover, according to Whitten, the labor unions were not acting on their own; they were calling for passage of the bill at the behest and connivance of the federal government, "with its board of economists, theoretical experts, long-haired dreamers, and college professors." [28] After similar harangues from southerners against Roosevelt, his advisers, labor unions, civil rights organizations, and the North in general, the House passed the bill on May 25 by 265 votes to 110. Only three congressmen from the South voted for it.[29]

The bill met a familiar fate in the Senate. Dixie Democrats were inexhaustible in their determination to filibuster. Theodore Bilbo of Mississippi assured a constituent that he was "stripped to waist for action. We are going to do what our daddies could not do—that is, whip 'the hell' out of these yankees." [30] The abolition of the poll tax, according to Bilbo, would not only enfranchise the Negro but would also pave the

27 *Congressional Record*, 78th Cong., 1st Sess., 4808.
28 *Ibid.*, 4880, 4882.
29 *Ibid.*, 4889. The three southern Democrats were Estes Kefauver and J. Percy Priest, both of Tennessee, and R. Ewing Thomason of Texas.
30 Bilbo to John McLaurin, November 23, 1943, in Bilbo Papers.

way for the elimination of segregation. No self-respecting southerner could acquiesce in this. "We are not going to bed with
the African negro. . . . We are not going to treat them as our
social equals. . . . we as a people are proud of our blood-
stream and are thoroughly possessed with race consciousness,"
he wrote.[31] His fellow southern Senators apparently agreed. In
the summer of 1944 they successfully killed the bill.

Dixie's voting laws were also at the heart of the imbroglio
over the soldiers' ballot. The attempt to revise an earlier soldiers' voting act toward the end of 1943 aroused more sectional
bitterness than any other item of legislation during the war. It
is worth recounting, therefore, at greater length the developments in this controversy, since its outcome prompted the first
serious reevaluation of the South's adherence to the Democratic
party.

The Soldiers' Voting Act of 1942 had attempted to facilitate
voting procedures for members of the armed forces who were
stationed outside their home state. However, the act had made
only a negligible impression on voting numbers. Members of
the armed services found the procedures for voting under this
statute both cumbersome and obstructive. Only 136,000 persons had actually overcome the obstacles against the mere application for a federal ballot and, of this total, only 28,000 had
actually cast an effective vote.[32] The president was embarrassed
at this denial of the suffrage and accordingly urged Congress to
pass a new bill that would avoid these pitfalls.[33] Eventually,
two almost identical bills were presented to the House and
Senate. The new bills, sponsored in the Senate by Democrats
Theodore F. Green of Rhode Island and Scott W. Lucas of
Illinois and in the House by Eugene Worley of Texas, proposed
to create a United States War Ballot Commission, consisting of
five members appointed by the president. At least two members would be Democrats, and two would be Republicans. The

31 Bilbo to Mrs. Thomas Phillips, November 17, 1943, in Bilbo Papers.
32 *Hearings to Amend the Soldiers' Voting Act,* 27.
33 FDR to Urban A. Lavery, August 9, 1943, in OF 1113, Roosevelt Papers.

War Ballot Commission would prepare federal ballots for use by members of the armed services. These ballots would be sent to military camps and to the battlefront well before election day. Soldiers and sailors would cast their votes in secrecy under the supervision of officers. The ballots would then be returned to the commission, which would forward them to the appropriate state election officials. In addition, servicemen would continue to be exempt from payment of the poll tax.[34]

The bill came before the Senate on November 22, 1943. While the Republicans showed anxiety about the partisan composition of the War Ballot Commission, southern Democrats, with the exception of Claude Pepper, challenged the very substance of the bill. They feared that it would provide a precedent for the "federalization" of all those elections in which certain segments of the population were supposedly deprived of the right to vote. Thus even a slight change in the election laws could pave the way for the eventual enfranchisement of the Negro. Consequently, they viewed the bill in strictly sectional terms. Senator James O. Eastland of Mississippi declared that under the terms of the bill the federal government "would send carpetbaggers into the South to control elections." [35] However, their fears in this instance were largely unwarranted. The administration and its supporters did not see the soldiers' ballot bill as an instrument for broadening the base of the southern electorate. After all, the sponsor of the House bill was a Texan. The bill admittedly would have removed many bureaucratic obstacles for members of the armed services. But the administration viewed it as a wartime measure, aimed at overcoming cumbersome state registration procedures. Despite this essentially democratic motive, southern senators felt that the bill deprived the states of their constitutional right to determine voting qualifications. No advocate of the bill was spared from their invective. "Cotton Ed" Smith of South Carolina thought the bill "disgusting and infamous" and argued that only the

34 *Hearings to Amend the Soldiers' Voting Act*, 1–12.
35 *Congressional Record*, 78th Cong., 1st Sess., 10064.

states could handle the problem of assessing voting qualifications. The bill would turn the country over "to an international group. We have never gotten anything out of the international group but some very unworthy immigrants," he exclaimed.[36]

Given the widespread unease at their opposition to a ballot for troops who were fighting for their country, Dixie senators felt constrained to offer an alternative for the Green-Lucas bill. The chief strategists were Senators Eastland, McKellar, and John L. McClellan of Arkansas, who accordingly offered an amendment in the form of a substitute bill. Their amendment recommended the several states to pass legislation which supposedly would enable members of the armed forces to vote in both federal and state elections. Under the terms of the substitute bill state ballots would be printed on postcards which would be sent to the secretaries of war and the navy for distribution to military personnel. The ballots would be marked and then returned to state election officials.[37] The Eastland-McClellan-McKellar amendment in effect froze all prospects of a soldiers' vote. There was only a slim chance that state legislatures would convene in time to pass such legislation. Indeed, only nine legislatures were scheduled to hold regular sessions in 1944. Even if special sessions could convene and pass the enabling legislation, the administration of forty-eight different types of ballot would prove overwhelmingly difficult—as, indeed, it had done under the 1942 law.

Nevertheless, southern Democrats welcomed the amendment, since it would keep the states' election machinery intact. Senator Eastland argued that the original bill was not only unconstitutional but also a license for a repetition of the machinations that had taken place at the polls during Reconstruction. He warned that "soldiers' voting is not an issue here; but the sole issue is . . . whether we are to turn the election machinery of the country over to an aggregation of power-crazy bureaucrats

36 *Ibid.*, 10067.
37 *Ibid.*, 10165.

in Washington." [38] His fellow senators agreed. They were not persuaded by the caustic comment of Majority Leader Alben Barkley, who snapped that "the adoption of the substitute will have no more effect upon procuring the right to vote among the men in our armed forces than the adoption of a pious resolution by the Ladies' Society or the Rotary Club." [39] The southerners carried the day with the help of the Republicans, who wished to cause partisan embarrassment to the administration. The Eastland-McClellan-McKellar substitute passed by forty-two votes to thirty-seven. Senator Pepper was the only southerner to oppose it. [40]

The passage of the amendment, however, did not terminate sectional rancor. A few days later, one of the South's leading New Deal critics, Josiah Bailey, drew attention to the growing sense of southern solidarity that had arisen as a result of the administration's policies. Indeed, his passionate statement on the Senate floor marked his personal conversion from a philosophy of conservatism to one of southernism. Bailey's sectional lambast was occasioned by the comments of Democratic Senator Joseph F. Guffey of Pennsylvania, chairman of the Senate Democratic Campaign Committee. Guffey had declared in a statement to the press that northern Republicans and southern Democrats, under the leadership of Harry Byrd, had conspired to deprive members of the armed services of the vote. Guffey had dubbed the maneuver the "most unpatriotic and unholy alliance that has occurred in the United States Senate since the League of Nations for peace of the world was defeated in 1919." On December 7, 1943, Bailey undertook to reply to the charge in detail after Harry Byrd had demanded Guffey's resignation as chairman of the Campaign Committee. [41]

---

38 *Ibid.*, 10172.
39 *Ibid.*, 10287.
40 *Ibid.*, 10290. Seventeen southern Democrats joined seven nonsouthern members of the party and eighteen Republicans to pass the amendment over the negative votes of Senator Pepper, twenty-three nonsouthern Democrats, and thirteen Republicans.
41 *Ibid.*, 10344–345.

The Senate listened in silence to this first major warning of a sectional split in the Democratic party. Bailey's dramatic and impassioned speech is worth quoting at length. "What is wrong with being a Southern Senator?" asked the septuagenarian senator. "We are southern Senators and we have no apologies, and no shame and no fear. . . . Southern Democrats have borne long and have been patient." But, said Bailey, "There can be an end of insults, there can be an end of toleration, there can be an end of patience. We can form a southern Democratic party and vote as we please in the electoral college, and we will hold the balance of power in this country. . . . We will assert ourselves—and we are capable of asserting ourselves—and we will vindicate ourselves; and if we cannot have a party in which we are respected, if we must be in a party in which we are scorned as southern Democrats, we will find a party which honors us, not because we are southerners, and not because of politics, but because we love our country and believe in the Constitution. . . ." [42]

This open and highly publicized threat of possible party secession from a nationally prominent politician had an instant effect. The speech released the latent political disquiet in Dixie and projected it into the open realm of public debate. Bailey himself was deluged with words of advice and praise for his stand. One woman wanted no more compromises: "Don't be moved by any tears of the *throne* and its parasites, but go ahead and secede from the bastard New Deal." [43] Other admirers shared Bailey's fears that the Democratic party would adopt policies inimical to the South in order to solder the coalition of workers and Negroes in the pivotal metropolitan states. One correspondent was "fed up to the gills with this being shoved around by the stooges of the Labor Racketeers and by a Supreme Court composed of their attornies, who, like the little dog in the ad, know 'Their Masters Voice'." [44] An Alabamian

42 *Ibid.*, 10346.
43 Edith Ryan to Bailey, December 8, 1943, in Bailey Papers.
44 Wand B. Duncan to Bailey, December 11, 1943, in Bailey Papers.

confirmed his desire for political independence and welcomed the prospect of "a Southern Democratic Party—to get away from the Tammany-Hague-New Deal Party." [45]

The Bailey-Guffey episode only intensified the battle over the soldiers' ballot. The emasculation of the original Green-Lucas bill prompted Roosevelt to intervene personally in the controversy. On January 25, 1944, before the House had even considered the measure, Roosevelt emphatically asked Congress to pass the original bill. He stressed the importance of insuring a soldiers' ballot and arraigned the Eastland-McClellan-McKellar substitute as "meaningless" and "a fraud upon the American people." [46] The president's message to Congress thus further heightened the sectional bitterness that had become associated with the matter. Southern Democrats, who had supported the bill, interpreted Roosevelt's remarks as a public insult. [47]

So, when the House took up the bill, the shadow of the president's message influenced the entire proceedings. The Republicans, who were anxious to reap the benefits from the split in the Democratic party, joined the southerners in condemning the president's message. [48] The debate in the House followed a pattern similar to that in the Senate. The "states' rights" bill in the House was sponsored by Congressman John E. Rankin

45 Horace Turner to Bailey, December 10, 1943, Tyn Cobb to Bailey, December 8, 1943, W. D. Malone to Bailey, December 10, 1943, Mrs. C. E. Houser to Bailey, December 8, 1943, in Bailey Papers. As a result of this episode, Alben Barkley, majority leader, forced Guffey to resign from the chairmanship of the Senate Democratic Campaign Committee. Guffey was succeeded by Senator Joseph C. O'Mahoney of Wyoming. See typewritten statement of Alben Barkley, n.d., Joseph Guffey to Barkley, January 26, 1944, in Alben W. Barkley Papers, University of Kentucky Library, Lexington.

46 Rosenman (comp.), *The Public Papers and Addresses of Franklin D. Roosevelt,* XIII, 56.

47 McKellar to E. H. Crump, January 28, 1944, in McKellar Papers; also, Josephus Daniels to Doughton, January 31, 1944, Doughton to Daniels, February 1, 1944, in Folder 1171, Doughton Papers.

48 Hamilton Fish, Republican from New York, for example, described Roosevelt's message as "dictatorial, intemperate and insulting." *Congressional Record,* 78th Cong., 2nd Sess., 1007.

of Mississippi. The Rankin substitute was reported out by the Committee on Rules which was dominated by the South. The House, therefore, had to vote against this amendment before it could consider the Worley bill, which provided for a federal ballot. Although proportionally more southerners supported the administration bill in the House than did their colleagues in the Senate, they still overwhelmingly endorsed the Rankin bill.[49] Again, sectional rhetoric dominated the discussions. Rankin, in his typically paranoid style, thought that the opposition to his bill had been organized by *PM*, the liberal New York daily newspaper, the Communists, and the Jews. Congressman John S. Gibson of Georgia blamed "the Congress of Industrial Organizations, which I believe to be the working organization of the Communist Party." Moreover, he attached sinister significance to the fact that nearly all his congressional mail which was critical of the states' rights position had apparently originated in New York.[50] The debate continued in this vein for three days. Finally, the Rankin bill, with amendments, was passed by 328 to 69 votes. After further restrictive amendments in the Senate, the different versions went to joint conference.[51]

While Congress went through the final deliberations, the advocates of the original bill mobilized their forces in an effort to stymie the southerners' designs. Cosponsor Theodore Green received at least five boxes of correspondence overwhelmingly in favor of the original federal War Ballot Commission. A naval chaplain affirmed that soldiers and sailors regarded the federal vote as a right and that "they will fight most valiantly for a Congress that honors not only their ability as warriors but also their dignity as citizens." [52] A member of the Marine Corps

49 Democratic Congressmen Kefauver of Tennessee, Cooley, Folger, and Morrison of North Carolina, Sparkman of Alabama, Robertson of Virginia, and Worley of Texas supported the Green-Lucas bill.
50 *Congressional Record*, 78th Cong., 2nd Sess., 1027–1028.
51 Only three southern Democrats voted against the Rankin bill, while ninety favored it. *Ibid.*, 1228–229; New York *Times*, February 9, 1944.
52 John F. Hayward to Theodore F. Green, February 25, 1944, in Box 348, Theodore F. Green Papers, Manuscripts Division, Library of Congress, Washington, D.C.

wrote to a southern editor: "I'm being extremely mild when I state that the armed services are disgusted with Congress," because they "believe that they are fighting for our form of government as well as our way of life." [53] Others took stock of the geographical divisions and blatantly accused the southerners of trying to perpetuate themselves in office by denying the franchise to young soldiers and to Negroes.[54]

Southern members of Congress, however, were not prepared to relent. The final bill, as reported out by the joint conference committee, passed both houses in an atmosphere "heavily saturated with political considerations." [55] This compromise represented a total emasculation of the original Green-Lucas bill. It permitted a federal ballot to be used only if a serviceman personally applied for a state ballot and subsequently failed to receive it. In addition, both the state legislature and the governor of an applicant's home state had to certify by July 15 that they would accept a federal ballot. The president, who now had to decide whether to sign the bill, fully understood just how restrictive these amendments were. He immediately consulted the

53 Jimmy Hayes to John Santford Martin, March 26, 1944, in John Santford Martin Papers, Duke University Library, Durham, N.C.
54 E. Bloom to Green, February 15, 1944, in Box 348, and J. F. Chisholm to Green, February 17, 1944, in Box 349, Green Papers; Walter White to Charles Edison, December 14, 1943, in Box 289/5, NAACP Files. Josiah Bailey acknowledged that his principal fear was that "certain of our Northern friends in the Party" want "to have Congress step right in and say to the Southern states that the negroes should be allowed to vote." Bailey to Raymond O. Christman, February 19, 1944, in Bailey Papers.
55 New York *Times*, March 15, 1944. In the Senate the twenty-four Republicans who voted for the bill were joined by fourteen southern and nine nonsouthern Democrats. Against the conference bill were four Republicans, three southerners, and twenty-seven nonsouthern Democrats. The three southern Democrats opposed to the new report were Russell of Georgia, Pepper of Florida, and Stewart of Tennessee. *Congressional Record,* 78th Cong., 2nd Sess., 2573. The House adopted the final bill by 273 votes to 111. The 175 House Republicans were joined by 97 Democrats—79 of whom were from the South. Against the compromise bill were twelve Republicans, twelve southern Democrats, eighty-four nonsouthern Democrats, and three minor party members. The twelve negative votes from the South were cast by Bulwinkle, Clark, Cooley, and Folger of North Carolina, Davis, Priest, and Gore of Tennessee, Flannagan of Virginia, and Johnson, Patton, Patman, and Thomas of Texas. See New York *Times,* March 16, 1944.

governors of the states as to whether the use of supplementary federal ballots, provided for in the bill, was authorized by the laws of their states or whether they could be made to conform to the laws by July 15. When three out of four replied in the negative, the president allowed the bill, which he considered "confusing" and "wholly inadequate," to become law without his signature.[56]

The debacle over the soldiers' ballot was probably the turning point in North-South relations. Although other issues more directly related to the interests of the South had divided the party in the past—and would provide the fuel for further antagonism in the future—the controversy over the Green-Lucas bill had marked the occasion of both a sustained sectional attack on the administration and the first serious exploration for means of asserting the South's political independence. Moreover, this new particularism was led by influential and respected southern conservatives. Josiah Bailey, for one, had put the seal of dignity on a southernism that had in the recent past been the hallmark of the demagogues and not of the more restrained representatives of the New South.

This revival of southernism was reinforced in anti–New Deal circles as the election of 1944 drew closer. Southerners felt that the president was insensitive to their political aspirations and indifferent to their solicitudes. Apparently, he was more eager to court the approval of his urban supporters in the North. This was in marked contrast to his somewhat relaxed attitude toward reform in the earlier stages of the war. This new boldness was underlined during the battle on the soldiers' vote when Roosevelt submitted his proposals for a "second Bill of Rights." Under this program all citizens would be given the right to a "decent

56 Rosenman (comp), *The Public Papers and Addresses of Franklin D. Roosevelt*, XIII, 101–102, 111–16; Olin D. Johnston to FDR, March 23, 1944, George Norris to Joseph Guffey, March 20, 1944, in OF 1113, Roosevelt Papers; Birmingham *News*, March 17, 1944; Columbia *Record*, March 23, 1944.

house," employment, sickness benefit, and education.[57] These proposals obviously abnegated any previous commitments to shelve "Dr. New Deal." Roosevelt confirmed his critics' suspicions further in February, 1944, when he repudiated the party leadership by vetoing a current revenue bill. Alben Barkley, who had never been associated with the southern bloc, promptly resigned as majority leader on the grounds that the president had become oblivious to the concerns and counsels of Congress and his party.[58] Although Barkley's resignation had little to do with sectional antagonism, it did serve to underscore the president's new sense of independence from the party stalwarts.[59] Robert Doughton thought somewhat dramatically that "the real fundamental issue was whether or not representative government should be supplanted by a one-man dictatorial government." And a number of newspapers in Dixie called for the South's withdrawal from the Democratic party.[60]

Thus, by the summer of 1944 the president had indicated not only that he would revive the New Deal after the war but also that he would no longer rely upon the South and other congressional conservatives for political support. His advocacy of the soldiers' vote, social welfare legislation, and noninterference with the rights of organized labor, despite the well-

57 Rosenman (comp.), *The Public Papers and Addresses of Franklin D. Roosevelt,* XIII, 41; Mary H. Hinchey, "The Frustration of the New Deal Revival, 1944–1946" (Ph.D. dissertation, University of Missouri, 1965), 9–12.
58 Rosenman (comp.), *The Public Papers and Addresses of Franklin D. Roosevelt,* XIII, 80–83; Alben W. Barkley, *That Reminds Me* (New York, 1954), chap. 12; George W. Robinson, "Alben Barkley and the 1944 Tax Veto," *Register of the Kentucky Historical Society,* LXVII (July, 1969), 197–200; *Congressional Record,* 78th Cong., 2nd Sess., 1965–966. A Democratic caucus, held immediately after Barkley's resignation, unanimously reelected him.
59 Frank M. Dixon to John Bankhead, March 8, 1944, in Frank M. Dixon Papers, Alabama Department of Archives, Montgomery. Also, John McDuffie to James Farley, February 26, 1944, in John McDuffie Papers, University of Alabama, Tuscaloosa.
60 Doughton to Walter H. Woodson, February 25, 1944, in Folder 1179, Doughton Papers; *Southern Weekly,* February 26, 1944; Baton Rouge *Morning Advocate,* February 24, 1944; Charleston *News and Courier,* February 24, 1944.

articulated wishes of many southern veterans, indicated that he valued more highly the support of those interest groups that had become associated with the urban coalition. Southerners were determined to show the president that he could not ignore Dixie in the formulation of domestic policy. Yet politicians in the South knew that anti–New Deal sentiment in their section was insufficient to arouse voters against the party that had represented their interests for at least fifty years. It thus became necessary to broaden the base of southern opposition. Ample opportunity would soon be afforded, however, as the Democrats, sometimes unintentionally, became more closely aligned with the cause of civil rights for Negroes.

CHAPTER THREE

Mobilization of the Urban Coalition: Washington and Dixie, 1942–1944

SOUTHERN DEMOCRATS were alarmed not only at the administration's policies on social welfare and the franchise but also at its predilection for the aspirations and programs of Negro and labor organizations. Southerners feared that if the party leadership became too responsive to these organizations, then they would ultimately form the backbone of the Democratic party. This would mean that the South would no longer hold dominion in the party, as it had done in the days of William Jennings Bryan and Woodrow Wilson. In such an eventuality, they reasoned, the entire social and racial fabric of the South could be destroyed. It is necessary, therefore, to examine the foundations of these fears. Did, in fact, the president deliberately and consciously seek an alignment with these groups? Or was he merely propelled toward them inadvertently by political forces that were ultimately beyond his control? And, equally important, what were the attitudes of the leaders and civil rights organizations themselves toward the South and the president?

The determination of the anti–New Deal faction to stymie the thrust of social welfare legislation and to move the fulcrum of power within the Democratic party to the right only hardened the resolution of the supporters of the New Deal. In particular, the leaders of civil rights, labor, and welfare organizations, together with their supporters in Congress, devoted their financial and intellectual resources in a drive to move the government to the left. The most attractive and forceful method of mobilizing support for their programs of social reform was to build up vast blocs of voters, who would be capable of wielding a decisive balance of power in elections in marginal states. The group most suited to this kind of mass political mobilization was, undoubtedly, organized labor. The Congress of Industrial Organizations was particularly well equipped to undertake preparations for concerted political action. It had spread rapidly during the war and was generally more capable of organizing its members, who tended to work in larger plants, than was its chief rival, the American Federation of Labor (AF of L). Moreover, it had had experience in political action in 1936, when it had formed Labor's Non-Partisan League, an organization that was partly responsible for Roosevelt's widespread support among workers.[1]

The experiences on the home front in the early part of the war convinced the CIO leadership that political action should be reactivated. Some union officials felt that certain war agencies were biased against the unions, and they wished to insure that the president's affirmed sympathies for labor's aspirations would be reflected in the decisions of the agencies concerned. They thought that the no-strike pledge had eliminated one of labor's most powerful weapons, the walkout. Thus, they deemed it necessary to secure their goals by exercising direct influence over government policy. This could most easily be done by arousing the electorate from the apathy reflected in the low turnout in the industrial cities of the North in the 1942 elections. It was this low participation, they reasoned, that had been responsible for the president's domestic reverses. The CIO determined, therefore, to pool its resources for the 1944

1 Overacker, "Labor's Political Contributions," 56–68; Josephson, *Sidney Hillman*, 468–89; Delbert D. Arnold, "The CIO's Role in American Politics, 1936–1948" (Ph.D. dissertation, University of Maryland, 1952), 34–60.

election to defeat those congressmen who had opposed protective welfare legislation and Roosevelt's veto of the Smith-Connally bill.[2]

Accordingly, Philip Murray, president of the CIO, planned for the mass participation of labor in the forthcoming election campaign. He discussed the matter with Sidney Hillman, who had by then become a close political associate of the president. Indeed, Roosevelt himself had earlier offered Hillman an appointment as special assistant to the president on labor matters, which, as interpreted by Roosevelt at the time, "will mean that your relationship with me in the Government will be very similar to that of Harry Hopkins."[3] Thus, Hillman's personal friendship with the president, together with his experiences of government war agencies and union organizing, fittingly equipped him for the task of galvanizing labor into a major political force. Hillman and Murray drew up plans together for the creation of the Political Action Committee (PAC), which would raise money for election purposes and also would plan and publicize its own legislative program. Most important, it would try to influence the ideology of the party leadership wherever possible.

In July, 1943, the Political Action Committee of the CIO was officially approved by the CIO's executive board. Sidney Hillman was appointed chairman and Van Bittner of the United Steelworkers of America, vice-chairman. The CIO unions initially pledged nearly $700,000 to the PAC. The money was to be used for the publication of materials and for the mobilization of voters.[4]

---

2 Philip Murray, "Labor's Political Aims," *American Magazine*, CXXXVII (February, 1944), 28–29; telegram, CIO Executive Board to Bilbo, May 14, 1943, in Bilbo Papers; E. L. Sandefur to Doughton, June 18, 1943, in Doughton Papers; Thirty Delegates Representing Approximately 300,000 Organized Workers (UAW-CIO) in Wayne County, Michigan, to FDR, June 26, 1943, in OF 407, Roosevelt Papers.

3 Telegram, FDR to Sidney Hillman, April 18, 1942, Hillman to FDR, May 1, 1942, in OF 4910, Roosevelt Papers.

4 Arnold, "The CIO's Role in American Politics," 94–98; also, U.S. House of Representatives, Special Committee to Investigate Campaign Expenditures,

This drive to bring workers to the polls was wholeheartedly endorsed at the CIO's annual convention in November, 1943. Murray told the delegates that the PAC would be labor's "political arm" and that it was an integral part of unionism. He believed that the immediate task before the PAC was to prepare for the 1944 elections. But he envisaged that the PAC should be "also looking beyond 1944 and planning for a permanent political organization for labor." He added, however, that "it is definitely not the policy of the CIO to organize a third party."[5] He affirmed that a new party would at that stage be superfluous since, presumably, Roosevelt's championship of an expanded social security system and a full employment program coincided in substance with labor's aims. Thus, although the CIO-PAC claimed it was nonpartisan, it leaned heavily in sympathy toward President Roosevelt. Indeed, it was this overt partisanship that was largely responsible for the refusal of the AF of L to associate with the PAC.[6]

This close association between the national Democratic party and the PAC was accentuated in January, 1944, when the latter convened in New York a two-day conference on full employment. The conference was attended not only by union officers but also by several government officials. The speakers openly endorsed Roosevelt's economic bill of rights and called for national economic planning in the postwar period.[7] Philip Murray told the convention that "labor's part in the coming elections is of the utmost importance" for the achievement of these goals.[8] The White House apparently concurred. Vice President Henry A. Wallace was sent to address the conference in New York, where he repeatedly stressed that the administration and

---

Hearings to Investigate Campaign Expenditures, 1944, 78th Cong., 2nd Sess., 3–94.
5 Quoted in Gaer, *The First Round,* 61.
6 Riker, "The CIO in Politics," 246–47.
7 CIO Political Action Committee, *Full Employment: The Proceedings of the Conference on Full Employment,* CIO-PAC (New York, 1944), 1–4, 56–59; Arnold, "The CIO's Role in American Politics," 100–21.
8 CIO-PAC, *Proceedings of the Conference on Full Employment,* 56.

the PAC shared the same ideals and goals.[9] Sidney Hillman, who was almost becoming a go-between for the CIO and the administration, shared the rostrum with Wallace. Hillman pleaded for a high turnout at the polls and also called for particular attention to the mobilization of the Negro vote in the North and South.[10]

The PAC thus began to campaign for the return of liberals to Congress with the tacit approval of the administration. Regional committees on political action were set up to scrutinize the political credentials of local candidates. The national Political Action Committee served as the coordinating agency for these regional committees, and itself made no endorsements of local candidates. Its main function was to raise money for organizing mass registration drives and to publicize its program for the benefit of aspirants to office. Its clearest statement of policy was to be found in a collated series of pamphlets, *The People's Program for 1944*. In this manifesto the PAC called for the establishment of a permanent national planning board, a guaranteed minimum wage, effective price and rent controls, a permanent fair employment practices committee, and the abolition of the poll tax.[11] Although the PAC insisted that it was nonpartisan and interested only in candidates' attitudes to these demands, it actually inclined overwhelmingly toward the Democrats. Nevertheless, it officially tried to maintain an independent stand so that its support would not be taken for granted automatically by the Democratic party.[12]

President Roosevelt and the Democratic National Committee were anxious to consolidate their informal alliance with the PAC. They recognized the need to court the PAC so that it could deliver the vital labor vote to the Democrats. They were acutely aware that its alienation could be electorally suicidal.

9 *Ibid.*, 67–74.
10 *Ibid.*, 126–27.
11 Pamphlet, CIO Political Action Committee, *The People's Program for 1944*.
12 *Hearings to Investigate Campaign Expenditures, 1944*, pp. 7–9; Gaer, *The First Round*, 110.

For his part the president remained on close terms and in frequent contact with Sidney Hillman—diplomatically, a very important step in insuring a binding relationship between the PAC and the administration. The party leadership was equally determined to woo the PAC. One such opportunity was presented in December, 1943, during the soldiers' vote controversy. Sidney Hillman, in his capacity as chairman of the CIO-PAC, had demanded the intervention of the Democratic hierarchy to press for the passage of the Green-Lucas bill. Frank C. Walker, Democratic chairman, publicly expressed complete agreement with Hillman on the importance of a federal ballot and released an exchange of telegrams on the subject at once.[13] The publication of this correspondence was, of course, as much a recognition of Hillman's influence as it was an endorsement of the original soldiers' ballot. Similarly, Democratic officials at the local level were impressed with the formidable power of the PAC. One proadministration Democrat from Texas, for example, advised Walker to join and encourage the PAC's voter registration drive. He recommended that "a campaign ought to be started immediately by the various labor organizations to get their members to register . . . and to pay their poll taxes in the states where that is the qualification required." [14] Solicitations such as these had their desired effect. In June, 1944, the PAC announced the inevitable—it endorsed President Roosevelt for a fourth term. The labor-Democratic alliance was now formalized.

The Negro population was equally watchful of political developments. Negroes understood that they constituted an important electoral bloc and that they too should organize to influence government policy. They recognized that their grievances

13 Release, Democratic National Committee, Exchange of Telegrams, Sidney Hillman to Frank C. Walker, December 27, 1943, and Walker to Hillman, December 27, 1943, in Box 46, DNC Files.
14 Clyde O. Eastus to Frank C. Walker, December 10, 1943, in Box 20, DNC Files.

could not be ignored in summary fashion while the United States was ostensibly engaged in a war against nations that espoused theories of national and racial superiority. Blacks, both north and south of the Mason-Dixon Line, thus determined to exploit this basic problem by questioning the moral basis of America's position—especially since they were being constantly reminded by the Office of War Information of the democratic ideals of the Allied cause. A Negro journalist commented that the slogans of justification for American intervention in the war had "built up his expectations for complete citizenship, have developed in the Negro a new critical approach to his position in the social structure of the country and the theory and practice of democracy." [15] This new militancy was more simply expressed in a warning to Senator Connally that "the Negro millions will *give* all *to* their Government; but not without, at the same time, *demanding* all *from* their Government." [16]

Negroes resolved that both their vigilance of government policy and the momentum of their national campaigns for social justice should be intensified. They took particular interest in the fate of the Fair Employment Practices Committee. However, their experiences in the campaigns to strengthen the FEPC demonstrated their greater weakness and vulnerability. As a result of their inability to bind both the administration and the party leadership to their cause, Negroes remained less committed to the Democrats than were the labor unions. The period of optimism following the creation of the FEPC reached an end in July, 1942, when the committee was transferred to the War Manpower Commission under Paul McNutt, who was

15 Horace Cayton in Pittsburgh *Courier,* February 27, 1943.
16 L. H. King to Tom Connally, September 16, 1942, in Box 113, Connally Papers. One historian has interpreted this new sense of race consciousness and militancy as a prolegomenon to the black revolution of the 1960s. See Richard M. Dalfiume, "The 'Forgotten Years' of the Negro Revolution," *Journal of American History,* LV (June, 1968), 90–106. Also, Rayford W. Logan, "The Negro Wants First Class Citizenship," in Rayford W. Logan (ed.), *What the Negro Wants* (Chapel Hill, 1944), 1–30.

generally unsympathetic to a federal nondiscrimination policy. McNutt's unwillingness to confront discriminatory racial practices was demonstrated by his refusal to allow the FEPC to investigate the employment policies of the southern railroads. Negro leaders echoed their disappointment unequivocally. A. Philip Randolph described McNutt's inaction as "a slap in the face of and insult to upwards of 20 millions of Negro Americans. It makes them feel that the President is surrendering to the race-prejudice-mongering political demagogues of the South."[17] After similar outcries, the FEPC was removed from the WMC in May, 1943, and established as an independent office, subject only to the authority of the president.[18]

This transfer temporarily renewed confidence in the Fair Employment Practices Committee, although the president continued to find it politically embarrassing. Roosevelt received constant counsel from his advisers that the FEPC, which was generally staffed by zealous and committed liberals, should pursue a cautious campaign against discriminatory hiring practices. Jonathan Daniels, White House administrative assistant with responsibility for racial matters, advised that the new FEPC, under the chairmanship of Monseigneur Francis J. Haas, "ought to be worked out as informally as possible in order not to set up another official point for pressure, and, therefore, for controversy."[19] By November, 1943, Daniels was warning Roosevelt that the missionary enthusiasm of the FEPC would invite southern leaders to seek a head-on clash with the administration. He advised the president to use his influence to prevent the FEPC from investigating the racial practices of the Washington, D.C., Capital Transit Company. Such an in-

17 Pittsburgh *Courier,* January 23, 1943.
18 *Ibid.,* April 3, 1943.
19 Jonathan Daniels to Marvin McIntyre, July 21, 1943, in Box 438, Jonathan Daniels Papers, Southern Historical Collection, University of North Carolina, Chapel Hill. Boris Shiskin, a member of the new FEPC, felt that FDR was ideologically committed to the spirit of the FEPC. Boris Shiskin, interview with author, October, 1969.

vestigation, admonished Daniels, might "in a jumpy situation create Southern fears that the government may be moving to end Jim Crow laws in transportation in the South under the guise of the war effort. It may also lift Negro hopes only to drop them." [20] The president was thus often tempted to vacillate on the FEPC issue in a deliberate endeavor to alienate neither the South nor the black community.[21]

Negro leaders were aware that the FEPC was also vulnerable to the whims of Congress, which could at any time deny it appropriations.[22] As a result, the civil rights organizations that wished to guarantee the permanence of the FEPC rallied to push for legislation which would give the FEPC statutory authority. In September, 1943, A. Philip Randolph formed the National Council for a Permanent FEPC. This organization was soon joined by other bodies, including the NAACP, the Urban League, the American Jewish Committee, the American Civil Liberties Union, and the ad hoc National CIO Committee to Abolish Racial Discrimination.[23] These organizations launched a full publicity campaign to achieve their goal. Randolph and Allan K. Chalmers, cochairmen of the National Council for a Permanent FEPC, planned to swamp key members of Congress with requests to hold hearings.[24] The NAACP adopted similar tactics. However, these strategies proved fruitless, because the Democratic leadership in Congress procrastinated. FEPC legislation was not even reported out of committee until the day Congress adjourned in 1944. The chairman of the House Committee on Labor, Mary D. Norton, Democrat from New Jersey,

20 Memo, Daniels to FDR, November 24, 1943, in Box 448, Daniels Papers.
21 See, for example, Ruchames, *Race, Jobs, and Politics*, 65–66; Pittsburgh *Courier*, November 13, 1943.
22 Ruchames, *Race, Jobs, and Politics*, 87; Will Maslow, "FEPC: A Case History in Parliamentary Maneuver," *University of Chicago Law Review*, XIII (June, 1946), 412.
23 Louis Coleridge Kesselman, *The Social Politics of FEPC: A Study in Reform Pressure Movements* (Chapel Hill, 1948).
24 A. Philip Randolph and Allan K. Chalmers to Roy Wilkins, April 29, 1944, in Box 280/5, NAACP Files.

who was sympathetic to the cause of a permanent FEPC, defended the political efficacy of this act of deliberate delay.[25] Alben Barkley also tried to exonerate himself from charges of indifference by attributing inaction to the absence of a quorum. Walter White, however, was unimpressed by their excuses. He told the majority leader that Negroes were greatly disappointed "that the Congress thought it more important to recess in order to participate in political campaigns . . . than to take action for the protection of human lives and destinies."[26]

The FEPC was only one area in which Negro leaders closed rank in a state of disillusionment. Jim Crow in the armed services and the reluctance of the military authorities to commit Negro soldiers to combat or other responsible assignments were condemned with equal energy. The War Department's persistent refusal to place Negroes in special units prompted William H. Hastie, a Negro, to resign in 1943 from his job as civilian aide in the War Department.[27] The instant outcry over Hastie's resignation again demonstrated the essential quandary in which Negroes found themselves. They were uncomfortably cognizant that the unprecedented number of overtures made to them by the Roosevelt administration had only raised their levels of expectation. Roy Wilkins spoke of "the amount of cynical discouragement spread through the Negro population."[28] Columnist George Schuyler was more ominous in his prognostications and predicted: "It seems to be definitely the end of the long honeymoon between the New Deal and the Negro."[29]

The NAACP, the Negro organization with the largest mem-

25 Walter White to Mary D. Norton, September 7, 1944, Norton to White, September 22, 1944, in Box 280/5, NAACP Files.
26 Alben Barkley to Walter White, September 22, 1944, White to Barkley, October 11, 1944, in Box 280/5, NAACP Files.
27 Pittsburgh *Courier*, February 6, 1943.
28 Roy Wilkins to Henry Stimson, February 5, 1943, in Box 274/2, NAACP Files.
29 See Commission on Interracial Cooperation Clip Sheet, Ser. 2, No. 10, May 31, 1943, in Ames Papers; also, Walter White to Martin Dies, September 25, 1942, in OF 93, Roosevelt Papers; Walter White to editor, *East Tennessee News*, February 16, 1943, in Box 274/2, NAACP Files.

bership, also crusaded for legislation that was not always of interest to Negroes exclusively. It supported and organized campaigns for bills on full employment, soldiers' votes, federal aid to education, social security, and the continuation of those New Deal agencies that were abolished in 1943.[30] Of course, all these matters affected Negroes, who formed, after all, a larger proportion of the working (and unemployed) population than whites. The NAACP kept special records of congressional voting behavior and was able to exert considerable influence on northern officeholders who represented areas with a substantial number of Negroes. Members of Congress who failed to vote for the bills supported by the NAACP might find themselves opposed by Negroes in their reelection campaigns. Thus, members with a large Negro constituency would often vie for the endorsement of the NAACP. Censure from this pressure group could sometimes cause embarrassment. On one occasion, for example, Congressman Hugh Scott, Republican from Pennsylvania, a staunch and sincere advocate of the anti-poll tax bill, threatened in a huff to withdraw his support from that measure when Walter White attacked the civil rights record of the Republican party as a whole. Scott, of course, recognized that the NAACP was as dependent upon his benevolence as he was upon that of the NAACP.[31]

Although the various civil rights groups campaigned energetically to secure favorable legislation, they did not attempt to mobilize the black vote in the fashion of the CIO-PAC. This desistance from mass political action was chiefly the result of two conditions, one structural, the other political. First, no Negro organization had the ability to rally Negro voters. None of the principal groups, such as the NAACP, the National Urban League, or the newly formed Congress of Racial Equality,

30 Memo, Leslie Perry to Staff (of NAACP), January 28, 1944, in Box 280/3, NAACP Files.
31 Hugh Scott to Walter White, March 12, 1943, in Box 263/4, NAACP Files. See also, Consuelo C. Young to editor, New York *Times*, August 15, 1944, in Box 280/4, George H. Bender to Walter White, June 9, 1943, in Box 263/4, NAACP Files.

wielded sufficient influence within the black community. These organizations could not claim that they represented the majority of Negroes as the AF of L or CIO could for organized labor. Although they challenged discrimination in everyday life and lobbied incessantly for protective legislation, they did not operate physically in the ghetto or on the factory floor. Thus, their degree of contact with the mass of Negroes was insufficient for large-scale political action. Second, Negroes had ultimately less to gain from partisan involvement. Although most Negroes had supported the Democratic party since 1936, they remained critical of the administration's waverings and, unlike the CIO, were disinclined to commit themselves completely to the party which had been dominated by the South for more than half a century.[32]

The president was fully aware that the Negro vote was more volatile than the labor vote. Roosevelt was thus careful to solicit the support of influential Negro leaders. He was helped in this respect by his wife Eleanor, who, he thought, could escape the notice of southern politicians. Mrs. Roosevelt corresponded frequently with Negro leaders and identified herself quite openly with the civil rights cause.[33] Her husband, however, was more cautious and tried to keep to the middle of the road, so that both Negroes and southerners would remain in the Democratic column. The president generally followed the advice of Jonathan Daniels, a North Carolinian, who was himself painfully torn between a commitment to social justice and a nagging penchant for the beneficence of the Old South. Daniels advised

32 It should be pointed out that black leaders did affiliate with the PAC in an individual capacity. Of the 142 members of the National Citizens' Political Action Committee, which was the nonunion counterpart of the CIO-PAC, 22 were Negroes. Riker, "The CIO in Politics," 225; also, Henry Lee Moon, *Balance of Power: The Negro Vote* (Garden City, N.Y., 1949), chap. 8.

33 The first lady often confided in Walter White. The NAACP files show that she gave her opinions and interpretations of events quite freely to the NAACP secretary. See, for example, various correspondence, in Box 316/4, NAACP Files, and White, *A Man Called White*, 190–94.

Roosevelt to open up communications with "some other Negro group beside that largely radical group in the North with which it has in the past been dealing." [34] Daniels knew, on the other hand, that if the president dissociated himself from leaders such as Randolph, Lester Granger, and White, northern Negroes, "in an over-militancy based on overexpectations," would return to the Republican fold.[35] The dilemma seemed insoluble. As early as 1942, Daniels had written: "I am more disturbed about race relations in the United States than I have ever been before. We seem to be almost back to the extreme abolitionists and the extreme slaveholders in the lines of the discussion." [36]

Anxious to hold both the "abolitionists" and the "slaveholders" in the Democratic column, Roosevelt made few commitments to Negro demands and always justified his decisions in terms of their contributions toward victory in the war. He was concerned as much with unity as with social justice, although he usually tried to make the latter instrumental in achieving his goal of national harmony. But his desire for political harmony within the party often precluded any positive encouragement to racial equality. For example, after the Detroit race riot of June, 1943, when thirty-four people were killed, the president condemned the violence and ordered federal troops into the area. He did not, however, use his moral authority to draw the public's attention to the underlying causes of the violence.[37] After a series of similar racial incidents he was advised to issue a statement condemning street riots. However, Daniels, who recommended the statement, counseled: "I do not think this is an occasion on which goals of ultimate justice for all need so

34 Memo, Jonathan Daniels to Marvin McIntyre, January 2, 1943, in Box 426, Daniels Papers.
35 Jonathan Daniels to Josephus Daniels, November 10, 1943, in Box 448, Daniels Papers.
36 Jonathan Daniels to Dr. Howard Odum, August 24, 1942, in Box 415, Daniels Papers.
37 Rosenman (comp.), *The Public Papers and Addresses of Franklin D. Roosevelt,* XII, 258–59; Alfred McClung Lee and Norman D. Humphrey, *Race Riot* (New York, 1943).

much to be stressed as your determination that no violence at home, regardless of cause, shall be tolerated." [38] The president, in fact, ignored even Daniels' caveat and took no subsequent action.

Roosevelt's ambivalence on the race issue may have encouraged various federal agencies to ignore the spirit of the FEPC's nondiscrimination orders. The director of the Office of Defense Transportation felt that he had "no mandate to deal with social questions" and that progress in race relations "can be jeopardized if steps are taken to force issues too rapidly and if decisions are made which fan the flames of prejudice." [39] In the South the War Manpower Commission and the United States Employment Service, according to FEPC officials, were not only reluctant to encourage equal opportunities but also were unwilling to cooperate or conform to FEPC orders. One report stated that the "WMC-USES at all levels within the region [*i.e.* the South] has been generally obstructionalist . . . and has displayed a minimum of cooperation and a maximum of opposition. Its occasional support for the principles of the Executive Order seems to vary inversely with size, importance and perhaps the political power of the party charged." [40]

Although caution was the hallmark of his racial policy, it must not be thought that Roosevelt acquiesced to the white supremacists in his party. He tried to convince Negroes surreptitiously and obliquely that his administration was deeply concerned about discrimination and the problem of inequality. Yet it was these cautious approaches that angered many white southerners. If the president seldom actually endorsed the campaigns of Negro leaders to secure specific protective legislation,

38 Memo, Jonathan Daniels to FDR, August 2, 1943, in Box 440, Daniels Papers.
39 Joseph B. Eastman to Walter White, August 15, 1942, in Box 240/4, NAACP Files.
40 Annual report of John A. Davis, Director, Division of Review and Analysis, and John Hope II, Fair Practices Examiner, Region VII, October 10, 1944, in RG 228–74, Office Files of George M. Johnson, FEPC Records; unsigned memo to Malcolm Ross, undated (probably from Will Maslow, 1944), in RG 228-70, Office Files of Malcolm Ross, FEPC Records.

he also never joined southern Democrats in condemning or criticizing their efforts. Many of Roosevelt's speeches and published letters contained general assurances of his commitment to the elimination of social injustice. For example, on the occasion of the Urban League's annual conference in Chicago he was constrained to write to Lester Granger that "we cannot stand before the world as a champion of oppressed people unless we practice, as well as preach, the principles of democracy for all men." [41] Neither is there any evidence in his personal papers that the president ever tried to restrain his energetic and uninhibited wife. And just before the 1944 election he decided to meet personally with Negro leaders to assure them of his interest in their race's welfare.

In October he conferred regarding future policy with Walter White, Mary McLeod Bethune, president of the National Council of Negro Women, and Dr. Channing Tobias of the Social Action Committee of the Colored Methodist Church. He promised them that he would desegregate the armed forces after the war and, when asked whether he supported the FEPC legislation, exclaimed proudly to the conferees: "Certainly, I invented the FEPC." [42] Nevertheless, although Roosevelt was eager to apprise Negro leaders of his concern, he hoped he could achieve his goal without unduly alarming the South. His promises were more forthcoming than his performance. The platform of the Democratic party in 1944 contained neither of the planks mentioned by Roosevelt in his conversations with Negro leaders.

Although the major Negro organizations rejected both large-scale political action and an alliance with the Democratic party, they recognized the need to present a coordinated program by which Negro voters could measure and judge individual candidates for office. It was considered particularly impor-

41 Quoted in Pittsburgh *Courier*, October 2, 1943.
42 Memo, October 3, 1944, re Memo on Conference with the President, 11:45–12:15, September 29, 1944, at the White House, in NAACP Files (no file number recorded). See also, memo, Jonathan Daniels to Samuel Rosenman, October 25, 1944, in Box 482, Daniels Papers; memo, James M. Barnes to FDR, August 28, 1944, in OF 93, Roosevelt Papers.

tant to translate the new militancy of the Negro into concrete
political terms and to destroy the belief that Negroes would
contentedly and humbly accept vague promises of federal action. To emphasize their new mood, Walter White organized
and sponsored a conference which was to convene in New York
in November, 1943. He considered it imperative for Negroes to
make a united, unambiguous stand, since "increasingly the administration [was] making concessions" to the South and to conservative Republicans. He feared also that the few gains Negroes had made could easily be lost after the war.[43] He told
Lester Granger in his invitation that the objectives of the conference

. . . will be for the purpose of drafting a strictly non-partisan statement of the Negro's position regarding the way in which various
political parties have treated him. Its essence will be the pointing out
to the American people and to the various political parties that the
Negro is tired of being treated as a football and that he does not
relish being thought of as a mental infant. On this premise will be
based a statement of the demands Negroes of all sections, parties and
affiliations make of the political parties as the price of their support
in the 1944 and succeeding elections. . . . it seems imperative that
Negroes should speak as a unit so as to make their position unmistakably clear.[44]

The conference met on November 20. It was attended by
prominent Negro leaders such as Walter White, Thurgood Marshall, William Hastie, Mary McLeod Bethune, Dr. Channing
Tobias, and George Weaver, who represented the National CIO
Committee to Abolish Racial Discrimination. Church, fraternal,
labor, civic, and educational organizations sent delegations to
the convention. The mood in New York was determined and
unequivocal.[45] After a brief debate, "A Declaration by Negro
Voters" was drawn up and approved. The declaration showed
that Negroes had become more emphatic and voluble in their

43 Walter White to Lester Granger, October 4, 1943, in Box 263/2, NAACP
Files.
44 White to Granger, November 11, 1943, in Box 263/2, NAACP Files.
45 Minutes of Political Conference at Hotel Theresa, New York, N.Y., November 20, 1943, in Box 263/2, NAACP Files.

demands and that compromise with prevailing racial sentiment, which had characterized so many civil rights groups during the depression, had been discarded for principle. The conference declared that "public officers who have not made a record of liberal and democratic action may expect the Negro to help remove them from office." Candidates for office were expected to support both the war effort and the social welfare proposals that Roosevelt would enunciate in his 1944 State of the Union Address. The conferees insisted upon the unconditional right to vote, with the concomitant abolition of the poll tax, the white primary, and gerrymandering. Racial integration in government housing and the armed forces, a statutory FEPC, and anti-lynching legislation were also demanded. Finally, the delegates resolved that no political candidate would be acceptable "unless he has clearly demonstrated opposition to and departure from the prevailing anti-Negro traditions." Thus, a political war had been declared on the most hallowed of all southern traditions: segregation.[46]

It has been argued that the president calculated that his policies should be sufficiently responsive to heightened Negro militancy without incurring the wrath of watchful southern Democrats. He recognized that the alliance between the Negro and the Democratic party was essentially fragile and was anxious not to weaken the already frail support he commanded among influential Negroes. So he deliberately eschewed all attempts to create a symbiotic relationship with the Negro bloc. He thus had to devise a method of convincing Negroes that his administration was cognizant of their handicaps in employment and the franchise, while, at the same time, reassuring southerners that he did not intend to dispense with their valuable support. Civil rights leaders exhibited little sympathy for Roosevelt's dilemma and insisted that the president should abandon his dependence upon the South. When it became clear that Roosevelt did not

46 "A Declaration by Negro Voters," draft, November 29, 1943 (issued December 1, 1943), in Box 263/2, NAACP Files.

intend to sacrifice Dixie's support, black leaders determined to sustain and even intensify their campaign for protective legislation. For, unlike the labor leaders, they felt little need to merge their campaigns with those of the Democratic party. Thus, the exhortations that emanated from the headquarters of the various civil rights groups were generally less compromising and more critical of Roosevelt's policies. Yet, paradoxically, while this would prove embarrassing to Roosevelt, it also reflected an uncomfortable political reality—Roosevelt wanted the support of the Negro, but he did not need it.

The energetic political activities of labor and Negro organizations weren't unnoticed south of the Potomac. Although both the CIO-PAC and the civil rights groups concentrated their efforts in the North and were thus more likely to wield an influence there in the political process, they did not shy away from mobilizing support in Dixie. For many white southerners this was to prove a sobering experience. They had repeatedly expressed a fear that workers and blacks were exercising too much control over Democratic affairs. Now they were apparently seeking not only to alter the composition of the Democratic party but also to transform the racial and economic structure of the South. Labor union leaders were guiding their flocks away from paths of southern mores, and officials of the NAACP were seeking to subvert the white primary and other fortresses of white supremacy. These very concrete attempts to change the political structure were especially portentous, argued the South's officeholders. For there was no longer any recourse for their grievances, since the Roosevelt administration had clearly aligned itself with these groups. This sense of frustration had a drastic effect on community relations, as well as on the partisan assumptions of southern Democrats.

Opponents of labor unions in the South had several reasons to be alarmed at the reinvigoration of the CIO. In the first place, they recognized that the rapid increase in industrialization and urbanization which had occurred as a result of the war would facilitate the general expansion of industrial unionism and thereby reduce the South's attractiveness for potential investors. The farm population of the South declined by 25.8 percent between 1940 and 1945, and this obviously raised the potential for growth in the labor movement.[47] Second, the CIO tended to confuse political patterns in the South. Workers in towns were less susceptible to political suasion or control by local officeholders, who had relied in the past upon the political malleability of the rural population for realizing electoral power. But, above all, the CIO threatened to subvert the racial structure of the South. The constitution of the CIO outlawed discrimination in its unions, while the AF of L had frequently acquiesced to segregation and racial exclusion in its locals.[48] If the CIO were permitted to organize a plant, it would have greater bargaining power than the more fragmented AF of L and would be in a position to insist, if it so wished, that Negroes be given equal opportunities in employment. Thus, since many small towns in the South were dominated by one or two basic industries, industrial unionism threatened not only to destroy competitive advantages and alter the framework of labor-management relations but also to transform the racial composition of the labor force.

The CIO intensified its campaigns to organize the South as the number of industrial workers increased during the war. But its drive to unionize workers was frequently met with violent resistance. The experiences of various union officials were viv-

47 Calvin B. Hoover and Benjamin U. Ratchford, *Economic Resources and Policies of the South* (New York, 1951), 91. The South here includes Kentucky and Oklahoma. Other studies of the demographic impact of the war include: Rudolf Heberle, "The Impact of the War on Population Distribution in the South," *Papers of the Institute of Research and Training in the Social Sciences,* Vanderbilt University, VII (January, 1945), 8–27; Dillard B. Lasseter, "The Impact of the War on the South and Implications for Postwar Development," *Social Forces,* XXIII (October, 1944), 20–26.

48 Herbert H. Northrup, "Unions and Negro Employment," *Annals of the American Academy of Political Science,* CCXLIV (1946), 42–47; Tindall, *The Emergence of the New South,* 571–73; Charles S. Johnson, *Into the Main Stream: A Survey of Best Practices in Race Relations in the South* (Chapel Hill, 1947), 115–22.

idly recounted by Lucy Randolph Mason, a leading organizer in the South throughout this period. Miss Mason, who described her role as that of "roving ambassador" for the CIO, was particularly concerned with the breaches in civil liberties in organizational drives.[49] She sought to minimize local friction and to insure that Negroes in particular were neither abused nor excluded in the CIO's campaign. She was uncomfortably aware that the CIO would be resisted in some quarters by remonstrations that multiracial unions would weaken the economic security of white workers and would result in desegregation and the promotion of Negroes to supervisory positions. For example, the *Textile Bulletin* had warned of the attempts "to force the white workers of the South to work side-by-side with negroes and to share with them their restaurants and their toilet facilities." [50] Miss Mason, who was apprehensive about the sensitivity of southerners on this issue, traveled through the South to record and, if possible, to prevent any violent incidents that might arise from the vitriolic rhetoric that accompanied so many organizers.

Lucy Mason found that union officials usually faced as much opprobrium and harassment from the law as they did from local business interests. For example, in Savannah, Georgia, pamphleteers for the CIO had been attacked after they had been given an enthusiastic response by Negroes. They had turned to the law for protection, but the police, who had sided with the AF of L, had turned a blind eye. Similar incidents were reported from Mississippi. According to George Brown, CIO director of organization, the police had arrested and molested union representatives without bringing charges.[51] On another occasion, the sheriff of Macon, Georgia, was alleged to have colluded with both a local manufacturing company, which the CIO had been

49 Lucy Randolph Mason, *To Win These Rights* (New York, 1952), 20–54.
50 *Textile Bulletin,* December 1, 1942.
51 Lucy Randolph Mason to Philip Murray, December 7, 1942, George Brown to Hall, March 15, 1944, in Lucy Randolph Mason Papers, Duke University Library, Durham, N.C.

trying to organize, and the Ku Klux Klan in an attempt to scare organizers away.[52]

Miss Mason frequently complained to the civil rights section of the Department of Justice. Typical was one filed in the spring of 1944. She alleged that organizers for the International Woodworkers of America (CIO) in Bolton, Mississippi, had been prevented from entering a hall where a union meeting had been scheduled. The police had taken the union officials to the station without charges for questioning. At the police station, reported John Hawkins, the southern representative for the woodworkers, "They asked us all sorts of questions and informed us that we were causing all sorts of trouble, and they thought if we were men the best thing we could do was to go North of the Mason-Dixon line to do our organizing. They said if we would organize the white men that would be all right, but they were not going to stand seeing the Negroes organized." [53] Lucy Mason believed that the root cause of the antagonism to the CIO was its proclivity for multiracial unions. Throughout the states of Mississippi and Tennessee, where Miss Mason had been traveling, she found "rage against the CIO that it is organizing Negroes." [54]

Although an organizational drive by the CIO perturbed industrialists and law enforcement officers, the projection of the CIO into the political arena caused greater alarm. The activists within the PAC strove to purge the Democratic party of some of its unremitting conservatives and thus implicitly threatened to upset the racial and economic precepts of the South. The PAC had specifically wooed Negroes, whose interests, they proclaimed, lay with "progressive labor" and the Roosevelt administration, under whom "we have made great gains in the South." It had reminded Negroes, however, that "there are in the ranks

52 Mason to Carroll Kilpatrick, February 15, 1944, in Mason Papers.
53 Mason to Victor Rotnem, April 6, 1944, in Mason Papers.
54 Mason to Beverley, April 6, 1944, in Mason Papers; Mason, *To Win These Rights*, 72–78.

of the Democratic Party men who are a stench in the nostrils of the just. . . . We must cleanse ourselves of the Rankins, the Bilbos, the Starneses. We have made a beginning and will continue to do all in our power to sweep them out of high office." [55]

The PAC fulfilled its pledge to try to oust those Dixie Democrats who espoused white supremacy and opposed New Deal legislation. It conducted an extensive campaign in selected urban districts to persuade voters to register and pay their poll taxes. In September, 1944, George Mitchell, southern representative of the PAC, reported that about 75,000 previously unqualified union members in eight southern states had paid their poll taxes and registered.[56] In Huntsville, Alabama, the local textile union alone paid the accumulated poll taxes of more than four thousand workers. These registration drives sometimes produced spectacular results. In the area around Beaumont, Texas, for example, the newly registered oil workers forced Martin Dies, the inquisitor of the PAC in his capacity as chairman of the House Committee on Un-American Activities, to resign from the congressional race.[57] Another member of the Committee on Un-American Activities, Joe Starnes of Alabama, was similarly defeated by Albert Rains, a state legislator who had been cultivated by the CIO as the result of his open sympathy for organized labor.[58]

The incursions of the PAC into the political arena naturally sent a stir through numerous courthouse circles. It was feared that the PAC might come to wield an electoral balance of power

55 CIO-Political Action Committee, "The Negro in 1944," in Gaer, *The First Round,* 452–69.
56 Unsigned report (presumably from Jonathan Daniels) to FDR, September 18, 1944, in Daniels Papers.
57 Riker, "The CIO in Politics," 310–12; also, William Gellermann, *Martin Dies* (New York, 1944), *passim.*
58 Noel R. Beddow to Philip Murray, December 23, 1943, in Box A4-4, Philip Murray Papers, Catholic University Library, Washington, D.C.; also, Martha Lee Saenger, "Labor Political Action at Mid-Twentieth Century: A Case Study of the CIO-PAC Campaign of 1944 and the Textiles Workers Union of America" (Ph.D. dissertation, Ohio State University, 1959), 538–41; Birmingham *News,* May 3, 1944; *Alabama News Digest,* July 7, 1944.

in the South.[59] Furthermore, since the administration had so openly courted the PAC, there was good reason to believe that this interference with the normal political process had the approval of Roosevelt himself. Dixie Democrats accordingly attempted to embarrass the president by demonstrating that the PAC was disreputable and politically dubious. For example, in March, 1944, Martin Dies's Committee on Un-American Activities issued a damning report on the PAC. The report, based more on assumptions than on evidence, found that Sidney Hillman, the bête noire of the PAC's foes, had "clearly deemed it expedient to collaborate with Communists for the attaining of his own political objectives." [60] It listed those members of the CIO-PAC executive board who were believed to be Communist sympathizers and consequently assumed that the entire PAC was dominated by fellow travelers. At the same time, Congressman Howard W. Smith of Virginia asked Attorney General Francis Biddle to investigate the PAC for possible subversive activities. When Biddle gave the PAC a clean bill of health, Smith acted unilaterally and set up a special Committee to Investigate Campaign Expenditures to expose the political and financial practices of Hillman's PAC.[61]

Howard Smith was only one of a number of influential southerners who expressed anxiety about the close ties between the PAC and the Democratic party. Senator Josiah Bailey, who was becoming the chief spokesman for the new, assertive South, warned Clyde Hoey, a candidate for North Carolina's other Senate seat, that, "the effort to convert our Party into a Labor Party of the most radical type is as plain to me as the nose on my face. . . . From the beginning he [Roosevelt] has tied his future in

59 *Southern Weekly*, October 23, 1943; *Alabama*, May 12, 1944; Josiah Bailey to William Watts Ball, December 4, 1943, in William Watts Ball Papers, Duke University Library, Durham, N.C.
60 U.S. House of Representatives, Special Committee on Un-American Activities, *Report on the CIO Political Action Committee*, 78th Cong., 2nd Sess., H. Rept. 1311, pp. 73–75.
61 Arnold, "The CIO's Role in American Politics," 136–41; *Hearings to Investigate Campaign Expenditures, 1944, passim.*

the CIO and I think he wishes the CIO to become a great and powerful political organization. I do not feel I am dealing here at Washington with my fellow Democrats so much as I feel I am dealing with men who care nothing whatever for the Democratic Party. . . ." [62] Bailey expressed the paradox of the situation even more poignantly to Harry Byrd: "The Committee for Political Action is moving through the country and especially the South. They will seek to purge us and every other self-respecting and honest man who runs for office. And the strange thing is they will do this in our own Party and in the name of our Party." [63]

Although the CIO's Political Action Committee was the most potent organization that fought for New Deal principles, it was not alone. The South, of course, had its native liberals as well as its conservatives. Among the former were politicians, such as Senator Claude Pepper of Florida and Congressman Luther Patrick of Alabama, who had supported federal anti-poll tax bills.[64] Other reformers were influential in their professional capacities as writers, journalists, professors, or lawyers and worked outside the political framework. A group of white liberals, centered largely around Virginia and North Carolina, worked quietly during the war years for the creation of a more racially tolerant South. Jessie Daniel Ames, the energetic director of the Southern Women for the Prevention of Lynching; Ralph McGill, editor of the Atlanta *Constitution*; Virginius Dabney, editor of the Richmond *Times-Dispatch*; Dr. Howard Odum, the sociologist; Will W. Alexander, former head of the Resettlement Administration; and Dr. Frank P. Graham, president of the University of

---

62 Bailey to Clyde R. Hoey, February 19, 1944, in Bailey Papers.
63 Bailey to Harry F. Byrd, May 22, 1944, in Bailey Papers.
64 These men were practically ostracized by their more senior and conservative colleagues. See, for example, Bailey to Judge Ollie Edmunds, April 8, 1944, in Bailey Papers. One amusing criticism of Pepper came from Governor Richard Jefferies of South Carolina. He wrote: "If he had a little more salt the Pepper would be much more attractive but it seems all Pepper without salt which would spoil any kind of food." Jefferies to James H. Hammond, October 16, 1942, in Box 13, Jefferies Papers.

North Carolina, all made lasting contributions in the quest for more enlightened attitudes toward the problems of poverty and race. They campaigned for an abandonment of racial discrimination although none was willing to advocate the termination of segregation.[65] They were active in convening conferences and holding seminars on race relations and related matters. In 1942 and 1943 they sponsored the Durham and Atlanta conferences, which were instrumental in the formation of the Southern Regional Council, an organization which provided a framework of participation for the advocates of change in the social structure.[66]

Even this group of very cautious white southern liberals did not escape censure. Frank Graham, for example, was accused of using the University of North Carolina "as an advance point in the South to break down race relationships as we have known them." [67] This condemnation may have been prompted by resentment of Graham's former chairmanship of the Southern Conference for Human Welfare (SCHW). This organization had been formed in 1938 in response to the National Economic Council's devastating *Report on the Economic Conditions of the South.* Dedicated to the economic improvement of the South, the SCHW sought to attain this end by bringing together liber-

65 Virginius Dabney to Harry M. Ayers, May 13, 1944, in Harry Mell Ayers Papers, University of Alabama Library, Tuscaloosa; Will W. Alexander to Ralph McGill, April 13, 1943, in File 13, Ames Papers. One outstanding dissident was Lilian Smith, author of *Strange Fruit* and *Killers of the Dream.* She actually declined to participate in the Southern Regional Council because it refused to condemn segregation. She believed that "we who do not believe in segregation must say so. We must somehow find the courage to say it aloud. For, however we rationalize our silence, it is fear that is holding our tongues today." Lilian Smith to Guy B. Johnson, June 12, 1944, in File 18, Ames Papers.

66 Edward F. Burrows, "The Commission on Interracial Cooperation, 1919–1944" (Ph.D. dissertation, University of Wisconsin, 1954), chap. 8; William Henry Leary, "Race Relations in Turmoil: Southern Liberals and World War II" (M.A. thesis, University of Virginia, 1967), chap. 2; Wilma Dykeman and James Stokely, *Seeds of Southern Change: The Life of Will Alexander* (Chicago, 1962), 283.

67 Dixon to B. B. Gossett, April 2, 1944, in Dixon Papers.

als who were willing to fight for New Deal legislation in the state legislatures and in other political forums.[68] Its participants included Eleanor Roosevelt, Charles S. Johnson, the Negro sociologist, Justice Hugo Black, Aubrey Williams, Will Alexander, and Claude Pepper. It favored the ultimate elimination of segregation and refused to observe segregation ordinances at its meetings. Unlike the Southern Regional Council, the SCHW advocated political involvement. It was ardently pro–New Deal and supported a permanent, statutory FEPC and abolition of the poll tax. In 1944 both the executive secretary of the SCHW, James Dombrowski, and the chairman, Clark Foreman, joined the National Citizens' Political Action Committee and worked for Roosevelt's reelection. The CIO executive board endorsed the SCHW and encouraged its efforts to abolish discrimination and to expand the voting rolls in the South.[69] The SCHW publicized the main issues of the 1944 election campaign, conducted voter registration drives, helped union organizers, and, like the CIO-PAC, endorsed individual candidates, including President Roosevelt.[70] Needless to say, those who inveighed against the CIO-PAC also inveighed against the SCHW. Theodore Bilbo hit it at its most sensitive spot. He warned Hugo Black, who was due to receive the SCHW's Thomas Jefferson Award, that the organization was "a scheme to break down the color-line that means so much to every red-blooded man and woman in the South." [71]

In sum, several well-established politicians in the South came to realize that the region was by no means ideologically monolithic and that certain groups, who traditionally had not played

68 Thomas A. Krueger, *And Promises to Keep: The Southern Conference for Human Welfare, 1938–1948* (Nashville, 1967), chap. 1.
69 *Ibid.*, 22–38, 123–25.
70 *Southern Patriot*, August, 1943, November, 1943, May, 1944, September, 1944.
71 Bilbo to Hugo Black, March 26, 1945, Bilbo to Forrest Jackson, April 14, 1945, in Bilbo Papers. In the same letter Bilbo reminded Black with indulgent cynicism that "you and I were good Ku Klux Brothers." Also, William D. Miller, *Mr. Crump of Memphis* (Baton Rouge, 1964), 292.

an assertive role in southern affairs, were now seeking to transform the political structure of the South by massive involvement. The configuration of politics was changing. Labor organizers were as concerned with the political process as with the problems of the union shop. Journalists and college professors were beginning to cooperate in seeking means to change the South. No longer did the cry for change emanate from lonesome individuals who could be easily isolated or ostracized by the community. Workers, in particular, were being urged to think in terms of economic self-interest, thereby transcending the regional preoccupations that had often destroyed effective unionism in the past. The transformation did not, of course, come as quickly as Lucy Mason, Sidney Hillman, and Claude Pepper had hoped. But the South's traditional leaders were being challenged. And, naturally, they tried to hold on to their position.

The promiscuous use of the race question by opponents of the labor unions was only one of several factors contributing to the deterioration in race relations that occurred in the South during the war. Other changes increased the degree of racial animosity and thus, unwittingly, hastened the demand for effective civil rights legislation. These other developments included the apparent overtures of the administration to black voters, the outmigration of Negroes from rural areas, the stationing of northern Negro troops in the South, and the spread of criticism among labor and civil rights leaders of the nation's racial practices. These demographic and political changes combined to harden racial attitudes in all parts of the social spectrum.[72]

There was one development, however, that was particularly galling to southern whites. Southern Negroes themselves were

72 See Charles S. Johnson *et al., To Stem This Tide: A Survey of Racial Tension Areas in the United States* (Boston and Chicago, 1943); Howard W. Odum, *Race and Rumors of Race* (Chapel Hill, 1943); Charles S. Johnson, "The Present Status of Race Relations in the South," *Social Forces,* XXIII (October, 1944), 27–32; Charles S. Johnson, "Social Changes and Their Effects on Race Relations in the South," *Social Forces,* XXIII (March, 1945), 343–48.

questioning the vortex of Dixie's caste system. Although most whites had probably always recognized individual grievances, they felt that Booker T. Washington's philosophy of compromise and acceptance still had a hold on the black leaders of the South. It now seemed, however, that the South's fundamental assumptions were being challenged by the indigenous black population. This left many southerners nonplussed. The whole racial edifice, which they had so carefully built up over the years, appeared to have cracked at the foundations. They had always boasted that Dixie was a natural haven for blacks; and yet the Negro population itself was repudiating this belief. A South Carolinian wrote: "The venom of many of the Negro newspapers and their supporters is undoubtedly one of the worst obstacles in their way. . . . All emphasis is laid by these agitators on what the negro does not get under our institutions and no mention is made of what he does get." [73]

This growing sense of resentment and suspicion had far-reaching manifestations. There occurred a blossoming of racial rumors and an increase in the incidence of racial violence. Racial rumors were easily fabricated. They spread at a time when it seemed that the war had produced economic and racial changes which would prove irreversible with the advent of peace. These rumormongers not only vented their suspicions against Negroes but also against northerners in general and President Roosevelt in particular. The "North," in the abstract, often became a scapegoat for the tension and violence in Dixie. Since many southerners believed that they had created a racial Eden, it was a simple step to find that the purveyors of social dislocation had come from outside the section. A newsagent and his wife from Biloxi, Mississippi, aptly expressed this sense of bewilderment and frustration: "We are kind to our darkies and treat them as they deserve to be treated, As far as their education they feel that they only need enough to read and write, but the Northern people seem to think that isn't enough and we

73 R. B. Herbert to Ball, December 8, 1942, in Ball Papers.

have the largest percentage of darkies here so why can,t they keep their hands off and their mouthes shut and let us handle this problem [*sic*]." [74]

Although racial rumors were by no means confined to the South, that region proved to be particularly receptive to them because of its large numbers of Negroes and the traditional susceptibility of southerners to prognostications of racial revolution. One almost exclusively southern rumor was that of the creation of Eleanor Clubs. The precise origin of the rumor is unknown, but the tale apparently arose as Negro women, who had always found employment in domestic service, left private households for more remunerative jobs in commerce or industry. A story circulated that under the sponsorship of Eleanor Roosevelt Negro women were organizing themselves into quasi unions and were threatening to leave for better paid jobs unless their employers paid them more and accorded them higher status. The motto of the Eleanor Clubs, according to these unsubstantiated reports, was "a white woman in every kitchen by 1943." It was also hearsay that Negro domestic servants were resigning if their employers expressed a dislike of the first lady.[75]

The rumors were credited widely. And there was no question in the minds of their purveyors that the activities of Eleanor Roosevelt and the economic policies of the government were responsible for the apparent assertiveness of southern Negroes. The head of a large corporation in Georgia complained that "we used to be able to work Negro women in the fields, but no more. Either their husbands are receiving fantastic wages from governmental projects, or they are getting $50 a month allowance on account of their husbands being in the army." [76] Several southern newspapers and journals added credibility to these tales in their harangues against Eleanor Roosevelt. *Alabama* magazine carried a front cover photograph of the first lady serving food to a racially integrated group of men and women and

74 Mr. and Mrs. J. D. Frazier to Bilbo, March 12, 1944, in Bilbo Papers.
75 Odum, *Race and Rumors of Race*, chaps. 8 and 9.
76 Samuel C. Dobbs to R. L. Russell, June 22, 1943, in File 15, Ames Papers.

reported that she had "served sandwiches and joined in singing love songs while white and Negro soldiers, white and Negro girls danced and fraternized on a full-fledged social equality basis." [77] The Glenville (Ga.) *Sentinel* predicted with a suspect hint of relish that the president's wife was "sowing seed that will cause one of the bloodiest wars in the history of our nation." [78] Others warned that Eleanor Clubs were Communist vanguards for a planned "black revolution" in the South.[79]

Fear of insurrection lay at the root of these numerous speculations about Negroes' plans for a confrontation with whites. The specter of this new self-assurance on the part of blacks convinced many whites that the wave of racial violence that had swept America during, and especially after, World War I would be repeated.[80] Not surprisingly, the most far-flung rumors were those suggesting that the verbal attacks by Negroes on Jim Crow were prolegomena to the use of violence. A rabid racist from Memphis warned that if Negroes "aren't put in their proper place very soon, mark my words, the United States is going to become embroiled in another very gory, bitter and unwanted battle. . . . Something MUST be done to either rid the country of all the members of the colored race or drastic steps taken to bring them back to their former state of humility and obedience." [81] Theodore Bilbo, always eager to jump on the bandwagon of racial friction, wrote that "a great many rape cases in the South" had been "brought about by the coddling, petting and associating of white folks." Bilbo inveighed against such various personages as Pearl Buck, the novelist, Norman Thomas, the Socialist leader, and A. Philip Randolph, all of whom, ac-

77 *Alabama,* March 10, 1944.
78 Quoted in Commission on Interracial Cooperation Clip Sheet, Ser. 3, No. 10, November 30, 1943, in Ames Papers.
79 Stanley Moore to Ball, August 1, 1942, in Ball Papers; also, Johnson *et al.,* *To Stem This Tide,* 28–29.
80 See Arthur I. Waskow, *From Race Riot to Sit-In: 1919 and the 1960s* (Garden City, N.Y., 1966), 12–142.
81 William Cathey to Bilbo, June 19, 1943, in Bilbo Papers.

cording to the senator from Mississippi, "are laying the foundations for a racial war when this war is over." [82]

These fears of revolution produced rumors that Negroes were preparing themselves for the bloody encounter. One of the more imaginative of these tales held that Negroes were buying ice picks, which would be used during a blackout for the racial Armageddon. According to one report, these uprisings by ice pick were expected in Washington, D.C., Norfolk, and Memphis.[83] Negroes were also suspected of buying up and storing large supplies of firearms.[84] This was not all. The NAACP received several inquiries about the apparent existence of "bumping clubs" from anxious northern and southern city dwellers, who alleged that "colored people have organized to push white people when they are in trains and buses." [85] In May, 1943, the rumor of an imminent insurrection over the dispute in the hiring practices of the Washington, D.C., Capital Transit Company were so widespread that some restaurants reputedly closed down in Washington in anticipation of riots.[86]

In South Carolina the rumors were taken seriously enough by the state administration to warrant an official investigation. Governor Richard M. Jefferies asked his chief law enforcement officer, S. J. Pratt, to look into the activities of the state's Negroes. In the tradition of the slave patrols and the South's "garrison psychology," the governor also ordered Pratt to insure that law officers were kept alert about the movements of Negroes and to make regular inquiries. Accordingly, local sheriffs and constables conducted investigations and sent their reports to Pratt.

82 Bilbo to Harry L. Lockman, June 14, 1943, in Bilbo Papers.
83 Memo, Julia E. Baxter to Walter White, May 24, 1943, in Box 273/1, NAACP Files; Odum, *Race and Rumors of Race,* chap. 12.
84 Lieutenant and Constable of Greenville County, S.C., to S. J. Pratt, September 29, 1942, in Box 14, Jefferies Papers.
85 White to Fiorello H. La Guardia, September 13, 1944, in Box 291/3, NAACP Files.
86 Memo, Baxter to White, May 24, 1943, White to FDR, May 10, 1943, in Box 273/1, NAACP Files.

These reports and Pratt's collated report to the governor revealed most of the rumors to be based upon fabrication, not concrete facts. Despite this evidence, law officers were not prepared to discredit the rumors. The stories about Eleanor Clubs were readily believed, especially since they were reinforced by articles in newspapers. Pratt reported that not only were Negro cooks demanding higher wages but also were "often demanding that they be addressed as Mister and Miss." He also recorded that "there have been several instances in which ammunition in small quantities have been shipped to Negroes," but found that some dealers had refused to trade in arms with the black populace. Interracial meetings also tended to raise public suspicions, he discovered. Pratt clearly assumed the rumors contained substance unless disproved.[87] Nevertheless, an independent investigation by the governor's officer, W. W. Brown, found that stories of arms hoarding were baseless and that the "customary organizations, such as burial societies, lodges and the like seem to be operating as usual, with no change in the direction of their interests." Brown concluded that only "white people appear to be considerably disturbed." [88]

Sometimes rumors of racial altercations flared into real violence. When friction in the North and South degenerated into physical violence, it reinforced the rumormongers' feelings of misapprehension. In 1943 major racial clashes occurred throughout the country. The first to receive full press coverage happened in the docks of Mobile, Alabama, where race relations had been tense for some time.[89] On May 25 Negro and white workers clashed in the shipyard of the Alabama Dry Dock and Shipbuilding Company. According to the company president, D. R. Dunlap, the altercation began after some black workers had been upgraded in their jobs in accordance with FEPC di-

87 S. J. Pratt to Jefferies, October 9, 1942, W. M. Swink to Pratt, October 17, 1942, in Box 14, Jefferies Papers.
88 W. W. Brown to Jefferies, September 10, 1942, in Box 14, Jefferies Papers.
89 As early as December, 1942, a union organizer had warned of potential racial violence, in the docks. See John Bouche to Mason, December 11, 1942, in Mason Papers.

rectives. Even though the work gangs remained segregated, rumors about the extent of the promotions circulated rapidly. Within a short time, a full-scale riot broke out between white and Negro workers. Governor Chauncey Sparks ordered 350 state guards into Mobile to keep the peace.[90] Three weeks later rioting erupted in Beaumont, Texas, after a white woman reported that she had been assaulted by a Negro in her home. A crowd of about one hundred men rallied before the courthouse to seek out the suspect who had been transferred to another jail. When they were told that the alleged assailant was not there, they marched into the Negro quarter of Beaumont. There, according to reports, Negroes were dragged from their automobiles and stripped of their clothing. The Texas state guard was sent in to restore order, which was not attained before two men had been killed in the fighting.[91]

The Mobile and Beaumont riots caused considerable stir in the South. They showed that the uneasy relations between Negroes and whites were capable of rapid degeneration into violence. Southerners also realized their boasts of racial control and feelings of contentment within the Negro community were based more on wishes than on reality. Most important of all, a number of people reacted to the violence by attributing its root causes to outside the South. Although some newspapers, such as the Dallas *Morning News*, felt that the burden of guilt rested primarily with the local white population, others took exception and found their scapegoats in the North and particularly in Washington.[92] For example, the president's Fair Employment Practices Committee was blamed for the Mobile shipyard riots. A correspondent from Dallas placed responsibility squarely upon "those great experimenters" and, in particular, Eleanor Roosevelt.[93] Moreover, three days after the Beaumont riot these censurers of "outsiders" felt that their views had been

90 Mobile *Register,* May 26, 27, 1943.
91 Dallas *Morning News,* June 17, 1943.
92 *Ibid.,* June 21, 1943.
93 *Ibid.*

completely vindicated by the events in the bloodstained streets of Detroit.

Full-scale street fighting between Detroit Negroes and whites had broken out after a local clash near Detroit's Belle Isle Bridge. The rioting continued unabated for nearly two days before federal troops finally restored an uneasy peace. Thirty-four people had been killed and over one thousand injured as a result of the violence.[94] The riot left a deep impression on southerners. It dramatically publicized the extent of racial animosity prevalent during the war and showed, with a certain degree of satisfaction to southerners, that friction was not merely confined to one region of the United States. Above all, the Detroit riot convinced white supremacists that the absence of segregation ordinances in the North was bound to result in racial holocaust. Determination to preserve the color line hardened. The Charleston *News and Courier* warned that the Detroit riot showed that "when separation is abandoned, trouble begins."[95] Theodore Bilbo fretted that "this is just the beginning of the real trouble we are going to have with these sons of Ethiopia when this world war is over" and determined to "open up on the mixing of negroes and whites that has taken place as a result of the war."[96]

Southern governors reacted to the riot in a similar way by asserting that they would act to preserve the southern caste system, which, they believed, was more conducive to racial harmony than the relative permissiveness of the industrial North. Their correspondence with Walter Davenport, associate editor of *Collier's* magazine, revealed their essential confidence in the cordiality that existed between the races in the South. The liberal governor of Georgia, Ellis Arnall, claimed that he would "be very surprised if we have any trouble in Georgia."

94 For further details of the Detroit riot, see: Detroit *News,* June 21, 22, 23, 24, 1943; Lee and Humphrey, *Race Riot*; Walter White and Thurgood Marshall, *What Caused the Detroit Riot?* (New York, 1943).
95 Charleston *News and Courier,* June 22, 1943.
96 Bilbo to William Cathey, June 25, 1943, in Bilbo Papers.

Governor Olin D. Johnston of South Carolina insisted that harmony prevailed, but admonished: "We intend to keep the Negro fair but we expect him to keep his place and this can only be down [sic] through segregation." Johnston warned against "outside interference from Washington or Northern agitation," as did Alabama's Chauncey Sparks, who blamed the riots on "inflammatory Negro newspapers" and "the attitude of certain ambitious politicians and misguided and emotional missionaries who place shibboleths above reality." Only Governor J. Melville Broughton of North Carolina felt that education and interracial action, rather than strictly enforced segregation and close police vigilance, would improve the situation. However, although he acknowledged that conflict arose from social deprivation he, too, scolded the Negro press for its militant stand on segregation and "the political juggling with Negro votes in pivotal Northern States." [97]

The wave of riots that spread through the country in the summer of 1943, together with the general exacerbation in race relations south of the Potomac, convinced a number of influential southerners that the new black militancy was receiving the silent blessing of the Roosevelt administration. The Jackson *News* commented acidly, "It is blood on your hands, Mrs. Eleanor Roosevelt." [98] Even those southerners who were not prepared to go as far as the editor of the Jackson *News* felt that the president's inattention to the South in the formulation of domestic policy had encouraged minority groups to ignore southern customs. Thus, throughout the South, in the state legislatures and the editorial columns of the county news-

---

97 Telegrams, Ellis Arnall to Walter Davenport, June 30, 1943, Olin Johnston to Davenport, July 2, 1943, Chauncey Sparks to Davenport, June 30, 1943, J. Melville Broughton to Davenport, June 30, 1943, in Box 273/5, NAACP Files.
98 Quoted in Commission on Interracial Cooperation Clip Sheet, Ser. 3, No. 1, July 15, 1943, in Ames Papers; also, Emory O. Jackson to Walter White, July 25, 1943, C. L. Harper to White, July 3, 1943, J. L. LeFlore to White, July 2, 1943, the Reverend Ralph M. Gilbert to White, August 17, 1943, in Box 273/5, NAACP Files.

papers, there was a flowering of sectional rhetoric and pride. This sectionalism paralleled that found on Capitol Hill. In South Carolina the state legislature gave this new sectional politics an official seal when it passed a resolution calling upon the "damnable agitators of the North" to "leave the South alone." [99] But the South was not left alone. Only four days later the Supreme Court handed down its monumental decision that the exclusion of Negroes from the Democratic primaries in Texas was unconstitutional.[100]

The *Smith* v. *Allwright* decision reversed the judgment in the case of *Grovey* v. *Townsend,* where the Court had ruled in 1935 that the Democratic party, as a private association, might exclude Negroes from its primaries without violating the equal protection clause of the Fourteenth Amendment, which applies only to state action.[101] In 1944, however, on the basis of its earlier decision in the *Classic* case, the Court ruled that the exclusion of Negroes from the Texas Democratic primary violated the Fifteenth Amendment's prohibition of discrimination in the right to vote because of color and was thus unconstitutional.[102] The Court reasoned that the Texas primary was an integral part of the election machinery and that since the primary was regulated by state law, the state itself endorsed and enforced the Democratic party's exclusion of Negroes.

Smith v. *Allwright* met determined resistance. Politicians throughout the South interpreted the decision as a major assault by the North under the supporting guidance of President Roosevelt, who had nominated most of the Supreme Court justices. One Democratic official from Texas described the de-

99 Columbia *Record,* March 1, 1944; also Ball to John D. Long, March 30, 1944, in Ball Papers.
100 *Smith* v. *Allwright,* 321 U.S. 649 (1944).
101 *Grovey* v. *Townsend,* 295 U.S. 45 (1935).
102 In this decision the Court ruled that "where the state law has made the primary an integral part of the procedure of choice, or where in fact the primary effectively controls the choice, the right of the elector to have his ballot counted at the primary is . . . included in the right protected." *United States* v. *Classic,* 313 U.S. 299 (1941).

cision as "a political opinion by a politically packed court in an election year." [103] "Cotton Ed" Smith called it "a culmination of the trend of events of the past eleven years: it's a very dangerous thing." [104] The specter of Reconstruction seemed to loom over Dixie. Southerners were warned that white supremacy would be undermined by the enfranchisement of the Negro. Indeed, an important weapon of Negro disfranchisement had been removed. If the South could not provide or reinforce other exclusive devices, a major political revolution would occur. The *Southern Weekly* termed the decision a "new Reconstruction of the South" and remonstrated that it was "only the beginning of a program which has for its ultimate object Federal coercion of the white people of the South in all their relations with Negroes." [105] Josiah Bailey mourned that the Court's judgment "practically gives the Federal Government control of our Party and our election machinery"; he predicted "a big battle ahead of us." [106]

Dixie prepared for the "big battle." Governor Sam Jones of Louisiana warned: "We've always handled that question—and always will." Even Claude Pepper, who had in the past made constant appeals for equal opportunity in the South, rashly proclaimed that "the South will allow nothing to impair white supremacy." [107] But it befell the bastion of nullification and secession, South Carolina, to become the first southern state to resist by positive action. Although the *Smith* v. *Allwright* decision had applied to the state of Texas, it seemed evident that other states which held primaries open only to whites would also be ordered to admit everyone without regard to race or color. Accordingly, the governor of South Carolina, Olin D. Johnston, who had been a notably loyal New Dealer, convened an extraordinary session of the state legislature to repeal "all

103 New York *Times*, April 5, 1944.
104 Columbia *Record*, April 6, 1944.
105 *Southern Weekly*, April 8, 1944.
106 Bailey to H. G. Gulley, April 5, 1944, in Bailey Papers.
107 New York *Times*, April 5, 1944.

laws on the statute books pertaining to the Democratic primary elections." [108] The rationale behind this move was that the Court had specifically ruled that discrimination in the primary was tantamount to state action, since state laws governed the procedures of holding the primary. Thus, Johnston hoped to circumvent this ruling by repealing all laws referring to the primaries in South Carolina.

The legislature, which convened on April 14, 1944, was in a militant mood. State Representative John D. Long vowed to "fight the Negro at the polls if I have to bite the dust as did my ancestors"; he completed his secessionist allegory by declaring that "it is a question of buckling under the dictation of the north." [109] Presidential politics also emerged in the debate. Combining the rhetoric of Robert Rhett and William Jennings Bryan, state Senator George Warren of Hampton announced that he would oppose Roosevelt for a fourth term and that "if it is necessary to be crucified politically in South Carolina, I am willing to be crucified provided it is on an anti-Roosevelt cross." [110] State Senator Richard M. Jefferies was less tempestuous on the floor, but confided resolutely: "We must meet this challenge and in the spirit of our fathers solve the problem for the protection of southern civilization." [111] In this spirit of defiance, the legislature completed the repeal of all the laws governing the primaries in under a week.

The uncompromising resistance to the white primary decision, which continued after 1944 in several other southern states, was symptomatic of a new bellicosity throughout the South. The Supreme Court's decision had confirmed Dixie's

108 Columbia *Record,* April 13, 1944; also, John E. Huss, *Senator for the South: A Biography of Olin D. Johnston* (Garden City, N.Y., 1961).
109 Columbia *Record,* April 17, 1944.
110 *Ibid.,* April 19, 1944.
111 *Ibid.,* April 20, 1944; Richard M. Jefferies to Joe P. Lane, April 17, 1944, in Olin D. Johnston Papers, South Carolina Department of Archives, Columbia. Since the Johnston Papers are in two different locations, their source will be abbreviated to SCDA (South Carolina Department of Archives, Columbia) and SCL (South Caroliniana Library).

worst fears that the administration, spurred on by powerful Negro and labor organizations, intended to pursue the policies demanded by the increasingly militant and influential "Roosevelt coalition." Although southern politicians probably discerned that the president was often only halfhearted in his policies, especially concerning race, they were cognizant of the numerous concessions the president had made to these groups. The Democratic leadership was no longer a haven for southerners, and after April 3 the Supreme Court no longer seemed to serve as a protector of states' rights. On the day the Court handed down the *Smith* v. *Allwright* decision, Josiah Bailey reflected bitterly: "The President is just as loyal to Frank Hague and the Kelly machine as he is to our Party. He is just as loyal to the American Federation of Labor and the CIO as he is to any Party and he is much more loyal to these institutions than he is to what we call Southern Democracy which I think he despises." [112] Southern Democrats determined to restore their influence in the councils of the Democratic party and to rid the party of the yoke of the northern urban coalition. The only problem was: how?

112 Bailey to C. L. Shuping, April 3, 1944, in Bailey Papers.

CHAPTER FOUR

The Southern Road
to Chicago,
1943–1944

I<small>T</small> WAS paradoxical, but perhaps appropriate, that the city of New York provided the stage setting for the South's first public sortie against the Democratic party. For it was at a meeting of the city's Southern Society, a club for Dixie émigrés, that the outgoing governor of Alabama, Frank M. Dixon, announced that dissident southerners were contemplating a revolt against the Roosevelt administration. Dixon knew, of course, that most southern voters still retained a deep affection for the president and that officeholders were wary of challenging any Democratic president, let alone the one who had reputedly saved America from total economic disaster. But he felt it was incumbent upon disaffected southerners to stake out a new path for a possible revolt. He informed the society's members that "suggestions are rife as to the formation of a Southern Democratic party" and that "ways and means are being discussed daily to break our chains." Apparently, Democratic supremacy was no longer the totemic goal of Dixie's politicians. Southerners, said Dixon, were prepared to risk defeat for the Democrats at the polls as the price of reasserting their influence.[1]

1 New York *Times,* December 12, 1942; *Textile Bulletin,* January 15, 1943; R. H. Powell to Dixon, December 23, 1942, in Dixon Papers.

Frank Dixon was not the only southern executive to call for breaking party bonds. In March, 1943, Governor Sam H. Jones of Louisiana wrote a well-publicized article in the *Saturday Evening Post* entitled, "Will Dixie Bolt the New Deal?" In this brief essay Jones assailed the New Deal, the political insensitivity of the president, and the blind allegiance of the South to the Democrats. The president, he complained, was "magnificently ignorant of the South," and his New Deal policies "continued to kick an already prostrate South in the face." Southerners could no longer trust Roosevelt, because he had shown an alarming predilection for the aspirations of the Negro. Furthermore, the South was being denied its due share of public investment. The differential in wealth between the two sections had not narrowed, and age-old grievances, such as discriminatory railroad freight rates, had not been alleviated. Because of these frustrations, concluded Jones, the solid South "is about to fall apart of its own absurdity," and "in the deepest South, the ferment is strongest and the rumbling loudest." Jones endorsed Frank Dixon's earlier trial balloon and hinted that the South might form an independent, regional Democratic party.[2]

Governor Jones's article was undoubtedly timed to stimulate further preparatory work at the Southern Governors' Conference, which met at Tallahassee, Florida, shortly after. At the conference Jones and Dixon urged their colleagues to follow in their footsteps, but were met with a cool reception. Although the other governors shared the rebels' misgivings about the administration, they believed a revival of sectionalism would only play into the hands of the groups they sought to usurp. Governors Ellis G. Arnall of Georgia and Melville J. Broughton of North Carolina were particularly anxious to preserve harmony. Arnall, who had a reputation as Dixie's most progressive executive, believed the South's grievances could be met best

2 Sam H. Jones, "Will Dixie Bolt the New Deal?" *Saturday Evening Post,* March 6, 1943, pp. 20–21, 42, 45; also, Sam H. Jones, "The Plundered South," Speech to Southern Farm Bureau Training School at Monroe, La., August 18, 1943, in File 9, Otis P. Morgan Collection of Sam Jones Campaign Speeches, Louisiana State University Library, Baton Rouge.

by normal consultative and judicial processes.[3] He urged that "sectionalism be buried in this land."[4] Broughton shared this view and strongly condemned one proposal for a joint statement on the race issue. He insisted that the problem "is national in its aspects and cannot adequately be solved on lines of section or geography."[5] Frank Dixon was clearly disappointed with these rebuffs. He wrote later that all the governors were opposed to a fourth term for President Roosevelt, but were afraid of operating outside the structure of the national Democratic party. Nevertheless, he was consoled by one agreement. The governors had decided that if Roosevelt were renominated, then someone other than Henry Wallace should be nominated as vice president. They regarded the outspoken Henry Wallace as "unsafe" and were mindful that if a fourth-term campaign were successful, the result, "in view of the age of the President, and in view of the inevitable wear of office, would be the elevation of whoever was Vice-President at the time."[6]

Most governors had resisted the idea of a Democratic revolt, because they knew the vast majority of southern voters still supported the president. A Gallup poll taken in the summer of 1943 revealed that 80 percent of southerners favored Roosevelt's renomination. Surprisingly, only 5 percent of FDR's critics specifically mentioned the race issue as a cause for their opposition.[7] Thus, in political terms, the race issue was not yet

3 Arnall, in fact, seemed more concerned about discriminatory railroad freight rates. See: Robert A. Lively, *The South in Action: A Sectional Crusade Against Freight Rate Discrimination* (Chapel Hill, 1949); Taylor, "A Political Biography of Ellis Arnall," 234–69; Hoover and Ratchford, *Economic Resources and Policies of the South*, 78–84; John P. Carter, "Recent Developments in Railroad Freight Rates," *Southern Economic Journal*, XV (April, 1949), 379–94.
4 Atlanta *Constitution*, March 26, 1943.
5 J. Melville Broughton to Forney Johnston, December 31, 1942, in Dixon Papers.
6 Dixon to Floyd Jefferson, March 29, 1943, Dixon to Lloyd C. Griscom, March 29, 1943, in Dixon Papers.
7 Tindall, *The Emergence of the New South*, 725; Atlanta *Constitution*, July 7, 1943. But see also John Temple Graves, "The Solid South Is Cracking," *American Mercury*, LVI (April, 1943), 401–406.

dominant enough in the minds of the electorate at large to warrant a revolt. The southern governors, who seemed far more concerned than their constituents about the matter, were still forcefully attracted to the Democratic party by the fruits of patronage and industrial contracts, which, of course, abounded in the war years.

Although most of the southern governors at Tallahassee wished to avoid a personal confrontation with the Democratic hierarchy, the state and county party organizations felt fewer ties to Washington. For example, in financial matters local party committees in the South were quite independent of the Democratic National Committee. To the contrary, the national committee usually relied upon these local committees to provide funds. Since the outcomes of general elections in the South were usually foregone conclusions, a large proportion of contributions raised by local party organizations were sent to the national committee for use in vital marginal elections in the North. Thus, southern state organizations which were critical of national party policies were in a position to threaten Washington with a withdrawal of funds until their grievances were corrected. Accordingly, in June, 1943, officials of the Democratic state executive committees of Georgia, Louisiana, and South Carolina announced that they would refuse to raise money until the national party leaders took steps to heal political wounds. The chairman of the Georgia committee, J. Lon Duckworth, explained that the allegiance of the state party was being taken for granted by the administration and that even in its appointments policies southern Democrats were being ignored. So, as far as Georgia was concerned, a basic incentive —patronage—for remaining within the party had been removed.[8] The Savannah *Morning News* hailed the withdrawal

---

8 Savannah *Morning News*, June 17, 1943. Even six months after the announcement, Georgia's grievances remained unaltered. See: J. Lon Duckworth to James M. Barnes, November 5, 1943, Duckworth to James E. Davies, January 5, 1944, H. T. Dobbs to Davies, December 14, 1943, in Box 4, DNC Files.

of funds as a "declaration of divorcement" and "a first step in the purging of our traditional party of the alien principles with which it has of late become infested." [9] In South Carolina the situation was more confused, as the state chairman, Winchester Smith, denied reports that his committee had decided to take similar retaliatory action. Senator "Cotton Ed" Smith, on the other hand, believed the story and, with his customary aplomb, exultantly congratulated the committee.[10]

The withdrawal of funds, however damaging to the national committee, could do little to help the South restore its voice to the decision-making process in Washington. Southern critics of the Roosevelt administration had to devise other methods to influence the future course of governmental policy. Sam Jones and Frank Dixon already had suggested one—the formation of an independent southern party. But the creation of a southern Democratic party would have had a number of drawbacks. First, not even the conservative leadership in the South was united, and clearly a third-party movement would have needed a broad base of support to have had any significant effect. Second, the creation of a separate party would have been, in many respects, self-defeating. Southern Democrats were striving to restore the old Wilsonian coalition of southerners and conservative, business-minded politicians from the North. The majority did not, at this stage, want to establish a particularist southern party. They aimed primarily to reduce the influence of the newer recruits of the urban coalition. If the South were to withdraw from the Democratic party, it would only pave the way for the complete preponderance in the party of Negroes and organized labor. Southerners wanted to dominate the party, not to surrender it to their foes. In the same way, a switch to the Republicans also would have defeated the South's avowed purpose, that is, to restore its influence in Democratic councils. Moreover, both Thomas E. Dewey and Wendell Willkie, the leading contenders for the Republican presidential nomination,

9 Savannah *Morning News,* June 18, 1943.
10 Charleston *News and Courier,* June 17, 1943.

were as solicitous of Negro support as Franklin Roosevelt. Some dissidents advocated an alternative means of asserting their power. Instead of forming a separate southern party, party organizations would retain the Democratic label, but would allow state electors to cast their votes in the electoral college for any candidate they might choose. However, this alternative was open to accusations of chicanery and could, conceivably, help the Republicans, especially in the upper South. In addition, if the Democrats were to win an election in spite of a bolt in the electoral college, then the southern bolters would undoubtedly suffer deprivation of party privileges. Thus, as far as most southern critics in 1943 and 1944 were concerned, the best method of trying to shift the political center of gravity was for state Democratic organizations to work within the traditional party framework and to elect a favorable presidential candidate on an acceptable platform. If this failed, then some other means could be tried.

Such was the intention of Mississippi's Democratic executive committee which voted in August, 1943, by twelve votes to eleven to submit an anti–New Deal resolution to the state Democratic convention, due to meet the following summer. The resolution, which condemned organized labor and the current criticism of southern racial practices, was passed shortly after that state's gubernatorial campaign, in which the racial policies of the New Deal had been at issue. The Mississippi primary had shown that the race issue could be easily whipped up for political purposes and that opposition to the New Deal in the South would center increasingly on the race question.[11]

This tendency was also apparent in the findings of a survey of county chairmen carried out by Democratic national chairman, Frank Walker, in November, 1943.[12] In a similar review of political feeling after the 1942 elections, it will be remembered, southerners had centered their criticism not on the treatment of the Negro but on bureaucracy, the power of the unions,

11 Jackson *Clarion-Ledger*, July 30, August 5, 22, September 1, 1943.
12 Analysis of letters from County Chairmen, n.d., in Box 38, DNC Files.

and the level of federal expenditures. Only twelve months later, however, these same officials were censoring the federal government for exacerbating the strains between the races and for ignoring southern sensibilities. The chairman of the Jasper County, South Carolina, Democratic executive committee wrote that "the South will stand for almost any kind of treatment from the party except on the race question. I believe the National Democratic Party will have to choose between the South and the negroes of the North." [13] Another South Carolinian complained that the administration had "ignored the rights of the Southern white Democrats" and that consequently the South "must devise some plan whereby we can bring back the interest we had at other times." [14] From Arkansas and Mississippi came familiar indictments of Eleanor Roosevelt, and a Macon, Mississippi, attorney warned that "many will bolt the Party," unless the administration changed its posture toward the South. [15]

Some southerners, however, hoped there would be no need to bolt the party. They believed, especially after a number of setbacks for the Democrats in the state elections of 1943, the president could be forced to retire from politics in 1944. This faith was not confined to disaffected southerners. James Farley, an experienced and well-qualified observer, felt that Roosevelt would not run again, because public opinion had turned against him. "I do not know whether anyone can win on our ticket," he wrote to his friend, John McDuffie. [16] It was thus necessary, argued Roosevelt's opponents, to exploit these speculations about Roosevelt's political demise and to encourage members of the party to seek a new candidate for the White House. Democratic Congressman Wesley F. Disney of Oklahoma recommended a simple course of action. Disquieted Democrats

13 H. Klugh Purdy to Frank Walker, November 26, 1943, in Box 38, DNC Files.
14 S. L. Brissie to Walker, December 2, 1943, in Box 38, DNC Files.
15 L. L. Martin to Walker, December 11, 1943, Jesse Taylor to Walker, November 23, 1943, in Box 38, DNC Files.
16 James Farley to McDuffie, December 1, 1943, in McDuffie Papers.

should form a "nucleus" to "organize a third party movement so strong that it will give these galloping wastrels so much food for thought that Mr. Roosevelt will voluntarily get out. Then we could nominate Harry Byrd and carry the Southern states." [17]

As Disney's matter-of-fact statement implied, Senator Harry Byrd had emerged by this time as the uncrowned leader and hero of conservative southerners (Josiah Bailey was too old to qualify as a viable presidential candidate). His continuous assault on the economic policies of the New Deal and his insistence on fiscal orthodoxy since the day of Roosevelt's first inauguration had won the unstinting admiration of the advocates of retrenchment and laissez faire. His close scrutiny of federal disbursements as chairman of the Joint Committee on Non-Essential Expenditures had probably made him the unrivaled head of the anti–New Deal bloc in the Senate. His political philosophy, enunciated tersely in an article in *American Magazine*, was a familiar echo of conservative preoccupations. He castigated improvisation in economic policy and complained of wastage, paper bureaucracy, and overstaffing on the federal payroll. He mourned for the decline in Congress' hold over the public imagination and feared an emergent personality cult, focused on Roosevelt.[18] Indeed, his stature increased still further in December, 1943, when Senator Guffey named Byrd the architect of the South's "unholy alliance" against the soldiers' vote bill.

Senator Byrd's economic creed particularly appealed to southern businessmen eager to have wartime restrictions removed and to curb the power of the unions. One notable exponent of this new frugality was John U. Barr, a wealthy New Orleans manufacturer and vice-president of the Southern States Industrial Council. In the winter of 1943 Barr formed the Byrd-for-

17 Wesley F. Disney to Dixon, November 15, 1943, in Dixon Papers. Also, R. Starnes to Rayburn, November 26, 1943, Clyde Eastus to Rayburn, November 4, 1943, in Miscellaneous Files 1943, Rayburn Papers.
18 Harry F. Byrd, "Are We Losing Our Freedom?" *American Magazine*, CXXXVI (September, 1943), 42–43, 132–34.

President Committee which aimed to coordinate southern efforts to cast off the yoke of the New Deal and to place Harry
Byrd in the White House. Although Barr had the sympathies of
numerous politicians, he was operating as a political outsider.
His initial task was to create publicity for his committee and
to convince party regulars that, since Roosevelt's policies ran
counter to southern interests, only the election of a southerner
could restore Dixie's influence in the Democratic party. He
strove, therefore, to secure the election or nomination of delegates pledged to vote for Byrd at the national convention.[19]

The Byrd-for-President Committee received encouragement
from various sources, including the southern press. Peter Molyneaux, editor of the *Southern Weekly*, endorsed the Byrd movement resoundingly on the grounds that "we can't see that anti–
New Deal Democrats in the South have anything to lose." [20]
Similarly, William Watts Ball, editor of the Charleston *News
and Courier*, supported Barr's activities in his columns and provided some financial help.[21] Although editorial publicity was
useful, Barr recognized the need to form grass roots organizations. He consequently encouraged sympathizers to develop
local committees. One such Byrd-for-President club was formed
in January in Indianola, Mississippi. At the open meeting, attended by about 250 people, local businessmen and farmers
vehemently lambasted the Roosevelt administration. A former
state senator cried that the South had been "too long a pack-
horse for the New Deal." A septuagenarian farmer reported that
he was "sick and tired of a government run by a handful of
men, assisted by the leaders of the labor unions." [22] In the same
month, after a number of other local rallies, Barr felt confident

19 Clifton L. Ganus to Clarke Salmon, May 15, 1944, in Box 466, Daniels Papers.
20 *Southern Weekly*, October 16, December 4, 1943.
21 Ball to John U. Barr, January 6, 1944, in Ball Papers; Charleston *News and
Courier*, January 7, 1944.
22 Baton Rouge *Morning Advocate*, January 12, 1944; Gordon L. Lyon to editor of *Life* magazine, January 12, 1944, in PPF 2834, Roosevelt Papers.

that his movement was "growing stronger and stronger each day."[23]

The Byrd-for-President Committee was only one of a number of organizations that aimed to prevent a fourth-term nomination. Other groups dedicated themselves to sending anti–New Deal delegations to the Chicago convention. They included the Constitutional Education League, Gerald L. K. Smith's America First party, Frank Gannett's Committee for Constitutional Government, and the American Democratic National Committee. Although these organizations were not sectional in their aims, they received the heaviest backing from the South. For example, the Committee for Constitutional Government reported that $100,000 of its total $255,000 in contributions had come from Texas alone.[24] The American Democratic National Committee was also well aware that most of its potential support would come from below the Potomac and gave special attention to its friends in the area.[25] By the spring of 1944 leaders were confident that anti–New Deal delegations could be sent to Chicago from eight southern states, as well as from New York and Massachusetts.[26]

These organizations all channeled their resources to defeat Roosevelt. The exact nature of their interrelationship is hazy, but they were all probably connected in some way by virtue of their common goals and of their members' multiple affiliations.[27] The Byrd-for-President Committee, the most active in the political sphere, concentrated on the South. The other organizations relied more on nationwide publicity than on direct political contact and lobbying to persuade local Democratic executive committees to free their convention delegates of their

23 Barr to Ball, January 3, 1944, in Ball Papers.
24 *Hearings to Investigate Campaign Expenditures, 1944*, pp. 377–463.
25 *Ibid.*, 557–87, 673–79.
26 Robert M. Harris to Ball, April 6, 1944, in Ball Papers; also, Stetson Kennedy, *Southern Exposure* (Garden City, N.Y., 1946), 143–55.
27 An unsigned report in the Daniels Papers alleges that there was "a clear connection" between the American Democratic Committee and the Committee for Constitutional Government. Memo, E. M. Biggers and Others, n.d., unsigned, in Daniels Papers.

ties to Roosevelt. Also, they did not adopt Byrd or any other person as their standard-bearer, while John U. Barr's committee pressed Byrd's candidacy continuously. However, Byrd himself gave no positive encouragement to Barr and did nothing to further his own candidacy. Indeed, he was conspicuously absent from a series of regional conferences sponsored by Barr to draw attention to his movement.

Whether the Byrd-for-President Committee actually converted anyone who was previously sympathetic to President Roosevelt is a conjectural problem that defies precise answer. It did, however, create a political climate which encouraged a number of anti-Roosevelt officeholders to challenge directly the policies of the national Democratic party. Tactics varied from politician to politician and from state to state. But throughout the South various county and state leaders raised the cry of insurgency and recommended a number of methods to discredit the president and his advisers. They all condemned the pervasive influence of labor leaders, the restrictions on prices, bureaucracy, and the racial policies of the president. However, local conditions usually determined the weight each of these issues would be given. In general, the race issue was emphasized more in areas with a proportionately high black population. Economic policy tended to be criticized more in regions dominated by commerce and industry. The success of these appeals in converting prejudices into political action usually depended upon the party loyalty and cohesiveness of the local political hierarchy, the party rules and laws of each state, and, of course, local public opinion.

The insurgents were always uncertain how the ordinary workers and farmers in the South would react to their campaigns. How prepared, they wondered, was the average white southern voter to turn his back on the party that had upheld the region's political culture for half a century? Could they seriously heed the advice of such rebels as Frank Looney, chairman of Louisiana's Democratic committee, "to even go far enough to follow the example of secession furnished by the states of the South at the cost of a war?" [28] Anyway, had the president lost his attractiveness to the ordinary southerner who had placed FDR's photograph on his living room walls during the depression? Or had his political fortunes declined only among business leaders and self-proclaimed racists? A Gallup poll, taken just before the *Smith* v. *Allwright* decision, showed that even though Roosevelt's popularity had declined considerably in the South, particularly in the Black Belt, he still remained Dixie's favorite candidate. Of the people polled in Alabama, 72 percent preferred Roosevelt for president to any other candidate—including Harry Byrd, James Farley, and James F. Byrnes, who were the darlings of the southern conservatives. In Mississippi and South Carolina, the two states with the highest proportion of Negroes, 62 percent and 60 percent, respectively, preferred Roosevelt.[29] If the polls were anything to go by, the president seemed safe. However, two key primary campaigns in May, 1944, served to gauge the extent of anti–New Deal sentiment in Dixie.

The senatorial Democratic primaries in Alabama and Florida essentially represented the current divisions of political opinion within the South. The two incumbents, Senators Lister Hill of Alabama and Claude D. Pepper of Florida, were both ardent supporters of the president. Although they were wary of the burgeoning agitation over civil rights, they had, nevertheless, believed that the best interests of the South lay in its continued allegiance to a party dedicated to social reform. They both had been consistent champions of Roosevelt's economic policies and were sincere advocates of unionism and protective legislation for workers. Their open sympathy for the urban coalition —both were endorsed by the CIO-PAC—became the central issue in their campaigns. Their opponents condemned them for betraying the South's interests and accused them of aligning themselves with Negro organizations. Indeed, in Alabama the

28 Baton Rouge *Morning Advocate,* January 30, 1944.
29 Columbia *Record,* April 10, 1944.

race question overshadowed everything else.[30] Thus, these campaigns served as trial balloons for disaffected Democrats. The Charleston *News and Courier* predicted that the outcome of the Florida contest alone would determine the tone and style of the southern revolt.[31]

Both primaries were held May 2. It came, therefore, as a double shock to the Democratic rebels that both Hill and Pepper had won resounding victories. Hill announced at once that his triumph represented an endorsement of Roosevelt's program.[32] The president himself rejoiced at the results and sent a congratulatory telegram to Hill.[33] These elections sounded the death knell for a bolt from the Democratic party in Alabama and Florida. For the time being, the insurgents were impressed with the view that "the race issue is no longer a short cut to political office." [34] They realized that even if leaders in the Black Belt were in revolt, most voters were still prepared to back their president. Nevertheless, they did not give up the fight completely. For in Alabama and those other southern states which were thenceforth unwilling to challenge Roosevelt's authority, the focus of opposition shifted to the movement to block the renomination of Henry Wallace as vice president and to replace him with a southern Democrat.

Not all Democratic organizations in the South, however, were prepared to surrender to the dictates of the national convention on the presidential nomination and the platform. Even if the defeat of Roosevelt seemed only remotely possible, die-hard anti–New Deal Democrats were determined to persist in their protests. For example, in South Carolina they broke away from the state party, headed by Governor Olin Johnston, and formed

30 Birmingham *News,* April 7, 16, 1944; *Alabama,* March 17, 1944; Ayers to Drew Pearson, April 10, 1944, in Ayers Papers; Bailey to Ollie Edmunds, April 8, 1944, in Bailey Papers; Stoesen, "The Senatorial Career of Claude D. Pepper," 181–84.
31 Charleston *News and Courier,* May 1, 1944.
32 Birmingham *News,* May 3, 1944.
33 Telegram, Stephen Early to Lister Hill, May 5, 1944, in PPF 3927, Roosevelt Papers.
34 Pittsburgh *Courier,* May 13, 1944.

their own separate group, the Southern Democratic party. These breakaway Democrats sought to win control of the state convention and then send a delegation to Chicago instructed to vote against Roosevelt's renomination and to insist on planks protecting states' rights and white supremacy.[35] If this failed, they would set up a slate of independent electors, pledged to support a southerner in the electoral college. They hoped that other states would follow suit, although they shunned association with other anti-fourth-term movements.[36]

The Southern Democratic party of South Carolina was unable to destroy Governor Olin Johnston's control of the state organization. Nevertheless, it did succeed in preventing the state convention from capitulating completely to party regularity. The state convention, held in May, was fraught with tension over the burning struggle to preserve the white primary.[37] The delegates were determined to prevent any further assaults on the caste system. A retired colonel from Greenville was prepared "to bolt the Chicago convention, hold a rump convention and put out a Southern Democratic ticket." [38] Sensibilities were further aroused when South Carolina Negroes began to organize their own independent party. In this heated atmosphere Governor Olin Johnston implored the convention to support the president for the sake of wartime unity. He wanted delegates to work for "the preservation of white supremacy," but to shelve other differences.[39] But many delegates were not prepared to bury their hatchets. Eugene S. Blease, leader of the anti-Johnston forces, sought to send an anti-fourth-term delegation to Chicago pledged to push for a white supremacy plank. Although Blease was defeated in his main aim, he did succeed in securing a delegation uninstructed as to the nomination but instructed to protect segregation and to oppose

35 Ball to Matthew B. Barkley, January 26, 1944, J. K. Breedin to Ball, May 9, 1944, in Ball Papers; Columbia *Record*, March 30, April 1, 1944.
36 Matthew B. Barkley to Ball, March 9, 1944, in Ball Papers.
37 See Charleston *News and Courier*, May 2, 1944.
38 Colonel C. Browning Smith to Ball, April 24, 1944, in Ball Papers.
39 Charleston *News and Courier*, May 16, 1944.

anything in the party platform that was "objectionable to the white Democrats of South Carolina." But the greatest victory for Blease's forces was the passage of a resolution requiring the state convention to reconvene after the Chicago convention to choose the state's electors. Thus, a path was left open to nominate electors who were not bound to vote for the Democratic nominee.[40]

The revolt in South Carolina had been limited because the Democratic loyalists, headed by Olin Johnston, had retained control over the state convention. Such was not the case in Texas, where, to the embarrassment of the Roosevelt administration, anti–New Deal forces won control over the Democratic organization of that state. Texas had been the center of Democratic recalcitrance for nearly a decade. Although the race question was an important ingredient of Texas politics, economic issues tended to dominate the political scene in the Lone Star State. V. O. Key has shown that in the 1940s the race issue was pushed into the background, while Texans divided broadly along liberal and conservative lines. "A modified class politics," Key has summarized, "seems to be evolving, not primarily because of an upthrust of the masses that compels men of substance to unite in self-defense, but because of the personal insecurity of men suddenly made rich who are fearful lest they lose their wealth." [41]

The men of wealth certainly took the initiative in 1944. They participated in full force in the precinct and county conventions in early May and were successful in securing anti–New Deal delegations from Texas' three largest cities to the state convention at Austin.[42] These delegations, on the advice of

40 *Ibid.*, May 18, 1944; New York *Times*, May 21, 1944; Resolution of South Carolina Democratic Convention, presented by Eugene S. Blease, May 17, 1944, in Johnston Papers, SCDA.
41 Key, *Southern Politics*, 255.
42 Clyde Eastus to Robert E. Hannegan, May 15, 1944, in Box 20, DNC Files; William Jean Tolleson, "The Rift in the Texas Democratic Party, 1944" (M.A. thesis, University of Texas, 1953), 26–28.

Texas' Democratic chairman, George Butler, hoped to persuade the state convention to go on record against a fourth term for Roosevelt and a second term for Vice President Henry Wallace.[43] The opponents of the New Deal had considerable backing not only from business interests, which had become particularly incensed over the president's use of his war powers, but also from key Democratic leaders, such as George Butler, Senator W. Lee O'Daniel, and, to a lesser degree, Governor Coke Stevenson.[44] However, they faced considerable opposition. As in South Carolina, a number of influential politicians who were sympathetic to the New Deal were determined to fight for control of the state convention. These party regulars included Congressmen Wright Patman and Lyndon B. Johnson, Tom Miller, mayor of Austin, former governor James Allred, and Speaker Sam Rayburn.

The Austin convention, held in the state Senate chamber, dramatized the deep schism in the state Democratic party. In the key battle for temporary chairman an anti–New Dealer, former governor Dan Moody, defeated James Allred, the pro-Roosevelt candidate. After this setback, the loyalists found themselves impotent in the struggle. Alvin J. Wirtz, former undersecretary of the interior, tried to introduce resolutions endorsing a fourth term and requiring the state's electors to vote for the party nominees. Pandemonium broke out after Wirtz had made his proposals. Anti-Roosevelt delegates insisted that the question of the status of electors should not be put up for a vote. When the chair sustained the objections to the Wirtz resolution, a Mrs. Alfred Taylor called upon "true Democrats" to walk out of the assembly and hold their own convention across the hall in the House of Representatives chamber. Be-

---

43 Clarence Miller to Rayburn, May 8, 1944, in Miscellaneous Files 1944, Rayburn Papers; Tolleson, "The Rift in the Texas Democratic Party," 30–31.
44 Copy, unsigned letter to Hannegan, February 25, 1944, in Miscellaneous Files 1944, Rayburn Papers; Eastus to Hannegan, May 15, 1944, in Box 20, DNC Files.

tween 250 and 500 Roosevelt supporters, including Wirtz, Allred, and Lyndon Johnson, walked out with heads high to a
chorus of jeers and hisses.[45]

The House convention declared itself a fully fledged convention of the Democratic party of Texas. It characterized the delegates in the Senate convention as "Republicans masquerading
as Democrats" and proceeded to select slates of delegates and
electors who favored a fourth term and would pledge themselves to support the party nominees. Meanwhile in the Senate
chamber, the "regular" convention, denuded of all New Dealers,
passed a series of resolutions that were to serve as ultimatums
to the Democratic National Convention. These resolutions
called for specific planks in the party platform. They required a condemnation of the *Smith* v. *Allwright* decision, together with a promise that the federal government would not
interfere in elections; denunciations of strikes, bureaucracy, and
"social equality"; and the readoption of the two-thirds rule. The
convention declared that if all these specifications were not
met, then delegates would be permitted to vote for a candidate
who supported these planks. In addition, the state's electors
would be considered free to vote for any candidate. Thus, if
the will of the regular convention prevailed, President Roosevelt would face not only the loss of twenty-three valuable electoral college votes but also the presence of a key nucleus for an
open revolt which could split the Democratic party irreparably.[46] James Farley certainly was convinced that the confusion
in Texas would have widespread repercussions.[47]

It is doubtful, however, that the state of Mississippi needed
encouragement from the Texans. Since the Negro had always

---

45 Tolleson, "The Rift in the Texas Democratic Party," 34–36; Seth S. McKay,
   Texas Politics, 1906–1944 (Lubbock, Texas, 1952), 433–36; New York
   Times, May 24, 1944.
46 Alvin Wirtz to Harold Ickes, May 25, 1944, J. B. Davis to Rayburn, May 24,
   1944, Lewis Carpenter to Wright Patman, May 25, 1944, in Miscellaneous
   Files, Rayburn Papers; G. C. Trout to Connally, May 26, 1944, in Box 102,
   Connally Papers; Tolleson, "The Rift in the Texas Democratic Party," 38–47;
   McKay, *Texas Politics, 1906–1944*, pp. 436–38.
47 James Farley to McDuffie, June 2, 1944, in McDuffie Papers.

set the tone of Mississippi politics, it was hardly surprising that the president's critics justified their determination to defeat Roosevelt in terms of race, rather than economic policy. For over a year the mutineers on the Democratic executive committee had been planning to seize control of the state convention.[48] So, when the convention officially met in June, 1944, the anti–New Deal bloc maneuvered with expected rapidity to win control by selecting sympathetic officers. They realized, of course, that the president still had a loyal following, even among such rabid racists as Senator Theodore Bilbo. They were careful, therefore, to emphasize not only race relations but also other acknowledged symbols of the South's social and political culture. Southernism was to be a major preoccupation of the rebels in Mississippi. The delegates at Jackson ignored Bilbo's counsel that "this is no time for shenanigans or 'monkey business,'" and proceeded to pave the way for a possible revolt from the Democratic party.[49] The speakers constantly harped on the dangers of the president's politics to southern civilization. The keynote speaker, Fred Smith, a Ripley attorney, told the convention that "the South is not the stepchild of the party, and will not permit itself to be treated as such." He inveighed against racial equality, warned of "the dangers of racial intermarriage and miscegenation," and prophesied that the CIO "will utterly destroy the peace and harmony of the South . . . unless we assert ourselves now in the council of the party." Delegates heeded these warnings and voted to send a delegation uninstructed as to the nominee to represent Mississippi at the Chicago convention. The delegates were also instructed to resist any kind of "social equality" plank in the party platform and to call for the restoration of the two-thirds rule. As in Texas and South Carolina, the Mississippi convention resolved

48 Dennis Murphree to FDR, January 11, 1944, in OF 300, Roosevelt Papers.
49 Bilbo to Forrest Jackson, June 1, 1944, in Bilbo Papers. Indeed, Bilbo was so overcome with feelings of loyalty that he swore, with obvious sarcasm, that he would stay with the party even if Henry Wallace were nominated! Bilbo to Jackson, June 11, 1944, in Bilbo Papers.

that the state's electors should be absolved from all obligation to vote for the nominees of the party if the national convention should adopt any plank in violation of their enunciated principles.[50]

In other southern states the revolt against the administration never assumed the same dimensions. For example, Louisiana was the only other state where there was any real danger that electors might be declared free agents, but the state committee, which nominated the electors, deferred action until after the national convention.[51] In Georgia Governor Ellis Arnall dismissed the race issue as an irrelevancy and made a well-publicized visit to the White House where he announced his support for a fourth term. Contrary to all other southern executives, Arnall also supported Henry Wallace for vice president.[52] Governor Broughton of North Carolina too advocated a fourth term, but he remained adamant that Wallace should not receive nomination as Roosevelt's running mate.[53] In Virginia, the Byrd organization, which controlled the state Democratic convention, selected a delegation instructed to oppose Wallace for the second place on the ticket, but uninstructed on the question of the presidential nomination. This action was tantamount to instructing for Virginia's favorite son, Harry Byrd—although Byrd himself was not particularly anxious to throw himself into the presidential race. The Virginia convention also refused to endorse any white supremacy planks and did not try to select independent electors. Such action might have played into the hands of the anti-Byrd faction, which had campaigned rigorously for a fourth term.[54]

50 Jackson *Clarion-Ledger*, June 8, 1944; New York *Times*, June 8, 1944.
51 New Orleans *Times-Picayune*, July 5, 1944.
52 Baton Rouge *Morning Advocate*, June 23, 1944; also, Ellis Gibbs Arnall, *The Shore Dimly Seen* (Philadelphia, 1946), 90–96; Taylor, "A Political Biography of Ellis Arnall," 295.
53 New York *Times*, June 11, 1944.
54 Washington, D.C., *Times-Herald*, July 9, 1944; New York *Times*, July 11, 1944. The anti-Byrd movement in Virginia was led by Martin A. Hutchinson, a Richmond attorney, and state Senator Lloyd M. Robinette of Jonesville. They helped set up a Committee of One Hundred for the Reelection of

Plans of action were, in sum, varied. Texas sent two delegations to Chicago, one committed to Roosevelt and the other decidedly opposed. The anti-Roosevelt delegations from Texas and
Mississippi were instructed to present specific planks on states'
rights, white supremacy, and labor relations to the national convention. If these planks were rejected, then the electors from
those states would be absolved from all obligations to support
the party nominees. South Carolina, which remained under the
control of Olin Johnston's faction, left the path open for the
selection of free electors but was unlikely to take such a drastic
step. The other southern delegations hoped to use normal representative methods to secure a platform and party rules that
were satisfactory to the South. They remained convinced that
unilateral action would only defeat their purposes. They realized, despite the alarm over Roosevelt's growing predilections
for the labor unions and the civil rights movement, that most
southern voters were still overwhelmingly in favor of the president. Roosevelt had, after all, presided over America's conversion from slump to boom and had provided moral guidance in
the struggle against the Axis. Indeed, it was deemed more necessary now than ever to maintain unity and continuity in the
wartime leadership, especially while the attention of the nation
was drawn to the invasion of France.[55] Above all, he had not instigated any single overt act to which southern voters could
point as being directly contrary to their regional interests. Dixie's rebellion was directed at tendencies and not at particulars.
Thus, as delegates from south of the Potomac prepared to travel
to Chicago, they determined to try to reverse these tendencies
by striking at one vulnerable particular—Henry Wallace.

Roosevelt. However, the Committee of One Hundred was powerless before
the Byrd organization. See Robinette to Hutchinson, May 29, 1944, Hutchinson to C. S. McNutty, June 5, 1944, Hutchinson to Robinette, June 19,
1944, in Box 7, Martin A. Hutchinson Papers, Alderman Library, University
of Virginia, Charlottesville.

55 John Odom to James Domengeaux, March 29, 1944, in Miscellaneous Files
1944, Rayburn Papers; William M. Kemper to Hutchinson, June 10, 1944,
in Hutchinson Papers.

Although he was the bête noire of the South, Wallace was the hero of the urban coalition of the North. Liberals respected his sense of vision. His dream of a postwar America that would dedicate itself to the elimination of poverty, injustice, and racism endeared him to many workers and to the struggling youths of the black ghettos. Except for Roosevelt himself, Wallace was the chief personification of the New Deal. But he was not only an uncompromising advocate of social welfare legislation. He had, of course, personally encouraged and associated with the massive campaigns of the CIO and the NAACP to create greater racial tolerance. After the Detroit riots in 1943, for example, he was one of the few members of the government to condemn the agitators of the race issue.[56] He was, consequently, a sitting target for dissident southerners. Those who understood the obstacles involved in repudiating the president in the midst of war served notice that the political execution of Wallace would be the minimum condition for preserving the unity of the party. Well before the convention southern leaders had planned to unite in their opposition to Wallace and to replace him with an acceptable southerner.[57] They wanted the symbolic satisfaction of knowing that they still could influence their own party. Remembering that Wallace had defeated William Bankhead of Alabama for the vice presidency in 1940, Gessner T. McCorvey of Alabama's Democratic executive committee affirmed: "I don't think that the President should undertake this year to dictate who should be his running-mate." He adamantly contended that "never before in the history of our Party had the position of Vice-President on the Democratic ticket been more important than it is this year." For he suspected, with a possible hint of malevolence, that "it will take a man of almost Herculean

56 Pittsburgh *Courier,* July 31, 1943.
57 Telegram, Chauncey Sparks to Olin Johnston, June 14, 1944, in Johnston Papers, SCDA; Gessner T. McCorvey to Sparks, July 7, 1944, in Marion Rushton Papers, Alabama Department of Archives, Montgomery; New Orleans *Times-Picayune,* June 10, 1944.

strength, great vigor and strong nerves to weather the storm." [58]

As McCorvey pointed out, the vice-presidential fight in 1944 was more than a campaign against symbols. Many other delegates and political observers seriously wondered whether Roosevelt could survive another four years of political office. His once long and fleshy face was, by the summer of 1944, thin and emaciated. He had lost weight and could not conceal his ashen complexion and sunken eyes. Although delegates to all conventions know that vice-presidential nominations are potentially presidential, the men and women at Chicago must have been uncommonly conscious of this fact. In August James Farley wrote to former vice president John Garner that "the question of the President's health will be quite a determining factor in the closing days of the campaign. There are all kinds of stories about, concerning his physical condition. . . . He doesn't look well in his pictures, except when a profile is taken." [59] The secretary of the NAACP, Walter White, who attended the convention, recalled that he had "never seen such cold-blooded speculation as there was among the Democrats, particularly those from the Deep South, as to how many years of a fourth term President Roosevelt could last." [60]

The determination of a number of southern delegates to drop Henry Wallace from the ticket only hardened the resolution of Negroes and labor officials to keep Wallace where he was. If, indeed, Roosevelt's life expectancy was a major consideration, labor and Negro leaders were equally aware of the necessity to secure the nomination of an established ally. They were determined to block the nomination of a southerner and to obtain an unambiguous liberal platform. To the chagrin of the southerners, they were permitted to put their case without interference before the credentials and platform committees. Walter White

---

58 McCorvey to Members of the State Democratic Executive Committee of Alabama, June 24, 1944, in Hobbs Papers.
59 Farley to John Nance Garner, August 23, 1944, in McDuffie Papers.
60 White, *A Man Called White*, 266; Ellender, interview.

told the Platform Committee that Negroes wanted the unrestricted right to vote and specific planks on the franchise, the FEPC, and antilynching. Edgar G. Brown, director of the National Negro Council, went further than White by advocating the use of federal troops to protect voting rights.[61] At the same time, White informed Senator Joseph Guffey that if James F. Byrnes or any other southerner were nominated for the vice presidency, "ninety per cent of Negroes would either vote Republican or go fishing on election day." He warned that "any substitute for Mr. Wallace would be construed as further surrender to the reactionary South by the Administration." [62]

The frankness of Negro leaders probably made a less lasting impression on the Democratic convention than the presence of the CIO-PAC. As will be shown shortly, the dominating influence of Sidney Hillman and the scattering of PAC representatives at Chicago would leave a deep-rooted mark not only on the Democratic party and the South's political consciousness, but also on the subsequent tone of the Republican opposition. Southerners were galled by the CIO's flagrant determination to keep Wallace on the ticket. "We believe that Mr. Wallace will strengthen the Democratic ticket and that any other candidate will weaken it," Sidney Hillman told the press. The Chicago *Tribune* hailed Hillman as the "king-maker." [63] He had, indeed, become one of the most powerful men in the Democratic party. The CIO-PAC and the National Citizens' Political Action Committee had contributed to the defeat of a number of anti–New Dealers in the primaries and alone had poured nearly $1.5 million into the Democratic campaign chests.[64] Hillman had become sufficiently influential within the party hierarchy to set up

61 New York *Times,* July 18, 1944; Baton Rouge *Morning Advocate,* July 18, 1944; Pittsburgh *Courier,* July 22, 1944; "A Message to the Republican and Democratic Parties," in Box 359/1, NAACP Files.
62 White to Joseph Guffey, July 19, 1944, in Box 291/1, NAACP Files.
63 See Josephson, *Sidney Hillman,* 617–22.
64 Louise Overacker, "Presidential Campaign Funds, 1944," *American Political Science Review,* XXXIX (October, 1945), 899–925.

his own separate headquarters in Chicago—next to those of Henry Wallace. Although only about one hundred PAC members were accredited as delegates or alternates, they were strategically distributed to be able to influence the delegations from the industrial states. Moreover, at least one CIO affiliate sat on each of the credentials, rules, permanent organization, and resolutions committees. Thus labor leaders were guaranteed a sympathetic hearing at Chicago.[65]

However, before the convention could consider the nominations and the wording of the platform, it had to resolve the claims for recognition of the rival delegations from South Carolina and Texas. An all-Negro delegation from South Carolina claimed recognition at Chicago on the grounds that the state Democratic party, headed by Governor Olin Johnston, had acted unconstitutionally in its exclusion of Negroes. The state Democratic convention had resolved to bar Negroes from membership in the state Democratic party. As a result, South Carolina Negroes had formed their own Progressive Democratic party under John McCray and James M. Hinton, who were both officials of the South Carolina branch of the NAACP. The Progressive Democrats had held their own convention where they had endorsed a fourth term and had resolved to contest the credentials of the white delegation in the light of the *Smith* v. *Allwright* decision.[66] White Democrats naturally viewed the Negroes' resistance with alarm. Eugene Blease feared that the national convention, in an attempt to woo Negroes further, would press for the seating of the black delegation. He recommended Olin Johnston to withdraw from the convention if any Progressive Democrats were seated.[67] But Johnston predicted that the credentials committee would not risk antagonizing the South by

65 Saenger, "Labor Political Action at Mid-Twentieth Century," 46–51; New York *Times*, July 19, 1944; Baton Rouge *Morning Advocate*, July 19, 1944.
66 Howard A. Quint, *Profile in Black and White* (Washington, D.C., 1958), 6–7; Charleston *News and Courier*, May 25, 1944.
67 Eugene S. Blease to Johnston, June 16, 1944, in Johnston Papers, SCDA.

accrediting the Negro delegation. He was right, for the committee voted, without challenge from the floor, to seat the white Democrats.[68]

The convention was not as acquiescent on the Texas question. Earlier in May both state conventions had nominated delegates to attend the national convention. The two delegations reported to Chicago after the Democratic National Committee had failed to reconcile the rival factions. Abe Murdock, chairman of the credentials committee, reported to the convention floor that his committee, after hours of wrangling, had decided to seat both contesting delegations and to divide their votes equally. After objections from Hart Willis, a representative of the anti-Roosevelt group, the Chicago convention compromised in grand tradition by agreeing to accept the recommendations of Murdock's committee. The Texans, on the other hand, were not satisfied. Immediately after the voice vote had been taken, thirty-three members of the anti-Roosevelt "regular" delegation, headed by Clint Small, walked dramatically from the convention hall.[69]

With all delegates seated and accredited, the Democratic convention proceeded to vote for its nominees and on the platform. The platform, which was accepted by voice vote over southern protests, consisted of laudatory appraisals of the New Deal and a pledge to continue the thrust of reform after demobilization. On the question of civil rights it fell between two stools. It merely affirmed the innocuous belief that "racial and religious minorities have the right to live, develop and vote equally with all citizens and share the rights that are guaranteed by our Constitution. Congress should exert its full constitutional powers to protect those rights." This plank satisfied neither Negro leaders

68 Johnston to Blease, June 24, 1944, in Johnston Papers, SCDA; Democratic National Committee, *Official Report of the Proceedings of the Democratic National Convention, 1944*, pp. 85–90.
69 Tolleson, "The Rift in the Texas Democratic Party," 57–61; McKay, *Texas Politics, 1906–1944*, pp. 444–45; New York *Times*, July 20, 1944; *Official Report of the Proceedings of the Democratic National Convention, 1944*, pp. 85–90.

nor the advocates of states' rights and white supremacy from the Deep South. Both groups had wanted specific provisions. In an attempt to alienate neither of them, officials had decided to adopt a plank open to the broadest interpretations. The *via media* had prevailed.[70]

Despite the earlier furor, Roosevelt was nominated with enthusiasm and without further ado. The southern delegates, however, complied with the instructions from their respective state conventions and party committees. The states of Mississippi, Louisiana, and Virginia gave all their votes to Harry Byrd, although he had made it clear beforehand that he was not a candidate. South Carolina, under the leadership of Olin Johnston, cast only three and a half of its eighteen votes for Byrd; the rest went to Roosevelt. The remaining Texas "regulars" gave Byrd twelve votes. Alabama cast two of its twenty-four votes for Byrd, and Florida gave him four of its eighteen votes. The final convention tally was 1,068 votes for FDR, 89 for Byrd, and 1 for James Farley.[71] Clearly, in spite of all the criticism and the handful of dissenting votes, the majority of southern Democrats had decided the time was not ripe to challenge the party leaders.

This was not the case when it came to the vice-presidential nomination. The intrigue that surrounded this fight has been recounted in a number of personal memoirs. The details, therefore, need be told only briefly. Although Roosevelt personally favored Henry Wallace, the leading party bosses, namely Ed Flynn, Ed Pauley, Frank Walker, and Robert Hannegan, believed that Wallace stood little chance of being nominated against the united opposition of the South. They also felt that no southern candidate could be nominated, since Roosevelt would subsequently lose the essential labor and Negro votes in the industrial states. Roosevelt took their advice. He informed James F. Byrnes, the South's favorite contender, that, contrary to ear-

70 New York *Times*, July 20, 1944; White to Eleanor Roosevelt, August 9, 1944, in Box 316/4, NAACP Files; McKellar to Crump, July 26, 1944, in McKellar Papers.
71 New York *Times*, July 20, 1944.

lier intimations, he was unacceptable on the ticket. Having considered all other eligible candidates, Roosevelt agreed with party leaders that Senator Harry S. Truman of Missouri was the most acceptable running mate. Truman had been selected for his loyal New Deal record, his scrupulous and efficient chairmanship of the Senate Committee to Investigate the National Defense Program, and for his domicile in the border state of Missouri. He seemed an ideal compromise for a convention that was to distinguish itself by compromise. The Democratic chairman, Robert Hannegan, persuaded Roosevelt to commit his choice to writing. In order not to appear to dictate to the convention, the president wrote that either Truman or Supreme Court Justice William O. Douglas would be acceptable as running mates. Sidney Hillman was informed of the president's preferences and, as soon as Truman arrived in Chicago, invited him to his quarters. Hillman found in Truman an acceptable substitute in the event of Wallace's defeat. Philip Murray and A. F. Whitney, president of the Railroad Trainmen, also approved. Truman himself was never an avowed candidate and told Hillman that he had promised to support James Byrnes. Indeed, even after Byrnes had been forced to withdraw from the race by party leaders, Truman insisted he was not a candidate. Only an arranged "eavesdropping" on a long-distance phone call from Roosevelt, who yelled (for Truman's hearing) that if the Missourian "wants to break up the Democratic party by staying out, he can, . . ." finally pursuaded him to stand as the president's running mate.[72]

Although Roosevelt had decided that Wallace's candidacy was no longer realistic, he felt he could not abandon his friend without at least offering a fight. He also wished to show the

---

72 The behind-the-scenes activities of the Chicago convention are recounted in Samuel I. Rosenman, Working with Roosevelt (London, 1952), 401–15; Harry S. Truman, Memoirs: The Years of Decision (Signet ed.; New York, 1965), I, 214–18; James F. Byrnes, All in One Lifetime (New York, 1958), 219–30; Flynn, You're the Boss, 181–83; see also Eleanor Roosevelt to White, August 3, 1944, in Box 316/4, NAACP Files.

labor leaders that he regarded compromise as a necessary last resort. He wrote, therefore, to Senator Samuel D. Jackson of Indiana, the permanent chairman, an open letter which was read to the convention. Roosevelt said of Wallace: "I like him, and I respect him and he is my personal friend. For these reasons I personally would vote for his renomination if I were a delegate to the convention. At the same time, I do not wish to appear in any way as dictating to the convention. Obviously the convention must do the deciding." [73] The southerners interpreted this message as yet another example of Roosevelt's obstinacy and insensibility. But their ire was capped by Wallace's seconding speech for Roosevelt's nomination. Wallace, in his impassioned style, told the assembly at Chicago:

The future belongs to those who go down the line unswervingly for the liberal principles of both political democracy and economic democracy regardless of race, color, or religion. The poll tax must go. Equal education opportunities must come. The future must bring equal wages for equal work regardless of sex or race. Roosevelt stands for all this. That is why certain people hate him so. . . . The Democratic party . . . is not only a free party but a liberal party. The Democratic Party cannot long survive as a conservative party.[74]

Wallace's nominating speech confirmed southern fears that he would encourage the party to associate solely with the urban coalition and break away from the South. The "certain people" of the South determined that Wallace should never be a heartbeat from the presidency.

Before delegates cast their first ballot, Robert Hannegan publicized Roosevelt's letter (dated July 19 but written, according to Samuel I. Rosenman, a week earlier) in which he had stated he would accept either Truman or Douglas on the ticket.[75] Although Sidney Hillman had agreed with Roosevelt's choice, he

---

73 Rosenman (comp.), *The Public Papers and Addresses of Franklin D. Roosevelt,* 199–200; Rosenman, *Working with Roosevelt,* 405, 411.
74 *Official Report of the Proceedings of the Democratic National Convention, 1944,* p. 79.
75 Rosenman, *Working with Roosevelt,* 408.

was determined to fight for Wallace on the first ballot. PAC delegates worked busily on the convention floor to rally votes for Wallace, but when the first count had been taken, the vice president had received only 429½ votes to Truman's 319½, John Bankhead's 98, Scott Lucas' 61, and a scattering of others. It was obvious that the first ballot had represented Wallace's greatest strength. From the South only Florida and Georgia cast votes for the incumbent vice president. The other southern votes went to Bankhead (who derived his entire vote from the South), Truman, Broughton, Barkley, and a sprinkling of minor favorite sons.[76] The Wallace movement had collapsed on the first ballot. The convention then swung in unison to the senator from Missouri. Louisiana led the South in joining sister states from the North to deliver a total 1,031 votes to Truman on the second ballot. Wallace polled a mere 105 votes.[77]

So, by taking a bellicose stand within the party framework, the South had succeeded in defeating the most important figurehead, except the president, in the Democratic party. Gessner McCorvey was "particularly delighted" with Wallace's defeat. He wrote to Hannegan of his confidence that Truman would "understand our problems" and that Alabama would go "overwhelmingly for the Democratic nominees." [78] McCorvey and the Dixie Democrats could find some cause for celebration. Although they had failed to secure a platform reflecting their preeminent interests, they had ousted Wallace and had prevailed over the PAC and NAACP by tempering the plank on civil rights. They could also claim, in the years ahead, that, had it not been for the South, Harry Truman would never have become president.

The South, therefore, had won a partial victory at Chicago; its opinions had not been ignored. On the other hand, it was

76 *Official Report of the Proceedings of the Democratic National Convention,* 1944, pp. 213–56.
77 *Ibid.;* Fred Odom to Ambrose Smith, August 30, 1944, in Box 7, DNC Files; Mrs. Roland B. Howell, interview with author, October, 1968.
78 McCorvey to Hannegan, July 25, 1944, in Box 1, DNC Files.

well aware that compromise had been necessitated by the need for wartime unity and by the sheer conflict of ideals within the party. Compromise had not drawn the South and the North together; on the contrary, it had only emphasized the gulf between these factions. The Democratic party came to be viewed increasingly as a marriage of convenience, a vehicle of political advancement. The grand coalition of 1936 seemed far removed. As they left Chicago, politicians from both sides of the fence felt the party had suffered for its abdication of principle. The southerners were relieved that a showdown had been averted but regarded the debacle as auspicious. Senator-elect Clyde R. Hoey of North Carolina, for example, was grateful that the South had ousted Wallace and had nominated in his stead "a very much safer and wiser man, from the Southern standpoint." But he regretted that a number of southerners had become estranged from the Democratic party. He hoped, however, that southerners would "not take any chance of hazarding the peace of the world hereafter by permitting divisions to arise in the Democratic party now." [79]

As the days passed, however, the dissidents took an increasingly sour view of the proceedings in Chicago. They were particularly piqued when Arthur Krock of the New York *Times* reported in September that Roosevelt had ordered that no vice-presidential candidate should be put forward without the express approval of Sidney Hillman. This story only served to reinforce their suspicion that the administration considered the South to be of minor importance.[80] As "Clear It Through Sidney" became the catchphrase of the election campaign, southerners became more convinced that the convention had sealed the power of labor and Negro leaders. Edward H. Crump, the political boss of Memphis, wrote that the ability of Hillman and Walter White to prevent the nomination of a southern vice pres-

79 Hoey to R. A. Doughton, August 12, 1944, in Clyde R. Hoey Papers, Duke University Library, Durham, N.C.
80 Arthur Krock, "Hillman and PAC Loom as a Big Campaign Issue," New York *Times*, September 17, 1944.

ident "was enough for any Southerner to pause for a moment, unless he was indulging in a gnat's eye view of the mountain." He was proud that Tennessee had been the only Dixie state to withhold its vote from Truman who had, after all, been instrumental in preventing the nomination of a southerner.[81] From Texas a party appointee reported that Hillman's activities during the campaign were handicapping the president. Hillman, felt southerners, "was drunk on power like a lot of men who get in that position and make themselves obnoxious by their arrogant attitudes." [82]

But southern Democrats were not the only pessimists concerning the future of the Democratic party. Liberals, who had found in Henry Wallace the embodiment of their own ideals, felt President Roosevelt had succumbed to the South and the machine politicians, who, they argued, were concerned only with electoral victory and not with the social purpose that underlay such a victory. These critics felt the strong leadership of the 1930s had degenerated into a politics distinguished only by compromise and expediency. Wallace had been a torchbearer of the New Deal; he was now its sacrificial martyr. A New York college student, depressed by the events at Chicago, wrote her father that the Democratic party had abandoned its progressivism and had "returned to the path of politics in every sinister connotation of the word." Wallace, lamented the girl, "whose greatness will be recognized too late has been thrown down and replaced by a machine politician, a Southerner, whose life-long environment has steeped him in narrowness and prejudice and sectional ethnocentricity." [83] Another admirer of the vice president condemned Roosevelt for deserting his friend and, raising a not altogether irrelevant point, asked Wallace: "If a couple of

81 Crump to Alfred Mynders, July 31, 1944, McKellar to Crump, July 26, 1944, McKellar to Hannegan, undated, in McKellar Papers.
82 Eastus to Hannegan, August 15, 1944, in Box 20, DNC Files.
83 Betty Himmelman to her father, undated (probably July 22, 1944), in Box 27, Henry A. Wallace Papers, Manuscripts Division, Library of Congress, Washington, D.C.

crooked City politicians like Hague and Kelly can eliminate you so easily, what in the world do you suppose will happen at the Peace table if Mr. Roosevelt is there and has to bargain with strong and able men like Churchill and Stalin?" [84] Wallace, however, seemed confident that his defeat did not mean the New Deal would be buried. He was sure other men would carry the battle flag of reform into the postwar world. "The lesson of the convention," he wrote, "is that the liberals will have to do everything possible to make a truly liberal party out of the Democratic party." [85]

The superficial healing of sectional antagonism at the convention took the sting out of the southern revolt. Although southerners had not had their way at Chicago, the convention had not produced any single *casus belli*. The majority of dissident southern officeholders were persuaded to continue the fight for southern supremacy within the Democratic party—especially when it seemed that they had little popular support at home. The thrust of the southern rebellion collapsed still further a few days after the convention when Olin Johnston defeated "Cotton Ed" Smith in South Carolina's senatorial primary. Smith had been campaigning on his anti-Roosevelt record and Johnston on his support of the administration. The repudiation of Smith showed that the vociferous southern critics did not always express popular sentiments. In recognition of Roosevelt's proven popularity, South Carolina's second state convention, which convened a week after the primary, endorsed the national Democratic platform and established procedures for selecting pro-Roosevelt electors. The convention lasted for only ten minutes. [86] Following on South Carolina's heels, Mississippi's electors voted one week later to support the Roosevelt-Truman ticket, although

---

84 Horace H. Kircher to Wallace, September 10, 1944, in Box 27, Wallace Papers. See also Felix Frankfurter to Wallace, July 23, 1944, in Box 27, Wallace Papers; Pittsburgh *Courier*, July 29, 1944.
85 Wallace to Hubert H. Jones, August 10, 1944, in Box 27, Wallace Papers.
86 Charleston *News and Courier*, July 26, August 3, 1944.

they reserved the right to change their minds. However, pressure from Roosevelt's supporters resulted in a full pledge to vote for the party nominees in the electoral college.[87]

Texas remained the final bastion of the southern revolt. E. B. Germany, leader of the anti-fourth-term forces, determined that Texas' electors should be bound to vote against Roosevelt in the electoral college. He remained confident that if he could persuade the electors of Mississippi and Louisiana to join Texas in voting for a southerner in the electoral college, then the South would be able to control the result of a close election.[88] However, Texas' national committeeman, Myron Blalock, a staunch party regular despite his personal antipathy to Roosevelt, moved to compel Texas' electors to vote for the party nominee.[89] When fifteen of Texas' twenty-three electors announced their refusal to sign pledges of support for the Chicago nominees, Roosevelt's followers resolved to bring the conflict to a showdown at the state's second convention.[90] The convention met on September 12. After a long struggle pro-Roosevelt delegates won control and proceeded to undo the work of the May convention. George Butler was removed as state chairman and was replaced by Harry Seay. Fifty of the sixty-two members of the state executive committee were ousted and a new list of electors, all of whom were pledged to support Roosevelt, was drawn up. However, the anti-Roosevelt delegates refused to give up their fight. After the Texas Supreme Court upheld the new arrangements, they convened at a closed meeting and set up their own independent slate of electors under the party title of Texas Regulars. The electors were pledged to vote for any Democrat other than

87 New York *Times*, August 12, 1944; A. B. Friend to Hannegan, August 21, 1944, in Box 11, DNC Files.
88 E. B. Germany to Richard C. Russell, August 10, 1944, in Box 11, DNC Files.
89 Myron Blalock to the Texas Democratic Electors, August 4, 1944, Blalock to State Senator Holbrook, August 12, 1944, in Miscellaneous Files 1944, Rayburn Papers.
90 Rayburn to W. A. Thomas, August 29, 1944, R. Lee Bobbitt to Rayburn, September 1, 1944, in Miscellaneous Files 1944, Rayburn Papers.

Roosevelt. In October E. B. Germany announced that the electoral votes of the Regulars would be cast for Harry Byrd.[91]

The attempts of disenchanted southerners to oust Roosevelt and to restore their eminence in the top echelons of the Democratic party had fizzled by October. Of course, dissidents had not become less dissident. They merely recognized that the combined forces of war, party loyalty, patronage, and Roosevelt's popularity had doomed the revolt. A bolt in the electoral college could be effected only if the respective state Democratic parties gave such action their full support. Usually individual heresies in the college were frowned upon as political chicanery —in Louisiana, for example, electors who had reserved the right to vote as they pleased were promptly ousted by the state committee, which was itself hardly sympathetic to Roosevelt.[92] Southerners realized that a revolt from the Democratic party would benefit only the Republican nominee, Thomas E. Dewey, who had stressed his personal support for a permanent FEPC and anti-poll tax legislation. Although Roosevelt also sought to win Negro votes, he chose to play down the civil rights issue in his campaign speeches. Just before polling day Senator McKellar admitted that although he had many criticisms of Roosevelt, he recognized that on the race issue Dewey was "quite as bad or worse in this respect." [93] The president's campaign staff also realized that he had to tread cautiously. Indeed, only a month before the election Roosevelt was advised to prevent the Department of Justice from prosecuting Alabama registrars for refusing Negroes the vote, in case such action "would translate impotent rumblings against the New Deal into an actual revolt at the polls." [94]

91 New York *Times,* September 13, 14, 1944; Tolleson, "The Rift in the Texas Democratic Party," 87–93, 99–103; McKay, *Texas Politics, 1906–1944,* 448–50, 452–54.
92 New Orleans *Times-Picayune,* September 26, 27, 28, 29, 1944.
93 McKellar to Jett Potter, October 30, 1944, in McKellar Papers.
94 Memo, Jonathan Daniels to FDR, September 28, 1944, in OF 93, Roosevelt Papers.

The die-hard insurgents, in fact, consisted largely of men who did not hold political office. The politicians who had been vehemently critical of the president earlier had either recognized the need for intraparty compromise or had been ousted from office. The political cost of a revolt, in the final analysis, was too expensive. Advocates of party secession had underestimated the allegiance of rank-and-file Democrats to the Roosevelt administration. The ordinary voter could see no overwhelming reason to forsake the party of his forefathers. Moreover, the predominance of big businessmen in the ranks of the insurgents made most people suspicious of their motives and provided party regulars with powerful campaign ammunition. The rewards of loyalty were too tempting to turn against the party leadership. Political tenure was always preferable to political oblivion, and those who did not hold office thus had little to lose. It was also difficult to keep up the momentum of the revolt. J. K. Breedin, chairman of South Carolina's Southern Democratic party, regretfully reported the demise of his party in October and gave up the fight. He complained that there was too much "lethargy" toward his movement.[95] In fact, in political terms his movement had become irrelevant. Gessner McCorvey, a constant critic of the administration—but also a perspicacious realist—best expressed the situation. He wrote that although many southern leaders had opposed the fourth-term nomination, they recognized it as necessary to the war effort. He saw that "the Southern people are finally waking up to the fact that by the South presenting a united front at our National Conventions we can regain in the councils of our Party the prestige which we formerly enjoyed." He warned, however, that "if the National Administration continues to meddle with our racial problems . . . I conceive that matters could get to the point where there would be danger of the South abandoning its traditional allegiance to the Democratic Party. However, I don't think we have as yet come to this point. . . . Of course, much has been done

95 J. K. Breedin to Ball, October 6, 1944, in Ball Papers.

by our Party that I do not approve of, but I believe in doing my fighting *within* my party, and not *without* it." [96]

McCorvey's analysis of the South's options proved correct. In the November election the American people for a fourth time elected Franklin D. Roosevelt as their president. Although Roosevelt polled only 3,500,000 more votes than Dewey, he won 432 electoral college votes to his opponent's 99. As always, the Republicans made a poor showing in the South. Even the Texas Regulars polled only 11.7 percent of the total vote in Texas, while Roosevelt received a massive 71.3 percent of the vote.[97] The quadrennial prophesies that the South was embarking upon a two-party system were again discredited by the voting statistics. The Democratic party was becoming increasingly a strange marriage of conflicting partners. While southerners flocked to cast their votes for Roosevelt, Chicago's Negroes gave Roosevelt a record 65 percent of their votes and Harlemites cast 80 percent of their votes for Roosevelt.[98] While southerners wrote congratulatory letters to the president and other Democratic leaders, FDR wrote his own letters of thanks. To Sidney Hillman he wrote: "One thing I want to make perfectly clear to Sidney is my appreciation. It was a great campaign and nobody knows better than I do how much you contributed to its success. I was glad to learn that the CIO in Chicago authorized the continuation of the PAC. I can think of nothing more important in the years to come than the continuing political education and political energy of the people." [99]

96 McCorvey to editor, Mobile *Press Register*, September 2, 1944, in Hobbs Papers.
97 U.S. Bureau of the Census, *Historical Statistics*, 684, 688.
98 Rita W. Gordon, "The Change in the Political Alignment of Chicago's Negroes during the New Deal," *Journal of American History*, LVI (December, 1969), 603; Florence Murray (ed.), *The Negro Handbook* (New York, 1947), 296.
99 FDR to Hillman, November 25, 1944, in PPF 8172, Roosevelt Papers. *Newsweek* commented that the president owed his victory to Hillman's PAC without which "his defeat would have been almost a certainty." The PAC "provided what the Democratic Party had plainly lost—organization." *Newsweek* (November 13, 1944). See also Joseph Rosenfarb, "Labor's Role in the Election," *Public Opinion Quarterly*, VIII (Fall, 1944), 376–90.

Both southern politicians and the leaders of the labor-Negro bloc were well aware of the paradox of the situation. As 1944 drew to an end, Democrats of both persuasions realized that coexistence under the same party roof would become increasingly precarious. How could southern planters and ghetto Negroes unblushingly continue to support the same party? Some saw a solution. One particularly galled southerner felt that "the only way to clean up the Democratic Party is to get new leadership, which can't be done by supporting, acclaiming, and condoning the present leadership. . . . Another four years of Mr. Roosevelt and his clique, and I think the Democratic processes in this country are gone." [100] But he did not know that by April, 1945, the occupant of the White House would be not the Harvard-educated aristocrat from New York, but a former haberdasher from Missouri—and the grandson of a Confederate sympathizer and slaveholder at that.

100 Robert M. Hanes to Martin, October 14, 1944, in Martin Papers.

CHAPTER FIVE

Harry Truman and
Reconversion: Washington,
1945–1946

O<small>N</small> APRIL 12, 1945, a shocked
American nation learned that Franklin D. Roosevelt had died.
His successor, Harry S. Truman, inherited not only the highest
office in the land but also the deep political divisions that Roosevelt had left behind him within his own party. The circumstances surrounding Truman's accession bore an almost bizarre
resemblance to those faced by Andrew Johnson when he succeeded Abraham Lincoln in 1865. Both presidents had been
originally selected for the vice presidency because they were
acceptable compromise candidates. Both hailed from border
states, an important consideration when a party is torn by sectional questions. As in the case of Johnson, Truman attained
the supreme office as America was drawing hostilities to an end.
Similarly, Truman headed a party whose members had been
divided during a war in anticipation of the political issues of
the postwar reconversion. And, as the status of the Negro had
divided the Republicans in 1865, so it divided the Democrats
in 1945. Equally important, certain members of the party had
become jealous and vigilant of the extraordinary executive powers of a wartime president. Like Johnson, Truman had received
only a limited education. And, like Lincoln's humble successor,
Truman faced the overwhelming personal handicap of succeeding a president, who, despite national divisions, had as-

sumed, if not during his lifetime then certainly at the moment of death, the mantle of a national folk hero.[1]

Harry Truman began his presidency with the confidence of the South, despite the fact that little was known of him. His Missouri upbringing, which included attendance at a segregated school, convinced southerners that he would be sympathetic to their concern about the race issue. At least he had had direct contact with the Negro and should, therefore, appreciate the delicacies of the caste system.[2] They admired his industrious and generally apolitical role as chairman of the Senate Committee to Investigate the National Defense Program and concluded from the record that he understood the necessity for an independent and critical legislative branch. Above all, southern Democrats felt that since they had been responsible for his initial election as vice president, Truman would be duly indebted to them. Of course, they did not think they would have a puppet in the White House. They sincerely believed, however, that Truman did not share his predecessor's enthusiasm for social reform and that he would bridge the sectional split in the Democratic party. Theodore Bilbo commended the new president for being "all wool, a yard wide, a straight-shooter and a good member of the Baptist Church."[3] Josiah Bailey, who seemed more relaxed in a period fraught with anxiety, confided: "The Congress was really distressed by the death of President Roosevelt, but as a general thing it is certain the members of Congress will get along better with President Truman than they did with him, and President Truman will get along better with Congress. He is a very thoughtful and very careful sort of man and does the intelligent thing in a tactful way."[4]

1 Truman, *Memoirs*, I, 15, 23–24, 31–32, 49–50.
2 Richard S. Kirkendall, "Truman and the South" (Unpublished paper delivered to the Southern Historical Association, October, 1969). I am indebted to Professor Kirkendall for making his paper available to me.
3 Bilbo to William H. Hooks, April 13, 1945, Bilbo to HST, April 13, 1945, in Bilbo Papers.
4 Bailey to Shuping, April 27, 1945, in Bailey Papers.

Southern Democrats looked forward to a new honeymoon with the executive branch and to a restoration of their influence in the party. Fresh appointments would be made, the details of reconversion would be worked out. They all hoped that their viewpoints and suggestions would be sought and accepted by the new president. After all, Truman had been a vigilant and dedicated senator and should, therefore, be sympathetic to those members of Congress who were anxious to realize the needs and aspirations of their constituents. They particularly wanted Truman to review the entire functions and responsibilities of government. He should not, they argued, be hampered or restricted by his predecessor's commitments. They were sure he would resist what they considered the more revolutionary aspects of Roosevelt's postwar plans. Olin Johnston advised him, "I think that your policies will be far enough to the right and not too far to the left. This in my opinion, will be most valuable in securing the fullest and best cooperation of the people and the Congress." [5]

Harry Truman moved cautiously in his first weeks of occupancy in the White House. His primary task was to grasp the reins of government as rapidly and as efficiently as possible. He realized the importance of asserting his own authority and of emancipating himself from the shadow of his predecessor. It was thus necessary to appoint to his cabinet and his White House staff personal supporters who would follow him loyally. His first move was to summon James F. Byrnes to Washington to become secretary of state, although his appointment was not finalized until after the San Francisco conference. This appointment was received with expected satisfaction in the South. Byrnes, of course, had been the South's principal choice for vice president in 1944; now, one year later, he was appointed the key architect of American foreign policy—and was also next in line to the presidency. Many former cohorts of Roose-

5 Olin D. Johnston to HST, April 18, 1945, in PPF 598, Harry S. Truman Papers, Harry S. Truman Library, Independence, Mo.

velt left the cabinet to be replaced by Truman's choices. Frances Perkins was replaced by Lewis Schwellenbach as secretary of labor. Tom Clark of Texas succeeded Francis Biddle as attorney general. Other familiar faces of the Roosevelt entourage left the White House to be succeeded by virtually unknown appointees, soon to be known as the "Missouri gang." Southerners were confident that this rapid change of personnel boded well for the reinstatement of more conservative policies and of a fluid channel of communication between the White House and Capitol Hill. The former governor of North Carolina, O. Max Gardner, could rejoice that the new president "has exercised a high degree of executive capacity" and that Truman's "political record" showed that "he understood the science of public opinion, and that he was of the type to delegate authority." [6]

Despite the rapid departure of New Dealers, Truman gave no definite indication that he would reverse or alter Roosevelt's policies. To the contrary, he wanted to convince the country he would act to implement the promises of the 1944 platform. The surrender of Germany in May made it imperative for the government to adopt immediate programs to meet new contingencies. The return of the soldiers and the decrease in production of war materials created nationwide fears of unemployment and economic contraction. Truman acted at once to make his intentions clear. He did not contemplate abdicating the tight economic controls that the government had established under the provisions of the war powers acts. Demobilization and reconversion would be an executive task and would incorporate the principles enunciated by Roosevelt. Truman, wanting to

6 O. Max Gardner to Russell, May 19, 1945, in Bailey Papers; Truman, *Memoirs,* I, 34–35; Hinchey, "The Frustration of the New Deal Revival," 89–98; Kenneth W. Street, "Harry S. Truman: His Role as Legislative Leader, 1945–1948" (Ph.D. dissertation, University of Texas, 1963), 89–90; Robert S. Allen and William V. Shannon, *The Truman Merry-Go-Round* (New York, 1950), 48–63; Patrick Anderson, *The President's Men* (Garden City, N.Y., 1968), 88–90; Elmer E. Cornwell, Jr., "The Truman Presidency," in Richard S. Kirkendall (ed.), *The Truman Period as a Research Field* (Columbia, Mo., 1967), 219–21.

expedite these powers, even requested Congress in May for authorization to reorganize the executive office of the president to insure maximum efficiency.[7] He also asked Congress to provide adequate unemployment compensation for the victims of industrial and military demobilization. Since state unemployment provisions were inadequate, he recommended that the federal government should provide an unemployment benefit of at least twenty-five dollars a week and that coverage should be extended to all workers. In a private conversation with Walter George, chairman of the Senate Committee on Finance, the president specified that the executive branch intended to exercise due vigilance over the demobilization process and that the long-awaited return to normalcy was not imminent.[8]

Truman thus showed that on social security matters he would use the full sweep of the executive powers granted to him. But beneath the preoccupying problem of reconversion lay the smoldering issue of racial discrimination. If reconversion was to be supervised and controlled by the government, then it would become necessary to adopt a policy, or at least some guidelines, regarding its own attitude toward the special handicaps of minority groups, especially Negroes. Truman may at one time have hoped this issue would somehow resolve itself, as it did, albeit unsatisfactorily, during Roosevelt's presidency. But within a few weeks of his accession to high office, Truman decided, though with possible regret afterward, to risk his entente with the South by lending support to the bill establishing a permanent FEPC.

Before discussing Truman's intervention in the FEPC controversy, however, it is necessary to unravel the legislative history of this issue. There were, basically, two FEPC bills under consideration in Congress in the spring of 1945. One was the

7 *Public Papers of the Presidents of the United States, Harry S. Truman: Containing the Public Messages, Speeches, and Statements of the President, 1945–1952* (8 vols.; Washington, D.C., 1961–1966), I, 69–72, hereafter cited as *Public Papers*, relevant date.
8 *Public Papers, 1945*, pp. 72–75; memo, Rosenman to HST, June 4, 1945, in OF 121 A, Truman Papers.

annual appropriations bill which was necessary to renew the functions of the extant FEPC. The other bill provided for the establishment of a permanent, statutory committee. On June 1 the House Appropriations Committee reported out the war agencies appropriations bill, but specifically withheld funds from the FEPC on the grounds that Congress should await developments on the pending bill creating a permanent FEPC. However, this latter bill, which would have established a permanent agency with enforcement powers, had come to a grievous standstill.[9] The bill in the House of Representatives had been sent to the southern-dominated Rules Committee which had bottled it without further consideration. For a brief period it seemed that it would die there. Most of the activity to release it from that sepulchral committee came from outside pressure groups, particularly civil rights organizations. But they not only agitated members of Congress. The National Council for a Permanent FEPC, for example, reminded the public that Truman himself had made "no public pronouncement as *President*" to date on the matter.[10] And, at the end of May, Walter White went to see Truman to discuss related problems.[11]

It was during this period of legislative inactivity over the FEPC that President Truman decided to intervene personally. It seemed that on the civil rights issue he was prepared to move beyond the wavering ambiguity of his predecessor by taking a firm stand against a recalcitrant Congress. There were several possible reasons for Truman's seemingly unequivocal intervention into the FEPC controversy. First, the president had been waiting for an opportunity to show that liberalism had not passed with the death of Roosevelt. Although he had not

---

9 *Congressional Record,* 79th Cong., 1st Sess., A 3266; also, U.S. Senate, Subcommittee of the Committee on Education and Labor, *Hearings to Establish a Fair Employment Practices Commission,* 79th Cong., 1st Sess., 8.

10 Circular, National Council for a Permanent FEPC, *Report to the Nation,* May 22, 1945, in Box 20/1, Philleo Nash Papers, Harry S. Truman Library, Independence, Mo.

11 Report of a phone call from Walter White, May 25, 1945, in Box 359/2, NAACP Files.

given left-wing Democrats cause for doubt at this stage in his career, there had not been a suitable occasion to prove his credentials as Roosevelt's ideological heir. Second, the president was probably eager, as a matter of personal conviction, to side with social justice. He must have realized that a planned reconversion policy would, in all fairness, have to include guarantees of equal employment opportunities for minority groups. Of course, his motive may have been less altruistic and even naive. For reasons that will become apparent, there is a possibility that he did not foresee at all the intensity of the southern reaction. Maybe he just acted impulsively. But whatever his precise personal motives, the FEPC bill provided Truman the first major opportunity to set the tone of his postwar domestic policies. He wrote, therefore, a letter, which was released for publication, to Democrat Adolph J. Sabath of Illinois, chairman of the deadlocked House Rules Committee:

To abandon at this time the fundamental principle upon which the Fair Employment Practice Committee was established is unthinkable.

Even if the war were over, or nearly over, the question of fair employment practices during the reconversion period and thereafter would be of paramount importance. Discrimination in the matter of employment against properly qualified persons because of their race, creed, or color is not only un-American in nature, but will eventually lead to industrial strife and unrest. It has a tendency to create substandard conditions of living for a large part of our population. The principle and policy of fair employment practice should be established permanently as a part of our national law.[12]

Truman had been at the president's desk for less than two months when he thus antagonized the southern wing of his party by aligning himself with the advocates of a permanent FEPC. Truman had done what Roosevelt had consistently refused to do—he had projected himself into the congressional debates on the increasingly pressing and explosive question of race.

12 HST to Adolph J. Sabath, June 5, 1945, in OF 40, Truman Papers.

The reaction to Truman's open letter was instant and revealing. Walter White hailed it as "magnificent" and proclaimed that minorities in America were "grateful" for his outspoken gesture.[13] Members of the FEPC also commended Truman.[14] The White House mail room reported that of about four thousand letters and telegrams received on the subject, only nineteen had expressed disapproval. Analysts in the mail room concluded that Truman's letter had "established him as a liberal in the eyes of liberals."[15] Exaggerated as this probably was, it seemed that Truman had certainly committed himself to the championship of liberal race policies. But, of course, there was a political price to pay. Columnist Thomas Stokes remarked that "it begins to look as though the orange blossoms and magnolias which symbolized the honeymoon of the new President and his Southern political leaders are about to wither."[16]

Predictably, Truman's letter to Sabath did not change the minds of those southern Democrats who found the FEPC abhorrent. In fact, it only hardened their determination to kill the FEPC. The missive indicated that southerners would have to fight the proposals alone and that they could expect neither sanctuary nor solace from the White House. Yet they were careful not to declare a political war on the president at once. Perhaps, they thought, Truman had sent the letter as a mere, once-for-all gesture to the liberal voters of the North and did not intend to continue bullying for the enactment of a permanent FEPC. A few days after the letter was published, southern Democrats caucused and selected Congressman Frank Boykin of Alabama to request an appointment with the president for the group to present its arguments against the FEPC. Boykin wrote to Truman of the caucus decision and warned him

13 Telegram, White to HST, June 5, 1945, in Box 359/2, NAACP Files.
14 Members of the FEPC to HST, June 7, 1945, in OF 40, Truman Papers.
15 Unsigned memo to HST, undated, in OF 40, Truman Papers.
16 Baton Rouge *Morning Advocate*, June 8, 1945.

of "this terrible thing that is not only tearing our Party to pieces, but the entire Nation." Boykin informed him that the southern caucus consisted of "strong Truman supporters," to emphasize, presumably, that the South hoped to repair the breach. The president, however, refused to see Boykin's delegation on the pretext that he did not have time. He realized he could not contradict his original stand and decided that silence was the best way to reconcile the southerners.[17]

However, they did not await further initiatives or gestures from the White House. On Capitol Hill southern Democrats proceeded to kill the FEPC. By a six-to-six tie vote, the House committee ignored Truman's request and denied a rule on the permanent FEPC bill. Roger Slaughter, a Democrat representing Truman's home district in Kansas City, was among the six southern and border-state Democrats who voted to stifle further action on the bill. Congress then shifted its attention to the appropriations bill for the FEPC. The Senate Appropriations Committee had agreed to restore the FEPC item in the war agencies appropriations bill. It had recommended a $446,200 appropriation—some $150,000 less than the sum recommended in the budget proposals. Theodore Bilbo, who wanted to liquidate completely the FEPC without further ado, led the southern fight to deny it any money at all. This time the president did not intervene directly, although Samuel Rosenman had advised him to make persuasive telephone calls to key Senate leaders.[18] For three days Bilbo held the Senate floor by reading out letters of opposition to the FEPC and quoting at length from books which discussed miscegenation and the chemistry of skin pigmentation. Bilbo ceased his filibuster only when Majority Leader Alben Barkley proposed a compromise amendment which appropriated $250,000 to the FEPC.

---

17 Frank Boykin to HST, June 29, 1945, in OF 40, Truman Papers; Thomas W. Carneal, "President Truman's Leadership in the Field of Civil Rights Legislation" (M.A. thesis, University of Kansas City, Mo., 1965), 26.

18 Memo, Rosenman to HST, June 15, 1945, in OF 40, Truman Papers.

Bilbo realized that this small sum was insufficient for the FEPC to function normally and so surrendered the floor.[19]

The circumstances that surrounded this episode had important political undertones and repercussions. In the first place, Truman reversed his previously unequivocal stand on the FEPC by deciding to keep to the sidelines. Barkley's compromise amendment, which in effect stripped the FEPC of any authority, removed the sting created by Truman's earlier intervention. The majority leader had thus reduced the hosannas that had accompanied Truman's open letter of support to whimpers of disappointment. The party leadership clearly had decided not to pursue further the new path laid out by Truman in his letter to Sabath. Indeed, Truman's somewhat checkered support was soon to become the characteristic political tool of his administration. This was only the first occasion in which Truman would advocate a particular policy or measure and then, either by silence or gesture, change his position. Not even Alben Barkley would admit that the Democratic leadership had capitulated on the issue. "It is within the truth to say," bragged Barkley, "that my efforts were largely responsible for its continuation for another year." [20]

Negro leaders, of course, were unimpressed by Barkley's defense, for the second and most lasting effect of this particular dispute was that Negroes began to lose their short-lived confidence in Truman's leadership. Roy Wilkins warned Barkley that Negroes had been "aroused and angered and disgusted" by the tone of the filibuster and that they were apprehensive about Truman's refusal to condemn it. Negroes were frankly bewildered by the sudden change of tone. They were disillusioned, said Wilkins, "not only with a Congress which seems to bow to the Rankins and the Bilbos, but with an executive family containing a substantial number of men not deemed

---

19 *Congressional Record*, 79th Cong., 1st Sess., 6803–824, 6885–906, 6991–7005, 7050–7068; Ruchames, *Race, Jobs, and Politics*, 127–32.
20 Barkley to Roy Wilkins, August 21, 1945, in Box 315/5, NAACP Files.

sympathetic to the Negro's aspirations." [21] Indeed, Truman had reverted to Roosevelt's strategy of appeasing both wings of the party, in spite of his initial dramatic gesture to the proponents of civil rights legislation.

The $250,000 appropriation for the FEPC, which under a House amendment had to cease functioning in June, 1946, meant that the concept of equal employment opportunity would be buried unless permanent legislation were passed. But the president did not press further for a statutory FEPC. Despite warnings from members of the FEPC that Negroes were experiencing considerable hardship from demobilization, the president chose to make only indirect gestures.[22] He did not mention the use of cease-and-desist orders in a new executive order, issued in December, 1945, nor did he go beyond mere mention of the FEPC in his State of the Union message of 1946.[23]

Congressional supporters of a permanent FEPC, therefore, did not wait for further nods from the president. After the House had failed to wrest the FEPC from the Rules Committee, Democratic Senator Dennis Chavez of New Mexico, author of the Senate version, determined to proceed with his own bill. On January 17, 1946, he introduced it on the floor. On the following day, before Chavez could continue, Senator John H. Overton of Louisiana seized the initiative by moving to amend the previous day's proceedings, as reported in the Senate *Journal,* by including the chaplain's prayer. This spurious device enabled Overton and his southern colleagues to

---

21 Wilkins to Barkley, August 28, 1945, assorted telegrams, White to various newspaper editors, June 30, 1945, in Box 315/5, NAACP Files.
22 Report to the President, August 27, 1945, in RG 228-69, Office Files of Malcolm Ross, FEPC Records.
23 Executive Order 9664, *Code of Federal Regulations, Title 3, 1943–1948,* p. 480, hereafter cited as *3 CFR, 1943–1948*; Circular to Heads of All Government Departments, Agencies and Independent Establishments, December 20, 1945, in OF 40, Truman Papers. See also the similar directives after the FEPC had expired: memo, HST to David Niles, July 22, 1946, in Box 21, Nash Papers.

conduct a filibuster against the Chavez bill under the guise of a discussion of the *Journal*.[24] There followed a filibuster that lasted for three full weeks.

The style of the subsequent debate was revealing. The southerners used this opportunity to give vent to their deep concern over the political mobilization of Negroes and organized labor. They repeatedly drew attention to the changes in the composition of the Democratic party and showed their determination to halt this process of political realignment. Grave misgivings were expressed about the Negro's affiliation with the Democrats. Eastland of Mississippi thought that Negroes had made a "grave mistake," and Overton prophesied somewhat sinisterly that "for a short term of political advantage the Negro made a very bad bargain." [25] Southerners also did not forget that the CIO had supported the FEPC. They indicated a desire to ban the closed shop and so destroy the authority of the CIO.[26] Eastland hardly had to remind his colleagues that the CIO was "a carpetbag organization which has come into the South and is attempting to destroy Southern institutions and Southern civilization." [27] John Bankhead of Alabama went even further. He declared that the bill reflected the views of "the Bolshevik crowd" and foresaw the creation of "star chamber" courts to subject the South.[28] But southern Democrats not only displayed contempt for Negroes and labor unions. They served notice to Truman that they would not support his postwar foreign and domestic policies unless he dissociated himself from the demands of the urban coalition. Walter George put their position quite bluntly: "If this is all that Harry Truman has to offer, God help the Democratic Party in 1946 and 1948." [29]

Truman did not intervene in the Senate filibuster. He hoped that his earlier endorsements of the FEPC would satisfy Negro

24 *Congressional Record,* 79th Cong., 2nd Sess., 114.
25 *Ibid.,* 88.
26 *Ibid.,* 178–207.
27 *Ibid.,* 242.
28 *Ibid.,* 318.
29 Atlanta *Constitution,* January 18, 1946.

voters. He had taken stock of the southern reaction to his letter to Sabath and presumably was unwilling to antagonize Dixie Democrats any further for fear of opposition on other matters. When questioned on his attitude toward the filibuster, Truman remarked that it "is a matter that the Senate itself must settle without outside interference, especially from the President." [30] Consequently he did not consult with the leaders of the administration forces in the Senate about possible means of ending the deadlock. Alben Barkley did nothing to keep the Senate in session into the late hours in the hope of breaking the filibuster. The majority leader finally acquiesced on February 9, when he called for a vote on a cloture motion. The motion was defeated by forty-eight votes for and thirty-six against—the affirmative votes were eight short of the two-thirds majority necessary to end the debate. Once again Senator Pepper was the only southern Democrat to vote for such a resolution.[31] Thus, the successful Senate filibuster and the restrictive appropriation for the extant committee doomed the FEPC to oblivion in the summer of 1946. The South had destroyed by legislative action an agency set up by executive fiat. It had learned that although it was powerless to initiate and direct legislation and policy, it could still act as a censor.

President Truman continued to conduct himself in this circumspect manner in matters relating to civil rights and the South. When an anti-poll tax bill was locked in the Senate, he refrained from interfering in yet another parliamentary squabble. He was determined to remain aloof. He did not want to reactivate the ill-feeling engendered by the filibuster of the FEPC bill. He wrote to a Virginian that his program had been "almost ruined by one filibuster, and I think that is enough for one season." [32] In April, 1946, he further conciliated the South when he told the press at Chicago that the poll

---

30 *Public Papers, 1946,* p. 94; also, *Crisis,* LIII (January, 1946).
31 New York *Times,* February 10, 1946; *Congressional Record,* 79th Cong., 2nd Sess., 1219–220; Pepper to Wilkins, February 4, 1946, in Box 293/5, NAACP Files.
32 HST to Irving Brant, March 9, 1946, in OF 465 B, Truman Papers.

tax was a matter for the South to "work out themselves" without outside interference.[33] Senator Bankhead was so encouraged by this apparent change of attitude that he wrote to Truman: "It was a statesmanlike declaration, and not withstanding the clamor in some excitable areas, I believe it will not injure you in the long run in politics." [34] However, Negro voters from the metropolitan states reacted with such outrage that David Niles, Truman's administrative assistant with responsibility for civil rights matters, advised the president to issue a statement at his next press conference to assure his supporters in the North that he was still fully committed to federal legislation. Truman acted on this advice a few days later.[35] Yet, despite his public volte-face, he replied to Bankhead that "there never was a law that could be enforced if the people didn't want it enforced." [36] Truman thus seemed to have adopted his predecessor's tactics—which he had discarded only temporarily in June, 1945, over the FEPC bill—by his adoption of a dualistic policy of public championship and private appeasement on the civil rights controversy.

The feuds over civil rights were, of course, only part of the larger problem of postwar reconversion. The surrender of the Japanese in August presaged the demise of a number of wartime government agencies and controls. Truman consequently addressed himself to two tasks, one long-term and the other short-term. The immediate problem was to continue the stabilization of prices and wages and to prevent a deflationary cycle. It was imperative to preserve consumer demand so that employment would remain at the highest possible level. Truman's long-term aim was to revive the New Deal, widen the

33 *Public Papers, 1946*, p. 185.
34 John H. Bankhead to HST, April 11, 1946, in OF 465 B, Truman Papers.
35 Memo, Niles to HST, April 11, 1946, in OF 465 B, Truman Papers; Houston *Post*, April 8, 1946; *Public Papers, 1946*, pp. 192–93.
36 HST to Bankhead, April 13, 1946, in OF 465 B, Truman Papers.

horizons and functions of government, and sustain the stable transition from war to peace. It was these long-range aims that were responsible for sustaining the ideological friction within the Democratic party.

The president's proposals, of course, required extensive legislation. Truman eventually consolidated his plans in a 21-Point Program for Reconversion which he presented to Congress on September 6, 1945. This lengthy sixteen-thousand-word document, which formed the basis of what was later to become the Fair Deal, reaffirmed Roosevelt's economic bill of rights and committed the Truman administration to long-term social reform, as well as to the more immediate task of a carefully controlled reconstruction. Among Truman's recommendations were proposals for an increase in the national minimum wage, the extension of the second War Powers Act to renew the authority of the stabilization agencies, full employment legislation, the creation of a permanent FEPC, a public works program, and comprehensive housing legislation. He also promised further messages on federal aid to education, expansion of the social security system, and a national health service.[37] Although the September message presented the Fair Deal program in general terms and avoided specific, detailed recommendations, Truman clearly intended to expand the functions of government and to retain the same electoral base of support his predecessor had enjoyed.

The political consequences of the Fair Deal program were apparent to all contemporary observers. Samuel Rosenman, who was chiefly responsible for drafting the 21-point program, pointed out that the message had placed Truman unambiguously in the liberal camp. Until September, he told the president, conservative Democrats had been speculating "that the New Deal is as good as dead—that we are all going back to

---

37 *Public Papers, 1945*, pp. 263–309. I shall adopt the term "Fair Deal" to describe Truman's reform program, even though the phrase is generally used to describe Truman's domestic policies after 1948.

'normalcy' and that a good part of the so-called 'Roosevelt nonsense' is now over." [38] It seemed that Truman had spurned an alliance with those Democrats who had led the crusade against Henry Wallace at the 1944 convention. There would be no substantial change in the direction of the political winds. *Southern Weekly* chided that "the whole program of the CIO-Political Action Committee and its allied left-wing groups, including the negro organizations, is adequately covered in this message." [39] Josiah Bailey warned the treasurer of the Democratic National Committee that "there is no need of artificial aids." If Truman went ahead with his program, the North Carolinian continued, he would have to "depend upon the radical element. No man can be radical enough to suit the radicals." [40]

Congress, however, did not give Truman what he wanted. Although the Senate passed an amended version of the president's unemployment compensation bill, a coalition of southern Democrats and Republicans on the House Committee on Ways and Means voted to shelve the bill indefinitely.[41] Also, contrary to Truman's known wishes, southern Democrats in the Senate, who were eager to restore local control over the labor market, voted to return the United States Employment Service to the states within ninety days. The president, convinced that immediate decentralization of the USES would cause "incalculable damage" and "grave disruption," proposed instead to create a permanent national system of employment offices.[42] Included in the new bill were provisions that no jobs should be

---

38 Truman, *Memoirs*, I, 532–33; Jonathan Daniels, *The Man of Independence* (New York and Philadelphia, 1950), 289–97; Hinchey, "The Frustration of the New Deal Revival," 140–50.
39 *Southern Weekly*, September 12, 1945.
40 Bailey to George Killion, September 19, 1945, in Bailey Papers.
41 Three southern Democrats voted to kill the bill: Camp (Georgia), Mills (Arkansas), and West (Texas). Columnist Thomas Stokes felt that Truman was "suffering from worse treatment from Congress and from his Southern Democrats than did his predecessor." Baton Rouge *Morning Advocate*, September 27, 1945.
42 U.S. Senate, Subcommittee of the Committee on Education and Labor, *Hearings to Provide a National System of Employment Offices*, 79th Cong., 1st Sess., 1.

offered either if the company in question forced potential employees to join (or to refrain from joining) a particular union or if the employer discriminated because of race.[43] Southerners particularly objected to these two clauses and thus rejected Truman's recommendations. An official of the Texas Trade Association Executives echoed southern sentiment on the matter when he protested before the House Committee on Labor that the president was only eager to keep the USES under permanent federal control because of pressure from the CIO-PAC.[44]

At the very heart of the administration's postwar economic policy was the proposal for full employment legislation. Under this scheme, which had been originally devised by the National Resources Planning Board, the federal government would assume full responsibility for maintaining full employment. Every individual would be granted the right to a job. The administration's bill provided for the use of monetary and fiscal policies to achieve full employment and for a public works program in the event that the private sector was unable to absorb the labor market. It presumed that sufficient resources for capital investment could be made available only through central planning and budgeting.

The bill aroused a great deal of criticism from both sides of the Mason-Dixon Line. Its opponents feared that it would give the whole ideology of the New Deal full statutory authority. Conservatives never had accepted the view that the federal government was ultimately responsible for sustaining an equitable economy. They believed the government should exert its authority in such a way as to insure that free competition could operate without encumbrance. Thus, it could claim to control banks, labor unions, and monopolies which often could exercise a pervasive influence over particular sectors of the economy. They denied it was the *duty* of government, in all

43 *Ibid., passim;* also, McKellar to HST, December 28, 1945, in McKellar Papers.
44 U.S. House of Representatives, Committee on Labor, *Hearings to Make the United States Employment Service a Federal Agency,* 79th Cong., 2nd Sess., 80.

circumstances, to plan the economy to provide full employment and adequate social security. Of course, in exceptional cases it could intervene with these goals in mind. However, intervention should not, they insisted, be actually prescribed by statute. Moreover, the executive branch should not be given the sole power to determine basic investment decisions. This could, they argued, result in a substantial decrease in congressional authority.

Their arguments were actually reinforced by the onset of the cold war. The concept of central economic planning now had strong emotive undertones. After Truman and Stalin had failed to agree on the future shape of central Europe, Soviet Russia emerged in American eyes as the principal threat to world peace. This had a profound effect on political rhetoric in the United States. The disciples of laissez faire created a kind of syllogism: the Soviet Union was evil; the Soviet Union had economic planning; therefore, economic planning was first, evil, and, second, Soviet or communistic. Conservatives, therefore, were particularly antagonistic to full employment legislation, viewing it as the first and most basic step toward socialism. The opponents of full employment legislation were not alarmed unduly when the bill passed the Senate in substantially original form in September, 1945. They knew they would be in a better position in the House of Representatives to eviscerate the objectionable components. They used, therefore, all the resources available to them to defeat what they considered the "dangerous experiment of a politically managed economy." [45]

The bill was introduced in the House by Wright Patman, a New Deal Texas Democrat, and cosponsored by 112 representatives. Only six of these cosponsors were southerners.[46] Most of

---

45 *Southern Weekly*, February 3, 1945; Stephen K. Bailey, *Congress Makes a Law: The Story Behind the Employment Act of 1946* (New York, 1950); Charles W. Collins, *Whither Solid South? A Study in Politics and Race Relations* (New Orleans, 1947), chaps. 12, 13, 14.

46 U.S. House of Representatives, Committee on Expenditures in the Executive

the opposition from the Democratic side came from the South. It was led by Carter Manasco of Alabama, chairman of the predominantly conservative Committee on Expenditures in the Executive Departments, to which the bill had been consigned. The committee hearings provided critics with a receptive platform from which to arraign it. Chairman Manasco and ranking Republican, Clare Hoffman of Michigan, were clearly sympathetic to witnesses hostile to the legislation. They agreed that economic forecasts were impossible in a volatile society and expressed concern that the president would be unfettered under the terms of the bill. The obvious enthusiasm of labor unions, civil rights groups, and social improvement organizations served to harden their own opposition to the proposals.[47] The committee was clearly quite skeptical of assurances from John McCormack, House majority leader, who tried to persuade the committee that, unlike Roosevelt, President Truman would use the bill only for economic ends and not to further social reform.[48] After a long delay, it voted seventeen to three against Patman's bill. Eventually, in December a subcommittee reported out a substitute bill which eliminated the declaration of a right to employment and demanded specific guarantees that there would be no competition between government and industry. The report climaxed that "it is either private enterprise or stateism." [49] The bill's opponents had a vital ally in the House Rules Committee, which subsequently allotted only one day for debate and ruled that no intervening motions, besides a motion to recommit, could be made from the floor. Thus, if the substitute were not adopted, nothing would be enacted at all. Cosponsors of the original bill were helpless, and the substitute was passed by 255 votes to 126.

The conservatives were thus successful in defeating this cor-

Departments, *Hearings to Establish a Full Employment Program*, 79th Cong., 1st Sess., 35–49.
47 *Ibid.*, 343–81, 558, 1150–152.
48 *Ibid.*, 1119.
49 Bailey, *Congress Makes a Law*, 170–71.

nerstone of the Fair Deal. There was nothing Truman or the congressional liberals could do in the face of such opposition. The final bill was devoid of the broad provisions of the original Senate version. The duty of the government was no longer to stimulate "full" employment, but "maximum" employment. The president was now required to submit only an economic report rather than a national production budget. The government would have no obligation to stimulate output to the point of full employment. Congressional conservatives had sought throughout the war to diminish the role of the federal government in economic affairs. They believed that the original full employment bill would have given the president almost infinite power over the economy and thus render their earlier efforts fruitless. This controversy was not particularly sectional, despite the broadly geographical division within the Democratic party. Southern Democrats did believe, however, that the final shape of the bill would determine the development of the Fair Deal. Carter Manasco was quite clear in his own mind about the portents of the president's proposals. "A planned economy leads to an absolute dictatorship, destroying liberties that were so hard-won," he lamented. "Our President is being poorly advised and unless he changes his course I fear he will go down in history as a complete failure." [50]

The adversaries of the employment bill also wished to destroy the remaining vestiges of the president's war powers over the economy. Truman's main instrument of control was still his authority to control prices through the Office of Price Administration (OPA). Conservatives particularly resented his policy of permitting wage increases without corresponding adjustments in prices. Truman, of course, aimed to create a high level of consumer demand, but his critics viewed this

[50] Carter Manasco to Dixon, January 16, 1946, in Dixon Papers; also, Bailey, *Congress Makes a Law*, chap. 11; Arthur F. Burns, "Some Reflections on the Employment Act," *Political Science Quarterly*, LXXXVII (December, 1962), 481–85; Frank C. Pierson, "The Unemployment Act of 1946," in Colston E. Warne (ed.), *Labor in Postwar America* (New York, 1949), 283–99.

policy as yet another example of the government's willingness to curry the favor of labor unions at the expense of business. Matters came to a head at the beginning of 1946 when Truman asked Congress to renew the authority of the OPA beyond its expiration date of June 30. The conservatives were determined to allow the OPA to lapse and to remove price controls as soon as possible.[51] Due to the absence of any other powerful countervailing group, such as labor unions, southern congressmen were particularly receptive to the pressures of agriculture and industry. They personally regarded the continuation of the OPA in peacetime as tantamount to an indelible recognition of the president's power to stabilize prices in the national interest, regardless of circumstances. The nation could not revert to private control over the economy as long as the government continued to fix prices. A member of Congress, they insisted, was better qualified to judge the needs of the community than was a remote administrator in Washington. Robert Doughton assured the textile magnate, C. A. Cannon, that he was "still unwilling to delegate to the President the right to do my thinking. I will go with the President as far as I can, but do not propose to jump off a precipice to please any high up official, even the President." [52]

The producers' principal argument for price decontrol was that they were operating at a loss and that the supply shortage was due to prohibitive price ceilings. They argued that decontrol or, failing this, substantial increases in price ceilings would provide the necessary incentives for increased production. For example, the South Florida Canners Association, which was particularly concerned with prices of fruit and vegetables, argued that the OPA's policies thwarted all incentives to produce. Its president claimed that tomato production had fallen by 65 percent. Tomatoes, apparently, had been allowed to rot in

51 For a general background on the OPA, see Mansfield *et al.*, *A Short History of OPA, passim.*
52 Cannon to Doughton, January 14, 1946, Doughton to Cannon, January 15, 1946, in Folder 1253, Doughton Papers.

the fields as the price ceiling on them was below the cost of production. "We are today economic slaves—slaves of rules and regulations of the worst sort—only thought possible in a totalitarian state," he told the House Committee on Banking and Currency. Airing the politicians' grievances, he also pointed out that OPA officials were not elective and were "hanging on to their jobs regardless of the misery they cause to others." [53] The largest and most dissatisfied group in the South was the cotton producers. In January, 1946, Chester Bowles, price administrator, announced that he would place a ceiling of 24.09 cents per pound on raw cotton. Cotton growers immediately cried out that the ceiling was unrealistic and that the current high costs of clothing were not due to the level of cotton prices. Cotton state senators and congressmen immediately took up the complaints. They threatened to join the Republicans in the move to abolish the OPA altogether, unless OPA's cotton policy was changed. As a result of this pressure, Bowles appeased a delegation of southern congressmen a few days later by assuring them that he had considered 24.09 cents to be only a minimum price ceiling for raw cotton. But they were still determined to protect local business interests by securing price decontrol on commodities produced in their constituencies.[54] Even Theodore Bilbo, who was generally sympathetic to the nonracial features of the president's reconversion program, swore he would fight to liquidate "this damnable, asinine, autocratic, bureaucratic agency known as OPA." [55]

The congressional fight over the future of OPA consisted largely of a complex plethora of amendments and amendments to amendments. Each member of Congress fought for specific concessions on goods produced in his district. The Republicans were anxious to reduce the OPA to impotence and sought the

53 U.S. House of Representatives, Committee on Banking and Currency, *Hearings to Amend the Emergency Price Control Act*, 79th Cong., 2nd Sess., 778.
54 Memphis *Commercial Appeal*, January 6, 1946; Atlanta *Constitution*, January 7, 8, 15, 19, 1946.
55 Bilbo to D. L. Webster, April 17, 1946, John G. Burkett to Bilbo, April 4, 1946, Bilbo to D. C. Funderburk, April 19, 1946, in Bilbo Papers.

cooperation of southern Democrats in securing exceptions for special interest groups. In March the Washington *Post* reported that Dixie Democrats and Republicans in the House had organized a formal committee to plan strategy to trim the OPA.[56] There is no record of just how successful such cooperation was. Nevertheless, most southern Democrats seemed united in their attacks on the pricing policies of the OPA. John Bankhead, longtime guardian in the Senate of the cotton interests, threatened that if the new bill did not raise ceilings substantially, he would vote to dismantle the agency entirely.[57] On the floor of both houses Republicans and southern Democrats frequently joined forces to pass limiting amendments. The most far-reaching amendment, introduced by Republican Senator Robert Taft of Ohio, enabled manufacturers to take the profit per unit of sales which the industry received for the particular product in 1941. Sixteen Democrats joined the twenty-eight Republicans to pass the amendment. Fourteen of the Democrats were from the South, the remaining two were from the border states of Maryland and Oklahoma. From the South, only Senators Hill, Pepper, and Ellender voted against the Taft amendment. In varying degrees Dixie Democrats helped the Republicans secure other amendments that seriously hampered the functioning of the OPA.[58] They succeeded thus in mangling one of the central features of Truman's floundering economic policies—and in forcing Chester Bowles, the object of their odium, to resign as economic stabilizer on the day the final conference report was passed.[59]

Truman took a firm stand against the mangled bill and delivered a resounding veto which was narrowly sustained.[60]

56 Washington *Post*, March 10, 11, 1946.
57 *Ibid.*, April 15, 16, 1946.
58 *Congressional Quarterly Almanac, 1946* (Washington, D.C., 1946), 401–19.
59 Washington *Post*, June 29, 1946; Hinchey, "The Frustration of the New Deal Revival," 222–24; Truman, *Memoirs*, I, 538–39. After Truman's capitulation on steel prices in February, Bowles had resigned as price administrator and was appointed to the almost defunct Office of Economic Stabilization.
60 For comments on Truman's veto see: Doughton to Captain W. Farley,

Since the bill was vetoed only one day before the OPA was due to expire, it had the effect of leaving the country without any price controls. Truman hoped in this way to force Congress to enact a more viable price control policy in the shortest time possible. Truman's strategy was carefully calculated. He intended to absolve himself from the collapse of price controls and accordingly blame the Republicans—and, in particular, the Taft amendment. In fact, Truman mentioned Taft by name eighteen times in his veto message.[61] The president thus prudently avoided implicating members of his own party for cooperating with the Republicans. But the struggle over price control had convinced him that only the president could resist and transcend the particularism and lobbying of special interest groups on economic affairs. He felt that any abdication of authority by the executive branch would undermine his plans for stabilization and social reform.

Wages policy was as central to the reconversion program as price controls. Truman had recognized the necessity to permit fairly substantial wage increases to sustain and stimulate demand. However, the president's entire attitude to wages and collective bargaining was a testy political issue. Organized labor supported the Fair Deal program, but regarded Truman's position on industrial relations as the acid test of his political sympathies. If Truman wanted to sustain the urban coalition, then he would have to show an appreciation of labor's concern about the union shop and declining purchasing power. Southern Democrats, on the other hand, expected the new president to be more sympathetic to their predilections. If Truman were to permit collective bargaining to be undertaken without control or restraint, then there would result only increased industrial strife and a further consolidation in the ties between the Democratic party and organized labor. Truman himself was

---

June 2, 1946, in Folder 1425, Doughton to R. A. Murdock, July 1, 1946, in Folder 1415, Doughton Papers; *Southern Weekly*, July 3, 1946.
61 *Public Papers, 1946*, pp. 322–29; New York *Times*, June 30, 1946; Washington *Post*, June 30, 1946.

well aware of this dilemma, and tried to steer a middle course by encouraging the unions and employers to cooperate in the creation of new mediation machinery. However, it happened that he satisfied neither group and was left for a short time out on a limb.

At first Truman hoped he could perpetuate the cooperative approach of the War Labor Board in solving industrial disputes. In November, 1945, he convened a labor-management conference for the specific purpose of discussing general wages policy. The conference, however, merely affirmed a few generalities and platitudes, such as faith in collective bargaining. It failed to produce any concrete proposals for settling disputes which might arise from wage claims or jurisdictional disputes. This failure was underlined a few days later when the country faced major strikes in the electrical and motor industries. The most spectacular of these was the General Motors strike in which 320,000 members of the United Auto Workers (CIO) were involved. Walter Reuther, vice-president of the UAW, had asked for a 30 percent wage increase. He claimed that General Motors could absorb the higher rate without a price hike and challenged the company to open its account books. Thus, prices and profits had become major considerations in collective bargaining. Truman realized that these added dimensions would make strike settlements even harder to obtain. He therefore recommended new legislation to improve the machinery for settling disputes.[62]

In December, 1945, and again in his State of the Union Address the following month, Truman asked Congress to establish fact-finding boards to which disputes in critical industries could be referred. Although under the terms of the proposed

62 Barton J. Bernstein, "The Truman Administration and Its Reconversion Wage Policy," *Labor History*, VI (Fall, 1965), 214–31; Barton J. Bernstein, "Walter Reuther and the General Motors Strike of 1945–46," *Michigan History*, XLIX (September, 1965), 260–77; Harry A. Millis and Emily C. Brown, *From the Wagner Act to Taft-Hartley* (Chicago, 1950), 300–13; R. Alton Lee, *Truman and Taft-Hartley* (Lexington, Ky., 1966), 23–25; Arthur F. McClure, *The Truman Administration and the Problems of Postwar Labor, 1945–1948* (Cranbury, N.J., 1969), 52–64, 69–71.

bill the boards were to have no enforcement powers, it would be illegal to strike while the board was deliberating.[63] Although the unions were unhappy about this restriction, employers were adamant that Truman's proposals were not firm enough and did not impose adequate restraint upon impulsive industrial action. They wanted the substance of the Wagner Act to be revised in order to prevent walkouts, such as those currently crippling the steel, electrical, and motor industries. They urged members of Congress to go beyond Truman's mild recommendations by passing legislation which would impede the right to strike and ban certain union practices that had been previously guaranteed under the National Labor Relations Act, such as the right to form a closed shop. The outcry from the South for control of the unions usually had a sharp political undertone. Now was the time, argued southern businessmen, to redress not only the industrial balance but political grievances as well. Two wagon manufacturers from Mississippi scoffed that fact-finding boards would be impotent and "just another political club over the employer's head." [64] The National Association of Manufacturers, the Southern States Industrial Council, and the Southern Coal Producers were but three of the major organizations that launched a full publicity campaign against the economic and political power of the labor unions after the war.[65]

Members of the House of Representatives responded promptly to these pressures. Republican Francis Case of South Dakota introduced his labor disputes bill which went much further than Truman's proposals. It created a Federal Media-

63 *Public Papers, 1945*, pp. 516–21; *Public Papers, 1946*, p. 52.
64 W. L. Fuller and Sam Lindsey to Bilbo, James O. Eastland, and William M. Colmer, January 14, 1946, in Bilbo Papers.
65 Clark Kerr, "Employer Policies in Industrial Relations, 1945 to 1947," in Warne (ed.), *Labor in Postwar America*, 43–76; Remmie Arnold to Bilbo, February 15, 1945, in Bilbo Papers; Arnold to HST, January 23, 1946, and pamphlet, Southern States Industrial Council, *The National Labor Relations Law Must Be Amended*, June 27, 1946, GF, in Southern States Industrial Council Folder, Truman Papers; U.S. Senate, Subcommittee of the Committee on Education and Labor, *Hearings to Provide Additional Facilities for the Mediation of Labor Disputes*, 79th Cong., 2nd Sess., 99–107, 174–88.

tion Board and provided for a mandatory thirty-day cooling-off period while the board deliberated. It prohibited employer contributions to welfare funds administered solely by the unions and made unions suable for breach of contract.[66] No hearings were held on the bill except those before the Rules Committee, before which only members of the House can appear. Southern Democrats, alarmed at the wave of strikes and eager to shackle labor's power, voted overwhelmingly for the Case bill, which passed the House within a month of its introduction. Joining the 149 Republicans to pass the bill were 87 southern Democrats, while only 9 from the South voted with 111 nonsouthern Democrats against it.[67]

While the Case bill awaited deliberation in the Senate, a new development occurred which not only put the entire program for the reform of industrial relations into jeopardy, but also resulted in a drastic, though temporary, reevaluation of political alignments. An imminent railroad strike threatened to throw the country into chaos, and Truman consequently arranged a five-day truce to try to settle the dispute. When Alvanley Johnston, president of the Brotherhood of Locomotive Engineers, and A. F. Whitney, president of the Brotherhood of Railway Trainmen, refused to accept a White House compromise, the railroad ground to a halt. Truman condemned Whitney and Johnston in a radio broadcast and gave the railmen eighteen hours to settle the dispute. When time under the ultimatum had expired at 4 P.M. May 25, Truman personally went before Congress to recommend special emergency legislation which would bestow the right to obtain court injunctions against union leaders responsible for walkouts in industries deemed vital to the national welfare. Then there came a major shock for organized labor. Truman climaxed his speech by re-

---

66 McClure, *The Truman Administration and the Problems of Postwar Labor,* 124–26.
67 *Congressional Quarterly Almanac, 1946,* pp. 100–101. All subsequent roll call voting analyses are taken from this source. See also, Doughton to Sandefur, February 6, 1946, in Folder 1367, Doughton Papers; Ida Fiske to Bilbo, January 7, 1946, Bilbo to Fiske, January 17, 1946, in Bilbo Papers.

questing immediate authority to draft strikers in industries that had been seized by the government into the armed forces. But before Truman could complete his address, Leslie F. Biffle, secretary of the Senate, handed Truman, with an almost theatrical gesture, a note to the effect that the strike had been settled.[68]

In political terms Truman's strike proposals were far-reaching. For labor leaders and other liberals, whose initial admiration of Truman had already diminished somewhat—as a result of his appointments, his acceptance of the mangled employment bill, and his capitulation on price increases during the steel strike—the president's proposals sealed the trend of disenchantment. James G. Patton, president of the National Farmers' Union, emotionally claimed that Truman, "for the first time in American history, proposes to use guns to coerce free citizens to work." Sidney Hillman, who bitterly remembered his approval of Truman's nomination at Chicago, condemned the president for being "autocratic." The CIO-PAC even considered plans for the formation of a third party.[69] On the other hand, southern Democrats, who had likewise become disaffected with the administration over its reconversion policies and had taken little cheer in the alienation of the left, felt the president finally had taken a positive step in asserting his full authority over the alleged excesses of the labor unions. Congressman Sam Hobbs of Alabama rejoiced that Truman's stand against the railroad workers had restored faith "in the belief that the Government has come to the realization that drastic legislation is essential."[70] For a short time, Dixie Democrats felt that Truman had at last dissociated himself from the labor leadership and would seek a new political alliance with

68 *Public Papers, 1946*, pp. 274–80; Truman, *Memoirs*, I, 550–52.
69 Alonzo Lee Hamby, "Harry S. Truman and American Liberalism, 1945–1948" (Ph.D. dissertation, University of Missouri, 1965), 97; Hinchey, "The Frustration of the New Deal Revival," 217; Daniels, *The Man of Independence*, 330–31. Even Robert Taft was horrified with Truman's proposals and refused to vote for a strikers' draft. See William S. White, *The Taft Story* (New York, 1954), 44–45; Washington *Post*, May 29, 1946.
70 Hobbs to Cecil H. Smith, May 28, 1946, in Hobbs Papers.

the South. However, they would soon realize that Truman's proposals did not signify any alteration in political strategy, but merely reflected the essential impetuosity and philosophical ambiguity that so characterized the early years of his presidency. He would soon soften his approach—as he had done with the FEPC letter to Sabath and in his price control policies.

Truman's message on the railroad crisis gave the movement for antistrike legislation a new impetus. Within hours of Truman's address the Senate passed a strengthened version of the Case bill.[71] Only two Dixie senators, Lister Hill and Claude Pepper, voted against it, despite hints from Alben Barkley that the president would probably veto it.[72] So, when the bill went to the White House for signature, Truman had to make a crucial decision. He could either make a positive commitment to southern conservatives by emphasizing his desire to control the unions, or he could try to recoup the losses incurred by his stand on the railroad strike by vetoing the bill and thus check the dwindling support of labor and liberal leaders in the party. Truman carefully sounded out opinions. All members of the cabinet, except John Snyder, recommended that Truman veto. Henry Wallace, the only remaining Roosevelt appointee, dubbed the bill "anti-labor" and said that it "cannot be supported upon calm, deliberate and analytical deliberation." [73] Labor leaders, of course, also clamored for a veto. Philip Murray pointedly criticized the voting alignments on the bill. In an open letter to Truman he flayed by innuendo those southern Democrats who had supported antistrike legislation. He saw a direct connection between support for the Case bill and the move "to deny the right of soldiers to vote on the specious grounds that the rights of the states were being invaded." South-

71 New York *Times,* May 26, 1946; Washington *Post,* May 27, 1946.
72 Washington *Post,* May 27, 1946; *Hearings to Provide Additional Facilities for the Mediation of Labor Disputes,* 153–74.
73 Unsigned memoranda to HST, undated, in Labor Files, Clark M. Clifford Papers, Harry S. Truman Library, Independence, Mo.

erners countered by urging the president to sign. Democratic
Senators Ellender, Byrd, and Carl Hatch of New Mexico
joined Republican leaders in giving an open, point-by-point
reply to Murray's letter.[74] Businessmen similarly urged Truman
to give his assent. Remmie Arnold, president of the Southern
States Industrial Council, informed the president that Americans wanted the "termination of the Governmental favoritism
which has produced a situation that permits labor leaders to
dictate to the Government." [75] However, it was John Rankin
of Mississippi who really appreciated the ramifications of Truman's decision. "If you should veto it, it would virtually destroy the gains you have made with public opinion in the last
few weeks, and cause us to lose the House this Fall," he wrote
with obvious reference to Truman's recent propensity to win
the South's approval. To emphasize the point, Rankin reminded
the president that "no administration has ever lost the House
at the mid-term election that [it] did not lose the presidency
two years later." [76]

Truman ignored Rankin's advice and vetoed the bill. The
House of Representatives sustained the veto by 255 votes to
135—a switch of 5 votes would have resulted in its overriding.
Voting or pairing with 159 Republicans to override it were 81
southern Democrats. Only 11 Dixie Democrats voted with 107
nonsouthern Democrats and 15 Republicans to sustain it.[77]
Truman had indicated that he was not prepared to impede the
strike weapon in the long run by delaying machinery and

74 Philip Murray to HST, May 31, 1946, Statement of Senators Ball, Byrd,
   Ellender, Hatch, Smith, and Taft, released June 8, 1946, in OF 407 B,
   Truman Papers.
75 Telegrams, Remmie Arnold to HST, May 31, 1946, R. R. Saunders to HST,
   May 31, 1946, John M. Ward to HST, June 4, 1946, W. Roy Ulrich to
   HST, June 5, 1946, in OF 407 B, Truman Papers.
76 John Rankin to HST, June 8, 1946, see also J. Percy Priest to HST, May 30,
   1946, in OF 407 B, Truman Papers.
77 There were two southern Democrats paired for passage of the bill. Five
   southern Democrats who had supported the conference bill voted to sustain
   the veto. These were Combs and Lyle of Texas, Mankin and Rains of
   Georgia, and Sparkman of Alabama. Congressional Quarterly Almanac, 1946,
   pp. 314–15.

cooling-off periods. Although he had responded somewhat dramatically to the railroad strikers, he realized that compulsory antistrike machinery would turn labor away from the party which had fostered its friendship and produced the National Labor Relations Act. The veto also convinced southerners that Truman just was not prepared to sacrifice the support of the urban coalition in an effort to appease them.[78] Truman presumably believed that traditional ties would force the South to overlook his overtures to labor. It was this calculation which prompted Truman to pursue his Fair Deal with renewed vigor.

Although social welfare and economic policies were the main sources of contention within the Democratic party in the first eighteen months of Truman's presidency, there was one other somewhat unrelated controversy that soured the relationship between the South and Washington. Large reserves of oil had been found beneath the offshore seabeds of California, Texas, Louisiana, Mississippi, and Florida. Other coastal areas were being prospected in the Gulf of Mexico. Considerable revenues had accrued to the states from leases and royalties on the oil discoveries beyond the low-water mark. In 1945, for example, Louisiana had collected $3,385,000 from oil and gas leases in the maritime belt; in the same year its peninsular parish of Plaquemines alone had received $141,000 from this source.[79] In order to conserve these valuable oil deposits, Secretary of

78 Hobbs to Roger Butler, June 15, 1946, in Hobbs Papers; *Southern Weekly,* June 12, 1946; Memphis *Commercial Appeal,* June 12, 1946.
79 U.S. Senate, Committee on the Judiciary, *Hearings to Quiet the Titles of the States to the Tidelands,* 79th Cong., 2nd Sess., 152–55. Two monographs have been written on the tidelands oil question. One gives a comprehensive legal history of this very complex case; the other attempts to show the pressures exerted in the political arena. These studies, however, analyze neither the political implications of the controversy nor the way in which the issue related to the wider sources of contention in the 1940s and 1950s. See Ernest R. Bartley, *The Tidelands Oil Controversy: A Legal and Historical Analysis* (Austin, 1953); Lucius J. Barker, "Offshore Oil Politics: A Study in Public Policy Making" (Ph.D. dissertation, University of Illinois, 1954); also, Lucius J. Barker, "The Supreme Court as Policy Maker: The Tidelands Oil Controversy," *Journal of Politics,* XXIV (May, 1962), 350–66.

the Interior Harold L. Ickes persuaded Truman shortly after his accession to claim right of ownership for the federal government. Accordingly, Truman issued in September, 1945, a proclamation which declared that in the interests of conservation the subsoil and seabed of the continental shelf beneath the high seas but contiguous to the coast of the United States were to be thenceforth subject to the jurisdiction and control of the federal government. At the same time, the Department of Justice claimed federal rights over the leased lands and filed suit against the state of California.[80]

The states' attorneys general and land commissioners immediately began to press Congress to pass a resolution which would force the federal government to relinquish its claims over the tidelands.[81] Congressman Hatton W. Summers of Texas introduced a resolution calling on the administration to quitclaim and vest title in the states. Representatives from the affected states of Florida, Texas, Louisiana, Mississippi, and California led the attack on the federal government's claim. Supporters of the quitclaim resolution based considerable weight on the legal history of the case. The states, they said, enjoyed *de facto* title to the continental shelf. Furthermore, the courts had previously upheld state ownership. They insisted that the states had entered the Union as sovereign territories on an equal footing with the original thirteen colonies, which had enjoyed sovereignty over their lands—including, in the unwritten tradition of international law, the marginal seas. They also had pragmatic objections to the president's proclamation. They argued that federal ownership would result in endless litigation to determine the limits of territorial waters. More important, the states had invested huge sums of money in oil drilling and were dependent on future returns for essential educational

---

80 Proclamation 2667, 3 *CFR, 1943–1948*, pp. 67–68; *Hearings to Quiet the Titles of the States to the Tidelands*, 3–13; Bartley, *The Tidelands Oil Controversy*, 141.
81 Barker, "Offshore Oil Politics," chap. 2.

funds. Opponents of the resolution, on the other hand, argued that the courts, in fact, never had ruled on the question of ownership and that Congress should not preempt the case, which was awaiting jurisdiction in the Supreme Court.[82] The proponents of quitclaim, however, won the day. The resolution passed both houses of Congress and was sent to the White House. Truman, despite warnings of dire political consequences in the Gulf states, naturally vetoed it. He could not have been expected to approve a measure aimed to nullify his own proclamation.[83]

Although the matter was basically a conflict between the vested interests of ownership in the states on the one hand and those who had no interests and thus wished to vest ownership in the United States on the other, there were important political undercurrents. In the first place, opponents of the president's proclamation felt that the nationalization of the tidelands represented a prime example of the much-feared widening of the dominion of federal government. The question of states' rights versus national rights, which was, after all, the quintessence of this particular dispute, was also the language of the sectional controversy. So, for some southerners, this was an especially loaded issue. Moreover, the proponents of quitclaim feared that if the Supreme Court were permitted to settle the matter, it would almost certainly rule in favor of the federal government. This was not a prospect southerners welcomed. The Court, they felt, was no longer the guardian of states' rights—especially in the matter of discrimination against Negroes. Congressman Leonard A. Allen of Louisiana echoed this view when he told the House that the Supreme Court "in the last years has upset so many long-standing decisions that I

82 *Congressional Record*, 79th Cong., 1st Sess., 8839–869; also, Bartley, *The Tidelands Oil Controversy*, chap. 9.
83 Telegram, Cotesworth Means to HST, July 30, 1946, memo, Matt Connally to HST, July 29, 1946, telegram, James H. Davis to HST, July 26, 1946, all in OF 56 F, Truman Papers; *Public Papers, 1946*, pp. 371–72; *Congressional Record*, 79th Cong., 2nd Sess., 10745.

think it is right and proper that the Congress should now step in and once and for all to settle this question." [84] The second political ramification of this controversy was more personal. Southern oil company executives and attorneys were very influential in southern politics, and deprivation of oil revenues could debilitate any support they might give to the national Democratic party. For example, the district attorney and political boss of oil-rich Plaquemines Parish in Louisiana, Leander Perez, who represented the oil interests at the congressional hearings, was to emerge in 1948 as an outspoken vilifier of Harry Truman.[85] Thus, although the tidelands question was not per se ideologically divisive, it did provide the administration's critics with yet one more piece of political ammunition.

By the summer of 1946 Harry Truman was in an unenviable position: he was a party leader without following. The trust that he had received from both the urban coalition and southerners in the weeks following his accession to the presidency had evaporated into disillusionment. The struggle over the future of the New Deal had ultimately left him out on a limb. Truman, sometimes through sheer political ineptitude but more often through intrinsic difficulty, had failed to endear either faction of the party to him. His bland impetuosity and his frequently contradictory statements could not create a spirit of trust and loyalty. But even without these political peccadilloes there was no chance that Truman could keep the Democratic alliance together. He could not extend the hand of support to one faction without alienating the other.

So, by mid-1946 Truman had fallen between two stools. Former New Dealers distrusted him, despite the fact that he had not only advocated all Roosevelt's policies but had gone further in his championship of housing reform and national

84 *Congressional Record*, 79th Cong., 2nd Sess., 8855.
85 *Hearings to Quiet the Titles of the States to the Tidelands*, 181–84, 225; Leander Perez, "Are You a States' Righter?" *Louisiana Police Jury Review*, XIV (April, 1950), 9–12; Leslie Velie, "Kingfish of the Dixiecrats," *Collier's*, December 17, 24, 1949.

health insurance.[86] They saw in Truman a president who had thrown himself into the civil rights arena only to cocoon himself afterward; a president who had vetoed the Case bill after he had threatened to draft strikers; a president who had embraced the New Deal and the memory of Franklin D. Roosevelt, but had dismissed all major New Deal officials, except Henry Wallace, within one year of his elevation to the White House; a president who had supposedly endorsed Roosevelt's *rapprochement* with the Soviet Union yet was talking of an iron curtain in eastern Europe.[87] But the alienation of the left did not comfort the South. To southern Democrats, Truman had shown clearly his intention to preserve the concept of a dynamic executive who would guide the direction of legislation. He had indicated that New Deal reform was to be institutionalized and expanded and that he did not regard it as a mere emergency program to be scrapped in periods of economic boom. Although southerners could applaud Truman's quarrels with A. F. Whitney and John L. Lewis, they also remembered his refusal to support legislation to weaken the unions. And, worst of all, he had used his office to support FEPC legislation.

But southerners not only complained about the conduct of the president. They also had grievances against the Democratic party organization which, under the chairmanship of Robert Hannegan, was dedicated to its preservation as a liberal party. They believed that Truman was being pressed against his instincts by the party bosses to promulgate his Fair Deal policies and that the Democratic hierarchy was prepared to dispense with the support of dissatisfied southerners in order to build up the party on liberal principles. This fear of the willingness of the top echelon to read dissidents out of the party was

---

86 Richard O. Davies, *Housing Reform During the Truman Administration* (Columbia, Mo., 1966); Monte Poen, "The Truman Administration and National Health Insurance" (Ph.D. dissertation, University of Missouri, 1967).

87 Hamby, "Harry S. Truman and American Liberalism," *passim*.

exacerbated in a number of incidents stemming from fund-raising activities prior to the midterm elections. In March, 1946, Henry Wallace told a women's group that Democrats who refused to vote for a British loan should "be put out of the party by not being allowed again on the Democratic ticket." About the same time, Robert Hannegan frankly castigated "dissident Democrats" who aligned with the Republicans—"a combination politically irresponsible," as the Democratic chairman dubbed it.[88]

A few days later, Hannegan and Wallace appeared together on the rostrum with President Truman at the Jefferson-Jackson Day dinner in Washington. Wallace did not repeat his call for a purge but reminded diners that "in our party we have been done great harm by those who have joined in a coalition against progress." He called upon dissidents "to honor our side with their 'mugs' as well as their 'wumps'." Truman also emphasized the importance of party unity so that a truly liberal program could be enacted. There was no doubt for whose ears these comments were intended. A dozen southern congressmen, according to Congressman Frank Boykin, had boycotted the gathering in anticipation of Wallace's remarks. Meanwhile at the dinner in Little Rock, Arkansas, dissenting Democrats did not content themselves with conspicuous absence from the function. Senator John McClellan condemned Truman's "strong trends and tendencies towards the left" and said that he could not support Truman so long as he consorted with Sidney Hillman, Henry Wallace, and "other political off-breeds." Governor Ben Laney announced that the proceeds of the dinner would be withheld from the Democratic National Committee in protest against the party leadership.[89]

To southerners, it seemed that the Democratic National Committee was conspiring to isolate them. Not only was there no

88 Washington *Post*, March 19, 20, 1946.
89 *Ibid.*, March, 24, 1946; Memphis *Commercial Appeal*, March 24, 25, 1946; *Public Papers, 1946*, pp. 165–69; Ronald F. Stinnett, *Democrats, Dinners, and Dollars: A History of the Democratic Party, Its Dinners, Its Rituals* (Ames, 1967), 173–74.

apparent room in the party for the supporters of laissez faire, but dissidents were considered unpatriotic and callous of the national welfare. The official party newspaper, the *Democratic Digest*, condemned their support of the Case bill as "a vote against the American people." Wallace had implied that southerners were "against progress." Congressman Charles E. McKenzie of Louisiana warned that the party was overreaching itself in its sense of self-righteousness. "The day is coming," he prophesied, "when the Administration is going to have to listen to us or else get no support from us." Southerners became even more suspicious that a purge was imminent when a Democratic National Committee circular was sent to county chairmen requesting them to select "proper" candidates who would support Truman's program. Although, after a massive outcry, a second letter was sent telling chairmen to ignore the original communication, the morale of southern Democrats sunk even lower. Despite Hannegan's apologetic retraction, it was self-evident to southerners that the party was devoting its time and resources to an all-out effort to regain the lost confidence of the liberal bloc—and not of the disgruntled South.[90] This was confirmed when Truman was persuaded to throw his weight against Congressman Roger Slaughter of Kansas City in the Missouri primary. For it was Slaughter's vote in the House Rules Committee that had so frequently blocked Fair Deal legislation, including the FEPC measures. The party leaders were continuing Roosevelt's strategy of giving political priority to the urban coalition.[91]

As the midterm elections of 1946 drew close, southern Democrats found themselves in a familiar paradox. Once again they were campaigning on a ticket whose leadership they had so often repudiated. In the second session alone of the Seventy-

90 Washington *Post*, April 3, 14, 18, 1946; Clipping, Louisville *Courier-Journal*, April 9, 1946, in Democratic National Committee Files, Harry S. Truman Library, Independence, Mo., hereafter cited as DNC Files, HSTL.
91 Truman had staked his prestige in the Missouri primary by endorsing Slaughter's opponent, Enos A. Axtell. "If he's right, I'm wrong," Truman insisted during the campaign. Washington *Post*, May 7, August 7, 1946.

ninth Congress, 43 of the 102 southern Democrats in the House had cast less than 50 percent of their votes with the majority of their party.[92] Although southerners were slightly compensated by Truman's dismissal of Henry Wallace in September because of differences over foreign policy, many were still apprehensive about the thrust of the president's program and his sources of advice.[93] They were not alone. A nationwide Gallup poll published in October, 1946, revealed that only 32 percent of the sample approved of Truman; a year before 82 percent had approved.[94] Not even Sam Rayburn could summon much enthusiasm for the president he served so loyally. "I think Truman is doing as well as practically anyone would do being catapulted into the position he was without too much training for it," he confided with rare superciliousness.[95] Theodore Bilbo was not so gentle. Southern Democrats, he suggested to Harry Byrd, should unite after the election to "defeat the plans and schemes of this communistic CIO-PAC crowd" and to curb the plans of "the long-haired economists and 'crackpots'." [96]

The Democratic chairman, Robert Hannegan, realized that his organization was in a state of disarray. Opinion polls and newspaper editorials seemed to confirm that the Republican slogan of "Had Enough?" was working favorably for the GOP. He labored hard to revitalize public sympathy for the Democrats. For the first time in a midterm election he created a speakers' bureau under the chairmanship of John J. Sparkman of Alabama. Sparkman organized speakers to address civic, labor, veterans', and business organizations on behalf of the party. He also enlisted southerners to help resuscitate the ebbing fortunes of the Democrats.[97] But Hannegan and Spark-

92 *Congressional Quarterly Almanac, 1946*, pp. 784–85. Speaker Sam Rayburn is excluded from this calculation. See also Hoey to Millard F. Jones, September 2, 1946, in Hoey Papers.
93 Hoey to James T. Potter, September 23, 1946, in Hoey Papers; Johnston to W. Stackhouse, September 24, 1946, in Box 251, Johnston Papers, SCL.
94 Houston *Post*, October 16, 1946.
95 Sam Rayburn to McDuffie, October 3, 1946, in McDuffie Papers.
96 Bilbo to Harry F. Byrd, August 20, 1946, in Bilbo Papers.
97 Washington *Post*, September 10, 1946; Robert Hannegan to Johnston, Au-

man realized only too well that the impediments were insurmountable. The pervasively low morale was underlined by their decision to keep Truman silent during the campaign and to play only taped speeches of Franklin Roosevelt at Democratic rallies.[98]

In November, 1946, Americans reacted to Truman as the British had to Churchill in the 1945 election—except the Americans voted out the liberals.[99] For the first time since Roosevelt had become president, the Democrats lost control of both houses of Congress. In the new House the Republicans would hold 245 seats to the Democrats' 188; in the new Senate the Republicans would hold 51 seats to the Democrats' 45. Three renowned champions of social reform lost their places in the Senate—Joseph Guffey of Pennsylvania, James Mead of New York, and Orrice Abram Murdock of Utah. All three had been active adherents of the CIO-PAC. In Chicago, Ed Kelley's machine was routed. In Kansas City Enos Axtell, the only candidate Truman had openly supported, lost to his Republican opponent.[100] Southern Democrats, of course, were reelected; no Republicans made any inroads into traditionally Democratic Dixie. The southerners seemed to have no doubts as to the meaning of these setbacks. To them, the Republican victories represented a direct repudiation of the Fair Deal and the views of the PAC. Memphis' E. H. Crump announced that "it will be foolish for Truman to offer himself for reelection in the 1948 Presidential campaign." [101] Senator William J. Fulbright of Arkansas was less patient. He called upon Truman to resign at

---

gust 15, 1946, in Box 261, Johnston Papers, SCL; Hannegan to Maybank, undated, in Maybank Papers; Hoey to Burke, September 12, 1946, in Hoey Papers; Democratic National Committee, *Campaign Issues, 1946: A Handbook for Candidates, Speakers, and Workers of the Democratic Party* (Washington, D.C., 1946), in Political Files, Clifford Papers; Hamby, "Harry S. Truman and American Liberalism," chap. 6.

98 Washington *Post*, October 27, 1946; Hinchey, "The Frustration of the New Deal Revival," 231–34.

99 For an interesting election eve prognostication, see O. Max Gardner to Holt McPherson, November 4, 1946, in Hoey Papers.

100 New York *Times*, November 7, 1946; Washington *Post*, November 7, 1946.

101 Memphis *Commercial Appeal*, November 7, 1946.

once and make way for a new leader. Southerners had been given a cue that the country had denied them throughout Roosevelt's presidency. The electorate had turned against its president.[102]

The Republican control of Congress meant, of course, that southerners would lose their numerous committee chairman-ships as well as the speakership of the House. On the other hand, they would constitute a comfortable majority of the Democratic membership in the House and one less of a full majority in the Senate. Thus, they could reorganize the party in Congress, dominate the Democratic caucus, and enjoy new bargaining power. The Shreveport *Times* summed up: "The task before the Democratic Party now, is to rebuild from the ashes, to let any smoldering flames of New Deal collectivism thoroughly burn themselves out, and then to kindle new and roaring flames of sound Democratic principle of the kind that have been trampled beneath a pseudo Democratic group in Washington for so many years." [103] Southern Democrats moved at once "to rebuild from the ashes."

102 Willis Robertson to Rayburn, November 9, 1946, in Miscellaneous Files 1946, Rayburn Papers; Washington *Post*, November 7, 1946; Houston *Post*, November 7, 1946; Memphis *Commercial Appeal*, November 11, 1946.
103 Quoted in *Southern Weekly*, November 13, 1946.

CHAPTER SIX

Racial Crisis in the South,
1946

Henry Grady, the apostle of the New South creed, once proclaimed: "The new South presents a perfect Democracy, the oligarchs leading in the popular movement—a social system compact and closely knitted, less splendid on the surface but stronger at the core." [1] This sentiment, articulated in 1886, proved to be timeless. It was destined to linger on in the political consciousness of the South for generations to come. Despite the almost incessant class strife and racial conflict that had characterized southern history since Grady's day, there were men and women who still believed that southerners, black and white, possessed a unique *esprit de corps*. Although they clung to this view with stubborn tenacity, it was becoming more and more apparent that a large section of the population, predominantly Negro but by no means entirely, did not subscribe to this idea at all. For, after World War II Negroes moved with rapid success to destroy the obstacles that had perpetuated the South's racial system. They successfully challenged the legal enforcement of Jim Crow and, to the bewilderment of many white southerners, began to assert their right to vote. Once again, Negroes were negating myths about themselves and the South, myths which had

1 Raymond B. Nixon, *Henry W. Grady: Spokesman of the New South* (New York, 1943), 348.

been created by white men. The South, after all, was not "stronger at the core." However, even this realization was to prove less traumatic than its political consequence. For when it became apparent that the state governments of the South would not accept the new reality, the federal government, spurred on by pressures from the urban coalition, began to seek methods of enforcing the law. The "southern question," after a dormancy of over half a century, once again became an issue of national concern. Only this time it was raised by Democrats.

When the Supreme Court in *Smith* v. *Allwright* had declared the Democratic primary open to all citizens, white southerners still believed that the Negro was sufficiently circumscribed to stay away from the polls. When to their consternation Negroes presented themselves for registration, whites felt constrained to act at once. Rhetoric would no longer suffice. They would have to either acquiesce in this new state of affairs or use all the political, judicial, and even physical means necessary to prevent a repetition of the Reconstruction experience.

Some states accepted the *Smith* v. *Allwright* ruling without much further opposition and grudgingly permitted Negroes to register—provided, of course, that they could overcome such obstacles as the payment of the poll tax or the literacy test. Texas, for example, capitulated to the Court's decision. Despite a few rumblings of resistance in the gubernatorial campaign of 1946, Texans decided to accept the inevitable, however distasteful. In the 1946 Democratic primary about 75,000 Texas Negroes voted.[2] Virginians, too, did not try to circumvent the decision. Despite a prohibitive poll tax and general electoral apathy due to the tight control of the Byrd organization, Negro registration increased considerably after 1944, although in total

---

2 Donald S. Strong, "The Rise of Negro Voting in Texas," *American Political Science Review*, XLII (June, 1948), 510–22; Key, *Southern Politics*, 521; Seth S. McKay, *Texas and the Fair Deal, 1945–1952* (San Antonio, 1954), chap. 2.

it remained small. In Richmond the registration of Negroes jumped from 6,374 in 1945 to 11,127 in 1948. Still more significant. Negroes began to run for political office. Blacks were candidates for seats in the House of Delegates and on a number of city councils. They appeared on the ballot in Norfolk, Lynchburg, Charlottesville, and Danville. In 1948 an important milestone was reached when Oliver W. Hill, a Negro, was elected to Richmond's city council.[3]

There was no such acquiescence, on the other hand, in the states of the Deep South. State officeholders there determined to resist black political participation. At first they declared that the Supreme Court's ruling would apply only to Texas. Other states would be unaffected. South Carolina was the only Dixie state to have taken any preventive action against enforcement of the ruling before the 1944 election. One reason, besides obstinacy and incredulity, for this apparent inaction was that the *Smith* v. *Allwright* decision came too late to affect the 1944 primary elections. In addition, white southerners thought that Negroes would be either too complacent or too scared to register. They presumed also that southern Negroes would not affiliate with the traditional party of white supremacy. But black leaders were not deterred by these conceptions. They decided to test local intentions. Throughout Dixie selected Negroes tried to register. In Alabama's Democratic primary of May, 1944, John LeFlore, head of the Mobile County branch of the NAACP, led a group of fifteen Negroes to the polling place only to find the deputy sheriff blocking the entrance defiantly.[4] In Macon County William P. Mitchell, a professor at Tuskegee Institute, filed suit against the board of registrars after he had been denied the right to register and vote. In the same year, 1945, a Florida circuit court ordered registrars to

3 Moss A. Plunkett to Hutchinson, June 28, 1946, in Box 9, Hutchinson Papers; Andrew Buni, *The Negro in Virginia Politics, 1902–1965* (Charlottesville, 1967), 151–57; Moon, *Balance of Power,* 156–65.
4 John LeFlore to Walter White, May 4, 1944, in Box 289/4, NAACP Files.

permit Negroes to vote after two Pensacola Negroes had complained that they had been barred from the ballot.[5]

Particularly notable for its political repercussions was the court action brought by Primus King, a Columbus, Georgia, Negro, who had been turned away at the local registrar's office. In March, 1946, the Fifth Circuit Court of Appeals upheld an earlier decision which had granted King the right to vote and had ruled against the defendants. The decision thus permitted Georgia Negroes to register and vote under the existing statutes.[6] White supremacists, fearing for their political skins, were naturally alarmed. If the laws were not changed, then they would inevitably be ousted from office by black voters. Roy Harris, speaker of Georgia's House of Representatives, announced that he was canvassing state legislators to petition Governor Ellis Arnall to convene a special session of the legislature to repeal all the primary laws, as South Carolina had done in 1944. Eugene Talmadge called upon Georgia's Democratic executive committee to bypass Arnall and act unilaterally in excluding Negroes from the primaries. The state chairman, J. Lon Duckworth, pointed out that his committee could do nothing by fiat until the legislature gave him its authority. But Governor Arnall refused to exercise his executive prerogative to convene an extraordinary session. Throughout his gubernatorial career he had rejected the temptation to stir up the race issue, and he did not intend to succumb to this new pressure. He called upon Georgians to accept the court's decision. "I will not be a party to any subterfuge or 'scheme' designed to nullify the orders of the courts," he proclaimed. Two days after Arnall's statement Eugene Talmadge announced he would be a candidate for the governorship in the forthcom-

5 *Mitchell* v. *Wright et al.*, 62 F. Supp. 580 (1945), 154 F. (2d) 924 (1946), 69 F. Supp. 698 (1947); Birmingham *News*, April 10, 1944; Luther P. Jackson, "Race and Suffrage in the South Since 1940," *New South* (June and July, 1948), 15; Murray (ed.), *The Negro Handbook*, 31–32.
6 *King* v. *Chapman*, 62 F. Supp. 639, 650 (1945), 154 F. (2d) 460 (1946); O. Douglas Weeks, "The White Primary, 1944–1948," *American Political Science Review*, XLII (June, 1945), 506.

ing election. His promise that the preservation of the white primary would be his principal platform came as no surprise.[7]

The challenge to white supremacy that so dominated the style and character of political campaigns in 1946 was not directed at the ballot sheet only. The postwar years also marked the incubation period of the judicial assault on and burial of Jim Crow. Although the Supreme Court's rulings did not visibly alter segregation patterns during the 1940s, white southerners were conscious that biracialism was beginning to tumble. Consequently, they devised systems to check the onslaughts which received encouragement from labor, Negro, civic, and church organizations. Proceedings had been initiated by NAACP lawyers in a variety of cases involving discrimination in housing, university education, labor unions, and interstate transportation. Although the details of the briefs need not be recounted, it must be realized that the protracted procedures involving these suits served as constant reminders that the racial caste system was essentially fragile. Southerners also viewed the Court's final decisions in these cases as further examples of the Supreme Court's prodigality in the matter of civil rights. With perhaps one notable exception, the Supreme Court, in case after case, struck penetrating blows at Jim Crow.[8]

The first blow to racial discrimination was in interstate trans-

---

7 Atlanta *Constitution*, March 19, 27, 29, 31, April 5, 7, 1946. Roy Harris was particularly determined to alter the laws in order to invalidate the court decisions. He has been quoted as saying: "If our system is held unconstitutional we will change the law at the next session of the legislature—but only by a period or a comma. We will hold our primary just as white as a clean sheet. If the Supreme Court invalidates that law too, then we will write it again for the next primary. That will go on *ad infinitum!*" Kennedy, *Southern Exposure*, 123; Herman Talmadge, interview.

8 The notable exception was in the case of *Screws* v. *U.S.*, 325 U.S. 91, 134 (1945). A Georgia sheriff, Claude Screws, had allowed a Negro to be murdered while under his charge. The Department of Justice successfully prosecuted sheriff Screws under a Reconstruction conspiracy statute, but the Supreme Court ordered a retrial on a technicality. However, it did not actually invalidate the section of the U.S. code under which Screws had been tried. Robert K. Carr, *Federal Protection of Civil Rights* (Ithaca, 1947), 106–15; see also Carl B. Swisher, "The Supreme Court and the South," *Journal of Politics*, X (May, 1948), 282–305.

port. In June, 1946, the Supreme Court, in a six-to-one decision, invalidated a Virginia statute requiring segregation on public buses moving across state lines. The Court reasoned that the great diversity of state statutes dealing with segregation in transport interfered with the uniformity of interstate commerce and thus made such laws invalid. But soon the Court was asked to reexamine the implications of the equal protection clause for Jim Crow.[9] In the same month NAACP lawyers filed a suit on behalf of a Texas Negro, Herman Sweatt, who had been denied admission to the University of Texas Law School. Texas legislators and educationalists had responded to Sweatt's application for admission by instituting a special law school for Negroes at Prairie View. But Sweatt contended that the improvised school lacked adequate facilities and claimed a denial of rights in contravention of the equal protection clause of the Fourteenth Amendment. Proceedings were begun, and, four years later, after considerable publicity in the press, the Supreme Court ruled unanimously that the special Negro law school did not furnish Negroes with true equality in legal education. This ruling followed an earlier, parallel ruling concerning higher education in *Sipuel* v. *Oklahoma*. The Court, however, refrained from any review of the "separate but equal" rule. Although the decision was handed down in 1950, Sweatt's registration application, as will be seen, became an important issue in Texas' 1946 gubernatorial election.[10]

The Supreme Court also struck blows at discrimination in labor unions. In *Steele* v. *Louisville and Nashville Railroad Co.*, for example, the Court reasoned that a union operating under a federal statute could not bar minority groups and still claim

9 *Morgan* v. *Virginia*, 328 U.S. 373 (1946); Pittsburgh *Courier*, June 8, 1946.
10 Houston *Post*, February 28, March 1, 1946; Pittsburgh *Courier*, June 1, 1946; *Sweatt* v. *Painter*, 339 U.S. 629 (1950); Robert J. Harris, *The Quest for Equality: The Constitution, Congress, and the Supreme Court* (Baton Rouge, 1960), 138; *Sipuel* v. *Oklahoma*, 332 U.S. 631 (1948); Memphis *Commercial Appeal*, January 13, 29, 1948; Pittsburgh *Courier*, January 17, 31, 1948.

the right to represent them in collective bargaining agreements. It reasoned that the Railway Labor Act imposed upon the statutory representative of a union the same obligations as those that apply to state legislatures. The Court was clearly disturbed by the way laws were used to enforce discrimination. Associate Justice Murphy, in a concurring opinion, declared that the Court could not decide "solely upon the basis of legal niceties, while remaining mute and placid as to the obvious and oppressive deprivation of constitutional guarantees." Such reasoning made "the judicial function something less than it should be." [11] And in the case of *Shelley* v. *Kraemer* the Court ruled that the judicial enforcement of restrictive covenants, used to exclude "undesirable" minority groups from buying real estate in certain zones, constituted state action and so violated the Fourteenth Amendment.[12]

Politicians in the South were uncomfortably aware that the Court was gnawing at the edges of Jim Crow. The Negro's "place" was now less certain. But they presumed, quite correctly, that the South's racial customs could be preserved if Negroes could be excluded from the political process. So they concentrated their political invective on the *Smith* v. *Allwright* ruling. Furthermore, they had a personal interest in sabotaging its implementation. Senator Burnet R. Maybank of South Carolina did not gloss over the reason for his recalcitrance: "When the negroes have an opportunity of voting they will naturally vote against any of us who run. However I hope this will be in the distant future." [13] So, a number of officeholders refused to play for time. They moved to forestall mass Negro registration by any means at their disposal. They usually relied upon publicity and electoral histrionics. Their impassioned defenses of the white Democratic primary usually proved politically lucra-

11 *Steele* v. *Louisville and Nashville Railroad Co.*, 323 U.S. 192 (1944); Emanuel Stein, "The Supreme Court and Labor," in Warne (ed.), *Labor in Postwar America*, 337–63. See also, Norfolk *Journal and Guide*, October 19, 1946.
12 *Shelley* v. *Kraemer*, 334 U.S. 1 (1948).
13 Maybank to W. J. Cormack, July 11, 1945, in Maybank Papers.

tive. The advocates of white supremacy found a ready popular response. They were either elected to office or they won endorsements of constitutional amendments which attempted to render the Court ruling irrelevant. However, their tactics brought about one unexpected result, one they had always feared but had never really expected to materialize. The president, a lifelong Democrat, decided to seek means to guarantee the civil rights of southern Negroes.

The white primary decision overshadowed all other issues in Georgia's gubernatorial contest in 1946. The incumbent, Governor Ellis Arnall, was constantly castigated by Eugene Talmadge, one of the principal contenders, for his refusal to convene the state legislature to repeal all the laws governing the primaries. Talmadge, who had himself been defeated by Arnall in 1942, staged his comeback by picturing the governor as a tool of northern Negro and labor organizations. These overt sympathies, according to Talmadge, had become apparent in 1944 when Arnall supported Henry Wallace for the vice presidency. Although Arnall was not even a candidate for the governorship, Talmadge succeeded in associating his most formidable opponent, James V. Carmichael, with the Arnall administration. Thus, the attitudes on the white primary were skillfully interwoven with a critique of the national Democratic party.[14]

Talmadge's exploitation of the *Smith* v. *Allwright* decision proved to be an effective political calculation. It was geared toward the country people, who were particularly afraid of the effects of Negro voting in areas where blacks often outnumbered whites. Furthermore, Georgia's unique primary laws gave rural voters an unquestionable electoral preponderance. These laws should be briefly explained. The Neill Primary Act of 1917 had created an essentially indirect system of nomination, whereby each of Georgia's 159 counties was given a specified

14 Taylor, "A Political Biography of Ellis Arnall," *passim;* Bernd, *Grass Roots Politics in Georgia,* 8–9; Arnall, *The Shore Dimly Seen,* chaps. 3, 4.

number of unit votes. The unit votes of a county went to the candidate with a popular plurality in that county. The winner of a state primary was the candidate who won the most county unit votes. But the votes of the most populous counties were deflated and the influence of the least populous inflated by assigning to each county twice as many unit votes as it had in Georgia's House of Representatives. Thus, the eight most populous counties which, according to the 1940 census, had 31.1 percent of Georgia's total adult white population, were allotted only 11.7 percent of the total number of unit votes, while 121 small counties with 39.9 percent of the total adult white population received 59.0 percent of the total unit votes. It was, therefore, to Talmadge's advantage to campaign for the electoral support of the rural counties. He knew, of course, that whites who lived in the rural Black Belt stood to lose the most from the collapse of the white primary.[15]

The specter of a powerful and vengeful Negro electorate was not mere fancy. Particularly in Georgia, Negroes had seized the opportunity to register and exercise their right to vote. They were encouraged by the relatively tolerant climate of the Arnall administration and the unequivocal decision in the *King* case. The shape of things to come was manifest in two special elections held in Georgia just before the state primary. In February, in a special congressional election in Atlanta, Mrs. Helen Mankin, who was supported by the CIO-PAC, was elected to serve in the House of Representatives. A number of Negroes had voted in this election, and they were quick to attribute Mrs. Mankin's victory to their support.[16] In April, Roy Harris, speaker of Georgia's House of Representatives, was defeated in the Richmond County primary by an independent, Bill Morris. Harris, a renowned white supremacist, had been the longtime leader of the local political machine, known to

15 The figures are from the analysis of Georgia's county unit system in Key, *Southern Politics,* 117–24.
16 Atlanta *Constitution,* February 13, 1946; Norfolk *Journal and Guide,* March 2, 1946.

Georgians as the Cracker party. He had broken with Ellis Arnall on the latter's refusal to repeal the primary laws and had based his campaign on this personal breach. When he was defeated, he blamed his reverse on the mass voting of Negroes in Augusta. Indeed, nearly two thousand Negroes had voted for Harris' opponent, while less than five hundred had supported the Cracker leader.[17] At the same time, throughout the urban counties of Georgia, Negroes were organizing registration drives. Special associations, such as the Georgia Association of Citizens' Democratic Clubs, were formed by black community leaders to direct and coordinate the campaign to place Negroes on the voting rolls. Although registrars in a number of counties attempted to prevent them from registering and at times went to the lengths of purging their names from the voting lists, the thrust of registration was unmistakable. Reliable sources estimated that by July, 1946, when the registration books in Georgia closed, some 120,000 Negroes had their names on the polling lists. This represented about 20 percent of the total adult Negro population and was, with the exception of Tennessee, the highest proportion of registered Negroes in any southern state.[18]

The county unit system, however, had minimized the effect of the voting drive among Negroes which had been concentrated in the cities. Talmadge, armed with the implacable

17 Atlanta *Constitution,* April 18, 1946; Hugh Carl Owen, "The Rise of Negro Voting in Georgia, 1944–1950" (M.A. thesis, Emory University, 1951), 17–21.
18 Owen, "The Rise of Negro Voting in Georgia," 48–49; Jackson, "Race and Suffrage in the South Since 1940," 3. Jackson estimated that, in 1947, 125,000 Georgia Negroes were registered out of a potential total of 663,000. In absolute terms this was the highest figure for any southern state. Texas had some 100,000 registered Negroes and Tennessee some 80,000. Registered Tennessee Negroes composed some 25.8 percent of the total black population of voting age. In the same year only 2.6 percent of Louisiana Negroes were registered; 1.2 percent in Alabama; and a mere 0.9 percent in Mississippi. NAACP estimates differ slightly, although these are probably less reliable. See Key, *Southern Politics,* 522–23n, 126; Atlanta *Constitution,* July 10, 1946; *Crisis,* LIII (September, 1946); pamphlet, Southern Regional Council, *The Condition of Our Rights,* in Box 16, Francis P. Matthews Papers, Harry S. Truman Library, Independence, Mo.

facts of Negro voting, based his gubernatorial campaign on this new phenomenon in Georgia politics. "The One Issue in this Race is White Supremacy," ran a headline in the *Statesman,* Talmadge's campaign newspaper. His opponents, James Carmichael and Eurith D. Rivers, both defended segregation and the almost sacrosanct county unit system, but they pledged themselves to abide by the court decisions on the franchise. Talmadge, however, equated their refusal to resist court orders with an endorsement of racial integration. He exploited fully any reported racial fracases and exacerbated the racial bitterness which was already prevalent. For example, after a reported racial altercation on a Savannah bus, the *Statesman* commented: "As the Arnall-Carmichael ideas of racial equality and non-segregation become more generally known among the negroes, more of these incidents can be confidently expected." [19] On a still more sinister level, at the height of the campaign the Ku Klux Klan held an open meeting and burned crosses at Stone Mountain, just outside Atlanta.[20]

The rural counties, particularly in the Black Belt, responded to Talmadge's campaign rhetoric. Although he received only 43 percent of the popular vote, he received 59 percent of the county unit votes and was thus nominated in the first primary. Carmichael had polled a sixteen-thousand-vote plurality, but his urban support was insufficient to offset the heavy rural county unit votes.[21] Talmadge interpreted the election result as an endorsement of his white supremacy campaign and consequently proceeded to consolidate his position. At the state Democratic convention, held in Macon in October, Arnall's supporters were ousted from the state party organization and replaced with pro-Talmadge officials under the chairmanship of James Peters of Manchester. The party platform endorsed all Talmadge's policies and pledged to preserve the white

19 *Statesman,* July 11, 1946.
20 Atlanta *Constitution,* May 30, June 21, 1946.
21 *Ibid.,* July 18, 19, 1946; *Crisis,* LIII (September, 1946); Bernd, *Grass Roots Politics in Georgia,* 7.

primary and the county unit system. Speakers at the convention unblushingly blamed northern politicians and officials in Washington for the recent attacks on white supremacy. Talmadge's selection, according to the new party platform, "was the answer of red-blooded white Georgians to attempted interference with their internal affairs by outside elements in the North who are seeking to destroy our Southern way of life, our Southern traditions, and our Southern institutions." Talmadge, however, did not live to put his promises into effect. And neither, as it happened, did his fellow white supremacist from Mississippi, Theodore Bilbo, who was nominated on a similar platform in the same month.[22]

Bilbo sought reelection in 1946 to another term in the U.S. Senate. Aware of the explosiveness of the registration drive being conducted by the Negro Mississippi Progressive Voters' League, he adopted Talmadge's tactics. Two weeks before the July primary Bilbo wrote to the other contenders for the Senate seat and implored them to appeal in clear-cut, unambiguous language to Negroes to refrain from voting. Their appearance at polling stations, he reminded them, was only the "first step, under the leadership of Northern Negroes, white Socialists, white Communists and white advocates of social and political equality, to destroy white control and white supremacy in the State of Mississippi." [23] In case Negroes would not respond to these imprecations, Bilbo also advocated the use of intimidation. On the stump he inveighed against Negroes in the crudest terms imaginable. On one occasion, for example, he remarked that "the nigger is only 150 years from the jungles of Africa, where it was his great delight to cut him up some fried nigger steak for breakfast." He laced his speeches with inflammatory appeals to white Mississippians to prevent Negroes from voting by "any means." And in a notorious broadcast he admonished

22 Atlanta Constitution, October 10, 1946; Herman Talmadge, interview.
23 Bilbo to Tom Q. Ellis, Ross A. Collins, Nelson Trible Levings, and Frank Harper, June 17, 1946, in Bilbo Papers; see also, Alexander Heard, A Two Party South? (Chapel Hill, 1952), 191.

whites to visit intending Negro voters the night before polling day.[24] His audience did not need to be told what to do on their visits.

Bilbo's vituperative campaign had its intended effects. Bilbo won the first primary with an absolute majority. He had succeeded in terrifying Negroes into remaining away from the polling stations. In Hinds County, where Jackson is situated, only 195 Negroes voted out of a total Negro population of 55,000. In Washington County, 25 of its 49,000 Negroes managed to vote. No blacks at all dared vote in Winston, Leflore, and Adams (Natchez) counties. According to reports by Senate investigators, court clerks made it impossible for Negroes even to register. Negroes were quizzed for their "understanding" of the constitution and were asked such questions as "what is *ipso facto* and *ex post facto* law?" In Tougaloo, just outside Jackson, a black minister was prevented from entering the polling place by three local whites, one of whom brandished a gun. Bilbo had thus managed to persuade his constituents to overcome the recent decisions on the Negro franchise by sheer brute force and terror.[25]

While politicians in Georgia and Mississippi employed public race-baiting as their principal means of keeping Negroes away from the polls, in other states of the Deep South they attempted to create legal obstacles. In Alabama, Democratic leaders rejected South Carolina's plan for the complete repeal of all primary laws and decided instead to tighten voting qualifications. They argued that a revision of the voting laws would be both more effective and more likely to be upheld in court. Moreover, this strategy would also prevent most Negroes from voting in the general elections as well as in primaries. Gessner McCorvey, state party chairman, feared that Negroes

24 U.S. Senate, Special Committee to Investigate Senatorial Campaign Expenditures, *Hearings on Bilbo Campaign, 1946*, 79th Cong., 2nd Sess., 331–61.
25 *Ibid.*, 14–16; U.S. Senate, Special Committee to Investigate Senatorial Campaign Expenditures, *Report 1 on Investigation of Senatorial Campaign Expenditures, 1946*, 8oth Cong., 1st Sess., 21.

would still be able to wield a decisive influence in Alabama politics if this loophole were not closed. Unless effective measures were taken to disqualify Negroes from registering in the first place, warned McCorvey, white politicians in predominantly black counties would be voted out of office.[26] Accordingly, party lawyers devised a constitutional amendment which would effectively bar Negroes from the polls at the discretion of registrars and clerks. The so-called Boswell amendment, named after its sponsor in the state legislature, provided that an applicant for registration should prove to the board of registrars that he could read and write, that he could "understand and explain" any article of the United States Constitution, that he had been regularly and gainfully employed for the preceding year, that he was of "good character," and that he could "understand the duties and obligations of good citizenship under a republican form of government." Clearly, the Boswell amendment delegated to registrars the power to reject would-be voters.[27]

After the amendment was passed by the state legislature, it was submitted to the electorate in November, 1946, for ratification. The campaign that was waged was reminiscent of the earlier contests in Georgia and Mississippi. However, the voters were divided on the merits of the Boswell amendment. Its opponents argued that it was so blatantly discriminatory that the already strained racial *modus vivendi* would collapse. They also feared the arbitrary power bestowed upon voting registrars. There was nothing to prevent them from disqualifying whites as well. The opposition, led by Senator Lister Hill and Governor-elect James Folsom, who had recently defeated the candidate of the powerful Black Belt bosses, knew that registrars would be in a position to perpetuate local machines by arbitrarily denying their critics the franchise. However,

26 McCorvey to Pat Robertson, October 21, 1946, in Hobbs Papers.
27 Dixon to McCorvey, October 12, 1944, in Dixon Papers; Key, *Southern Politics*, 632–33.

McCorvey and Horace Wilkinson, a bigoted but powerful Birmingham attorney, refuted this view. They insisted that the sole purpose of the amendment was to preserve white supremacy. In a circular *To the Voters of Alabama,* McCorvey stated that "the vast majority of negroes have not yet fitted themselves to vote intelligently on important governmental matters." The new measures would "protect our state from the veritable flood of negro registration and negro domination, which the Supreme Court decision has released." [28] However, many Alabamians did not share this view. There were, after all, less drastic solutions. The amendment passed by a slim majority vote of only 53.7 percent. As expected, those counties with a high proportion of Negroes were the most enthusiastic advocates of the amendment. Two years later, however, a federal district court invalidated the amendment. The Supreme Court refused subsequently to review this decision.[29]

South Carolina's attempts in 1944 to evade the *Smith* v. *Allwright* decision were also struck down in court. In 1947 the NAACP filed suit on behalf of a Negro who had been denied the right to vote in the 1946 primary. The case came before Justice J. Waties Waring of the U.S. district court, a member of an old, aristocratic Charleston family. Waring ruled that the repeal of the primary laws did not alter the fact that Negroes were still being denied the right to vote. "Racial distinctions cannot exist in the machinery that selects the officers and lawmakers of the United States," he concluded. "It is time for South Carolina to rejoin the Union. It is time to fall in step with the other states and to adopt the American way of conducting elections." [30] This judgment was upheld by

28 Circular, McCorvey, *To the Voters of Alabama,* September, 1946, in Dixon Papers; also, McCorvey to Pat Robertson, October 21, 1946, in Hobbs Papers.
29 Key, *Southern Politics,* 633–35; *Davis* v. *Schnell,* 81 F. Supp. 872 (1949), 69 S. Ct. 749 (1949); McCorvey to Dixon, January 28, 1949, Horace Wilkinson to Dixon, January 31, 1949, in Dixon Papers.
30 *Elmore* v. *Rice,* 72 F. Supp. 516 (1947); Atlanta *Constitution,* July 13,

the circuit court of appeals. Thus, legislative attempts to prevent Negroes from voting in the Democratic primaries proved fruitless. It seemed that the more extreme solutions, as advocated by Theodore Bilbo, were the only effective means of preserving the status quo.[31] However, die-hard advocates of the white primary vowed to continue their resistance.

These blatant attempts to nullify or evade the rulings of the Supreme Court were to have major political repercussions. Although discrimination at the polls had been practiced throughout the South since the end of the nineteenth century, it had generally been exercised under the umbrella of legality. Now the Court had specifically ruled that the white primary, a major means of exclusion, was unconstitutional. It was difficult, therefore, for the chief executive to permit states to defy the laws so flagrantly. Furthermore, it was difficult politically. The president had already committed himself, albeit capriciously, to the cause of civil rights and could not, without losing total credibility, ignore the demands from the urban coalition for intervention.[32] Too, the race issue had assumed a transcendent, international dimension. Dean Acheson, undersecretary of state, had advised Truman that the nation's racial practices were often "a formidable obstacle to the development of mutual understanding and trust between . . . two countries." [33] Acheson's observation may have been an exaggeration, yet it was not merely a pietism. Three members of the British House of Commons, for example, were sufficiently aroused by Bilbo's campaign techniques to demand the pro-

1947; New York *Times*, July 13, 1947; James M. Hinton to Maybank, July 14, 1947, in Maybank Papers; Weeks, "The White Primary, 1944–1948," 509; Moon, *Balance of Power*, 185–86.

31 Atlanta *Constitution*, December 31, 1947; statement of Burnet R. Maybank, July 13, 1947, in Maybank Papers.

32 See, for example, Mason to A. R. Klemmer, September 11, 1946, Mason to Herbert Lehman, September 19, 1946, in Mason Papers; telegram, Hillman to HST, June 24, 1946, Frank Kingdon to HST, June 25, 1946, in OF 93, Truman Papers; Aubrey Williams to C. C. Davis, July 8, 1946, in Bilbo Papers.

33 Dean Acheson to Malcolm Ross, May 8, 1946, in RG 228-67, Office Files of Malcolm Ross, FEPC Records.

tection of "basic human rights." [34] Truman knew that he would soon have to risk a break with the South.

The white primary ruling did not affect all the elections in the South in 1946. In many states conservatives were more preoccupied with the activities of the CIO and the CIO-PAC than with white supremacy. The CIO had decided to launch a massive union organization drive in the South after the war. The drive, known to friends and foes as Operation Dixie, was formulated and begun in the spring of 1946. Under the direction of Van Bittner, the CIO Southern Organizing Committee deliberately selected native southerners to conduct the campaign and hold union elections. Labor leaders had decided that the rapid industrialization during the war would ease their task. Thus, not only the CIO but also the AF of L mobilized to unionize southern workers. However, the AF of L's strategy was carefully geared to win acceptance from business leaders and conservative politicians. It attacked the CIO with the same vehemence used by their southern mentors. It promiscuously charged the rival CIO with harboring "communists." George L. Googe, southern representative for the AF of L in Atlanta, described CIO organizers as "picnic junkets of Northern radicals and a motley crew of parlor pink intellectuals squandering funds and bestirring hatred to the trade union movement as a whole." [35] Thus, southern politicians could, without embarrassment, claim that they were sympathetic to unionism, while they simultaneously lambasted the CIO.

Despite this barrage from the AF of L, Bittner proceeded with his plans to unionize southern workers. Within a short time CIO organizers were traveling through Dixie, holding

---

34 Telegram, Donald Bruce, Tom Driberg, and Richard Crossman to HST, June 14, 1946, in OF 93, Truman Papers.
35 Marshall, *Labor in the South*, 246–65; U.S. Department of Labor, *Labor in the South* (Washington, D.C., 1947), *passim;* Atlanta *Constitution,* March 22, 1946; American Federation of Labor, *Report of the Proceedings of the 66th Convention of the American Federation of Labor,* held at San Francisco, October 6–16, 1947, 172–76.

meetings and instigating union shop elections. In addition, they publicized the activities of the PAC and emphasized the need for comprehensive social welfare legislation. Although they were not as successful in converting workers as they had hoped, they made some important penetrations. In February, 1947, North Carolina's state director boasted that the CIO had enrolled 22,000 new members since the drive had begun.[36] In fiscal 1947 the CIO won precisely as many union elections as did the AF of L, although in numbers the CIO probably had an edge over its rival. Van Bittner announced in January, 1948, that the CIO's membership in the South had increased to about 800,000.[37]

Even the limited successes of the CIO were feared by businessmen and many community leaders. They believed that the CIO constituted a nuclear organization dedicated to the overthrow of the South's political and economic system. The CIO, through the instrumentality of the Democratic party in Washington, had already attempted to subvert the South's civilization. If it went unimpeded, it would soon have a firm foothold in Dixie. Once entrenched, it would wield a decisive balance of power in the political process. This would result, said the Southern States Industrial Council, in "the kiss of death" for the South as a distinctive region. It would "establish political control over the nation and supplant our democratic institutions with centralized federal control." Furthermore, it would destroy the racial *modus vivendi.* "By advocating a system of social and economic equality . . . these people are promising the Negro an earthly utopia which they know they cannot deliver, and which they really have no intention of attempting to deliver," wrote Remmie Arnold, the council's president.[38] Most intolerable of all, this revolutionizing process

36 Atlanta *Constitution,* March 20, 1946; Mason to Philip Murray, October 30, 1944, in Mason Papers; *CIO News,* February 24, 1947.
37 U.S. Department of Labor, *12th Annual Report of the National Labor Relations Board* (Washington, D.C., 1947), 79; *CIO News,* January 5, 1948.
38 Circular, Southern States Industrial Council, *The Kiss of Death,* April 29, 1946, in GF, Southern States Industrial Council Folder, Truman Papers.

would be conducted under the auspices of a reconstituted Democratic party. This would leave southern conservatives politically homeless.[39]

Thus the activities of the CIO-PAC were vehemently assailed in the election campaigns of 1946. Even though the PAC itself had lost some of its vitality, it was pictured by many politicians as a formidable threat to the South's political institutions.[40] Candidates for office usually found that endorsements by the PAC were liabilities rather than assets. In a number of primary elections, candidates accused their opponents of collusion with the PAC in the belief that this would cast a stain on their adversaries. Even where the PAC had no interest in a particular campaign, political aspirants, eager to capitalize on the unpopularity of the PAC, labeled their opponents "tools" of the CIO-PAC. Thus in the South, the PAC frequently served a politically symbolic function in the way that the "interests" had done in the Progressive era.

The emergence of the PAC as a major political issue was particularly notable in Alabama, where, contrary to experience in other southern states, the candidates who had been endorsed by the PAC actually won the election. The eventual victor in Alabama's gubernatorial contest in 1946 was the large-framed James E. Folsom. In the tradition of Tom Watson and Huey Long, Folsom, one of nature's extroverts, made direct appeals to voters who had never really identified with the planter-politicians of the Black Belt. His blustering performance on the stump, which included music from a hillbilly band and marathon sessions of kissing women and children, was to many voters an attractive contrast to the earnestness of the plantation elite. Furthermore, his "People's Program" was welcomed by workers in the thriving cities of Birmingham and Mobile. He promised protective legislation for work-

---

39 *Southern Weekly*, May 1, 1946. For the racial arguments against unionization see: Ransome J. Williams to A. W. Hopson, November 29, 1945, in Ransome J. Williams Papers, South Carolina Department of Archives, Columbia; *Textile Bulletin*, June 15, 1946.
40 Arnold, "The CIO's Role in American Politics," 259–86.

ers, free school textbooks, the repeal of the poll tax, and reapportionment in the state legislature "to break the old political machine." The CIO-PAC was also impressed by Folsom's policies on social welfare and labor. It endorsed "Big Jim" and helped him raise funds for the campaign. His opponents, who between them had the support of nearly all of Alabama's major newspapers, quickly pointed to Folsom's backing from the PAC and translated the campaign into a plebiscite on the PAC. Folsom was bracketed with the CIO as a threat to the established racial and political order. However, he overcame this criticism and won resoundingly in the runoff primary. Only in counties with a high proportion of Negroes did Folsom fare badly. Although the PAC may have influenced the outcome, Folsom's personal magnetism and his ability to arouse the white farmers in the hill counties were his major sources of strength. His triumph was, as former governor Frank Dixon pointed out, "a sort of people's revolution against old-line politicians." [41] Folsom had indeed shown that there was more demand for governmental paternalism than the old-line politicians had ever cared to admit. He had also eschewed the race question. His victory was a source of encouragement to liberals throughout the South. Perhaps, after all, social change could be accomplished indigenously, rather than from without. There were, however, limitations to Folsom's powers. He could not, for example, persuade the voters to reject the Boswell amendment in November. Thus, his earlier electoral triumph was dwarfed by the triumph of white supremacy only a few months later. He had demonstrated the frailty of southern progressivism, as well as its potential.

In other southern elections the PAC was unsuccessful in securing the electoral victory of its supporters. Although it is difficult to determine the extent to which the PAC itself was

41 Dixon to B. B. Gossett, May 16, 1946, in Dixon Papers; William D. Murray, "The Folsom Gubernatorial Campaign of 1946" (M.A. thesis, University of Alabama, 1949), *passim*; W. Bradley Twitty, *Y'All Come* (Nashville, 1962), 47–59; Key, *Southern Politics*, 42–44, 56–57; *Southern Weekly*, June 5, 1946.

responsible for the defeat of the liberal candidates, there seems little doubt that it was a handicap to the weaker ones. In Virginia, William Tuck, a protégé of Harry Byrd, had won the 1945 gubernatorial contest easily on a specifically antilabor platform. Afterward, on his recommendations the state legislature passed a series of laws hampering organized labor. It restricted the collective bargaining rights of state employees and prohibited the reemployment of any public worker who had gone on strike. In March, 1946, Tuck called for the induction of striking electrical workers into the state militia.[42] It was hardly surprising, therefore, that the CIO-PAC in Virginia resolved to try to defeat all machine candidates. Their most enticing opportunity came in 1946 when Harry Byrd sought reelection for another term in the Senate. He was opposed by Martin A. Hutchinson whom the CIO-PAC instantly endorsed. The antimachine organization, however, was weak. Hutchinson stood little chance against Virginia's powerful oligarchy. Moreover, Hutchinson's CIO-PAC backing was turned against him by Byrd's stalwarts. Byrd realized that the PAC was potentially powerful and strove to discredit it before it could exert any lasting influence in Virginia politics. "When the CIO gets into action they must be taken seriously," Byrd wrote to Senator Hoey after his resounding victory.[43]

The CIO-PAC was attacked in nearly all southern primaries. In South Carolina, where the PAC did not make any endorsements at all, the gubernatorial contenders still made and denied allegations that they were PAC affiliates.[44] In Texas, the fourteen contenders for the governorship behaved as if Sidney Hillman, by then an ailing man, was the most formidable rival for office. The most liberal candidate, Dr. Homer P. Rainey,

42 J. Harvie Wilkinson, III, *Harry Byrd and the Changing Face of Virginia Politics, 1945–1966* (Charlottesville, 1968), 56–61.
43 Harry Byrd to Hoey, September 10, 1946, in Hoey Papers; Robinette to Hutchinson, May 25, 1946, in Box 8, Hutchinson Papers; clipping, Lynchburg *News*, May 13, 1946, in DNC Files, HSTL.
44 Charleston *News and Courier*, September 4, 1946; New York *Times*, September 3, 1946.

was constantly accused of colluding with Hillman to subvert the South's customs. His opponent in the runoff primary, Beauford Jester, state railroad commissioner, managed to stigmatize Rainey as a cat's-paw of the CIO-PAC. Moreover, Jester skillfully exploited the current furor in Texas over the application of Herman Sweatt, a Negro, to the University of Texas. He intimated that since Dr. Rainey, who had been president of that college until his dismissal in 1944, was being abetted by the PAC, he was logically bound to favor desegregation in higher education. Despite Rainey's avowed championship of segregated schools and his bizarre advocacy of separate polling booths for Negroes, he was unable to cast off the PAC's stigma. Jester was swept into office on a decidedly antilabor, anti-"radical" vote.[45]

The PAC was almost the sole target of attack in Tennessee, where Senator Kenneth McKellar, aided by Ed Crump's powerful Shelby County organization, sought another term to the Senate. The CIO was less of an imaginary threat in Tennessee than in Virginia or Texas. It had scored some important union successes in the Memphis area and seemed capable of posing a serious challenge to Crump's hold over West Tennessee. Crump thus had good reason to try to discredit it, especially when McKellar's opponent, Edward W. Carmack, was endorsed by the PAC for his advocacy of protective legislation for organized labor. Crump and McKellar were particularly alarmed when the PAC began to organize block-by-block canvassing operations. Its national director, Jack Kroll, came to Tennessee to give local workers his personal support. It was becoming clear that the PAC regarded Tennessee as a test area for its potential strength in the South. In Chattanooga Kroll condemned McKellar publicly as "the leader of Southern reactionaries in Congress."[46] McKellar himself almost ignored

45 McKay, *Texas and the Fair Deal, 1945–1952*, chap. 2; Houston *Post*, March 3, May 5, 26, June 5, August 4, 1946; *Southern Weekly*, July 31, 1946.

46 Memphis *Commercial Appeal*, April 16, May 10, June 17, 27, July 22, 1946; Miller, *Mr. Crump of Memphis*, 312–20.

Carmack in his campaign (he did not even go to Tennessee to make speeches, but fought from Washington) and reserved all his invective for the CIO, which, he insisted, was the central election issue. "All those who want a Communistic Senate or a Communistic House or a Communistic Government should vote for the CIO candidates," he declared.[47] Tennesseans obviously preferred to protect their government from these forces of revolution. In August McKellar was comfortably renominated in the primary. Nevertheless, the divisive campaign had its toll in lives, if not in its political institutions. In the small town of Athens in McMinn County, a deputy sheriff was killed and twenty persons were wounded in an affray outside the courthouse after a disagreement about counting the ballot papers.[48]

Athens was not the only southern town to experience violence that summer. In a number of other communities there occurred armed clashes which were usually preceded by divisive election campaigns or a sudden upsurge in political activities among Negroes. Indeed, these altercations were nearly always racial in character. In most instances they happened in areas where the local populace, spurred on by its political leaders, had determined to apply the rules of the color line rigidly to discourage Negroes from voting. Although it cannot be shown categorically that the white supremacy campaigns caused the spread of violence, there was a pervasive determination among southern whites to find ways to fortify the crumbling conventions of Jim Crow. The advocacy of employing "any means" to preserve segregation and disfranchisement by such politicians as Theodore Bilbo might well have encouraged people to resort to physical methods. Thus, in certain areas, violence appeared to have official condonation. Certainly, the perpetrators of lynchings and riots found numerous apologists for their activities. The special importance, however, of these

47 Memphis *Commercial Appeal*, July 6, 1946; McKellar to Crump, July 1, 1946, Crump to McKellar, July 5, 1946, Paul B. Carr to McKellar, June 28, 1946, in McKellar Papers.
48 Memphis *Commercial Appeal*, August 2, 3, 1946.

interracial conflagrations lay less in their causes than in their political effects. Civil rights leaders became more determined to force the federal government to provide protection for Negroes in the South against discrimination. A new campaign was undertaken to publicize their plight. This time they were successful. President Truman decided that he had more to lose by inaction. He therefore finally agreed to order a review of the whole racial system in the United States.

There was one riot in particular which attracted public attention in the North. This occurred in February, 1946, in the small town of Columbia in central Tennessee. There were conflicting versions of what actually happened, but it appears that the facts were as follows. Columbia was the seat of Maury County, which had about twelve thousand Negroes in its total population of forty thousand. Columbia itself was a typical small southern town, with Negroes living in a separate residential section. It was not noted for its amicable race relations. There had been two lynchings within the previous twenty years, and in 1943 there had been a minor racial disturbance. Suspicion and animosity had risen to a new peak after the war when soldiers returned home to find a shortage of jobs and Negro veterans demanded voting rights. In this atmosphere of mistrust, a black woman and her son had a disagreement with a white radio electrician, who fell, perhaps as the result of a push, through the plate glass window of his repair shop. The two Negroes were immediately arrested on an assault charge. However, this did not prevent rumors of a pending riot and lynching from circulating throughout the white and black sectors of town. Negroes began to fear for their lives. Within a short period four policemen were wounded in a shooting incident. The state highway patrol subsequently descended on Mink Slide, the local nickname for the Negro business section, and arrested about a hundred residents. The police swoop, however, was conducted with considerable lack of restraint. The black community had barricaded itself into shops and houses. The police forcibly entered homes, arrested their occupants, and caused devastating damage. A number of Negroes were wounded in these raids—estimates of the injured varied from ten to sixty.[49]

Tension remained high in Columbia, while about seven hundred state guardsmen kept vigil. The local gaol was overcrowded with the victims of the police raid. On February 28, under mysterious circumstances, two of the Negro prisoners were shot to death and a deputy sheriff was wounded in an affray inside the cells. The deaths of these prisoners converted the Columbia affair into a national *cause célèbre*. Malcolm Ross, chairman of the FEPC, expressed his "deep concern" about the riot and recommended that Truman authorize an official investigation into community tensions.[50] Attorney General Tom C. Clark ordered the local U.S. attorney to investigate possible infringements of civil rights statutes and to draw any such violations to the attention of the convening grand jury.[51] Walter White announced that the NAACP would carry out its own investigation and promised free legal counsel to Columbia's Negroes. He was also instrumental in forming the National Committee for Justice in Columbia, Tennessee, under the cochairmanship of Dr. Channing Tobias and Eleanor Roosevelt. This committee sought to publicize the proceedings in Columbia and to raise funds for the defense of the twenty-five Negroes who were finally indicted.[52]

The grand jury hearings and the trial of the Columbia Negroes were reported fully in the national press. This was due largely to the publicity tactics of the NAACP and one or two

---

49 Guy B. Johnson, "What Happened at Columbia?" *New South*, I (May 1946), 1–8; White, *A Man Called White*, 309–12; Memphis *Commercial Appeal*, February 26, 27, March 1, 2, 1946; memo for the file, February 26, 1944, in Box 4, Nash Papers.
50 Memo, Malcolm Ross to HST, March 1, 1946, in RG 228–69, Office Files of Malcolm Ross, FEPC Records (copy also in OF 93 C, Truman Papers).
51 Memo, Tom C. Clark to Horace Frierson, March 21, 1946, in OF 93 C, Truman Papers.
52 Memphis *Commercial Appeal*, March 3, 1946; memo, Walter White to Eleanor Roosevelt, Arthur Spingarn, and Channing Tobias, April 22, 1946, in Box 342/1, NAACP Files.

other rival organizations which sought to boost their reputations by aiding the defendants. The trial, with its national press coverage, its rivalry between civil rights organizations for the right to represent the defendants, and its elevation into a showcase of southern justice, bore considerable resemblance to the Scottsboro affair of the 1930s. For a while, outsiders viewed Columbia as a microcosm of the South. Walter White hoped that if the matter were kept in the public eye it might help "prevent a repetition of the use of police and mob terror against Negro communities."[53] Civil rights organizations were determined to convince southerners that the nation as a whole would no longer tolerate the speedy justice usually meted out to Negroes. Furthermore, they warned that "downtrodden Negroes" would resort to "a policy of resistance" if "their lives were endangered."[54] Needless to say, defensive southerners reacted with hostility to the adverse publicity. They were particularly disturbed by the NAACP's assumption of responsibility for the defense and by the embarrassing fund-raising campaigns by the National Committee for Justice in Columbia in the North. A white Tennessee banker chided: "The people of the South are getting fed up with the offensive propaganda by self-appointed ignoramuses who feel themselves divinely appointed to evangelize the South."[55]

Despite the efforts of the NAACP and defense counsel, there were no prosecutions arising from the killing of the two Negro prisoners. Nor, indeed, was the case moved to a federal court, which could, of course, consider possible violations of federal civil rights laws.[56] Their only preliminary victory lay

53 Walter White to Ulric Bell, June 11, 1946, in Box 342/1, NAACP Files. The Civil Rights Congress, which had been frequently dubbed "Communist," vied with the NAACP to represent the defendants. White, *A Man Called White*, 315–17.
54 Norfolk *Journal and Guide*, March 9, 1946; *Crisis*, LIII (April, 1946).
55 Walter McElreath to Carl Van Doren, May 14, 1946, in Box 342/1, NAACP Files.
56 Pittsburgh *Courier*, June 22, 1946; Memphis *Commercial Appeal*, March 23, June 15, 18, 1946; Johnson, "What Happened at Columbia?" 6. Defense

in their ability to persuade the judge to order the case to be heard in a neighboring county, where the all-white jury might be less biased. The trial itself was characterized by cantankerous charges from the prosecution, which reserved most of its invective for the defense and its backers. Paul Bumpus, the prosecuting attorney, continuously harped upon the Yankee origins of the defense and the unfavorable press coverage. His summing up, described by the Washington *Post* as a "really terrifying flood of hatred," was a constant barrage of expletives against northerners, Negroes, and "ski's" ("Eleanorski"). In spite of these tactics, only two of the twenty-five defendants were found guilty; the others were acquitted. The civil rights groups were understandably encouraged.[57]

The profound sectional animosity which prevailed at Columbia worsened whenever new racial incidents arose. Each time a case of violence or overt discrimination was reported, civil rights organizations and other liberal groups would hail the new atrocity as further examples of endemic southern bigotry. The defendants of southernism would retaliate by accusing these critics of self-righteous interference. Furthermore, they blamed the militancy of Negroes and the aggressive defensiveness of southern whites on the unjustified exhortations from Yankees. The upholders of the racial status quo insisted that the wave of violent incidents would never have occurred without this intrusion. Governor Fielding Wright of Mississippi insisted that a recent shooting incident in Sullivan's Hollow was caused by hatred generated "by meddling outside interference."[58] Civil rights leaders had no need to refute

---

lawyers claimed that the FBI had been biased against the defendants when it had conducted its own separate investigations. See Thurgood Marshall to J. Edgar Hoover, May 10, 1946, Marshall to Eleanor Roosevelt, October 28, 1946, in Box 342/1, NAACP Files; Pittsburgh *Courier*, July 13, 1946.
57 Washington *Post*, October 6, 7, 1946; Pittsburgh *Courier*, October 12, 1946; Memphis *Commercial Appeal*, October 5, 1946.
58 Fielding Wright to Walter White, August 20, 1946, White to Wright, August 27, 1946, in Box 236/5, NAACP Files; White to NAACP Branch

these charges. As far as they were concerned, the revival of the Ku Klux Klan, the rantings of Bilbo and Talmadge, the horrifying blinding of a uniformed Negro veteran in South Carolina, and the Columbia riot fully justified their criticisms of Dixie's racial practices. And, whether southerners liked it or not, as a result of profound political and demographic changes over the previous decade, the race issue was no longer a southern question but a national one. Or, rather, it was a national issue which had not yet been politicized. Civil rights leaders still needed a dramatic event that would finally persuade the federal government that it could no longer deal with the problem of civil rights on an impromptu basis. It was time, they argued, for the government to commit itself to the obliteration of the root causes of racial prejudice, not merely its manifestations. Such an incident soon occurred.

At the end of July, 1946, a brutal murder was perpetrated near the small town of Monroe in Georgia. The incident had come only one week after Talmadge's victory in Georgia's vituperative gubernatorial contest. Walton County, where the murders were committed, had been tense on election day when a number of Negroes had voted for the first time in a Democratic primary. Just before the crimes, according to the testimony given by a Walton County Negro to the NAACP, two blacks had been involved in an altercation with a group of whites after they had registered to vote. The tension and suspicions in the community finally exploded a few days later when a band of whites shot two Negroes, Roger Malcolm and George Dorsey, who had been traveling by car with their wives and a white Georgia farmer. (The farmer had just put up bond for Malcolm, who had been charged with stabbing

---

Presidents, August 21, 1946, in Box 236/4, NAACP Files; Statement of J. Edgar Hoover, Proceedings of the President's Committee on Civil Rights, April 30, 1947, pp. 79–113, in Records of the President's Committee on Civil Rights, Harry S. Truman Library, Independence, Mo.; White, *A Man Called White*, 325–28; Kennedy, *Southern Exposure*, 171–76.

a former employer.) When one of the wives recognized a member of the lynch party, the mob riddled the two women with bullets.[59]

Public reaction was instant and horrified—especially when it was learned that on the same day another Negro in Georgia's Taylor County had been murdered after he had voted. It seemed that lynch law would become widespread unless the Department of Justice acted promptly to bring the murderers to court. In the North, journalists readily attributed the shootings directly to Talmadge's racist incitements. The headline of the Pittsburgh *Courier* ran: "Talmadge 'Hate Campaign' Responsible for Georgia Mass Murders." [60] An article in *PM*, a leftist New York daily, proclaimed that "the season on 'nigger' was automatically opened, and every pinheaded Georgia cracker and bigoted Ku Kluxer figured he had a hunting license." [61] Even the less involved critics believed that the lynchings were a culmination of recent political developments in the South. Everywhere, liberals believed that the apprehension of the lynch mob was insufficient. It was time, they said, for federal legislation to protect the basic civil rights of southern Negroes.[62] Within hours of the news, the National Association of Colored Women organized picket lines outside the White House. President Truman was inundated with protests from all parts of the country. He was clearly sympathetic to their cause. He immediately instructed the Justice Department to investigate the lynching and "any other crimes of oppression" and to ascertain whether the perpetrators could be indicted under federal law. The day after he ordered the

59 Atlanta *Constitution*, July 27, 28, 1946; Washington *Post*, July 27, 1946; copy, testimony of Willie Johnson, White to Tom Clark, August 12, 1946, in Box 236/4, NAACP Files.
60 Pittsburgh *Courier*, August 3, 1946.
61 Clipping, *PM*, July 28, 1946, in Box 236/4, NAACP Files.
62 Eugene M. Martin to White, July 24, 1946, Martin to White, July 26, 1946, telegram, White to Arnall, July 31, 1946, in Box 236/4, NAACP Files; Atlanta *Constitution*, July 28, 1946; *New South*, I (August, 1946).

FBI investigation, Truman confirmed his belief in the necessity of a federal anti-lynching bill.[63]

The nation had scarcely recovered from the shock of the Monroe massacre, when another brutal lynching was carried out two weeks later near Minden, in North Louisiana. After a survivor of this new atrocity recounted his horrendous experience, the Negro press and other civil rights organizations intensified their campaigns to persuade Truman to take measures to improve the lot of Negroes in the South. Piecemeal legislation would no longer suffice. They wanted the president personally to lend his moral support in a campaign to ameliorate the racial climate and to use his political authority to secure comprehensive civil rights legislation. Walter White warned that Negroes were so pessimistic about governmental protection that they might soon resort to "armed resistance." [64]

Civil rights leaders made speeches, produced press releases, and organized demonstrations in their campaign to enlist the president's support. Their activities were coordinated by the National Emergency Committee Against Mob Violence, which was formed in August. This new interracial group was successful in securing an appointment with Truman, and its executive committee went to the White House on September 19 to confer with the president about the racial crisis in the South. The delegation consisted of Walter White, James Carey, secretary of the CIO, Boris Shiskin, an economist for the AF of L and a former member of the FEPC, Dr. Herman Reissig of the Federal Council of the Churches of Christ in America, Dr.

---

63 *Public Papers, 1946,* p. 368; Washington *Post,* July 30, 31, 1946; assorted telegrams, in OF 93 A, Truman Papers.
64 Statement by Walter White, NAACP Release, August 16, 1946, NAACP Release, August 29, 1946, affidavit of Albert Harris, Jr., in Box 236/3, NAACP Files; Atlanta *Constitution,* August 16, 1946. In the spring of 1947 the local jury, in an atmosphere of sectional prejudice, racism, and public antipathy to the FBI, acquitted the Minden defendants. Memo, Fred Folsom to Robert K. Carr, re *U.S.* v. *O. H. Haynes, Jr.,* in Box 15, Matthews Papers; statement of J. Edgar Hoover, Proceedings of the President's Committee on Civil Rights, March 20, 1947, statement of Tom Clark, Proceedings of the President's Committee on Civil Rights, April 3, 1947, in Records of the President's Committee on Civil Rights.

Channing Tobias, director of the Phelps-Stokes Fund, and Leslie Perry, an NAACP administrative assistant. The president spoke with the men at length. He seemed clearly disturbed by their assessments. "We've got to do something," he agreed in an apparent tone of desperation. David Niles, a White House administrative assistant, who was also present, suggested that Truman should set up a special committee on civil rights to investigate the status of minority groups and to recommend a program of corrective action. The president and the National Emergency Committee concurred that the establishment of such an investigatory body was desirable. Truman envisaged that this would be a first step toward the formulation of a comprehensive federal program. He assured the delegation that he regarded existing laws as imperfect and that further legislation was "imperative." [65]

Truman kept the promise he had made to White, although he deliberately stalled for time. In December he issued an executive order which established the President's Committee on Civil Rights, consisting of fifteen distinguished leaders of business, religious, and academic organizations. The committee, under the chairmanship of Charles E. Wilson, president of General Electric, was directed to advise the president how current law-enforcement measures "may be strengthened and improved to safeguard the civil rights of the people." In addition, it was to recommend "adequate and effective" means, "by legislation or otherwise," of protecting these rights.[66]

The announcement of the creation of the Committee on Civil Rights was timed to minimize any political repercussions

[65] White had also wanted Ellis Arnall to join the group, but the latter was unable to attend. White to Arnall, September 21, 1946, Arnall to White, September 23, 1946, in Box 359/3, NAACP Files; White, *A Man Called White*, 329–31; William C. Berman, "The Politics of Civil Rights in the Truman Administration" (Ph.D. dissertation, Ohio State University, 1963), 36–46; Shiskin, interview.

[66] Executive Order 9808, *3 CFR, 1943–1948*, p. 590; *Statement of the President*, December 5, 1946, in Box 26, Nash Papers; Harry S. Truman, *Memoirs: The Years of Trial and Hope* (Signet ed.; New York, 1965), II, 210–11.

from the South. The president realized that its establishment might cause a stir south of the Potomac. He therefore waited until after the midterm elections and deliberately announced its formation while Congress was in recess. He knew that some southerners might view this development as another milestone in the disintegration of the Democratic party. Although Truman had not made any new, specific commitments to Negroes since his letter to Sabath in 1945, he had now authorized a full-scale study of the South's racial practices. There was more potential danger in this for the South than the occasional gesture on the poll tax or employment opportunities. Truman hoped, however, that southerners would not view the committee in this light. Perhaps they could see it as a temporizing measure, a mere investigatory and fact-finding commission. But there was really little chance of this. Southerners knew where his personal sympathies lay and were unhappily aware of his commitment to the urban coalition. They noticed that the only two southerners serving on the committee were renowned liberals—Dr. Frank Graham and Mrs. Dorothy Tilly of the Women's Society of Christian Science. Indeed, Truman had not made a mere moral and personal gesture. He had made an irreversible commitment to the cause of civil rights. Racial discrimination would no longer be a problem for individuals to solve among themselves. The gamut of race relations had become a political issue—probably the most divisive one of the twentieth century.[67]

67 Looseleaf notebook, interview notes for Daniels' biography of the president, in Box 85, Daniels Papers; White to William Hastie, September 26, 1946, in Box 359/3, NAACP Files; clipping, Shreveport *Times*, February 13, 1947, in Box 25, Nash Papers; Memphis *Commercial Appeal*, December 16, 1946; Truman, *Memoirs*, II, 210–11; Reynold J. Davis, "A Study of Federal Civil Rights Programs During the Presidency of Harry S. Truman" (M.A. thesis, University of Kansas, 1959), 51.

CHAPTER SEVEN

"The South Can Be Considered Safely Democratic": Washington, 1947

Sᴇᴄᴛɪᴏɴᴀʟ ill-feeling among Democrats was translated into personal terms before members of the Eightieth Congress even took their seats. Neither southerners nor northerners seemed prepared to seek means of restoring unity to the party. Both factions were anxious to mold the Democratic party in their own image. Each wing hoped the party would stake out its ideology clearly and unequivocally for the electorate. Northern Democrats, particularly from urban areas, generally hoped that the Fair Deal would be vigorously championed and firmly imprinted on the party's platform. Most southerners, on the other hand, wanted to change the direction of the administration's policies. It should, they argued, be more sensitive to the needs of business, more sympathetic to the ideals of individualism, and less missionary in its egalitarianism. Yet these conflicting goals were not expressed in words or votes only during debates on individual bills. Each side believed it was essential to enjoy strategic supremacy on the floors of Congress. It was thus necessary to expunge their opponents from positions of influence or prestige. This emphasis on the composition and hierarchial structure of the Democratic party resulted in several affrays that were not only political in their nature, but personal as well—and personal differences often left more lasting scars.

Southern Democrats in the House of Representatives thought about the problem of leadership as soon as the results of the 1946 election were known. They were determined that their minority leader should be a fellow southerner. The position of floor leader is especially important, because he is the instrument of accommodation between conflicting forces within his own party and is responsible for keeping the president informed of opinions within the rank and file. Since southerners constituted a majority of House Democrats in the Eightieth Congress, they felt entitled to a party leader from their section. They believed a northerner would ignore their political preferences to bulldoze reform legislation through Congress. Accordingly, Dixie Democrats overwhelmingly supported the outgoing speaker of the House, Sam Rayburn, for the post. Rayburn himself was initially reluctant to assume the position. He felt that he could exercise more influence as an ordinary member of the House and was himself more interested in results than in ideology. He therefore believed that on pragmatic grounds the one official floor leader should be a northerner, since, "if we ever come into power again, we must have a great many Northern votes." [1] Democrats from the North obviously agreed with him. They favored the staunch New Dealer from Massachusetts, John W. McCormack, who had been majority leader in the previous Congress. Because of this overwhelming preference among northerners, Rayburn, true to his sense of political realism, endorsed McCormack for the leadership.

Representatives from Dixie, however, united to persuade Rayburn to accept their draft. They pointed out that McCormack would not have the confidence of the majority of House Democrats and that his selection would accentuate the ascendancy within the party of ideas totally alien to southerners. Eugene Cox of Georgia reminded Rayburn of the sectional fragility of the party and warned that if the Bostonian were

---

1 Rayburn to John H. Kerr, December 16, 1946, Rayburn to Estes Kefauver, December, 1946, Rayburn to Harold D. Cooley, December, 1946, in Miscellaneous Files 1946, Rayburn Papers.

elected to the leadership, "the rift within the rank of the House Democrats will be wider than that between the Democrats and Republicans." [2] The traditionalists were not the only ones who feared this degree of disaffection and isolation. Southern liberals also wanted Rayburn. They even feared the possible creation of a third party if the southerners were not courted.[3] The most articulate argument for Rayburn's nomination, however, came from Congressman F. Edward Hébert of Louisiana. In a long letter to Rayburn, Hébert explained the South's reasons for drafting him. He argued that the Democratic setback in the 1946 elections was due to the failure of the party leadership to follow "more closely the ideals and principles espoused by those of us who make up the old fashioned Democratic Party from the South." Hébert was convinced that a more conservative orientation would insure success for the Democrats in 1948. McCormack, he said, was not popular in the South and would be resented for the duration of the Congress. The Democrats had reached a crucial stage in their history. "Now with the members from the so-called solid South in irrefutable domination of the Democratic side," he admonished, "I am sure you readily recognize the fact that this schism on the part of the Southern members becomes more widened instead of being closed." Hébert closed his letter by pleading that "you and you alone can heal this sore." [4] John McCormack, too, realized that his own nomination would exacerbate divisions. He thus urged Rayburn to accept the leadership to reconcile the North and South. Rayburn reluctantly acquiesced, but realized within a short time that he was quite powerless to prevent further splintering in the Democratic party.[5]

2 Eugene E. Cox to Rayburn, December 30, 1946, in Miscellaneous Files 1946, Rayburn Papers.
3 Kefauver to Rayburn, November 9, 1946, John Sparkman to Rayburn, November 11, 1946, Cooley to Rayburn, December 5, 1946, Kenneth Romney to Rayburn, November 9, 1946, in Miscellaneous Files 1946, Rayburn Papers.
4 F. Edward Hébert to Rayburn, November 22, 1946, in Miscellaneous Files 1946, Rayburn Papers.
5 John McCormack to Rayburn, November 22, 1946, clipping, Dallas *Times-Herald*, January 2, 1947, in Miscellaneous Files 1946, Rayburn Papers.

There was an even more controversial dispute in progress in the Senate. Again, the basic point at issue was the South's growing isolation from the mainstream of the Democratic party. In this particular case, the focus of contention was on Senator Theodore Bilbo of Mississippi. After his virulent primary campaign in the summer of 1946, a number of civil rights leaders had pressed the Senate to conduct an official inquiry into Bilbo's tactics. They hoped if the allegations of impropriety were substantiated by an investigating committee, then Bilbo could be expelled from the Senate. An extensive crusade was waged by Negro leaders to press for Bilbo's exclusion from the Senate. The Pittsburgh *Courier* conducted a "Bilbo Must Go" campaign, and the Civil Rights Congress formed a National Committee to Oust Bilbo.[6] In response to these demands the Senate had created a Special Committee to Investigate Campaign Expenditures to inquire into the charges against the Mississippian. However, all three Democratic members of this ad hoc committee came from the South. Chairman Allen Ellender of Louisiana, Burnet Maybank of South Carolina, and Elmer Thomas of Oklahoma were all notoriously antipathetic to the Negro.

The committee went to Mississippi at the beginning of December to hold open hearings on the charges against Bilbo. A few witnesses who appeared before it were scared or overawed by the blatantly hostile posture of the Democratic members. Nevertheless, it was apparent from the testimony of the members of the predominantly Negro Mississippi Progressive Voters' League that Bilbo had acted in a threatening and intimidating manner. The complainants convincingly showed that Negroes had been "subjected to a campaign and reign of terror" during the primary.[7] Altogether, 102 witnesses testified. Two thirds of them were Negroes, most of whom recounted—or implied by

6 Pittsburgh *Courier*, September 14, November 23, 30, 1946.
7 *Hearings on Bilbo Campaign, 1946*, pp. 3–6. See also Charles M. LaFollette, "The Case Against Bilboism," unpublished document, October 21, 1946, in Box 42, Stephen J. Spingarn Papers, Harry S. Truman Library, Independence, Mo.

their silence—their fears and ordeals during the July primary. There was hardly any contradictory or conflicting evidence from the black witnesses. A few were bulldozed into a telling bout of stammering, but most of them confirmed the allegations that had been leveled against the senator earlier.

However, it came as no surprise when the majority report, signed by Ellender, Maybank, and Thomas, vindicated Bilbo by accepting his argument that Negroes had not been entitled to vote in the primary anyway. Under Mississippi law, a voter had to agree to support the primary winner in the general election, and he had to have been in accord with the party's principles for the previous two years. The majority argued that no Negro would have supported Bilbo in the November election under these conditions, since blacks naturally did not advocate white supremacy. They excused Bilbo's vituperative remarks and deemed them "justifiably directed at the attempted and unwarranted interference with the internal affairs of the state of Mississippi by outside agitators, seeking not to benefit the Negroes but merely to further their own selfish ends." On the other hand, the two Republican members, Styles Bridges of New Hampshire and Bourke Hickenlooper of Iowa, found that Bilbo had violated the law by his use of coercion and intimidation and that his conduct had been a "mockery of the democratic process and a prostitution of majority rule." [8]

The findings of the majority did not convince Bilbo's opponents. They realized it was unlikely that, as southerners, the three Democrats would have condemned their colleague. To his critics Bilbo represented the typical product of a bigoted, benighted South. They hoped to strike a blow at southern racism by persuading the Senate to expel its most notorious racist. The NAACP conducted a massive campaign to persuade senators to proceed with banishment. They pointed out that the record of the Ellender hearings provided overwhelming evidence that Bilbo had conducted a virulent campaign in violation of basic

8 Report 1 on Investigation of Senatorial Campaign Expenditures, 1946, p. 22.

political ethics. Bilbo, they claimed, had scant respect for the law. He had even accepted graft from war contractors and was not deserving of public office.[9] Nevertheless, Bilbo had a contingent of defenders. His southern associates realized that expulsion from the Senate would represent an official repudiation of the political system upon which Bilbo and his fellow Dixie senators relied for their continual reelection. Bilbo himself emphasized this aspect in his personal campaign to secure solidarity among southern senators. He wrote to Richard B. Russell of Georgia: "Because of my militant representation of my racial views and my fight for the South and the white race that there are a lot of folks who would like to unseat me for no other reason than that they do not agree with my racial ideologies." He attributed the expulsion movement to the desire to attract northern Negro votes.[10] His fellow members appreciated the sectional undertones of the exclusion campaign and determined to support their colleague. "Regardless of the merits of the Bilbo case," prejudged Tennessee's Kenneth McKellar, "I am more opposed to those who are fighting him than I could ever possibly be opposed to him." [11]

The controversy came to a head as soon as the Senate convened in January, 1947. The Senate Republican Steering Committee, headed by Robert Taft of Ohio, led the move to exclude Bilbo. Taft, the architect of the plan, resolved that the Senate should bar Bilbo at the door and refuse him his seat. Under Senate rules this could be done on a simple motion, requiring only a majority vote. If Bilbo had been allowed to take his seat,

9 Charles H. Houston to Allen Ellender, December 16, 1946, Thurgood Marshall to Tom Clark, January 23, 1947, in Box 359/1, NAACP Files; the Reverend C. R. White and L. M. Jackson to Hoey, December 16, 1946, in Hoey Papers; *Southern Weekly*, October 30, 1946; Washington *Post*, January 3, 1947; Ellender, interview; A. Wigfall Green, *The Man Bilbo* (Baton Rouge, 1963), 113–17.

10 Bilbo to Richard B. Russell, December 23, 1946, in Bilbo Papers; Bilbo to McKellar, December 30, 1946, in McKellar Papers.

11 McKellar to A. B. Broadbent, January 4, 1947, in McKellar Papers; Hoey to the Reverend C. R. White, December 21, 1946, in Hoey Papers; Ellender, interview.

then a two-thirds majority in the Senate would have been necessary to expel him. Such a majority would have been more difficult to obtain and would have enabled Bilbo, an experienced
practitioner of the filibuster, to use this device to prevent such
a motion from ever being put. Taft's own interest in the matter
was a mixture of principle and political expediency. He genuinely believed that Bilbo was a slur on the Senate's reputation.
He had always eschewed demagogy and emotionalism in politics and was an exponent of the genteel political tradition of
the mugwumps. But he also knew that he could embarrass the
Democrats by excluding one of their senators. In this way he
could focus public attention on the fact that the Democratic
party consisted of confirmed racists as well as committed liberals.[12]

On January 3, 1947, senators who had been elected before
November, 1946, and were, therefore, already sworn in, took
their seats. They then agreed to swear in the newly elected
senators in alphabetical order. When Bilbo, who was second on
the list, was called upon to take the oath, Democratic Senator
Glen Taylor of Idaho submitted a resolution which maintained
that Bilbo's credentials were "tainted with fraud and corruption"
and requested the Senate to exclude the Mississippian until further investigations were carried out.[13] Senator John Overton of
Louisiana immediately rose to offer a substitute amendment to
seat him, but "without prejudice" to Bilbo or to the right of the
Senate to consider his case subsequently. Overton's substitute
motion was overruled by a curious combination of votes. The
Republicans were unanimously in favor of excluding Bilbo without further ado. The Democrats, however, were split in an embarrassing fashion. Two southerners, Claude Pepper of Florida
and William Fulbright of Arkansas, voted with the Republicans
as did eight other nonsouthern Democrats. However, some of
the Senate's most notable leaders, such as Scott Lucas of Illinois,

12 Ellender, interview; White, *The Taft Story*, passim.
13 *Congressional Record*, 80th Cong., 1st Sess., 7–8, 13–31.

James Murray of Montana, and Alben Barkley, supported the southerners in their opposition to exclusion. Clearly the Democratic leadership was unwilling to repudiate Bilbo at this stage. To do so would be seen as an affront to all Dixie Democrats. The southerners, however, did not trust their volatile allies. They kept talking to prevent a motion to exclude Bilbo from being put. Senator Ellender led the southern force. He told his associates that the proceedings were an unwarranted assault on his section. Bilbo, he argued, had become the South's sacrificial martyr. Senators were using the case to establish their credentials with liberals. He complained that while 75 percent of American Negroes lived in the South, "the North has been trying to tell us what to do about them." He condemned the administration for courting the black vote and revealed his real fear that if Bilbo were expelled, then other white supremacists could be similarly excluded. "The march is on to destroy Southern traditions which are as deeply rooted as the giants of the forest," he exclaimed.[14] However, it was neither Taft nor Ellender who resolved the impasse. It soon became known that Bilbo had to return South to undergo surgery for a throat complaint. Barkley requested unanimous consent that Bilbo's credentials should lie on the table and that the remaining senators should be sworn in. This consent was given. Fortunately for the Democratic leaders, the issue never arose again. Bilbo did not return to Washington. In August of that year he died from cancer.[15]

Senator Ellender, who recalled that the dispute over Bilbo's seat was "the only black mark between me and Senator Taft," could not commend his relationship with Truman as highly.[16] Personal rebukes may be harder to forget than philosophical differences, and in the saga of Dixie's political estrangement there were important, though infrequent, personal clashes which

14 *Ibid.*, 77–79.
15 *Ibid.*, 108–109; New York *Times*, January 5, 1947; Washington *Post*, January 5, 1947.
16 Ellender, interview.

turned Democrats away from the president. Personal grudges, of course, are familiar landmarks on the political landscape. All politicians have to face repudiation and ostracism. Nevertheless, when these are sufficiently dramatic, or, alternately, where the people concerned are sufficiently sensitive, political configurations can change dramatically. One dispute in the opening weeks of the Eightieth Congress involved the prestige of a veteran southern senator. This was Kenneth McKellar of Tennessee, who found himself embroiled once again with the president in a bitter conflict over his personal bugbear, David Lilienthal. As a result of this dispute, McKellar decided to withdraw his support from the administration on a number of key issues. His grievance serves to remind one that ideology and material interest were not the sole factors determining political attitudes.

The president had nominated Lilienthal to serve as chairman of the newly created Atomic Energy Commission. Throughout his distinguished career as chairman of the Tennessee Valley Authority, Lilienthal had been faced with Senator McKellar's continual personal attacks. McKellar had resented Lilienthal's broad powers to organize TVA finances and appoint personnel and had previously accused him of harboring communists.[17] When Truman, to McKellar's horror, nominated Lilienthal to head the Atomic Energy Commission, the Tennessean found another opportunity to smear him with charges of radicalism— and also to refute the popular belief that he had opposed Lilienthal earlier mainly because of differences affecting the pork barrel. The senator determined to defeat his new appointment. His resolve not only constituted a vendetta against Lilienthal but also was in retaliation against Truman's circumvention of senatorial courtesy.

Hearings on the Lilienthal nomination were held before the Senate Committee on Atomic Energy. Although McKellar was not a member of this committee, he exercised his right under

17 Thiel, "Kenneth D. McKellar and the Politics of the Tennessee Valley Authority," 76–127.

Senate rules to attend the hearings and to interrogate witnesses. His examinations were often intemperate, unjust, unsupported by facts, and occasionally tainted with anti-Semitism.[18] He said that Lilienthal was "the head Communist in my state,"[19] "an errant rascal and I believe a lying thief."[20] However, McKellar was unable to persuade a majority of his colleagues to join his crusade. Robert Taft, somewhat ironically, was the only major Republican leader to support him. His fellow southerners were equally unimpressed by his arguments and made it clear they approved of Lilienthal's nomination. Thus, McKellar was unable to create a sectional issue of the controversy.[21] When it became apparent that Truman would stand by his decision to nominate Lilienthal and that the appointment would be endorsed by the Senate, McKellar decided to strike a personal blow at the president by withdrawing his cooperation, particularly on foreign policy.[22] He knew that Truman was developing a new approach toward Soviet expansion in Europe and that the president would rely heavily on Senate leaders to foster a bipartisan alliance in foreign affairs. So, only five days before Truman was due to make public his program for aid to Greece and Turkey, Mc-Kellar, obviously in a distressed state, wrote to the president and declined an invitation to attend a White House conference on loans to Europe. In a classic example of psychological projection the senator informed Truman:

My attendance at such a conference would not accomplish much in the present state of your mind concerning me and therefore I

18 Joseph P. Harris, *The Advice and Consent of the Senate* (Berkeley and Los Angeles, 1953), 155–77; David E. Lilienthal, *The Journals of David E. Lilienthal, II: The Atomic Energy Years, 1945–1950* (New York, 1950), 132–33, 144–47.

19 Memphis *Commercial Appeal*, January 27, 1947.

20 McKellar to John Wisdom, January 17, 1947, telegram, Murrel Holderby to McKellar, February 13, 1947, Edward O'Neal to McKellar, January 27, 1947, in McKellar Papers.

21 John Folger to HST, February 14, 1947, in OF 692 B, Truman Papers; Rayburn to Miss Reeves, March 14, 1947, in Miscellaneous Files 1947, Rayburn Papers; Washington *Post*, March 5, 1947; Harris, *The Advice and Consent of the Senate*, 163.

22 See *Public Papers, 1947*, p. 131.

must decline. In October you appointed David E. Lilienthal. . . .
You did not consult me or my colleague concerning this appointment.
. . . I had always been friendly with you while you were in the
Senate and when you became President you invited me, of course
because of my holding the position of President pro tempore of the
Senate, as a quasi member of your cabinet. I was also one of the
four members of Congress, Mr. Barkley, Mr. Rayburn and Mr.
McCormack being the others, who met you every Monday morning
at the White House to confer about all kinds of legislative and governmental matters. I always gave you the best I had to offer in these
conferences. I thought you and I were friends. But to appoint him
[Lilienthal] to what may be the foremost place in the world and
after you knew that I had opposed his former appointment to the
TVA and in view of his record as above stated, without a word to
me or to my colleague, seemed to me to be an intentional affront.[23]

Truman's reply that "there has never been anything but the
kindliest feelings on my part towards you," did not deter him.
Thereafter, McKellar opposed his party with increasing fre-
quency and vehemence.[24] And Lilienthal's appointment was
confirmed in the Senate by fifty votes to thirty-one.

Besides the heat produced over the Lilienthal nomination, relations between the president and Congress were relatively calm
for the first five months of the congressional session. After the
1946 elections, Truman thought that the electoral tide was
against him and accordingly played down his Fair Deal program
in his annual messages. Observers also believed that, as a result
of the November polls, Truman would not be a candidate in
1948 and would defer in the formulation of domestic policy to
his more conservative advisers and Capitol Hill. Indeed, a num-

23 McKellar to HST, March 7, 1947, in McKellar Papers.
24 HST to McKellar, March 11, 1947, in McKellar Papers. In 1947 McKellar
   voted in only 44 percent of roll call votes with the majority of his party on
   partisan divisions. On bipartisan roll call votes he voted only 65 percent
   of the times with the majority. The only Senate Democrats to vote more
   frequently against a majority on foreign policy were Taylor of Idaho,
   Murray of Montana, and O'Daniel of Texas. Murray and Taylor reflected
   the tradition of midwestern isolationism, while O'Daniel, who consistently
   voted against any majority, was a breed of his own. *Congressional Quarterly
   Almanac, 1947* (Washington, D.C., 1947), xxvi, xxvii; Susan M. Hartmann,
   "President Truman and the Eightieth Congress" (Ph.D. dissertation, University of Missouri, 1966), 119.

ber of associates counseled him to try to bridge some of the differences with his congressional critics, since they commanded a majority in Congress and could thwart the president's welfare designs. Truman also realized the need for solid bipartisan support in the embryonic stages of his European economic aid program and was unwilling to sour relations further.[25] He thus sought to meet some of the demands of congressional conservatives. As early as November, 1946, he ended all price controls except for those on sugar, rent, and rice—thus preempting the designs of southern Democrats and Republicans. Furthermore, on the last day of 1946 he proclaimed the official cessation of hostilities, thereby ending twenty government powers instantaneously and some thirty-three others at the end of six months, including those powers granted under the Smith-Connally Act.[26] Congressmen in both parties consequently anticipated a dampening of executive initiatives in domestic affairs commensurate with the extinction of the president's war powers.

In June, however, Truman changed his tactics. He began to understand that his conservative opposition could be converted from a source of hindrance to a source of strength. If he could demonstrate to disaffected liberals that his administration was prepared to forsake further support from the right, then they might be persuaded to proclaim him as their standard-bearer once more. The person most responsible for apprising Truman of this view was his young special counsel, Clark M. Clifford, who had become by mid-1947 the most intimate and influential of his advisers. This former St. Louis lawyer headed a small group of liberal White House aides who had been urging the president to move leftward and to reaffirm his position as the champion of the urban coalition. Clifford recalled years later: "Most of the Cabinet and congressional leaders were urging Mr. Truman

25 Richard E. Neustadt, "Congress and the Fair Deal: A Legislative Balance Sheet," *Public Policy*, V (1954), 360–62; Hartmann, "President Truman and the Eightieth Congress," 28.
26 *Public Papers, 1946*, pp. 475–77, 512–14; Executive Order 9801 and Proclamation 2714, 3 *CFR, 1943–1948*, pp. 583, 99–100.

to go slow, to veer a little closer to the conservative line. They held the image of Bob Taft before him like a bogeyman. We were pushing him the other way, urging him to boldness and to strike out for a new high ground . . . it was two forces fighting for the mind of the President, that's really what it was." [27] Truman saw his opportunity to strike out for this "new high ground" when he was presented in June with the Taft-Hartley labor-management relations bill, which had formed the core of the Republicans' domestic program. He realized that whatever course he took on the bill, there would be far-reaching consequences. If he approved the bill he would further alienate organized labor. If he vetoed it, he would incur the wrath of many southern Democrats, who had supported the measure overwhelmingly. Truman calculated that the latter result would reap its own paradoxical rewards.

After the president's veto of the Case bill in 1946, manufacturing and commercial organizations had intensified their campaigns for the revision of the Wagner Act. They claimed that the statute was unjust because it forced obligations on employers without corresponding restrictions on employees. Their greatest grievance was the guarantee under the Wagner Act of a closed-shop contract. The closed-shop guarantee provided that a union could insist on all workers becoming members as a condition of employment. Labor organizations contended that if workers were given "the right to work" (that is, permitted to opt out of union membership), their collective bargaining position would be undermined, since their agents then would not represent all the employees in any one unit. They reasoned, also, that nonunion members would receive benefits which they would not have paid for in dues and that workers would compete with one another and force down wage rates. Opponents of the closed shop, on the other hand, argued that

27 Irwin Ross, *The Loneliest Campaign: The Truman Victory of 1948* (New York, 1968), 19; also, Allen and Shannon, *The Truman Merry-Go-Round*, 58–59; Anderson, *The President's Men*, 115–18.

it frequently resulted in actions which were not approved of by the mass of employees and that it was un-American, because it deprived an individual worker of the right to choose between affiliation and independence. The closed shop, however, was only one of their complaints. Secondary and sympathy boycotts and jurisdictional strikes had sometimes crippled entire industries. In the same way, argued the advocates of union control, walkouts had often occurred before the collective bargaining process had been exhausted. Employers were thus eager to enforce a compulsory cooling-off period to prevent impulsive strike action.[28]

These demands for a major revision of the Wagner Act touched the right chords among members of Congress who were eager to dampen the labor and welfare reforms of the New Deal. Responding to the examples set in several state legislatures, they proceeded to amend the National Labor Relations Act in favor of the employers.[29] The House of Representatives, under the guidance of Fred Hartley, Republican from New Jersey, passed a bill severely hampering the operations of the unions. In addition to outlawing the closed shop and sympathy strikes, it also banned industry-wide bargaining—a stab at the

28 Circular, Southern States Industrial Council, *The Year of Opportunity*, January 10, 1947, in Southern States Industrial Council Folder, Truman Papers; E. G. Lackey to Hoey, January 13, 1947, Hoey to Lackey, January 17, 1947, Hoey to J. D. Wilkins, December 10, 1946, in Hoey Papers; Kerr, "Employer Policies in Industrial Relations, 1945 to 1947," 43–76; Lee, *Truman and Taft-Hartley*, 45–47; Millis and Brown, *From the Wagner Act to Taft-Hartley*, 334–40; Congress of Industrial Organizations, *The Case Against "Right to Work" Laws* (n.p. [presumably Washington, D.C.], n.d. [probably 1955]), 73–96.

29 Sixteen state legislatures outlawed the closed shop in 1947. Of these, six were in the South. See David Ziskind, "Countermarch in Labor Legislation," in Warne (ed.), *Labor in Postwar America*, 317; Millis and Brown, *From the Wagner Act to Taft-Hartley*, 326–32, 345–46; John A. McPherson to J. Strom Thurmond, April 18, 1947, J. C. McKinney to Thurmond, April 16, 1947, in Anti-Closed Shop File, J. Strom Thurmond Papers, South Caroliniana Library, Columbia, S.C. (All references to the Thurmond Papers, unless otherwise stated, are from the collection in the South Caroliniana Library.) Frank T. De Vyer, "The Present Status of Labor Unions in the South, 1948," *Southern Economic Journal*, XVI (July, 1949), 1–22; CIO, *The Case Against "Right to Work" Laws*, 43–44, 60.

CIO that southerners particularly welcomed. Indeed, southerners gave the bill their overwhelming support. Only sixteen of the ninety-five southerners who passed through the division lobbies voted against the bill. By contrast, only fourteen non-southern Democrats voted with the proponents of the Hartley bill, and most of these came from rural areas. In the Senate, where the somewhat milder Taft bill was passed by sixty-eight votes to twenty-four, only three Dixie senators, Hill, Pepper, and Olin Johnston, voted with northern Democrats against the proposal. The final conference measure, the Taft-Hartley bill, met most of the criticisms that had been leveled against the Wagner Act by employers. It outlawed the closed shop, banned jurisdictional and sympathy strikes, imposed a sixty-day cooling-off period, prohibited a compulsory checkoff, made unions suable for breach of contract, and forbade unions to spend money during election campaigns. The advocates of the Taft-Hartley bill were confident that these provisions would curb the economic power of the unions and their political influence.[30]

President Truman was well aware of the profound political implications of the Taft-Hartley bill. It was a highly controversial measure about which few people felt indifferent. There had not been a more controversial bill before Congress since the New Deal, at least in domestic policy. The White House mail room received about half a million telegrams on the subject in one week. Public meetings were held throughout the country either to praise or condemn the measure.[31] Truman knew that his attitude toward the bill would determine his political image for the 1948 election, so he needed to be sure that his forthcoming veto had substantial support within the party as a whole.

30 *Congressional Record*, 80th Cong., 1st Sess., 3670, 5117; Lee, *Truman and Taft-Hartley*, 75–77; Millis and Brown, *From the Wagner Act to Taft-Hartley*, 395–481.
31 Memo, mail room to Clifford, June 12, 1947, in Labor Files, Clifford Papers; Lee, *Truman and Taft-Hartley*, 81–85. See also, memo, Louis Sherman to Lewis Schwellenbach, June 5, 1947, in RG 174-190, General Subject File, Department of Labor Archives, Files of Secretary Lewis B. Schwellenbach.

There is no evidence that he even seriously considered signing the bill. After all, he had presented himself as a champion of social welfare legislation from the beginning of his presidency. But he still felt the need to measure the intensity of feeling within the party, particularly among southern Democrats.

Truman decided to sound out opinion among local party officials. He instructed Gael Sullivan, executive director of the Democratic National Committee, to discover the views of party members on the Taft-Hartley bill. The results of Sullivan's queries were revealing and provided Truman with a useful yardstick for future political strategy. Taken as a whole, a sizable majority of the respondents to Sullivan's questionnaire recommended that Truman veto the bill. Ninety-five officials urged him to veto, while sixty-four wanted him to sign it. However, the southerners did not reflect this nationwide trend. Of the thirty-seven replies from southern Democrats, twenty-nine recommended that Truman sign the bill, while only eight advised disapproval. Thus, Dixie's local leaders, who in electoral terms were so influential, overwhelmingly advised Truman to ignore the strong representations of the labor unions by approving the revision of this cornerstone of New Deal legislation. Party officials from below the Potomac believed that Truman could rehabilitate himself politically if he emancipated himself from organized labor. If he did not take this final opportunity to do so, then southerners could no longer realistically support the Democratic party. They believed a veto would be "disastrous" and could result in the final breakup of the solid South. Gessner McCorvey of Alabama wrote that if the president acted in accordance with the wishes of Alabamians and signed the bill, his state's delegation "will have the pleasure in placing you in nomination for the Presidency." Alabama's vice-chairman believed that endorsement of the bill would be politically astute. "I cannot conceive of labor leaving the Democratic party, they have nowhere else to go," he advised. This comment had grave implications for Truman. It implied that the South was not as tied to the Democratic party as northern workers were and that to ignore southern opinion would drive the South from the party in national elections.[32]

Ironically, however, Truman reversed the logic. He believed labor was the unpredictable quantity and that the South would ultimately stay with the Democrats as there was "nowhere else to go." He rejected further advice from the party stalwarts and determined to push ahead with his plan to consolidate his position with the liberals.[33] On June 20, therefore, Truman delivered a firm, bellicose, five-thousand-word veto. He argued that the Taft-Hartley bill undermined collective bargaining, weakened the trade union movement, and injected political considerations into normal economic decisions. After an analysis of its flaws, he concluded that its few merits were overshadowed by its many faults.[34] Congress clearly did not agree. The House of Representatives immediately overruled the president's objections by voting to override his veto by 331 votes to 83. Only nine southern Democrats voted or paired to sustain the president. Obviously, Truman had lost any semblance of authority he may have had over the southerners. Last minute plans to speak to southern senators personally and to implore them to sustain him were of no avail. After a last-ditch filibuster, the Senate overruled the president—only Johnston, Sparkman, Hill, and Pepper from the South supported him.[35] However, this defeat was soon to be converted into a political asset. Truman had redeemed himself in the eyes of organized labor, whose coolness to the president now began to evaporate.

Of course, Truman could not rest on the laurels of one veto. He still would have to press vigorously for social reform in

---

32 Memo and enclosure, Gael Sullivan to Clifford, June 14, 1947, in Labor Files, Clifford Papers; McCorvey to HST, June 3, 1947, in OF 300, Truman Papers.

33 Sid Gregory to HST, May 17, 1947, John Nance Garner to HST, June 19, 1947, Overton Brooks to HST, June 5, 1947, in OF 407, Truman Papers; Lee, *Truman and Taft-Hartley,* 90.

34 *Public Papers, 1947,* pp. 288–97.

35 New York *Times,* June 21, 1947; *Public Papers, 1947,* pp. 298–301; unsigned list of senators, undated, in Labor Files, Clifford Papers; *Congressional Record,* 80th Cong., 1st Sess., 7538.

order to assert his claim as the undisputed and also sincere leader of the liberal bloc. Yet, despite some indiscreet and impulsive utterances, there could be no substantial cause for doubt about his ideological predilections. Truman, at least until 1947, had been admittedly inept in projecting his philosophical image publicly. Appearances to the contrary, his consistencies were more durable than his contradictions. The southerners perceived this phenomenon, while the liberals were more prone to judge Truman on his clumsy mien and unsophisticated exercise of *Realpolitik* than on his indisputable sympathy for his own Fair Deal. Truman lacked political acumen; he did not lack a basic inner consistency. It was this quality that ultimately alienated the South from his administration. Roosevelt had possessed both qualities—hence his ability to retain the allegiance of both Dixie Democrats and the urban coalition.

The administration thus continued to urge Congress to enact the Fair Deal proposals. With varying degrees of intensity, southerners opposed such measures as comprehensive housing legislation, federal aid to education, and national health insurance.[36] But the South did not turn against Truman until he moved toward adopting the most controversial of all his Fair Deal proposals, civil rights legislation. It was when Truman reassumed the stance he had taken on the race question in the opening weeks of his presidency that the South converted its sense of disenchantment into revolt.

Truman's first public incursion into the race issue in 1947 occurred nine days after his veto of the Taft-Hartley bill. Walter White, secretary of the NAACP, had invited Truman to address a rally at the NAACP's annual conference in front of the Lincoln Memorial in Washington at the end of June. Truman accepted the invitation, rejected the advice of his aides

36 Hartmann, "President Truman and the Eightieth Congress," 73; Street, "Harry S. Truman: His Role as Legislative Leader, 1945–1948," 267; Davies, *Housing Reform During the Truman Administration*, 59–72; Poen, "The Truman Administration and National Health Insurance," 121–24; Wilfred E. Binkley, *President and Congress* (Vintage Books ed.; New York, 1962), 342–43.

"not to exceed a minute" in his oration, and asked two members of his Committee on Civil Rights to help him draft a speech.[37] Truman intended to make a statement of policy and not a platitudinous benediction. In his address before a crowd of ten thousand persons, he reaffirmed his determination to secure the passage of comprehensive civil rights legislation and, with obvious reference to the South, avowed: "We cannot, any longer, await the growth of a will to action in the slowest State or the most backward community." "We cannot wait," he proclaimed, "another decade or another generation to remedy these evils. We must work, as never before to cure them now." [38] These outspoken words impressed leaders of the Negro community, who, like the labor leaders, again changed their posture toward Truman. The Pittsburgh *Courier* aptly commented, "We cannot recall when the gentleman who now sleeps at Hyde Park made such a forthright statement against racial discrimination. . . ." [39] Walter White was equally impressed and recalled in his autobiography that Truman told him after the rally: "I said what I did because I mean every word of it—and I am going to prove that I do mean it." [40]

Truman's pledge was not destined to be just another empty gesture. Throughout this period the President's Committee on Civil Rights had been deliberating. It was largely preoccupied with assessing the difficulties faced by minority groups and with suggesting means of removing these obstacles and enforcing the law where breaches might occur. It consulted sociologists, political scientists, lawyers, and civil rights workers in its investigations. The committee considered most aspects of racial, religious, and ethnic discrimination. But it concentrated first on finding ways in which legal loopholes could be over-

37 Barton J. Bernstein, "The Ambiguous Legacy: The Truman Administration and Civil Rights" (Unpublished paper read before the American Historical Association, New York, December, 1966).
38 *Public Papers, 1947*, pp. 311–13.
39 Pittsburgh *Courier*, July 12, 1947; *Crisis*, LIV (August, 1947).
40 White, *A Man Called White*, 348–49; statement of Walter White, July 3, 1947, in PPF 200, Truman Papers.

come to enable the Department of Justice to secure more prosecutions for infringements of civil rights and, second, on suggesting legislation to guarantee everyone the right to vote and the other privileges of citizenship. There was little discussion about methods of eliminating the socioeconomic differences between various racial groups. This was assumed to be a problem of economic policy and not of community relations and thus beyond its area of jurisdiction. Most members of the committee accepted such traditional cures as a fair employment practices committee and the enforcement of a nondiscrimination policy in government services as means to eliminate the worst forms of economic discrimination.[41]

On the whole, the committee was afraid that if it made proposals which were not politically acceptable or feasible, the president might ignore its recommendations altogether. One member, Charles Luckman, president of Lever Brothers, was particularly sensitive on this matter. He felt he could not recommend action that would fail even to be considered. He was also particularly eager not to single out the South too frequently for its racial malpractices.[42] He was supported in this by Robert E. Cushman, a professor of government at Cornell. Cushman told the committee that it would command no respect if it proposed drastic changes in the law and its machinery.[43] But this sentiment was not felt unanimously. Another member, Morris L. Ernst, a prominent civil liberties lawyer and former special consultant to the War Production Board, felt the committee should not hesitate to recommend what was morally right—even if there were doubts about its political feasibility. Ernst originated the proposal that the government should withdraw federal funds from institutions that practiced discrimination or sanctioned racial violence. "Our money from up North is a

41 These conclusions are based on the Records of the President's Committee on Civil Rights in the Truman Library.
42 Proceedings of the Committee on Civil Rights, March 6, 1947, in Records of the President's Committee on Civil Rights.
43 Proceedings of the Committee on Civil Rights, April 3, 1947, in Records of the President's Committee on Civil Rights.

much better weapon than a local grand jury and a petit jury to get a conviction," he reminded the committee. He suggested that the federal government begin with the District of Columbia as "a guinea pig" and a "laboratory" in its war on Jim Crow.[44] Ernst's advocacy of federal sanctions eventually was accepted, despite the opposition of Dr. Frank P. Graham, president of the University of North Carolina, and V. O. Key, the political scientist. But it rejected Ernst's other proposals for an unequivocal, all-out attack on segregation and the entire economic syndrome of the caste system.[45]

In October the committee published its report, entitled *To Secure These Rights*. It undoubtedly was far bolder than Truman had expected, although he had made no effort to control or influence the committee.[46] The report surveyed the condition of civil rights and painted a dismal picture of poverty, violence, and discrimination in all areas of employment and the social services. It discussed the handicaps experienced by all the main minority groups, but most of its analysis centered on the plight of the Negro. The report blamed segregation for the general socioeconomic malaise of southern blacks and concluded that so long as "separate but equal" remained, inequality would prevail. It did not recommend the complete illegalization of segregation, although it recognized that Jim Crow was largely responsible for the depressed status of the Negro. The report said the federal government should assume the duty of correcting these social evils and should begin in Washington, D.C., which, it maintained, constituted a moral blight on the nation. Its

---

44 Proceedings of the Committee on Civil Rights, March 6, 1947, minutes of the second meeting of the Committee on Civil Rights, February 5, 6, 1947, in Records of the President's Committee on Civil Rights; Shiskin, interview.
45 Memo, Robert K. Carr to Committee on Civil Rights, statement of V. O. Key, "Use of Federal Grants-In-Aid as a Device for Preventing Discrimination in the Providing of Public Services," in Records of the President's Committee on Civil Rights; Daniels, *The Man of Independence*, 342.
46 Shiskin, interview; Barton J. Bernstein, "America in War and Peace: The Test of Liberalism," in Barton J. Bernstein (ed.), *Towards a New Past: Dissenting Essays in American History* (Vintage Books ed.; New York, 1969), 305.

other recommendations included: the creation of a new FEPC; an anti-poll tax bill; federal legislation to guarantee to all citizens the right to vote in primaries; federal antilynching legislation; the reorganization and expansion of the civil rights section of the Justice Department; the establishment of a permanent commission on civil rights in the executive office of the president; the elimination by statute and executive order of discrimination and segregation in the armed services and in all other government departments; and the prohibition of Jim Crow in interstate transportation. The most novel and controversial recommendation was that federal grants-in-aid to the states should be made conditional on compliance with the report.[47]

The publication of *To Secure These Rights* served to clarify political alignments. Negroes became more evocative in their support of Truman. Mary McLeod Bethune, president of the National Council of Negro Women, hailed it as "a document which will forever live in the hearts of all liberty loving people." [48] Walter White thought it "beyond all question the most forthright Governmental pronouncement . . . which has yet been drafted," and the editor of the Pittsburgh *Courier* praised the committee which "pulled no punches and evaded no issues.[49] Most southerners, on the other hand, were as despondent as Negroes were elated. They inundated the White House with letters protesting that the committee, in wanting to terminate segregation, had encouraged racial anarchy and rape. Nearly all the critics made the familiar claim that race relations in Dixie were harmonious and that only southern whites genuinely held the Negroes' interests at heart. They also warned Truman of the political, as well as the sexual, consequences of the report. The chairman of the Danville, Virginia, Democratic

47 U.S. President's Committee on Civil Rights, *To Secure These Rights* (Washington, D.C., 1947), 151–73.
48 Telegram, Mary McLeod Bethune to HST, October 31, 1947, in OF 596 A, Truman Papers.
49 Pittsburgh *Courier*, November 8, 1947.

committee wired: "I really believe that you have ruined the Democratic party in the South. We were in hopes we would not expect another Smith campaign." [50] A North Carolinian wrote: "Your recent stand and utterances on the Negro question will no doubt cause many thousands of Negroes to vote for you, but this stand of yours will cost you hundreds of thousands of white votes." [51] And a minister from Florida warned icily: "If that report is carried out you won't be elected dog-catcher in 1948. The South today is the South of 1861 regarding things that your committee had under consideration." [52]

To Secure These Rights was a political bombshell. Truman could hardly ignore the recommendations of a committee which he had personally set up. To have done so would not only have been an admission of self-defeat and hypocrisy but would also have driven the Negroes and the mass of northern sympathizers out of the Democratic party. But Truman knew that if he accepted the report without qualification, he would completely lose the already fragile support of the "solid" South. He resolved to retain the support of the Negro voters at all costs and hoped a carefully formulated strategy would save the South at the same time.

These political permutations were complicated further by the threat of a split from the left wing of the Democratic party. This faction was loosely led by Henry Wallace, who, since his dismissal from the cabinet, had condemned the administration in a number of speeches and written articles for unnecessarily antagonizing the Soviet Union by the adoption of the Truman Doctrine and the Marshall Plan. Wallace felt that the president had ruled out a *rapprochement* with the Russians by accepting the concept of an irreconcilable, bipolar world. He constantly castigated Truman for bypassing the United Nations in his con-

50 Telegram, John B. McDaniel to HST, October 31, 1947, in OF 596 A, Truman Papers.
51 Charles Doggett to HST, October 30, 1947, in OF 596 A, Truman Papers.
52 Telegram, the Reverend A. C. Schuler to HST, October 30, 1947, in OF 596 A, Truman Papers.

tainment policies and, during a well-publicized tour of Europe, called for reconciliation with the U.S.S.R. When he returned from abroad, he hinted that he was considering the formation of a third party and undertook a nationwide speaking tour. Wherever he went, he criticized Truman's foreign policy and his reputedly unequivocal attitudes on labor and civil rights legislation, as well. His political style was markedly antipodal to that of the president. He refused to address racially segregated audiences during a tour of the South. And, on one notorious occasion, he visited a union organizer, one Horace P. White, who had been imprisoned in Atlanta for cutting the throat of a textile worker after the latter had attempted to pass through a picket line. The blaze of publicity which followed the former vice president, together with the frequent calls for a third party by the newly formed Progressive Citizens of America, convinced most political observers that Wallace would run for the presidency as an independent in 1948.[53]

In order to create a viable third party, Wallace needed the support of those who were generally associated with the Democratic left—in particular, Negroes, labor unions, and intellectuals. However, most leaders of these groups shunned the Wallace movement. Their overriding reason was that since third parties had almost always failed, they preferred to exercise as much influence as possible within the Democratic party itself. In addition, Truman's apparent swing to the left in his veto of the Taft-Hartley bill and the creation of the Committee on Civil Rights had caused leaders of the urban coalition to reconsider their temporary antipathy to the Democratic party. This change in attitude was particularly noticeable in the case of A. F. Whitney, who had pledged in May, 1946, to use the entire treasury of the Brotherhood of Railway Trainmen to defeat Truman after the latter's threat to draft the railroad strikers. Only one year later, after Truman had vetoed the Taft-

---

53 Hamby, "Harry S. Truman and American Liberalism," 170–207; Curtis D. MacDougall, *Gideon's Army: The Components of the Decision* (3 vols.; New York, 1965), I, 220–23.

Hartley bill, Whitney proclaimed that the president had "vindicated himself in the eyes of labor" and pledged his union's support. Philip Murray, president of the CIO, had similarly praised Truman after the veto and had promised to reinvigorate the PAC to oust supporters of the Taft-Hartley bill from Congress. He recommended that members of the PAC dissociate themselves from Wallace's Progressive Citizens of America and refrain from joining the other leading liberal organization, the Americans for Democratic Action.[54] And, as previously noted, Negro leaders were confident of the president's good intentions in the field of civil rights.

Wallace's greatest potential pool of support might have come from liberal intellectuals, who were uneasy about Truman's blunt pugnacity. However, many liberals could not identify with Wallace. Although he possessed their mental qualifications, many refuted his interpretation of the state of world affairs. They were often militantly anticommunist and wanted to contain Soviet expansion in Europe. In January, 1947, these progressive Democrats had formed the Americans for Democratic Action (ADA), an organization dedicated to the principles of the Fair Deal and the extirpation of communism at home and abroad. It believed that the Democratic party should be converted into a totally liberal party without its conservative trimmings. It endorsed containment and the Fair Deal but remained cool to Truman, who was thought to be a political dilettante. Wallace's plans for a third party were unequivocally condemned as divisive and misguided. A breakaway movement "would be a catastrophe for American liberalism," claimed Wilson Wyatt, chairman of the ADA.[55] Thus, the hard core of the urban coalition, the labor unions, the Negroes, and the intellectuals, were still basically affiliated with the Democratic party. It was up to Truman to inspire their confidence.

54 MacDougall, *Gideon's Army*, I, 174–75, 178; Clifton Brock, *Americans for Democratic Action: Its Role in National Politics* (Washington, D.C., 1962), 58–59.
55 Brock, *Americans for Democratic Action*, 44–45, 65–66, 68–71.

The Democrats were as troubled in the South as they were in the strongholds of liberalism. Until the Committee on Civil Rights issued its report, southerners had not seriously considered implementing their occasional threats to bolt the Democratic party. Officeholders, particularly at the local level, had for a long time felt they were the incompatible bedfellows of the Fair Deal liberals but could not point to any one single catalytic proposal which would have forced them to withdraw from the national party. The Taft-Hartley veto alone would not have resulted in a final severance, since it was not startling enough to persuade the voting masses to discard their political habits. Experienced politicians were aware that the South's ties to the party were too entrenched to warrant a revolt and a subsequent realignment in the party system. Indeed, only four weeks before the publication of *To Secure These Rights*, the governor of South Carolina, J. Strom Thurmond, who would shortly become the leader of the anti-Truman forces, commended Truman's "seasoned experience, demonstrated ability, and tact in international affairs" and predicted his renomination "without delay." [56]

Thurmond's remarks notwithstanding, southerners still hoped to exercise more influence in the party during the forthcoming election year. Their success in overriding Truman's veto of the Taft-Hartley bill had shown that at least in Congress they still possessed the power to thwart the president's legislative goals. But if southerners wished to set the tone of the 1948 election campaign and determine the choice of candidates, they would have to be able to exert more power in the policy-making committees and the national convention of the party. One way to assume greater authority would be to select a national party chairman who would be sympathetic to the South's political aspirations. They had frequently attacked the national chairman, Robert Hannegan, for his sympathy for Negroes and organized labor. When in 1947 Hannegan announced his decision to retire, southerners saw an opportunity to redress the balance.

56 Speech, J. Strom Thurmond, delivered at Louisville, Ky., October 2, 1947, sent to HST, October 7, 1947, in PPF 2873, Truman Papers.

They hoped that his successor would stem from below the Mason-Dixon Line, but Truman nominated another northerner, Senator J. Howard McGrath of Rhode Island, to succeed him. Southern expectations of increasing their influence through the office of a congenial national chairman were thus dashed. At the full meeting of the Democratic National Committee, held on the same day as the release of *To Secure These Rights* (before its contents could be read and digested), they acquiesced in McGrath's appointment. However, they tried to increase their representation at the national convention by a reapportionment of delegates. They demanded that extra seats be assigned to districts which had returned a Democrat to Congress in the previous election. Gessner McCorvey advised the committee that if this plan were adopted, the South would feel more reassured that it was being given "proper recognition." Eurith Rivers of Georgia also complained about the absence of southerners in the most important party offices and urged the restoration of the two-thirds rule. The committee, however, thwarted these proposals and voted to keep its current apportionment and nominating rules.[57]

The Democratic party was thus in a state of disarray. The intellectuals mistrusted Truman, labor leaders had returned to the fold but were scarcely faithful bedmates, and the southerners felt they had been ostracized and pushed aside in favor of the urban coalition. Truman and his advisers had to devise a viable political strategy for the forthcoming election. They realized that conscious compromise, in an attempt to bring the factions together, really was not feasible. Compromise, until the middle of 1947, had often been mistaken for inconsistency. Truman would have to appear to be more decisive and ideologically committed as a rejoinder to his censors. The issue, therefore, seemed fairly clear-cut. The president continually had espoused the extension of the New Deal but somehow had conveyed the impression that he was insincere or insufficiently determined to

57 Proceedings of the Democratic National Committee, October 8, 1947, in J. Howard McGrath Papers, Harry S. Truman Library, Independence, Mo.; Jack Redding, *Inside the Democratic Party* (New York, 1958), 86–93.

pursue his proposals. As a result, Henry Wallace had managed to assert himself as the philosophical successor to Franklin Roosevelt. Thus, if Truman in any way gave the impression of trying to dilute his own policies, the charges of hypocrisy or fence-sitting would ring true and play into the hands of the Republicans. The president would then lose ground with former New Deal supporters. He would, of course, renew southern confidence, but the South's loyalty would provide no additional electoral votes. Working on these assumptions, his political aides, particularly Clark Clifford, Oscar Ewing, and Charles Murphy, believed that Truman's only course was to reemphasize all his Fair Deal proposals, including those on civil rights, and to reestablish himself as a leading liberal in the coming election campaign.

In November, 1947, Clark Clifford set out the current political configurations in a forty-three-page memorandum to the president. This document was remarkable both for its foresight and as an illustration of the political considerations endemic in the decision-making process. In addition to suggesting an election strategy, it presented a penetrating analysis of the problems and consequences of the ideological differences among the Democrats. Clifford correctly predicted that Wallace would lead a third party and that Thomas E. Dewey would head the Republican ticket. He believed that Negroes, organized labor, farmers, and independent progressives would hold the balance of power in the 1948 election. Most important was the Negro and labor vote, which could not be ignored at any costs. "Unless there are new and real efforts (as distinguished from mere political gestures which are today thoroughly understood and strongly resented by sophisticated Negro leaders)," he advised Truman, "the Negro bloc . . . will go Republican." Truman also should consult openly with labor leaders, who "must be given the impression that they are once more welcome in the councils of the Administration." Clifford recognized that Wallace posed a real electoral threat and advised Truman to insulate Wallace as rapidly as possible. There were two ways to do this: one was to stigmatize him by publicizing the Communist affiliations of some of his supporters and the other was to adopt some of Wallace's proposals himself. Truman could demonstrate his new leftward path by making unequivocal demands for a comprehensive housing bill, reestablishment of price controls, total revision of the tax structure, and a rigorous civil rights bill. Clifford realized that a firm stand on racial matters "would obviously cause some difficulty with our Southern friends, but that is the lesser of the two evils." The southern vote, he believed, was less crucial than that of the urban coalition. He recommended that the president pursue a deliberate, uncompromising campaign to keep Negro and labor voters in the Democratic column—irrespective of the consequences south of the Potomac. Clifford counseled: "The *only* pragmatic reason for conciliating the South in normal times is because of its tremendous strength in the Congress. Since the Congress is Republican and the Democratic President has, therefore, no real chance to get his own program approved by it, particularly in an election year, he has no real necessity for 'getting along' with the Southern conservatives." [58]

Truman agreed with this strategy. He would thenceforth give primary consideration to the urban coalition. In the first few weeks of 1948, when Truman had the opportunity to outline his political program, there were few sops to southern sensibilities. This new, hard-hitting posture was based upon one other prognostication made by Clark Clifford in his November memorandum. Clifford had predicted that, despite the protests that would come from below the Mason-Dixon Line, "it is inconceivable that any policies initiated by the Truman administration no matter how 'liberal' could so alienate the South in the next year that it would revolt. As always, the South can be considered safely Democratic. And in formulating national policy it can be safely ignored." [59] On this particular prophesy, he erred.

58 Memo, Clifford to HST, November 19, 1947, in Political Files, Clifford Papers.
59 *Ibid.; Public Papers, 1948,* pp. 1–10; Ross, *The Loneliest Campaign,* 23–24; Cabell Phillips, *The Truman Presidency: The History of a Triumphant Succession* (New York, 1966), 162–65.

CHAPTER EIGHT

The Democratic Party Divides: Dixie and Philadelphia, January to July, 1948

FEBRUARY 2, 1948, was a historic day. For the first time in the twentieth century, a president had sent Congress a legislative package dealing solely with the issue of civil rights. Both Harry Truman and southern Democrats, albeit with differing degrees of awareness, realized that these proposals would not only cause a political storm but might also radically alter the course of the country's political history. True enough, the president's recommendations were scarcely revolutionary. He did not raise all the points discussed in *To Secure These Rights* and conspicuously omitted the most controversial suggestions. He may have already begun to realize, perhaps as the result of an anticipatory furor in Mississippi, that the South was not as politically submissive as he originally thought.[1] He did not, for example, mention the demeaning effects of segregation, nor did he recommend, as his committee had done, the integration of the District of Columbia—he merely hoped to iron out "the inequalities arising from segregation" in the schools and other public facilities in Washington. He also temporized by dropping the proposal to withdraw federal aid to penalize intransigent states and by saying nothing definite about Jim Crow in the armed services. Besides these very important ex-

[1] New Orleans *Times-Picayune*, January 21, 1948; Memphis *Commercial Appeal*, January 21, 1948.

ceptions, Truman accepted the committee's other proposals. He recommended that Congress strengthen the Justice Department, abolish the poll tax, create a permanent FEPC, protect citizens against lynching, and outlaw segregation in interstate transport. He did not suggest anything new. What was unprecedented was that the president had undertaken personally to press for a comprehensive civil rights bill and that he had cited such legislation as his "first goal." [2]

Most southerners reacted with expected horror to the president's message. The fears and even the political shibboleths of yesteryear had suddenly materialized. Reconstruction was no longer part of their historical folklore but had assumed a new, urgent reality. Many southerners suspected that Truman's proposals were mere prolegomena to the elimination of segregation and the eradication of the South's stratified social system. Although some admitted that Truman had tempered the more radical recommendations of the Committee on Civil Rights, they argued that he could be easily influenced to go beyond his proposals.[3] After all, *To Secure These Rights* had regarded true equality as the quintessential goal and had acknowledged that this could not be attained until Jim Crow had been eliminated. Their first reaction, therefore, was to despair that their special institution, segregation, would be swept aside by a political coalition openly hostile to the white South. Once segregation was destroyed, they argued, the entire racial *modus vivendi* would collapse. "The South we know is being swept to its destruction," lamented Mississippi's Senator James O. Eastland. "It is a real danger—it is an imminent danger." [4]

Fear of the eradication of Jim Crow was the principal response, although not the only one, of white southerners to Truman's message on civil rights. Closely connected with this ap-

2 *Public Papers, 1948,* pp. 3, 121–26; Report of the Conference in Charles Murphy's Office, January 28, 1948, in Spingarn Papers.
3 *Arkansas Gazette,* February 5, 1948; Raleigh *News and Observer,* February 5, 1948.
4 Address of Senator James O. Eastland, in States' Rights Scrapbook, Mississippi Department of Archives and History, Jackson.

prehensiveness was the feeling that certain pedestals and icons of the South's political culture had finally collapsed. The Democratic party had been in the past more than a vehicle of political advancement. To many it had been the much-needed symbol of southern white unity and historical continuity. Whites had differed with one another on social welfare, monetary matters, agricultural reform, and even race. Nevertheless, many southerners believed, there had been an underlying sense of cohesion, a cohesion that had been shared in a slightly different way with northerners as a means of sectional conciliation after Reconstruction. The Democratic party, however, was now in ruins. It was no longer the agreed protector of the South's institutions, but a profoundly split organization. The Democratic party was no longer a historical idea. "This much is certain, if the present Democratic leadership is right, then Calhoun and Jefferson Davis were wrong," assured Senator Eastland rhetorically.[5] Governor Fielding Wright of Mississippi would not even brook Eastland's small degree of uncertainty. "Vital principles and eternal truths transcend party lines," he exclaimed.[6] He meant, of course, that the civil rights issue had removed the *raison d'être* of the South's allegiance to the Democrats.

The Democratic party, then, no longer represented the South's interests. It had become dominated by intellectuals, self-seeking labor leaders, and most poignant of all for white southerners, insensitive Negroes. These groups, demurred Dixie's politicians, now enjoyed so much influence within Democratic councils that southerners had been relegated to an almost emblematic position. This was intolerable. Not only had the South been dispossessed of a political sanctuary but also it was in danger of being transformed by people who had no connections below the Potomac. Senator Eastland believed that "northern mongrel groups" had devised a plot to subvert the South's racial

5 *Congressional Record*, 80th Cong., 2nd Sess., 1193–195; see also, "The President's Program: Civil Rights, States' Rights, and the Reconstruction Background," *Staple Cotton Review*, XXVI (April, 1948).
6 Memphis *Commercial Appeal*, January 21, 1948.

system and singled out Walter White of the NAACP as "a negro, who, I am afraid to say, has more power in your government than all of the Southern states combined." [7]

Dixie Democrats did not believe that this change had come about by chance. The Democratic leadership in Washington was held culpable, and, in particular, Truman himself. They believed that he had pressed for civil rights legislation as the result of Henry Wallace's decision at the end of 1947 to run for president. Truman, they argued, had decided to salvage his presumed declining fortunes with Negro voters in order to counteract Wallace's obvious appeal. This strategy was particularly galling to them. They felt that Truman, who owed his nomination as vice president in 1944 to southerners, had double-crossed them. Eugene Cox of Georgia wondered "if, after all, Henry Wallace is such a bad man. . . . The whole thing sickens me." Wallace had at least always been forthright in his views and had shied from southern support. Truman, on the other hand, had welcomed their support at Chicago and should thus have been indebted to them. Congressman John Bell Williams of Mississippi best expressed this sense of betrayal. "If it were not for Southern Democrats," he said, "Henry Wallace would be in the White House today instead of Harry Truman. Southern Democrats have always been the best friends that President Truman or the Democratic party ever had. . . . This is a mighty poor way for him to evince his gratitude." [8]

Fear of racial integration, disenchantment with the Democratic party as a whole, and personal antipathy to Truman, who had become something of a Judas figure overnight, provoked southerners into finding effective means to protect their special interests. A number of spontaneous calls for a revolt were made after Truman's special message had been delivered, but these were still uncoordinated and unplanned. However, a few southerners, none of them officeholders, already had penned dis-

---

7 Address of Senator James O. Eastland, in States' Rights Scrapbook.
8 *Congressional Record*, 80th Cong., 2nd Sess., 975, 976.

courses on the political problems of Dixie and had thus cleared the path for a possible rebellion. These writers had been prompted by earlier rumblings during the war to find ways of increasing their region's influence without, in fact, sacrificing the fruits of the one-party system. At least one of these tracts was to provide Dixie's politicians with a firm theoretical and practical basis for political action.

The most influential tract on the theme of southern impotence and isolation was composed by Charles Wallace Collins, an Alabama lawyer who practiced in Washington. Collins took a keen interest in political and constitutional developments and had written books on a variety of subjects ranging from banking to the Fourteenth Amendment. In 1947 he published *Whither Solid South?*, a lengthy book which portrayed the South's sense of frustration and alienation over recent political developments. Collins firmly believed in the innate inferiority of the Negro and ardently defended segregation. Racial integration, he believed, would dilute the achievements of the white race and would destroy the South's individuality and unique corporate existence. Collins argued that the Democratic party would soon obliterate the fabric of southern society. The party, he said, was in the control of Negro and labor union leaders who were intent on creating a monolithic welfare state. The Employment Act of 1946 was the first step toward total paternalism. There could, according to Collins, be only one result. "The two virulent issues —Negro equality and state capitalism . . . are bound to meet in a head-on collision with the South unless a means of diversion can be found," he predicted.[9]

Collins felt that a realignment of the political parties along conservative and liberal lines would enable the South once more to gain control over its own affairs. But he knew that a realignment into a national conservative alliance was only a remote possibility. He advocated, therefore, that the South use its constitutional powers in the electoral college to block the election

9 Collins, *Whither Solid South?*, 253–54.

of any candidates who espoused policies alien to southern traditions. In a close election, theorized Collins, the South's 127 electoral college votes would hold the balance of power. Electors could be either uninstructed, and thus vote for whomever they pleased, or they could represent a southern party. In either case, the southerners would possess unparalleled power in the electoral college and could conceivably effect the election of a southern president. For if neither of the two main parties polled an electoral majority, the South could force the election into the House of Representatives where each state has only one vote in the event of a presidential election. In this way the South could reassert its influence in political life.[10] Although Collins' strategy was scarcely original, his ideas were enthusiastically welcomed by disaffected officeholders. *Whither Solid South?* became their ideological manifesto. The book was sent to several renowned politicians, who not only read it carefully, but also continued to consult with him.[11]

Although Collins was the most articulate and most "southern" of the postwar ideologues, other writers also emphasized the uniqueness of the southern experience and saw in the Fair Deal and the civil rights program an imminent threat to Dixie's historical legacies. For example, a Texan, Peter Molyneaux, published personally a volume entitled *The South's Political Plight*. This book, like *Whither Solid South?*, was a scathing indictment of the economic and racial policies of Roosevelt and Truman. Molyneaux argued as a dedicated economic conservative as well as a self-conscious southerner. He castigated recent social reforms and postulated that the president, through the instrumen-

10 *Ibid.*, chap. 17; Richard Hofstadter, "From Calhoun to the Dixiecrats," *Social Research*, XVI (June, 1949), 143–48.
11 Hofstadter, "From Calhoun to the Dixiecrats," 143; Sarah M. Lemmon, "The Ideology of the 'Dixiecrat' Movement," *Social Forces*, XXX (December, 1951), 162–71. References to *Whither Solid South?* were found in a number of letters to various southern politicians. Collins' role in the States' Rights party is discussed below. See, for example, W. R. Withers to John Sparkman, August 20, 1948, McCorvey to Charles W. Collins, July 14, 1948, in Dixon Papers.

tality of the Democratic party, wanted to "institute a new Reconstruction of the South by the Federal Government." Southern Democrats, he insisted, had become blinded by the fruits of political spoils and had allowed concepts of party loyalty to supersede sectional allegiance. He eschewed Collins' counsel to opt out of the two-party system and called upon southerners to abandon the Democratic party and align on an experimental basis with the Republicans, who, he thought, might welcome them into their political councils.[12]

Most southern Democrats, however, were not as hasty as Molyneaux might have wished. They recognized the need for coordinated action to stem Truman's reforming zeal, but did not want to act with finality until they were sure of widespread public support. At the Southern Governors' Conference, held in February, 1948, at Wakulla Springs, Florida, they agreed—with the exception of Fielding Wright of Mississippi who wanted the South to dissociate itself from the Democratic party without further ado—to go through certain diplomatic motions before embarking upon a dramatic course of action. After extensive deliberations they decided to form a special committee under the chairmanship of Governor J. Strom Thurmond of South Carolina. Members were instructed to consider the various courses open to the South and to make representations to the national Democratic chairman in order to clarify the precise intentions of the president. The governors agreed that the committee should report back to them forty days thence.[13]

---

12 Peter Molyneaux, *The South's Political Plight* (Dallas, 1948), 16, 118. A third polemic, written by a Louisianian, Stuart O. Landry, concerned itself more narrowly with the race issue. The author, a respected commentator on southern affairs, was less concerned in this volume with the regional implications of Truman's proposals. Indeed, his work was an extremist racist diatribe. Nevertheless, his ideas and his uncompromising sectionalism were sufficiently influential to be quoted in the official handbook of the States' Rights party. See Stuart O. Landry, *The Cult of Equality* (New Orleans, 1945); National States' Rights Democrats Campaign Committee, *States' Rights Information and Speakers Handbook* (Jackson, 1948), 51, 54.

13 New York *Times*, February 7, 8, 1948; Atlanta *Constitution*, February 9, 1948; New Orleans *Times-Picayune*, February 9, 1948; Thurmond to Hobbs, February 9, 1948, in Hobbs Papers; motion of Thurmond at Southern

Two weeks later Thurmond's special committee met with Senator J. Howard McGrath, national Democratic chairman, in his Washington office. Thurmond and Ben Laney of Arkansas did all the talking and tried to pin down McGrath more precisely on the administration's attitude toward segregation. McGrath was in a difficult position. He wanted to appease the southerners without, at the same time, repudiating any of the president's proposals. His tone, therefore, was accommodating and reassuring. He emphasized that Truman had no intention of interfering with segregation in schools and agreed that education as a whole was a state prerogative. He made a few appropriate strictures about racketeering in labor unions and predicted that the Democratic convention would be content to adopt a general, innocuous plank on civil rights. Nevertheless, despite McGrath's apparent concern for the governors, it was clear that he was not prepared to use his influence to persuade Truman to reverse his proposals. The administration had already calculated its political priorities, and, while it was happy to soothe the southerners, it was not going to revise its strategy. In substance, therefore, McGrath had little to offer. He would manipulate the wording of the plank on civil rights and thus help Dixie Democrats to save face, but this would not, on his own admission, really change anything. The conference, therefore, was something of a sham. The southerners would not budge on the race question, and McGrath's hands were also tied. Thurmond himself realized that an impasse had been reached. He was convinced that the South was destined to play only a subordinate role in policy making. "The present leadership of the Democratic party will soon realize that the South is no longer 'in the bag'," he said in a statement afterwards.[14]

Governors' Conference, February 7, 1948, in States' Rights Papers, Thurmond Papers.

14 Transcript of conference of southern governors with Senator J. Howard McGrath, chairman of the Democratic National Committee, February 23, 1948, in Publicity Division Folders, Democratic National Committee, John M. Redding Papers, Harry S. Truman Library, Independence, Mo.; Redding, *Inside the Democratic Party*, 136–40; New York *Times*, February 24, 1948.

However, not all the governors shared his view. North Carolina's R. Gregg Cherry chided later: "There was just a lot of talk, talk, talk. McGrath handled himself pretty well." He even refused to leave North Carolina for the next meeting of the southern governors on the grounds that "my work down here is more important than going up there to listen to Mr. Thurmond lecturing." [15]

The failure of the southern governors to induce the administration to drop its recommendations on civil rights stimulated a searching debate below the Potomac on the most effective way of forcing the national Democratic party to respect the wishes of its southern members. Southerners were by no means united on the method of transforming the Democratic party. A few wanted to withdraw without delay and act unilaterally in the electoral college. Some were willing to bolt but were uncertain about the timing and even the mechanics of such a move. Others believed that the Democratic party best represented Dixie's economic and political interests and that southerners should therefore combat the proposals from within the party. The political landscape was confused. Only protracted discussion in the state legislatures, party committees, and newspaper columns would clarify the situation.

The insurgents, the politicians who advocated a unilateral withdrawal from the national Democratic party, were wary of repeating the mistakes of 1944. They believed that the South now had good reason to break its bonds from the party but realized that historical ties and political inertia did not make this an easy task. The election of 1944 had shown that a political revolt could not be successfully executed unless a majority of the members in any individual state party organization was coherently in sympathy with insurgency. The revolt against Roosevelt, furthermore, had fizzled because there had not been a single *casus belli*, one particular act to have captured the rebellious

15 Memphis *Commercial Appeal*, February 23, 24, 1948; Raleigh *News and Observer*, March 12, 1948.

imagination of southerners. Above all, the insurgents were aware that they had made inadequate preparations at the local level. The voters had not been persuaded to submerge their deep-rooted political habits, and local officials had not had sufficient faith in the success of a bolt. So, cognizant of the mistakes of 1944, the proponents of a party revolt in 1948 were determined to sustain the momentum of their campaigns against Truman and, above all, to build a grass roots organization that was prepared to undo the political ties of half a century.

The first thing that the insurgents did was to undermine the personal authority of President Truman. They tried to demonstrate that Truman himself had been responsible for the civil rights program and that the unfavorable changes in the structure of the Democratic party had been encouraged by him. Truman became the new scourge of the South, the archvillain of the political drama about to unfold. Dixie Democrats of various persuasions made it clear that their minimal condition of party loyalty was that Truman should not be renominated. Their personal contempt for him was manifested in a variety of ways. In the first place, Truman was virtually ostracized. At the annual Jefferson-Jackson Day dinner in Washington, D.C., the table in front of President Truman's table was conspicuously empty. The parties of Strom Thurmond and Olin Johnston had deliberately booked the seats and then boycotted the dinner in protest of both Truman's leadership and McGrath's symbolic insistence that no special provisions should be made to segregate Negro guests. A number of other senior Democrats from the South absented themselves. Congressman John Bell Williams of Mississippi chided that southerners "cannot join in such a hypocritical gesture and you will find most of us having our own Jefferson-Jackson Day dinners in gatherings in which white supremacy is the order and segregation is the rule."[16] And at the

16 New York *Times,* February 20, 1948; Stinnett, *Democrats, Dinners, and Dollars,* 178–79; Huss, *Senator for the South: A Biography of Olin D. Johnston,* 158–59; Memphis *Commercial Appeal,* February 20, 1948.

state dinner in Little Rock, Arkansas, about half of the nine hundred guests left the dining room before Truman's Jefferson-Jackson Day message was due to be relayed over the radio.[17]

Expressions of discontent with Truman were not limited to speeches and boycotts of dinners. Disaffected southern governors had to demonstrate that they were willing to break their ties with the national party if Truman neither tempered his proposals nor abdicated from office. However, they were circumscribed by political considerations. No skillful politician would take measures if they were not politically viable. So, in general, the governors, as the titular heads of their respective state parties, would seriously consider a bolt only if they could carry the support of key party officials at the state and local level. This, in turn, depended upon whether they enjoyed control over the party machine. Where more than one faction was represented in the governor's circle and the state Democratic organization, executives tended to avoid divisive steps. If they found that insurgency was not endorsed by officeholders, particularly within the powerful state Democratic executive committees, then they usually shied away from plans to divorce themselves from the national party. Thus the main test of feasibility was usually official local support. However, there were other considerations, such as personal predilections, the attractiveness of the race issue as a political device, and the threat, particularly in the upper South, of a strong Republican alternative within the state.[18]

The first Dixie governor to seek means of freeing his state's electors from all obligations to the Truman Democrats was William Tuck of Virginia. On the surface Virginia's early entry into the movement for southern independence was somewhat surprising. The race issue, as in neighboring North Carolina, really had never molded the style of politics in Virginia where, after

17 *Arkansas Gazette,* February 20, 1948.
18 In his authoritative study of southern politics, V. O. Key confined himself to only two of these conditions. He argued that a state was more likely to bolt if the risk of Republican opposition was negligible and the proportion of Negroes (and hence, presumably, the intensity of feeling on the race issue) was high in any one state. Key, *Southern Politics,* 329–44.

all, Negroes had begun to run for state and municipal offices without intimidation. But Virginia had been a heartland of the anti–New Dealers. Harry Byrd, the powerful boss of Virginia politics, had agitated against the reform impulse of successive Democratic administrations for fifteen years. A considerable degree of public sympathy with his views, plus his absolute control over the state's party machine, facilitated his decision to challenge the national Democratic party. To Byrd, Truman's civil rights proposals merely represented the climax of the Democrats' profligacy. But he realized that this finally gave him sufficient cause to rebel. Tuck had his emphatic blessing when, three days after the southern governors' meeting with McGrath, he asked the state legislature to enable the electors to be selected without obligatory ties to the nominees of the major political parties. Tuck proposed that the state convention should instruct Virginia's electors at a future session to cast their votes for persons other than the nominees of the national party, if the Democratic National Convention, "dominated by pressure groups from the larger cities, has adopted policies and principles destructive of the sovereign rights of the State of Virginia." [19]

Tuck's proposals were eventually modified after an outcry from the anti-Byrd Democrats, led by Martin Hutchinson, Byrd's adversary in the senatorial primary of 1946. The Byrd organization was, of course, sufficiently powerful to withstand criticism from an ineffective political faction. However, there were some restraints operating even against this indomitable machine. In the first place, there was a small but nevertheless influential Republican party in Virginia. A sharp division among Democratic voters could have resulted in a formidable Republican resurgence. This threat of a real two-party system might have encouraged Tuck's eventual retraction. Second, Byrd, as a U.S. senator, undoubtedly would have lost patronage from the administration in the event of a Democratic victory. He

[19] Memo, Henry Fowler to McGrath, Virginia Democratic Situation, March 19, 1948, in McGrath Papers; New York *Times*, February 27, 1948.

may well have remembered what happened to Virginia's "Hoovercrats" in 1928. Ultimately, therefore, he calculated that there were no real rewards to be gained from a bolt. His political supremacy was undisputed, and he did not need "issues" to sweep himself or his cohorts into office. Nevertheless, he kept alive the possibility of repudiation; but both he and Tuck intended to do this in the name of the Democratic party.[20]

This determination to retain the party label at all cost was a feature common to all the other rumblings of revolt in the southern states. Throughout Dixie, insurgents insisted that Truman, not they, had deserted the party and that they, in fact, were the regulars. This was not merely a matter of semantics. It raised the fundamental question of whether the national Democratic party consisted of anything more than the sum of the state parties. If, as southerners insisted, the national party was merely a canopy for the various state organizations, then individual state parties could not, by definition, leave the Democratic party, as they constituted its core in the first place.

While there were protests from certain quarters in Virginia against plans to repudiate the decisions of the national convention, in Mississippi there was scarcely any public outcry against Governor Fielding Wright's militant stand on this question. Wright had established himself as a fire-eater even before the president had delivered his special message on civil rights.[21] He had guessed correctly that white Mississippians would be almost universally aroused by the recommendations in *To Secure These Rights*. The race issue had always played a predominant role in Mississippi's election campaigns. Concern about racial matters, as Wright well knew, had increased since the *Smith* v. *Allwright* decision. Mississippians, after all, would be more affected by the Negro's participation in political affairs

20 Hutchinson to Philip B. Yeager, March 11, 1948, Hutchinson to N. Clarence Smith, March 2, 1948, in Box 14, Hutchinson Papers; Raleigh *News and Observer*, March 5, 1948; Key, *Southern Politics*, 336.
21 Elbert Riley Hilliard, "A Biography of Fielding Wright: Mississippi's Mr. States' Rights" (M.A. thesis, Mississippi State University, 1959), *passim*.

than would fellow whites in other southern states. In 1940 Negroes had composed 49.2 percent of Mississippi's population, and about one fifth of its counties had a black population of over 70 percent. The political and social repercussions of Truman's program did not have to be articulated to opinion leaders in Mississippi. Nearly all the major editors (with the one notable exception of Hodding Carter of the *Delta Democrat-Times*), the officials in the state party organization, and the entire congressional delegation in Washington welcomed Wright's initiative. In no other state was there such wide agreement that the South and the national Democratic party had reached the political crossroads.[22]

The sole issue in Mississippi, then, was race. The advocates of severance from the party resolved to emphasize this question in their campaign. Wright was particularly anxious that a revolt should be instigated by public demand and not merely by oligarchic fiat, as had happened in 1944. He labored hard for the southern cause by traveling throughout the state to publicize what he regarded as the dangers of the president's proposals. He wanted Mississippi to lead the South in its mission to force the Democratic party to drop both its program and its leader.[23] Wright was willing, however, to pool the resources of the state party to persuade white Mississippians to rally in defense of their social system. Accordingly, he encouraged the state executive committee to adopt a militant plan of action at its meeting on March 1. Such a strategy, he hoped, would help his movement gain momentum. Herbert Holmes, state party chairman, consequently steered through a resolution requiring Mississippi's delegates to walk out of the Democratic National Convention unless the party repudiated both the civil rights program and its sponsors and nominated a presidential candi-

---

22 Key, *Southern Politics*, 229; Hodding Carter, "The Civil Rights Issue as Seen in the South," New York *Times*, March 21, 1948; clipping, Jackson *Daily News*, February 24, 1948, clipping, Jackson *Clarion-Ledger*, January 30, 1948, in States' Rights Scrapbook.
23 New York *Times*, February 29, 1948; New Orleans *Times-Picayune*, February 13, 1948.

date on a strong states' rights plank. If a walkout were to occur, resolved the committee, then another state convention would be called. This, in turn, would call for summoning a States' Rights convention, which would invite other southerners to join with Mississippi in nominating a president and vice president on a States' Rights ticket.[24]

In accordance with his desire to place Mississippi at the helm of a southern revolt, Governor Wright helped fellow dissidents publish a special newspaper and create a People's Committee of Loyal States' Rights Jeffersonian Democrats. The functions of these extra organizations were to publicize the southern cause, to raise funds, and to foster and coordinate local movements under the leadership of county chairmen. Wallace W. Wright, president of a Jackson grocery firm, was appointed chairman of the new committee. The governor was honorary chairman.[25] Together they founded its official organ, the *States' Righter*. This newspaper advertised the various southern movements against the national Democratic party and sought to give the revolt a political and philosophical rationale. Its editors reasoned, in line with the Virginians, that "we do not feel we are bolting the party. We feel that the party has departed far away from the principles of Jefferson and left us high and dry." These remarks were clearly aimed at those people who feared the political consequences of dropping the Democratic label. But they knew that it was the race question that would ultimately spur the rank and file into revolt. Consequently, they constantly harped upon—and distorted—the ramifications of the president's civil rights program. The "anti-segregation bill," as they termed it, "would abolish the separation of the races as now practised throughout the South generally. . . . Soon

24 New Orleans *Times-Picayune*, March 2, 1948; Richard Dallas Chesteen, "The 1948 States' Rights Movement in Mississippi" (M.A. thesis, University of Mississippi, 1964), 50–51.
25 New Orleans *Times-Picayune*, February 23, 1948; Chesteen, "The 1948 States' Rights Movement in Mississippi," 51.

there would be no difference in hotels, restaurants, theatres, schools and other public places." [26]

Because white Mississippians exaggerated Truman's intentions, it did not mean that their fears were not real. The series of Supreme Court decisions on the question of discrimination and the emergence of civil rights in general as a major issue in Washington convinced white supremacists that the movement to create equal opportunities for Negroes would gain momentum—especially since the black population of the North, with its concomitant voting power, was increasing rapidly. They felt that there were only two ways to offset the political effects of this development. One was to show that the South was capable of counteracting the Negroes' influence by threatening to withdraw its support from the national Democratic party, thus depriving it of future electoral victories. The other was to reverse somehow the trend toward federal responsibility for social welfare. Mississippi's leaders believed that if they could halt the tendency toward paternalism in the federal government and increase the power of the state authorities, then civil rights as a national issue might also diminish. They argued that "the whole case seems to boil down to the fact that in this twentieth century the country is getting away from the belief in free enterprise and states' rights. . . . The rising tide of centralization and federal ownership must be reversed." [27] This emphasis on states' rights served two additional purposes. It attempted to exonerate white supremacists from charges of racism—even though they unhesitatingly used racial fear as a political weapon. And second, the rebels hoped to attract anti–New Deal southerners, who were equally concerned with the federal government's policies on labor, social security, and economic planning. But, for many of the insurgents this was a mere

26 *States' Righter,* I (April, 1948); also, pamphlet, Mississippi state Democratic party, *Know All the Fact About Truman's So-Called "Civil Rights" Program and What It Means to You,* in States' Rights Scrapbook.
27 *States' Righter,* I (April, 1948).

facade. Fielding Wright was the first to admit that Truman's civil rights program was "the straw that broke the camel's back, and caused Southern Democrats to flare up into open threat of rebellion." [28]

Antagonism toward the Democratic party's sponsorship of civil rights legislation was no less pronounced in South Carolina, which ranked second only to Mississippi in its proportion of Negroes. As in Mississippi, the state's leading critic was its governor. J. Strom Thurmond, like Fielding Wright, was backed fully by the state machine. However, Thurmond differed from Wright in his general approach to insurgency and in his style of presentation. Wright had unequivocally favored unilateral action in Mississippi and had opposed attempts to mediate with the national Democratic leadership. Thurmond, on the other hand, appeared to be more compromising. He initially hoped to prevail over the national party leaders to make some concessions on the civil rights proposals and to drop Truman from the ticket. Although these were fanciful ideas, they do illustrate that Thurmond wished to show that his actions were cautious and well considered. Furthermore, he did not want to appear to be concerned solely with the race issue. Indeed, he had had a relatively progressive record as governor. He was sympathetic to organized labor, had sponsored some important state welfare reforms, and had acted with uncommon speed to secure the apprehension of the perpetrators of a particularly brutal lynching in 1947.[29] He was particularly anxious, therefore, not to be portrayed in 1948 as a southern bigot. He continually insisted that the civil rights program constituted only one of his grievances, albeit the most deeply felt, against the federal government. He could point to the renowned anti–New Deal reputation of most of his followers, such as H. Klugh Purdy, chairman of Jasper County's Democratic executive committee. But

28 Fielding Wright, "Give the Government Back to the People," *American Magazine* CXLVI (July, 1948), 36, 37, 126, 127.
29 Thurmond to J. B. Finley, February 25, 1947, Osceola E. McKaine to Thurmond, March 12, 1947, in Thurmond Papers.

there was an inconsistency between his claims and the reality of his own behavior. Despite his claim that he was equally aroused by the economic policies of the Roosevelt and Truman administrations, there is no evidence that he ever made a sustained attack on the national leadership before February, 1948. Indeed, as already noted, as late as October, 1947, he had delivered a speech eulogistic of Truman. Although he insisted that "we are making this fight, not from the standpoint of racial discrimination or on the theory of white supremacy, but on State sovereignty or local State government," there is good reason to believe that the issue of centralization and governmental paternalism was an afterthought.[30]

Thurmond was projected into the leadership of the southern movement in his capacity as chairman of the special committee of the southern governors. After the meeting with McGrath in February, Thurmond became convinced that bargaining within the party would not move the administration to dilute its proposals. He then joined Fielding Wright and the other southern governors in their March resolution to work for the withholding of electoral college votes from the Democratic nominee, if that nominee did not disown the civil rights proposals.[31] Thurmond had the full support of the state executive committee, although South Carolina's congressional delegation was not as overwhelmingly in favor of an electoral college bolt as was Mississippi's. Members of Congress, of course, had more to lose than state politicians from open rebellion. Seniority and patronage could be denied them. Moreover, if one or more of them decided to fight Truman from within the party, the bolters stood a greater risk of political punishment, which can be visited more readily upon a few than upon the many. If, as in Mississippi, the entire congressional delegation supported the plans for independence in the electoral college, then depriva-

---

30 Thurmond to Colonel Damon Gunn, March 22, 1948, in Box 7, Thurmond Papers; J. Strom Thurmond, interview with author, October, 1969.
31 Committee Report Adopted by Southern Governors' Conference, Washington, D.C., March 13, 1948, in States' Rights Papers, Thurmond Papers; New York *Times,* March 14, 1948.

tion of congressional privileges would be more difficult to accomplish.[32]

Thurmond's most vocal opponent in South Carolina was Senator Olin D. Johnston. Johnston in many ways typified the Democrat who was torn between the principles of partisan loyalty (based on firm ideological principles, not romantic delusion) and white supremacy. Johnston, despite his notorious antipathy to the black franchise and protective legislation for Negroes, had been an ardent supporter of the New Deal and Fair Deal. He had advocated most of the social reforms of the previous decade and had been outspoken in his opposition to the Taft-Hartley Act. He did not, therefore, wish to repudiate the party that had sponsored so many measures with which he was sympathetic. He believed southerners should concentrate on preventing Truman from being renominated. This was the most effective kind of rebuff and could be accomplished only by working within the Democratic fold. He was confident that another nominee could repudiate the civil rights program without adverse political repercussions. Truman, he knew, was bound by his February proposals. He wanted a presidential candidate "with ability to harmonize the discordant elements within the Party." [33] Unlike the more obdurate insurgents, Johnston realized that the party had to represent a coalition of geographic and class interests. He was unalterably opposed to Truman, but he knew that a national party could not merely reflect the views of the South. He told Governor Fielding Wright: "It is my belief that most of us would prefer to fumigate the Democratic party than abandon it to those who have temporarily gained control. As I have stated previously, it is imperative that we be for somebody rather than merely against Truman." Nonsoutherners also, he pointed out, felt that Truman "cannot possibly win in the November election." They were "unwilling to back a candidate predestined to defeat."

32 Courtney Pace, interview with author, September, 1969.
33 Johnston to A. C. Tobias, Jr., March 22, 1948, in Box 240, Johnston Papers, SCL.

The southerners should, therefore, in cooperation with other party members, find a potentially successful candidate who could command the support of both regions.[34]

Local party officials, however, did not share Senator Johnston's views. They were unencumbered by the fear of political punishment and had fewer ideological ties to the administration. They proceeded, therefore, to pave the way for independent action in the electoral college. In February alone two county committees relinquished their ties with the national Democratic party and resolved to exercise their votes in the convention and electoral college without restriction.[35] The state executive committee, headed by William P. Baskin, was understandably influenced by the rumblings in the counties. In its March meeting it resolved to oppose Truman's nomination in all circumstances and to name only anti-Truman electors in order to help southern Democrats develop "joint and effective action."[36] This resolution was later confirmed by the state convention, held in Columbia on May 19, and attended by an overwhelming majority of antiadministration delegates. The convention nominated Strom Thurmond for president and instructed South Carolina's delegates to the Philadelphia convention to withhold their votes from Truman. In the event of Truman's nomination, the state executive committee was empowered to decide for whom the state's electoral votes should be cast. However, state officials typically rejected the formation of "anything resembling an outright third party movement" in favor of the selective exercise of its electoral college votes.[37]

While South Carolina's politicians were paving a course for a possible electoral college bolt, Alabama's Black Belt leaders asserted such absolute control over the party that they were

---

34 Johnston to Fielding Wright, March 22, 1948, in Exhibition Case, Johnston Papers, SCL.
35 Charleston *News and Courier*, February 10, 24, 1948.
36 *Ibid.*, January 17, 1948.
37 *Ibid.*, May 4, 20, 1948; Robert M. Figg, Jr., to Dixon, May 25, 1948, in Dixon Papers.

able to exclude completely all avenues of protest other than party secession. Even though there were a number of men in high office in Alabama, including Governor Folsom, who advocated an intraparty struggle, their views were thwarted by a series of political manipulations. These maneuvers were possible because the loyalist faction was not effectively represented in the key party committees. Alabama would become the only state which compelled an electoral college bolt and actually omitted the national Democratic nominee from the ballot. An examination of the anti-Truman movement in Alabama illustrates how the party machine in one state was able to bring to its logical conclusion the theory that the state party owed no obligation to the national party. It also shows how an important progressive element in the Democratic party of Alabama could be rendered completely powerless by an omnipotent and cohesive state executive committee.

Gessner T. McCorvey, Alabama's state Democratic chairman, had issued a number of insurgent warnings to Presidents Roosevelt and Truman and national Democratic chairmen prior to 1948. It was hardly surprising, therefore, when, after Truman had made his proposals on civil rights, McCorvey announced his intention to sever relations with the national Democratic party unless it forthrightly rejected Truman's recommendations. In conjunction with a Birmingham lawyer, Horace Wilkinson, a vocal white supremacist and a former "Hoovercrat," McCorvey proceeded to carry out his threat. Together, they requested from candidates for elector signed statements which pledged that votes would be cast against any Democratic nominee who failed to disown the entire civil rights program. McCorvey also asked Alabama's delegates to the Philadelphia convention to pledge themselves to walk out if a civil rights plank were adopted. By mid-March they had secured pledges from most of the candidates for elector.[38] However, the candidates for dele-

38 Horace C. Wilkinson to Hobbs, March 18, 1948, in Hobbs Papers; Wilkinson to McKellar, March 18, 1948, in McKellar Papers; W. R. Withers to John Sparkman, August 20, 1948, in Dixon Papers; Key, *Southern Politics*, 332.

gates to the national convention were more divided on the question of a walkout. The militants unhesitatingly favored a walkout in the event of the adoption of a civil rights plank. They argued that a withdrawal would save the South from the criticism that it had bolted—since it would not have participated in the actual nomination proceedings in the first place.[39] They also stressed that dissociation would be an appropriate buffet to the representatives of the urban coalition at Philadelphia. Birmingham's police commissioner, Eugene "Bull" Connor, was confident that a dramatic gesture of this kind would "help roll back the attempt of meddlers, agitators and Communist stooges to force down our throats, through our own Democratic Party, the bitter dose they are now offering us under the false name of Civil Liberties."[40] On the other hand, the opponents, who included Senators Sparkman and Hill, Governor Folsom, and former governor Chauncey Sparks, argued that a walkout defied democratic principles and that the South should fight the proposals from within the party councils.[41] Lister Hill reasoned that if the South disengaged itself from the Democratic party, "we would but weaken the very arm with which we battle these measures in the House and Senate."[42] Sparks emphasized the broader implications. "A re-

39 McCorvey to Members of the State Democratic Executive Committee of Alabama, April 1, 1948, in Dixon Papers; Robert T. Albritton to Rushton, April 20, 1948, in Rushton Papers.

40 Circular from Eugene "Bull" Connor, March 8, 1948, in Rushton Papers; Eugene "Bull" Connor to Candidates for Delegate at Large to the Democratic National Convention, April 23, 1948, in Chauncey Sparks Papers, Alabama Department of Archives, Montgomery.

41 All these politicians had publicly opposed Truman's civil rights proposals. However, there was a small but influential group of white Alabamians who endorsed the recommendations of *To Secure These Rights*. These were various labor leaders and former members of the Southern Conference of Human Welfare. Most famous of all was Aubrey Williams. He accused Fielding Wright "that you want to fight the Civil War all over again. Failing to hold the Negro in legal slavery, you now want to deny him the freedom which was so dearly bought. . . . Your stand . . . is brutally undemocratic and brazenly un-Christian, and far from easing the tensions of race antagonism in the South, what you are doing will increase them ten-fold." Aubrey Williams to Fielding Wright, February 25, 1948, in Hobbs Papers.

42 Memphis *Commercial Appeal*, March 12, 1948.

quest to walk out after I have made the fight and lost is little different from asking a member of Congress to walk out when that body passes laws to which he or his state or his region objects," he said. Even in sheer practical terms, nothing would be achieved. Secession, said Sparks, would be "evidence of the continued frustration and indecision of the South. We would have no particular place to walk to, certainly not to Republicans and get a worse dose of civil rights; nor to Wallace's Third Party, which is worse still." [43]

In spite of this formidable and outspoken opposition to a divorce from the national Democratic party, the views of McCorvey and the insurgents prevailed. In the May primary, Alabama's voters selected eleven electors pledged to vote against a nominee who supported in any way the civil rights program.[44] This meant, of course, that if Truman or any other Democratic liberal were nominated in Philadelphia, there was no means by which regular Democrats in Alabama could vote for the national ticket. Alabama law permitted only the names of candidates who were supported by the state's electors to appear on the ballot. Anybody, therefore, who tried even to place a pro-civil rights candidate on the ballot, would be considered a bolter from the state party and could conceivably be deprived of his vote in future primaries.[45] Thus did Alabama succeed in compelling an electoral bolt in the event of an unfavorable nomination.

The controversies in Alabama, Mississippi, and South Carolina, in short, showed that if the state executive committees overwhelmingly supported a Democratic bolt, then it was both feasible and likely that a bolt would occur. Moreover, since none of these states faced gubernatorial elections that year, the

---

43 Sparks to McCorvey, April 6, 1948, Sparks to Sidney M. Sayer, April 9, 1948, also speech, Chauncey Sparks, "What of Alabama and the Democratic Party?" March 25, 1948, all in Sparks Papers.

44 John Fagg Gillis to Rushton, May 4, 1948, in Rushton Papers; New York Times, May 6, 1948. The primary was dominated by the race issue. Potential bolters portrayed Truman's proposals as an assault on segregation.

45 McCorvey to Joseph N. Langan, August 13, 1948, in Hobbs Papers.

Democratic committees were able to devote more time and energy to the forthcoming presidential campaign. In Mississippi and South Carolina, the two southern states with the highest proportion of Negroes, there was a substantial grass roots movement against the national Democratic party. Local county committees drew up their own resolutions of party severance and fostered local meetings and conventions to impress upon the respective state organizations that white southerners were determined to take positive measures against the civil rights proposals. In Alabama, where there was considerably more opposition to a bolt, Black Belt leaders took full advantage of party rules to foreclose any alternative action. All the rebels justified their course by pointing to Truman's civil rights program. In most cases, however, the dissidents had been censorious of the national Democratic party before 1948—Thurmond was a notable exception to this pattern.

The nucleus and model for a revolt, then, was to be found in these three states. In no other southern state did the revolt against the national Democratic party assume the same dimensions. Throughout the rest of the South the arguments against a bolt usually prevailed. The majority of politicians were reluctant to leave the national Democratic party because they were uncertain about their own political positions. Sometimes they were afraid to interfere with traditional Democratic loyalties; sometimes they were loath to inject this explosive issue into their own complicated election campaigns. Usually, however, they eschewed a revolt if the state party organization was split into different factions. A very brief examination of the movement in some other Dixie states should suffice to illustrate that a revolt was more likely to occur in states with relatively monolithic organizations and, very important, in states which were not involved in their own political campaigns in 1948.

Perhaps the most notable of the recently converted rebels in 1948 was Edward H. Crump, Memphis' powerful political boss. Crump had been a loyal, if not always uncritical, follower of President Roosevelt. He had fully recognized the extent of

Roosevelt's popularity in the South and admired his political acumen. He had also respected Roosevelt personally. Crump, who himself stemmed from a planting family, empathized with FDR's exuding sense of *noblesse oblige* and his unabashed love for comfort and rural serenity. Crump, however, had never transferred his enthusiasm to Truman. At the Chicago convention in 1944 he had even refused to vote for him. Crump's contempt for Truman became greater when he announced his civil rights program and, equally important, when it became increasingly apparent that the president could not hold his party together. Crump had never tolerated losers. Yet there was an ironic twist to Crump's break with the administration. He, too, was losing ground in his native Tennessee. His grip over Memphis had been somewhat weakened by the incursions of the CIO. Similarly, in other cities the unions had made substantial gains and, through political action, had secured the election of a number of liberals, including Estes Kefauver, to Congress and the state legislature. Indeed, the anti-Crump forces put up a formidable ticket for the congressional and gubernatorial elections in 1948.[46] Crump decided that the use of the race issue, together with his call for a "showdown in the South," would enable him to retrieve his waning political fortunes. However, he miscalculated. Even his oldest political ally, Senator Kenneth McKellar, realized that Tennesseans would not respond to these tactics.[47] The state had few predominantly Negro counties, so the race issue was scarcely preoccupying. Indeed, since Crump himself had never invoked white supremacy before, his crusade lacked credibility. Consequently his strategy rebounded. Despite calls for a bolt in a sprinkling of counties, most Tennesseans found Crump's attitude either outmoded or irrelevant—as illustrated by the fact that in the August primaries Crump's candidates for governor and U.S. senator were beaten by the liberals. Needless to say,

46 Miller, *Mr. Crump of Memphis,* 322; Key, *Southern Politics,* 62–75.
47 Memphis *Commercial Appeal,* March 2, 1948; statement by Kenneth McKellar, July, 1948, in McKellar Papers.

Crump's repudiation at the polls was the death knell of a bolt in Tennessee.[48]

In Arkansas, as in Tennessee, the absence of any unified political machine stifled any effective move to bolt in the electoral college. Governor Ben Laney and the state party chairman, Arthur Adams, were early converts to the cause of a revolt, but found other party members unwilling to commit themselves in the same way. Arkansas had no distinct political alignments or controlling factions. Each politician generally looked after his own interests. Election campaigns were usually centered around personalities. "Causes" and factionalism played a lesser role in Arkansas than in a number of other southern states.[49] Thus, Laney's associations with Thurmond and Wright offered few political attractions to state officials who did not depend on the goodwill and patronage of the party hierarchy for their tenure in office. The state Democratic executive committee remained noticeably silent while Laney and Adams inveighed against the national party leadership and advocated united southern action.[50] Many of its members were more concerned about the impending campaign for the office of governor. Laney himself was not a candidate and could, perhaps, afford the luxury of an independent stand. One of the gubernatorial candidates, Jack Holt, tried to make political capital out of the civil rights issue, but found that his opponents were reluctant to delve into the hazardous territory of political revolts. They were particularly unwilling to inject this issue into the campaign, since one of the principal lobbyists for an electoral college bolt was the renownedly anti–New Deal business organization, the Arkansas Free Enterprise Association. Given the early indifference of the party machine, Holt should have realized that an alliance with an ultraconservative business

48 Memphis *Commercial Appeal*, August 6, 1948.
49 Key, *Southern Politics*, 184–200.
50 *Arkansas Gazette*, March 3, 15, April 27, 1948. See also, Sam Rorex to Louis Johnson, May 15, 1948, Charles E. Goodman to Matt Connelly, April 20, 1948, in OF 300, Truman Papers.

association could be exploited by the other contestants to raise the suspicions and doubts of the electorate.[51] In sum, political interests in Arkansas were too varied and heterogeneous for an effective revolt from the national party.

Veteran anti–New Dealers also led the insurgents in Louisiana and Texas. In Louisiana former governor Sam Jones and John U. Barr, head of the Byrd-for-President Committee in 1944, agitated for the selection of independent electors. The emergence of the race issue enabled them to arouse voters and local party officials in a way they had failed to accomplish in 1944. But they received no encouragement from Governor Earl Long. Long was busy overhauling and consolidating the party machine, which had been under the control of the anti-Long faction for eight years. In addition to the task of reinvigorating his own faction, he was eager not to antagonize officials in Washington, as he hoped to secure federal aid to fulfill his election promises for higher social security benefits. His opponents had also accused him of income tax evasion, and Long consequently may have wished to keep on friendly terms with the administration to avoid investigations into his personal finances.[52] But he was unable to prevent the agitation for concerted action against Truman—although until September, 1948, the state central committee avoided any positive commitment on the question of secession from the national party. In May and June the state legislature passed a series of resolutions condemning the president and urging the state of Louisiana to "take its rightful place at the side of all sovereign states that will oppose this unconstitutional and undemocratic

51 John L. Daggett to Dixon, May 28, 1948, in Dixon Papers; *Arkansas Gazette*, April 28, May 12, July 23, 1948. The Free Enterprise Association, headed by John L. Daggett, a leader of the anti-fourth term forces in 1944, had also carried the anti-closed shop banner in Arkansas after the war.

52 Sam Jones to Dixon, May 24, 1948, in Dixon Papers; New Orleans *Times-Picayune*, February 6, 23, 1948; *Congressional Record*, 80th Cong., 2nd Sess., 1335–336, A3607–609; Allan P. Sindler, *Huey Long's Louisiana: State Politics, 1920–1952* (Baltimore, 1956), 212–13, 220–21.

'civil rights' program." [53] The Louisiana Police Jury Association (the organization of county governments), which was predominantly anti-Long, similarly endorsed Fielding Wright's call for a coordinated southern strategy. But no official action was taken by the state party prior to July, as one vital element for an electoral bolt—the support of the governor—was not forthcoming.[54]

Texas' Governor Beauford Jester similarly did not lend his support to the move to dissociate from the Democratic party. Admittedly, he castigated Truman frequently and issued a number of threats to sever his ties with Washington. However, he did not want to be associated with either the racist fringe or the formidable contingent of conservatives within his own state. Although he retained control over the state party organization, he reasoned that a bolt in a state with a Negro population of only 14 percent would realize few political bounties. Thus, after some preliminary flirtations with the advocates of a bolt, he announced his intention to work within the party. A number of observers believed that Jester's initial proclivity for the rebels was the result of pressure from the oil interests, who had been incensed over the federal government's claim to the offshore seabed. One critic cynically referred to Jester's followers as "Tidelands Democrats." [55] However, although many politicians were indeed censorious of Truman's handling of the tidelands issue, it is improbable that their fundamental attitudes were molded or changed by this particular controversy.

53 Louisiana, *Official Journal of the Proceedings of the House of Representatives,* 14th Sess., 24, 57.
54 New Orleans *Times-Picayune,* April 27, 29, 1948; John U. Barr, "Louisiana Can Be Proud," *Louisiana Police Jury Review,* XIII (April, 1949), 13–17.
55 Statement and release of letter, Creekmore Fath to Beauford Jester, February 20, 1948, in OF 56 F, Truman Papers. Radio address of Jester, November 17, 1947, in Box 64, McGrath Papers; speech, Jester, delivered at Fort Worth, Texas, April 20, 1948, Harry L. Seay to HST, June 1, 1948, in OF 300, Truman Papers; U.S. Congress, Committees on the Judiciary, *Joint Hearings to Confirm and Establish the Titles of the States to the Tidelands,* 80th Cong., 2nd Sess., 118–51.

There is little evidence to substantiate the charges that the supporters of the movement to nominate independent electors were either inspired or financed by the oil barons. Indeed, many of the more renowned businessmen were confirmed anti–New Dealers long before the issue of ownership of the tidelands had arisen. And Governor Jester not only decided to disengage himself from the former "Regulars" but also was sufficiently reconciled to the administration to accompany Truman on a tour of Texas in September.[56]

To summarize, there was a common pattern to the revolt throughout the South. In each state the proponents of independence tried to persuade the respective party organization to pledge itself to oppose Truman or any other Fair Deal Democrat in the national convention. If this step failed, they hoped the electors would vote in the electoral college for a candidate who was acceptable to the South as a whole. The insurgents always wanted to work within the regular Democratic organization of each state. They were reluctant to found a third party for two main reasons. First, they recognized that the Democratic party was too firmly entrenched in the political culture of the South for a radical realignment in the party system. The party had been an umbrella of white unity for fifty years; the rebels were loath to discard it now. Second, they argued that the South should not be required to sacrifice its political establishment for the vagaries of the Democrats in the North. At any rate, they insisted, each state party was autonomous and could wield its powers in any way thought fit. They found, however, that Democratic leaders would consider committing themselves to independent action only if there was no serious danger of division within the hierarchy

56 See, for example, Thomas Sancton, "White Supremacy: Crisis or Plot?" *Nation* (July 24, 1948); "High Cotton," *New Republic* (August 20, 1948); clipping, Washington *Post*, October 20, 1948, in DNC Files, HSTL; Barker, "Offshore Oil Politics: A Study in Public Policy Making," 92–93; telegram, HST to Jester, September 17, 1948, telegram, Jester to HST, September 17, 1948, in PPF 3214, Truman Papers. The finances of the States' Rights Democrats are discussed in the following chapter.

of the state party. Thus, bolters from states with loose factional systems, imminent gubernatorial primaries, loyalist governors, small concentrations of Negroes, and influential second forces (such as labor unions or Republicans) generally found that they could not carry the incumbent party machine. They were, however, successful in states which were preoccupied with the race issue or where, as in Alabama, the state executive committee was powerful and cohesive enough to thwart the activities of the party faithful.

The insurgents were not discouraged unduly by the absence of substantive support from the top echelons. They believed that most southern whites were disturbed by recent developments and hoped to create a popular crusade. However, they were aware that their movement would flounder if the rebels in the states did not coordinate their activities. They recognized that the revolt would have to be southwide to be at all effective. Each state comprised an organizational nucleus for action at the national convention and in the electoral college, but it was essential for the state parties to agree on one alternative ticket and platform. If the South were merely against Truman and miscellaneously presented a variety of favorite sons to the Democratic convention, then the choice of the North would easily prevail. So, the leaders and organizations prominent in the States' Rights movement undertook to rationalize and unify their forces and to create for southern voters a sense of regional solidarity and identity.

The person who was most concerned with broadening the appeal of the States' Rights movement was Fielding Wright. The Mississippi governor believed that if southern dissidents could get together in appropriate conditions, then the cause would gain a momentum of its own. It was necessary, of course, to meet before the Democratic convention so a strategy could be worked out and publicized. His dream of a southern assembly, representing all dissident elements in the South, finally materialized in May, when the rebels gathered at Jackson, Mississippi, for a conference of States' Rights Democrats.

Wright and his associates intended to establish a formal organization at Jackson, to lay down formally its principles and to formulate contingency plans in the event of victory for the Truman Democrats at Philadelphia. However, there were already a few bad omens for Wright at the conference. A majority of the delegates were from Mississippi anyway. There were active delegations from Alabama, South Carolina, and to a lesser degree, from Arkansas, but the remaining Dixie states did not send any official representatives. In fact, many of them were either disgruntled businessmen or dedicated "unreconstructed rebels." [57]

The conferees, however, were apparently not deterred by this limited attendance. They showed an unhesitating determination to use all possible means to preserve white supremacy and to challenge the Democratic leadership. After a defiant keynote speech from Strom Thurmond, the participants, under the guidance of Governor Ben Laney, permanent chairman, drew up their declaration of principles. They resolved to "reestablish the Democratic Party on the principles for which it has always stood and to make use of the electoral vote to again demonstrate that no longer may the individual states be ignored in party councils and in the formulation of party policies." They advised all southern delegates to the national convention to come to a prior agreement about strategy at Philadelphia and recommended that they insist on certain motions. The Democratic nominees would be required to repudiate the civil rights program and affirm their belief in states' rights. If these provisos were not met, the southerners were advised to reconvene in Birmingham on July 17 to select alternative candidates for president and vice president. These nominees would then become the official candidates of the respective state parties. Voicing a familiar theme, the Jackson conferees insisted that "in no sense can this action be described as bolting the

57 James S. Peters to Dixon, May 20, 1948, in Dixon Papers; New York *Times*, May 11, 1948; Atlanta *Constitution*, May 11, 1948; Charleston *News and Courier*, May 11, 1948.

party, forming a new party, nor as the holding of a rump convention. The national party organization is merely an association of the various state party organizations." [58] Thus, by the middle of May, Dixie's insurgents had carefully formulated plans to take independent, unilateral action if the Democratic National Convention refused to take account of their complaints. It was indeed ironical that even at this stage they could not tolerate any suggestion to drop the Democratic label.

Meanwhile, opposition to the renomination of President Truman was arising in other sections of the party—and for different reasons. Public opinion polls repeatedly showed that the Republicans would beat Truman in November. The poll of the *Public Opinion Quarterly* showed that Dewey had an 8.5 percent lead over the president in April; by June, Dewey's margin increased to 12 percent.[59] For this reason a number of outstanding liberal northern Democrats, who were anyway apprehensive about Truman's personal capacities, decided that they would try to nominate someone else at the Democratic convention in Philadelphia. They feared that Henry Wallace, who had revealed his strength in a special congressional election in the Bronx in February, 1948, would win a substantial number of votes in the North unless the Democrats produced a viable alternative candidate.[60]

The attitude of these Democratic liberals was somewhat anomalous. Truman had clearly adopted and extended Franklin Roosevelt's domestic policies—especially on civil rights. Throughout the early part of 1948 the president had sent a barrage of special messages to Congress, requesting the enactment of his own Fair Deal proposals. Truman's public actions simply gave lie to insinuations from some quarters that his

---

58 Declaration of Principles of Conference of States' Rights Democrats, May 10, 1948, various resolutions of States' Rights Democrats, May 10, 1948, in States' Rights Scrapbook.
59 "The Quarter's Polls," *Public Opinion Quarterly*, XII (Winter, 1948), 767.
60 New York *Times*, February 18, 1948; Brock, *Americans for Democratic Action*, 58–98.

commitment to social reform was essentially fragile. However, the anti-Wallace liberals felt that Truman simply could not win and that it was in the Democrats' interests to replace him. They could not forgive the president's earlier waverings in his economic policies and disliked his general political style. Even his voice, which was flat and unvaried, was criticized for its failure to inspire the popular imagination. They believed that despite his stands on civil rights and social welfare, he did not possess Roosevelt's sense of vision. Of course, Truman had never tried to emulate his predecessor—yet this seemed only to reinforce the liberals' conviction that Truman lacked Roosevelt's personal qualities. Above all, they felt he was a loser. There seemed to be no doubt that he would be resoundingly beaten in November and that other progressive Democrats, such as Adlai Stevenson and Paul Douglas, both of Illinois, would be defeated on Truman's coattails.[61] The national board of the Americans for Democratic Action declared: "Our political crisis is essentially a crisis of leadership. As never before, we need greatness in the Presidency of the United States." It praised Truman's endeavors in the field of civil rights, labor legislation, and foreign policy, but added rather limply, "We cannot overlook the fact that poor appointments and faltering support of his aides have resulted in a failure to rally the people behind policies which in large measure we wholeheartedly support." The Chicago chapter of the ADA calculated that only 4 percent of its members favored Truman's reelection.[62]

In view of the divisions within the Democratic party, Truman and his inner council of campaign strategists had to devise means of reuniting the party. The president had drawn up the

---

61 Hamby, "Harry S. Truman and American Liberalism," 226; Alonzo Lee Hamby, "The Liberals, Truman, and FDR as Symbol and Myth," *Journal of American History*, LVI (March, 1970), 859–67; Jules Abels, *Out of the Jaws of Victory* (New York, 1959), 14–24; James A. Stayer, "A History of the Presidential Campaign of 1948" (M.A. thesis, University of Virginia, 1958), 83.
62 ADA statement on political policy, adopted April 11, 1948, in Clifford Papers; Brock, *Americans for Democratic Action*, 91–93.

issues clearly in the earlier part of 1948. In terms of policy-making initiatives, therefore, there was little else that could be done. Truman had to keep Wallace isolated, he had to keep Negro voters in the Democratic column, and he had to insure that the revolt in Dixie could be contained. Truman perceived that the only course open to him was to bide by his own pronouncements and commitments. However, he was prepared to change certain emphases and to reshuffle his priorities. He would continue to court Negro and labor voters, but would endeavor not to antagonize the South any further. Truman had not anticipated that the Dixie revolt would attract so many followers. He realized that although the rebels were irretrievable, he could not afford to alienate the southern moderates who still advocated compromise and debate within the party. This meant that he would have to defuse the civil rights issue.

There were several means employed by the Truman forces to dampen the race question and thus prevent the bolt from spreading. There were unsuccessful attempts to appoint special liaison officers to keep channels of communication open with southern congressmen.[63] The president abandoned his plan to make civil rights reform the "first goal" and publicly defended his refusal to send Congress the White House draft of the omnibus civil rights bill. Truman also did not issue, as he had promised in his February message, executive orders outlawing discrimination and segregation in the armed forces and the federal civil service. His personal staff had already prepared drafts of orders, but Truman deliberately delayed any formal announcements until after the Democratic convention. Truman's retreat in this matter was underlined by his decision to mention civil rights only once in a total of seventy-three speeches delivered during his "nonpolitical" tour in June.[64]

---

63 Redding, *Inside the Democratic Party*, 128–37.
64 Donald Dawson to Clark Clifford, March 8, 1948, in OF 596, Truman Papers; *Crisis*, LV (May, 1948); New York *Times*, June 3, 5, 8, 1948; Dalfiume, "Desegregation of the United States Armed Forces," 239–43; Ross, *The Loneliest Campaign*, 64–65; Ruth L. P. Morgan, "The Presidential

The most significant concession that Truman was prepared to make was on the wording of the party platform. He left the actual bargaining on the platform to his lieutenants. Led by McGrath, they tried to appease southerners by permitting a repetition of the 1944 plank on civil rights, which had been worded in a general way and had excluded any specific recommendations. But McGrath knew that he was caught in a dilemma. If the indefinite 1944 plank were accepted, northern Negroes would protest that Truman had reneged on his promises and had retreated to the equivocation so characteristic of his predecessor. So, although the Truman forces tried to persuade southerners to accept a vague civil rights plank, they were forced to do so surreptitiously for fear of alienating the black vote. Indeed, the southerners themselves realized that these peace feelers were aimed at preventing an open breach and did not really constitute an intention to revise the civil rights program. As Harry Byrd commented, "If Truman is nominated, he has made his own platform. I don't think anyone would pay much attention to what the party platform says about civil rights, when the President has made it clearer than any platform could, what he wants to do along these lines." [65] Not all southerners, however, shared Byrd's cynicism. Congressman John Rankin of Mississippi, who paid a well-publicized visit to the White House in June, felt convinced that if the 1944 plank were adopted, Truman would no longer feel obliged to press for protective legislation for Negroes. It is im-

---

Executive Order as an Instrument for Policy-Making" (Ph.D. dissertation, Louisiana State University, 1966), 32–39; Berman, "The Politics of Civil Rights in the Truman Administration," 77, 88–89; Harvard Sitkoff, "Harry Truman and the Election of 1948: The Coming of Age of Civil Rights in American Politics," *Journal of Southern History,* XXXVII (November, 1971), 609–10. In his *Memoirs* President Truman has implied that he favored and encouraged a strong civil rights platform all along. The bare facts of the case just do not correspond with Truman's account. Truman, *Memoirs,* II, 212–13.

65 Memo, William L. Batt to Clifford, June 8, 1948, in Clifford Papers; New York *Times,* June 8, 9, 1948.

probable, however, that the president would have retreated and maintained a stony silence. For despite his anxiety to appease southerners, his fundamental political calculations concerning the importance of the metropolitan vote had not changed.[66]

Despite pressures from the southerners and McGrath, who led the conciliatory contingent, Truman still was being urged to resume his militant posture. Although McGrath's supporters seemed to have the upper hand, as evidenced by Truman's sudden muteness on the race issue, there were still pressures from within the administration and the party organization to forsake further temptations to appease the South. Clark Clifford, for example, never proffered contrary advice to the champions of an aggressive policy on civil rights. The members of the new research division of the Democratic National Committee, which worked closely with Clifford and had ties with the ADA, counseled continually that the South should be given only secondary consideration in the formulation of electoral strategy—although, of course, they were never oblivious to the South's potential power to destroy the party. William L. Batt, Jr., director of the research division, urged the administration to gamble with the South's allegiance in order not to alienate Negro votes. Black ward leaders, he said, were warning him that Negroes would flock to Wallace unless Truman openly championed his own civil rights program. Batt recommended that Truman issue an executive order ending discrimination in the armed forces at once and reexamine the validity of his fears that such an order might exacerbate the southern revolt. He also proposed "the judicious use of appointments" of Negroes to counteract "the depredations of the Wallaceites." [67] Similarly, Senator Francis J. Myers of Pennsylvania, chairman

66 New York *Times*, June 23, 1948.
67 Memo, William L. Batt, Jr., to Gael Sullivan, April 20, 1948, memo, Batt to Clifford, June 8, 1948, memo, Kenneth Birkenhead to Batt, May 21, 1948, in Clifford Papers.

of the platform committee of the Democratic convention, brought McGrath's attention to a letter which urged his party leaders to publicize the Democrats' record on civil rights.[68]

Although the president equivocated on the race issue, he did not compromise his earlier position on labor legislation. Truman realized that despite the euphoria following upon his veto of the Taft-Hartley bill, he still had failed to gain the confidence of labor leaders. At the beginning of 1948, for example, the CIO's executive board had rejected association with Henry Wallace's Progressive party but had failed to endorse the president. Union leaders shared the ADA's skepticism about Truman's ability to lead the Democrats to victory. They believed that Truman was essentially chameleonic and was capable of altering political course for short-term advantage. Even the CIO-PAC, which had warmly endorsed Truman after his veto of Taft-Hartley, allocated funds only to candidates for Congress.[69] The president was determined to demonstrate that labor's apprehensions were ill founded. During his "nonpolitical" tour, he hammered at the Republicans for their supposed indifference to the welfare of workers and pledged his administration to support protective labor legislation. Furthermore, as the election drew nearer, he planned to consult with labor leaders on domestic policy. Just after the Democratic convention, but before the CIO finally endorsed Truman, Clifford advised the president to keep in constant communication with Philip Murray's group in order to persuade it of its political indispensability.[70]

Despite Truman's overtures to labor leaders, liberals still wanted to deny him the Democratic nomination. The group most active in the preconvention maneuvers to drop Truman from the ticket was the Americans for Democratic Action. The

68 Raymond P. Alexander to Francis J. Myers, May 11, 1948, in McGrath Papers.
69 CIO News, January 26, February 23, 1948; Arnold, "The CIO's Role in American Politics," 301–304; Brock, Americans for Democratic Action, 74.
70 Memo, Clifford to HST, July 22, 1948, in Clifford Papers; Baton Rouge Morning Advocate, July 8, 1948.

ADA had announced publicly that it regarded the president as a political liability. It resolved, therefore, to find a new leader who could be presented to the convention in place of Truman. The ADA reasoned that a substitute would not be so haunted by his previous declarations and actions and would, consequently, be able to reinvigorate the despondent and diffident supporters of the Democratic party. Accordingly, it began to search for a new candidate, and by March, General Dwight D. Eisenhower had emerged in ADA circles as the most popular choice for the presidency. One by one, such notable New Dealers as Chester Bowles, Leon Henderson, Adolf Berle, and, rather symbolically, the three sons of FDR, announced that they regarded General Eisenhower as the political savior of the Democratic party. They were joined by key Democratic officials, including Mayor William O'Dwyer of New York, Colonel Jacob Arvey, Chicago boss, and Jersey City's Frank Hague. The draft-Eisenhower movement received official endorsement in April from the executive board of the ADA, which called for an open convention (with no instructed delegates) and the nomination of Eisenhower and Justice William O. Douglas as his running mate.[71]

The draft-Eisenhower movement made strange bedfellows. Those very southern Democrats who found the ADA platform so alien to their own political philosophy joined the Eisenhower bandwagon in an attempt to ditch Truman at the convention. There was, of course, no formal association between the southerners and the Democratic liberals, but both felt that their own needs would be served by nominating the popular war hero. They did not appear to have given thought to the probability that if Eisenhower had been nominated, an intraparty battle on the platform would have occurred. Without any evidence, the ADA assumed that Eisenhower was sym-

71 Atlanta *Constitution,* July 4, 1948; Brock, *Americans for Democratic Action,* 91–93; Stayer, "A History of the Presidential Campaign of 1948," 80–83; Abels, *Out of the Jaws of Victory,* 73–82; Ross, *The Loneliest Campaign,* 114–15.

pathetic to their views, while the southern insurgents were equally confident that Ike was "safe." This bizarre alliance over Eisenhower's candidacy was a telling paradigm of Truman's decline. Both northerners and southerners were so convinced that Truman would lose the election that they were prepared to take the almost unprecedented step of depriving the incumbent president of the nomination and opting for a dark horse. Above all, it showed how both the South and the urban liberals appreciated that neither of them could exercise paramount influence over the party hierarchy and the White House. Each faction consequently sought a sympathetic and pliable leader who might restore its respective authority. And General Eisenhower seemed well endowed with these qualities.

The determination to find a candidate who sympathized with Dixie's political predicament and who offered a chance of success at the polls confused southerners of various ideological shades. They all seemed to see Eisenhower as the embodiment of their own political philosophies—liberal or conservative. Olin Johnston, who was himself sympathetic to the Fair Deal, wrote that Eisenhower was "the only possible hope of Democratic victory in November" and that he was "extremely liberal—probably to a much greater extent than Truman, who seems to have finally succeeded in getting himself tied hand and foot by the ultraconservatives—except for the race issue." [72] The staunch conservatives of Alabama's Black Belt were equally convinced that Eisenhower held the key to peace and harmony within the party. Eisenhower apparently was "the proper man and the best man for us to nominate for President." The fact that he was born in Texas (his family had moved to Kansas when he was a baby) was thought sufficient proof that he had "Southern sympathies." [73] Even Gessner McCorvey, one of the most recalcitrant and hardened of all Tru-

[72] Johnston to John B. Culbertson, March 25, 1948, in Box 240, Johnston Papers, SCL.
[73] Handy Ellis to Rushton, April 20, 1948, Rushton to McCorvey, April 19, 1948, in Rushton Papers.

man's critics, was prepared to give the general the benefit of the doubt. He wrote to Charles Wallace Collins, the southern ideologist, that Eisenhower "knows and understands the Southern negro and appreciates our problems, and I, for one, would be willing to risk him as our President without getting any positive commitment from him as to propositions on which I would wish to have other candidates definitely declare themselves." [74] Thus, the most dissident of southern Democrats were prepared in their desperation to give Eisenhower a carte blanche.

Eisenhower, on the other hand, did not want the nomination. He announced on three separate occasions that he would not be a candidate for the presidency.[75] With these firm rebuttals, the southerners and the Democratic liberals parted political company once more. Thenceforth, they concentrated on securing a platform representing their particular interests. It was inevitable that the race issue, which had so dominated domestic politics in the preceding nine months, should now emerge as the prime source of contention and ultimately split the party asunder.

There were three main groups at the Democratic convention in Philadelphia. The liberal forces consisted of representatives of Negro and labor organizations and members of the ADA, which sent approximately 110 delegates. They were led by the ebullient young mayor of Minneapolis, Hubert H. Humphrey, an affiliate of the ADA. They had agreed that if Truman were nominated, he should be bound to a plank on civil rights that specifically reiterated his earlier proposals.[76] The southerners, who made up the second group, were determined that the Democratic nominee should be elected on a plank that affirmed states' rights and omitted mention of Truman's civil rights program. Between these two groups came the administration cadres who hoped to prevent a schism by adopting a general

74 McCorvey to Charles W. Collins, July 14, 1948, in Dixon Papers.
75 New York *Times*, July 6, 1948; Atlanta *Constitution*, July 6, 1948.
76 New York *Times*, July 5, 1948.

plank on racial policy on the model used in 1944. These "moderates" assumed that since Roosevelt had managed to hold both the South and the urban coalition together, there was no reason why Truman could not achieve the same result. But they should have realized that circumstances had changed considerably. For Roosevelt had never overtly or consciously made civil rights a central party issue and thus party professionals never had been forced to confront the question separately. By 1948, on the other hand, civil rights had become the most pressing question of domestic policy, and equivocation would not have had the same effects as in 1944.

Senior officials of the Democratic National Committee hoped to smooth over the ill feeling generated over the race question by presenting a platform that did not specifically mention Truman's civil rights proposals. A majority of members of the convention platform committee, under the chairmanship of Senator Francis Myers of Pennsylvania, favored the compromise. However, they were obliged under party rules to conduct hearings on the platform and to permit the formulation of amendments, which could, with the permission of the permanent chairman and the committee on rules, be presented to the floor. The main outside pressure for a specific plank on civil rights came from Negro leaders who testified that failure to publicize the recommendations of *To Secure These Rights* would undermine the attachment of black voters to the Democratic party. A *Declaration of Negro Voters*, endorsed by twenty-one major Negro organizations, presented specific demands for inclusion in the platform. In a statement on behalf of the organization, Walter White warned the committee that if the party continued "to permit bigots to dictate its philosophy and policy" then the Democrats would lose their reputations as agents of reform and ultimately "perish." [77]

77 Pamphlet, *Declaration of Negro Voters*. This manifesto was modeled on the experiment first tried in 1944. (See Chapter 3.) Statement by Continuation Committee of 21 Negro Organizations in Presentation of *Declaration of Negro Voters* to the Democratic National Committee, July 8, 1948, in Box 367/1, NAACP Files; New York *Times*, July 9, 1948.

Walter White's admonitions did not fall entirely on unreceptive ears. There were four members of the ADA on the platform committee and, in accordance with previous plans and resolutions, they presented a plank which included nearly all the main proposals of Truman's earlier stand on civil rights. However, members of the platform committee who represented the administration's position rejected it by voice vote. They argued that this explosive issue should be stifled in the interests of party harmony and that Truman himself should be permitted to determine the matter. Hubert Humphrey, leader of the ADA group, said that he would not give in and that he would try to present his plank to the convention floor.[78]

The southerners were both as active and determined as the ADA. In the hectic days immediately preceding the nominations at Philadelphia, Dixie Democrats held innumerable caucuses and meetings to plan for all possible contingencies. They still remained divided on the question of a walkout and an electoral college bolt, but were all determined (with the possible exception of the uncompromisingly militant Mississippians) to prevail over the administration and the ADA by substituting a states' rights plank and, if possible, by defeating Truman. They gave top priority to the attempt to secure a plank on states' rights. Former governor Dan Moody of Texas, together with fourteen other southern members of the platform committee, presented an amendment which reserved to the states "the power to control and regulate local affairs." However, as with the ADA plank, the platform committee rejected the resolution by voice vote.[79]

Southern delegates also made elaborate preparations for the nomination. After the draft-Eisenhower movement had col-

78 Clipping, Kansas City *Star,* July 11, 1948, in DNC Files, HSTL; New York *Times,* July 8, 1948; Ross, *The Loneliest Campaign,* 120–21; Brock, *Americans for Democratic Action,* 97.
79 New York *Times,* July 11, 12, 13, 14, 1948; Baton Rouge *Morning Advocate,* July 10, 1948; clipping, New York *Herald-Tribune,* July 12, 1948, in DNC Files, HSTL; *Democracy at Work: The Official Report of the Democratic Convention* (Philadelphia, 1948), 178–79.

lapsed, Governor Ben Laney of Arkansas emerged as the South's most favored candidate for the presidency. The selection committee of the southern Democratic caucus accordingly agreed on July 11 to put the Arkansas governor into nomination. Laney thus became, albeit ephemerally, the chief coordinator of southern plans and objectives.[80] However, not all Dixie delegates trusted Laney. After all, he had flirted with the fire-eaters from Mississippi and Alabama and seemed committed to a bolt. The Texas delegation, for example, was split between those who unreservedly wished to concentrate on defeating President Truman and nominating Laney and those who were more concerned about the wording of the platform and subsequent party loyalty than about the personalities involved. The leaders of this latter group were Governor Jester, Senator Tom Connally, and Sam Rayburn. Rayburn, who was permanent chairman of the convention, argued that he could best use his influence "by looking in on the drawing of the platform." Wright Morrow, a senior party official, similarly felt that Texas should honor its pledge to support the nominee, even though "there is no man or woman on the floor who despises the idea of voting for Truman any more than I do." However, Laney's supporters had the upper hand. After Laney's pathetic plea to the effect that "the truth is that I'm just about all you've got," the Texas caucus agreed to oppose Truman and support a southern candidate.[81] The meetings of other southern delegations followed a similar course.

Against this background of activity the delegates to the convention began their formal deliberations. Alben Barkley, temporary chairman, started by making a rousing speech in which he extolled the virtues of Democratic rule and ritualistically castigated the Republicans as the purveyors of economic depression.[82] After similar speeches from a number of senior Dem-

---

80 Memphis *Commercial Appeal*, July 12, 1948.
81 Minutes of the caucuses of the Texas delegation to the Democratic National Convention, in Miscellaneous Files 1948, Rayburn Papers.
82 *Official Report of the Democratic Convention*, 33–47.

ocratic officials, the convention sat down to the business at hand. It was characteristic that nearly all the resolutions of major importance concerned the sectional antagonism produced by the race issue. The first source of contention was over the minority report of the committee on credentials—its authors included Adlai Stevenson and Hubert Humphrey. This report proposed that the Mississippi delegation not be seated. It was introduced onto the floor by a Negro delegate from Missouri, George Vaughn. Vaughn argued that since Mississippi's delegates were pledged to walk out in the event that Truman were nominated on a civil rights plank, they were disloyal and should thus be denied the right to participate in the proceedings. The resolution was rejected by voice vote.[83] But the sight of a Negro from Truman's home state moving on the exclusion of the Mississippi delegation had a lasting impression on southern members. An unflattering photograph of Vaughn was soon circulating among white supremacists in the Deep South.[84]

The southern delegates then attempted to restore the two-thirds rule. They felt that the abrogation of this rule in 1936 had enabled the Negro-labor bloc to emerge as the most powerful single group in succeeding conventions. The southerners, who no longer cherished illusions about Democratic brotherhood, wanted to end nominations by majority vote in order to veto unfavorable nominees. Accordingly, Wright Morrow of Texas introduced the motion, pointing out with rather unconvincing altruism that it would produce greater unanimity in the choice of president. State Senator Edgar Brown of South Carolina, who seconded the motion, did not mince words. He complained that a majority vote would result in the selection of "some outstanding liberal . . . the people of the solid Democratic states have been buffeted around long enough and they

83 *Ibid.*, 102–103; clipping, Jackson *Clarion-Ledger*, July 14, 1948, in States' Rights Scrapbook; clipping, Baltimore *Sun*, July 14, 1948, in DNC Files, HSTL.
84 McCorvey to Dixon and Horace Wilkinson, August 21, 1948 (including photograph), in Dixon Papers.

are not going to stand it for any longer." The southerners, however, were overwhelmed by voice vote, and the two-thirds rule remained a matter of history.[85]

The main battle was over the wording of the platform. Senator Myers introduced the majority report of the committee on platform and regulations. This reiterated Truman's Fair Deal program and included pledges to raise the minimum wage, repeal the Taft-Hartley Act, and institute a national health service. The platform, however, did make some concessions to the South. It omitted mention of the tidelands question. And, of course, it made only a vague, general commitment to civil rights. It stated that minorities "must have the right to live, the right to work, the right to vote, the full and equal protection of the laws, on a basis of equality with all citizens as guaranteed by the Constitution." [86]

In accordance with agreements in committee, the dissenters from the majority report rose to present their own minority resolutions to the convention. The southerners were particularly angered. Although they had accepted an almost identical plank in 1944, they had thought at the time that it was meaningless, since Roosevelt had never committed himself personally on the matter. But in the four years that had passed since the Chicago convention, the president had unambiguously committed himself to protective legislation for Negroes. Because of this radical development, the southerners had pledged themselves to fight for the omission of any mention of civil rights and for the substitution of a plank on states' rights. Accordingly, former governor Moody of Texas moved that the convention affirm its belief in states' rights, as the southern minority had suggested in committee. The minority report pointedly proclaimed that historically states' rights was a Democratic credo. It called for confirmation of the doctrine that "under the Constitution the general Federal Government and the separate states have their separate fields of power and have permitted activities" and that

85 *Official Report of the Democratic Convention*, 109–16.
86 *Ibid.*, 169–78.

the individual states had the authority to "control and regulate local affairs and act in the exercise of police powers." [87]

The Moody resolution was not the only one proffered by the South. A shorter report to the same effect was submitted by Cecil Sims, a delegate from Tennessee. And Walter Sillers, speaker of Mississippi's House of Representatives, submitted his own minority report which specifically mentioned the rights that were to be exercised exclusively by the states. These included "the power to provide by law for qualifications of electors, the conduct of elections, regulation of employment practices within the states, and segregation within the states." [88]

After the southerners had submitted their resolutions, Congressman Andrew J. Biemiller of Wisconsin submitted the minority report of the ADA affiliates. Introducing this version, Biemiller almost cynically pointed out that the majority report did not "give due recognition to the courageous fight of President Truman for civil rights." Biemiller thus reminded delegates that their party leader had taken a firmer stand earlier in the year. He and cosponsor Hubert Humphrey felt that further appeasement of the South would destroy the urban coalition. They also presumed that since the South would not even accept the administration's compromise, the convention had nothing to lose by adopting a more specific plank. The Humphrey-Biemiller resolution called upon Congress "to support our President" in guaranteeing the rights to "full and equal political participation," to "equal opportunity of employment," to "security of person," and to "equal treatment in the service and defense of our nation." [89]

Debate and supporting arguments followed the submission of the reports. The southerners emphasized that the states' rights plank was the basic pedestal of Democratic philosophy and had been confirmed at countless previous conventions. They maintained that the purpose of the plank was to restore harmony

87 *Ibid.*, 178–79.
88 *Ibid.*, 179–81.
89 *Ibid.*, 181–82.

and strengthen the party. Cecil Sims warned that the final vote would "determine whether or not the Democratic Party is to be destroyed in the South." [90] But the most electrifying statement came from Mayor Hubert Humphrey. In words alien to convention floors since Reconstruction, he pleaded: "My friends, to those who say this civil rights program is an infringement of states' rights, I say this, that the time has arrived in America for the Democratic Party to get out of the shadow of states' rights and to walk forthrightly into the bright sunshine of human rights." [91]

Humphrey's climactic speech had an instant effect. Delegates representing Negro, labor, and progressive interests were aroused from their spirit of resignation and gloom. The ADA contingent had been busy throughout the proceedings trying to rally support for the Humphrey-Biemiller resolution. They had finally persuaded the big city bosses to agree to the minority report. Ed Flynn of the Bronx agreed with the ADA that a forthright stand on civil rights was "what we need to stir up this convention and win the election." [92] Humphrey's oratory effectively kindled the enthusiasm of the big city delegations. After the minority resolutions on states' rights were shouted down by voice vote, Sam Rayburn permitted, in accordance with an agreement he had made the night before, a roll call vote to be taken on the Humphrey-Biemiller and Moody resolutions. The convention defeated the Moody resolution by 925 votes to 309. Every delegate from the South voted in favor of it; only eleven votes from outside the old Confederacy were cast with Dixie. Then came the vote on the ADA plank. After a breathtaking count, Rayburn announced that the plank had been carried by 651½ votes to 582½. The southern states had unanimously op-

90 *Ibid.*, 184–85.
91 *Ibid.*, 189–92; New York *Times*, July 15, 1948; Atlanta *Constitution*, July 15, 1948.
92 Quoted in Ross, *The Loneliest Campaign*, 124–25; Brock, *Americans for Democratic Action*, 98; New York *Times*, July 15, 1948.

posed it. They were joined by the delegations from Arizona, Idaho, Kentucky, Maryland, Nevada, North Dakota, Rhode Island, and Utah. But the industrial states of the North, with their crucial Negro electorate, voted overwhelmingly for it. Only one dissenting vote was cast from Illinois, California, Minnesota, Wisconsin, Michigan, New Jersey, Washington, Pennsylvania, and New York. The urban coalition had triumphed.[93]

It is unlikely that anybody in the convention hall could have misinterpreted the events that had just passed. Since his accession to the presidency, Truman had been vying for the continued support of liberals, Negroes, and workers. Their allegiance to Truman had seldom been more than lukewarm. But when they reconciled themselves to the fact that he was indisposable, they maneuvered to saddle him with his own civil rights proposals. Truman had courted the urban coalition more successfully than he had intended. He was not only unable to soft-pedal the program when southerners began to contemplate a political revolt but also had inadvertently lost control over his party. Southerners, too, had realized what had happened. They were not interested in the fact that the president had tried to tone down the plank on civil rights. So far as they were concerned, Truman had deliberately forced the convention into a showdown. He had been the helmsman of a convention which "ran roughshod over everything the South asked for." [94] Dixie Democrats had once controlled the party. Even under Roosevelt they had managed to circumscribe the thrust of social reform. But in 1948 they seemed powerless and impotent, victims of a political strategy almost intrinsically designed to alienate Dixie.

The southern rebels consequently proceeded to disown the party. Indeed, as soon as the tally on the Humphrey-Biemiller

---

93 *Official Report of the Democratic Convention,* 210.
94 Edith Susong to McKellar, July 16, 1948, in McKellar Papers; see also, Rushton to Grover C. Hall, July 23, 1948, in Rushton Papers; Doughton to Thad Wasielewski, July 26, 1948, in Folder 1584, Doughton Papers.

resolution was announced, the Mississippi delegation, joined by half of Alabama's delegates, walked out of the convention hall.[95] Although the other Dixie states remained, they refused to associate themselves with Truman's nomination. They joined forces and rallied behind Senator Richard B. Russell, who was nominated "as a protest against the outrageous violation of states' rights" and as a warning of the South's refusal to be "the whipping boy of the Democratic party." Of course, this last-minute bid was swamped by the northern delegates. Russell secured only 263 votes to Truman's 947½. Every ballot he received came from the South. North Carolina was the only Dixie state to cast a proportion of its votes for Truman. In fact, the convention was so split that nobody even bothered to move, as is customary, to make the nomination unanimous.[96]

95 George Wallace to Gladys King Burns, September 18, 1964, in Gladys King Burns Papers, Alabama Department of Archives, Montgomery. This letter, written in response to a query about a master's thesis, describes the factional split in the Alabama delegation. New York *Times*, July 19, 1948; *Official Report of the Democratic Convention*, 228–30.

96 *Official Report of the Democratic Convention*, 223; Atlanta *Constitution*, July 15, 1948; clipping, New York *Sun*, undated (presumably July 16, 1948), in Redding Papers; New York *Times*, July 15, 1948; Paul McNutt polled the remaining half vote, and Mississippi was not represented at the time of the roll call. The movement to nominate Governor Laney had collapsed, due largely to his unpredictable waverings on the question of an electoral college bolt.

CHAPTER NINE

The Dixiecrat Movement

NOT ALL southern delegates re-
turned to the apolitical serenity of their homes after the Democratic National Convention. A small number of them followed
the example of other disenchanted Democrats and converged
on Birmingham, Alabama, where they proceeded to hold their
own separate, southern convention. The organizers of this as-
semblage were eager to convey the impression that it was spontaneous, firmly dedicated to its cause, and "grass roots." [1] The
meeting was consequently open to anyone who cared to attend.
Approximately six thousand persons were present at the convention, but the vast majority of the self-styled delegates had
no official standing in the Democratic party. Furthermore, all
but a few came from either Mississippi or Alabama. Those who
did come from outside these two states were veteran anti–New
Dealers who had previously fought against the Democratic
party in an unofficial capacity. They included John U. Barr,
former head of the Byrd-for-President Committee, John Daggett of the Arkansas Free Enterprise Association, and some
notable Texas businessmen. *Newsweek* later dubbed them as

---

1 Horace Wilkinson to Ben Laney, July 1, 1948, Wilkinson to Merritt Gibson,
July 1, 1948, in Dixon Papers.

"successful amateurs who are more at home at Rotary and Kiwanis luncheons than in smoke-filled rooms." [2]

The leading figures at Birmingham were Strom Thurmond; Fielding Wright; Frank Dixon, former governor of Alabama; Horace Wilkinson; Merritt Gibson, a Longview, Texas, judge; and Wallace W. Wright, a Jackson grocery magnate, who led the States' Rights movement in Mississippi. The organizers had dismissed the idea of a separate southern party. They planned instead to recommend to the southern electors a special southern ticket, "with the idea," according to Dixon, "that through the use of the electoral college and the independence of our electors, we may be able to recapture some of the strength to which we are entitled in the councils of the Party." [3] In short, the insurgents intended to nullify the decisions of the Philadelphia convention by putting forward a slate of candidates who would be recognized in the South as the official nominees of the state Democratic parties. Accordingly, Strom Thurmond and Fielding Wright were recommended for the presidency and vice presidency respectively as States' Rights Democrats. They were obvious choices, since they were the only two southern governors to attend the meeting. And governors could most easily carry the state party organizations. [4]

The organizers of the Birmingham convention were largely preoccupied with defining and publicizing the issues upon which they were making their stand. Clarification of their intentions would not only be self-advertisement for the southern electorate

2 "Report on the 'New South'," *Newsweek* (October 25, 1948); also, Atlanta *Constitution*, July 18, 1948; *Arkansas Gazette*, July 18, 1948.
3 Dixon to Charles W. Collins, July 14, 1948, in Dixon Papers.
4 The chameleonic governor of Arkansas, Ben Laney, also went to Birmingham, but remained in his hotel room throughout the proceedings. He said in a statement that he was opposed to the setting up of a new party and that "whatever is done must be done through and by the official Democratic organization in each state." The paradox, of course, was that the Birmingham delegates insisted that they were not setting up a fourth party and recommended official action within the state Democratic organization. However, even this comment did not represent Laney's last words. In September he again switched sides, when he announced he would support Thurmond's States' Rights Democrats. *Arkansas Gazette*, July 18, September 24, 1948.

but also would enable the party organization in each southern state to make a coherent decision about its future course of action. The resolutions and speeches that were made closely resembled those heard at Jackson earlier in May. There were unequivocal condemnations of the Philadelphia convention, Harry Truman, and the social welfare policies of the administration. Of course, the civil rights program came under the heaviest fire. Although Strom Thurmond declared that he wished to center the campaign on the constitutional question of states' rights, and not on the racial issue per se, the organizers felt that it was impossible to create a mood of solidarity and defiance without emphasizing the very issue that had sparked off the revolt in the first place—that is, race. Frank Dixon, who gave the keynote address at Birmingham, deliberately exaggerated the portents of Truman's civil rights proposals to stimulate widespread opposition to Truman's reelection. Dixon warned, quite falsely, that the president meant to eliminate segregation in transport, restaurants, churches, hospitals, housing, labor unions, and public schools. "What will it mean in immorality, in vice, in crime?" he asked. He was sure that "violence will follow" any implementation of Truman's recommendations. When Dixon had completed his speech, he was cheered enthusiastically. Other publicists, cognizant of the prevailing mood, similarly drew upon the race issue.[5]

The overall response of the delegates to the speeches and the selection of a States' Rights ticket was effusive, messianic, and unmistakably southern. Confederate flags were ubiquitous in the municipal auditorium at Birmingham. Speakers were greeted not only with customary applause but also with distinctive "rebel yells" and rambunctious renditions of "Dixie" and other Confederate marching songs. As the Birmingham *News* commented the following day, there was "all the pent-up fever of a giant, boisterous revival meeting. . . . It was a responsive, excited, sometimes hysterical crowd—and the convention orators

5 *States' Rights Information and Speakers Handbook*, 42–43; Birmingham *News*, July 18, 1948.

made the most of it." [6] However, the leaders of the Dixiecrats, as they were widely nicknamed after July, knew that they could not rely upon this infectious southernism to achieve their goals. They appointed a fourteen-man executive committee under the direction of Judge Merritt Gibson to rationalize and plan political strategy. As a first step, these officials were required to persuade the Democratic executive committees of the various southern states to instruct their electors to cast their votes for the nominees of the States' Rights Democrats. If this tactic failed, they still intended to place Thurmond and Wright on the ballot as independents. [7]

The organizers arranged for another convention to be held at Houston on August 11. They hoped that by this date a number of state committees would have declared Thurmond and Wright as the official Democratic candidates, so that the two governors could subsequently accept their selection by the state parties. In the three weeks between the Birmingham and Houston conventions, the state central committees of Alabama, Mississippi, and South Carolina adopted Thurmond and Wright as their official nominees. [8] This meant that Truman would not appear on the ballot as a Democrat in these three states. Thus, when Thurmond and Wright attended the second convention at Houston, they formally accepted the nominations although they were disappointed that so few states had endorsed them. The mood at Houston was similar to that at Birmingham. Thurmond, despite his repeated repudiations of demagogy, lambasted "the Reds, the pinks and the subversives" in his acceptance speech. [9]

6 Birmingham *News*, July 18, 1948; also, clipping, Birmingham *Post*, July 17, 18, 1948, clipping, Jackson *Daily News*, July 18, 1948, in States' Rights Scrapbook; Eugene Peacock, "Why Are the Dixiecrats?" *Christian Century*, LXV (September 22, 1948), 975–77.
7 Baton Rouge *Morning Advocate*, July 29, 1948; Charleston *News and Courier*, July 29, 1948.
8 Transcript of radio interview with Strom Thurmond, Baltimore, October 1, 1948, in States' Rights Papers, Thurmond Papers; Atlanta *Constitution*, August 4, 1948; Charleston *News and Courier*, August 8, 1948.
9 New York *Times*, August 12, 1948; New Orleans *Times-Picayune*, August 12, 1948.

After the Houston meeting one Thurmond supporter wired: "I cried as I listened to your compelling voice. . . . You saturated the sensibilities of us . . . in the South who take off our hats and shed tears when we see a Confederate flag. The Lord willing I'll vote for you with every fibre of my being and every drop of blood in my body." The significance of this telegram was not that Thurmond attracted such passionate support, but that he chose to make it available for immediate release to the press.[10] Despite his craving for political respectability, he could not resist the temptation to exploit the emotive components of his cause.

The mood and style of the Dixiecrat revolt remained a source of continuous controversy. Strom Thurmond knew that his movement attracted a number of blatant racists and cranks still instilled with the spirit of the Lost Cause. But he was anxious not to permit these elements to dominate or even color his campaign. He wanted to present himself as a serious candidate, who was concerned about the entire confluence of recent government policy. He did not want his party to appear to represent merely an organization of white supremacists. Although Thurmond had turned away from Truman because of the civil rights program, he hoped to emphasize the broader issue of centralization and federal paternalism of which civil rights was only one, albeit the most objectionable, offshoot. More important still, he recognized that the controversy would not have arisen at the time it did had not Negro and labor groups succeeded in infiltrating the Democratic ranks. Accordingly, Thurmond repeatedly insisted—especially to the press—that the Dixiecrats were principally concerned with slowing down the rate of centralization and with restoring Jeffersonian principles of states' rights to the Democratic party.[11] He was obviously embarrassed by the reputation for racial intolerance of some of his

10 Copy, unsigned telegram to Thurmond, August 12, 1948, in States' Rights Papers, Thurmond Papers.
11 Statement by Thurmond on 1948 States' Rights Campaign in possession of the author; New York *Times*, July 20, 1948; Thurmond, interview.

supporters. For example, only two days after the Birmingham meeting, Thurmond rejected an offer of support from the fascist leader, Gerald L. K. Smith, and warned that he would spurn "any other rabble-rousers who use race prejudice to influence the emotions of the people." [12]

Other Dixiecrat leaders also recognized the importance of portraying themselves as persons who were concerned as much about the growth of the federal government and the realignment within the Democratic party as about the race issue. Marion Rushton, who had been Alabama's Democratic national committeeman until his resignation in July, when he assumed the chairmanship of the executive committee of the Alabama States' Rights Democrats, warned supporters against overemphasis of the Negro question. He wrote to Congressman Sam Hobbs: "Personally, I think the issue is entirely too serious to be settled by telling lynching jokes, negro jokes, or in any way tending to support the attitude upon which the old Ku Klux Klan flourished. The time is gone in my judgement when we Southerners can quit thinking and simply express ourselves by shouting 'nigger' and singing Dixie. We must have a positive as well as a negative program for 35% of our people." [13]

Dixiecrat leaders, however, never developed fully any "positive" proposals. Despite their sometimes hollow disavowals of demagogy, racism, and romanticism, they were unable to propound a coherent ideology that was politically meaningful for all southerners, black or white. Their main conception of a concrete program was to harp on the shift in both the popular and ideological basis of the Democratic party and to promise voters that once the South was able to gain control of the party, the states would be given full authority over civil rights, electoral reform, and the administration of social welfare programs. They were never more specific than this. The South would have to create its own firm political base, the States' Rights candidates argued, before detailed programs could be devised. The imme-

12 Atlanta *Constitution*, July 20, 1948.
13 Marion Rushton to Hobbs, August 20, 1948, in Hobbs Papers.

diate problem before the South was to effect a realignment in the political parties. The Jeffersonian idea of government had been subverted by Roosevelt and Truman, and it had to be restored before the racial and economic structure of the South would be completely destroyed. But, reasoned the Dixiecrats, it could be restored only through the decisive exercise of power. They never coherently articulated what the purpose of this power would be.

Thurmond and his followers were preoccupied with the mechanics of their operation. This was not a reflection of personal obsessions but the result of a need to justify their existence and strategy. It was self-defeating, they demurred, for southerners to vote for a candidate who had sponsored a program that threatened to destroy the region's social fabric. Since the Democratic party had approved of principles counter to southern interests, the South owed the national party no allegiance. The Dixiecrats reasoned that Dixie's state parties should consequently instruct their electors to nominate a States' Rights Democrat in the electoral college. In the event of a close election, the region's potential 127 electoral votes could force the election into the House of Representatives, where the South would hold 11 of the 48 votes. In the House election, southern Democrats would be able to deadlock the election until the Republicans agreed to drop their own civil rights plank. Strom Thurmond himself believed that the States' Rights candidates even stood the chance of being elected, on the ground that both parties might prefer to elect a southern Democrat rather than to concede a victory to their immediate opposites. Thus, Thurmond felt that Dixie could display its political strength most effectively by the careful exercise of its electoral votes.

Of course, the calculation that the outcome of the November election might be resolved in the House of Representatives was based on the assumption that neither the Republicans nor the Democrats would win an electoral majority. The Dixiecrats assumed, as did all the pundits and pollsters, that Truman could not, in any circumstances, win the election without, or even with, the South's votes. They thought that the Republicans might win an outright electoral majority, in which case, of course, there would be no House election. In the event of a Republican landslide, they argued, they would still have shown the national Democratic party that it could not survive politically without the support of the South. They were convinced that once Truman had been repudiated by the electorate, the South would take the leading hand in reorganizing the Democratic party. In such an event, reasoned the Dixiecrats, the Negro-labor bloc would no longer have any single person or group within the Democratic party in a position influential enough to determine party policy.[14] Thurmond confidently believed that "having thus shown its unity and strength, and aided by a powerful protest vote in outside States, the South could never again be treated as a political doormat." [15]

The States' Rights Democrats also thought that unilateral action in the electoral college would enable southerners to assert themselves as a separate political entity. Although a number of theorists wanted a national political realignment on conservative and liberal lines, they recognized that as a preliminary step the South should form a regionally based bloc. It was necessary for the South to define itself politically and to exercise power before embarking upon new ideological adventures. In fact, the rebels hoped to create a vast countervailing machine that would play a role similar to that of the urban coalition in the North. Negro and labor organizations had managed to exert a transcendent influence in party politics. The South, it was reasoned, should be able to command such authority. Strom Thurmond felt that independence in 1948 "is the best opportunity the South has had since the War between the States to regain the respect of the nation politically. Therefore it is important that we stick together toward that end." [16]

14 Statement by Thurmond on 1948 States' Rights Campaign in possession of the author; Thurmond, interview; also, McCorvey to editor, Roanoke *Leader*, October 9, 1948, in Hobbs Papers.
15 Thurmond to Martin, September 2, 1948, in Martin Papers.
16 Thurmond to Hobbs, July 21, 1948, in Hobbs Papers.

Gessner McCorvey was "absolutely confident that four years from now we will have the National Conventions of all political parties wooing and courting the South. . . . we are certainly going to let every citizen of America realize that we constitute a group to be reckoned with and that we are fighters and are not going to be kicked around any more." [17]

The Philadelphia convention had demonstrated to southerners that the wishes of well-organized pressure groups could prevail even over those of the president. They now wanted to emulate that example. It was necessary, therefore, to convince the Democratic leadership that the South would not return to the fold unless the liberal coalition was stripped of its influence. This could be done only by showing the national Democratic hierarchy that the South was electorally more crucial than the Negro-labor bloc of the industrial North. Southerners were confident that if they could impress this view on politicians from the North, then state sovereignty would be respected. "I know that already this is a 'shooting war', in which the survival of our right to govern ourselves and to develop in our own way is at stake," philosophized Alabama's Marion Rushton. "I know that the vigor of our protest will be the measure of our success and that if we fail now we will be in a sadder position in 1952 than that in which we find ourselves today." [18]

Rushton was not alone in his rhetoric on "survival." The Dixiecrats believed that the South was a distinctive region, with unique social, economic, and racial patterns. These characteristics had made the South a civilized and even exemplary place in which to live. Southerners had previously resisted unsolicited programs of societal change and would do so again. They thought that resistance was historically obligatory. To surrender to enforced desegregation and nationally determined election laws would be tantamount to a repudiation of the past which had provided political yardsticks to so many south-

17 McCorvey to editor, Roanoke *Leader*, October 9, 1948, in Hobbs Papers.
18 Rushton to Grover C. Hall, July 23, 1948, in Rushton Papers.

erners. Indeed, they believed it to be incumbent upon them not only as southerners but as Americans to emphasize the importance and sanctity of tradition in the promulgation of laws. Sam Hobbs of Alabama recognized the historical role that Dixie was now asked to play, although he seemed unembarrassed by his manipulation of history. "Dixie leads the fight against the impending doom of the nation, because she has learned the lesson of Appomattox and in three wars since. . . . she has earned the right to take up Lincoln's battle to save the Union." [19] Thurmond was similarly stimulated by his own perceptions of the past. "The South's problem is not a pure question of logic and law. It involves a sense of bitter *history* and bitter *pride*," he told supporters in Georgia.[20]

Thus the Dixiecrat leaders were imbued with a deep-rooted historical consciousness, which was often, though inadvertently, laced with a romantic view of their history and society. Occasionally, of course, they sanctioned a sense of the past that was intellectually unsustainable or crudely iconoclastic. They expressly never repudiated their followers for their promiscuous use of rebel paraphernalia, such as the waving of Confederate banners.[21] Despite their tacit encouragement (or at least the absence of any explicit discouragement) of a resurrection of the spirit of the Lost Cause, they firmly believed—however mistaken they might have been—that they were involved in a moral crusade that offered to save the South from the clutches of political modernism and maintain the continuum of history.

19 Speech, Sam Hobbs to States' Rights Democrats, September 11, 1948 (printed as a pamphlet, *The Ramparts We Watched*), in Hobbs Papers.
20 Address of Thurmond, Augusta, Ga., September 23, 1948, in States' Rights Papers, Thurmond Papers.
21 This kind of hullabaloo probably reached its most absurd peak in Mississippi, where the state legislature considered a bill which would have required all radio stations within the state to play "Dixie" at the end of each day's programs. One legislator, who was not satisfied with this stipulation, even proposed an amendment outlawing the playing of the "Missouri Waltz" on the radio. (Missouri was, of course, Truman's home state.) See *Arkansas Gazette*, March 26, 1948.

Charles Wallace Collins, the South's foremost ideologue, expressed these sentiments forcefully in a long, contemplative letter to Merritt Gibson, director of the States' Rights party. Beneath his obvious self-indulgence, there is a missionary sense of dedication in his words: "In this ordeal a civilization is fighting for its life. This is the highest challenge that can be made to man. It calls for great moral courage and for heroic effort in a rededication of the individual to his native soil. And in this fight the soul of the South will be purified, her wits sharpened and her hands strengthened. When those on the other side of the Mason and Dixon Line, who love the Constitution, see the quality of the fight the South is making, they will respond with respect and admiration." Indeed, Collins was convinced not only that southerners were being loyal to the traditions of their forefathers but also that they were acting in a way predetermined by general, historical laws: "The States' Rights movement is following a well known law of history which holds that when a group has lost the use of a particular instrumentality it is apt to respond to this challenge by specializing in the use of some other instrumentality to offset its handicap in the first. The States' Righters lost the use of the machinery of the National Democratic Party. They turned to the use of the Electoral College and to a balance of power bloc in the House and in the Senate." [22]

Nevertheless, despite all the verbiage about historical legacies and southern distinctiveness, the Dixiecrats recognized that the South's treatment of the Negro had set the region apart from the rest of the nation. As already mentioned, the States' Rights Democrats frequently insisted that the civil rights issue was subordinate to the larger problem of the growth of the federal government. Thurmond claimed in Houston: "We have constantly refused to permit the racial issue to dominate our campaign. . . . We have taken the position that the racial

22 Charles W. Collins to Merritt H. Gibson, November 8, 1948, in Dixon Papers.

questions involved are secondary to the broad principles of constitutional government that are under attack." [23] But Thurmond knew that if he did not emphasize the question of race relations, he would fail to attract solid support for his cause. The States' Rights movement had come into existence because of Truman's proposals, and, in the end, the leaders necessarily had to justify all their arguments in terms of race. So, despite affirmations that they were motivated by growing governmental paternalism, a concern for local self-determination, and their adherence to the concept of historical continuity, Thurmond and his colleagues ultimately had to swallow their words and emphasize the Negro issue to its full extent.

The most blatant use of the race issue was the technique traditionally employed by white supremacists. The Dixiecrats warned southern voters that failure to vote for independent electors would result in the full enfranchisement of the Negro, a police-enforced fair employment practices program, and, eventually, the elimination of segregation. The official sample ballot of the Mississippi state Democratic party warned that "a vote for Truman electors is a direct order to our Congressmen and Senators from Mississippi to vote for passage of Truman's so-called civil rights program in the next Congress. This means the vicious FEPC-anti-poll tax-anti-lynching and anti-lynching and anti-segregation proposals will become the law of the land and our way of life in the South will be gone for ever." [24] At a rally in Memphis, Senator James O. Eastland warned that if Truman won the election, "our traditions and our culture will be destroyed and mongrelized by the mongrels of the East." [25]

The States' Rights Democrats only deluded themselves if they thought that they had toned down the race issue. Ala-

---

23 New York *Times*, October 21, 1948; see also, Wright, "Give the Government Back to the People," 36, 37, 126, 127; William G. Carleton, "The Fate of Our Fourth Party," *Yale Review*, XXXVIII (March, 1949), 449–51.

24 Broadside published by Mississippi state Democratic party, in States' Rights Scrapbook.

25 Memphis *Commercial Appeal*, September 11, 1948.

bama Dixiecrats contemplated circulating a rather menacing photograph of the Negro, George Vaughn, who had sponsored the motion at Philadelphia to deny the Mississippi delegation its seats. Gessner McCorvey was convinced that the distribution of the photograph "would make many a vote." [26] Sometimes this kind of racism was employed even more crudely. And it was used not only in spontaneous outbursts on the stump. The official *States' Rights Information and Speakers Handbook* warned that if the poll tax were abolished and Negroes voted freely, "there would not be a business or industry operating in the country twelve months after they took over—unless violence was resorted to." The *Handbook* explained, "The negro is a native of the tropical climate where fruits and nuts are plentiful and where clothing is not required for protection against the weather. The negro has never been under the necessity of producing anything through voluntary cooperation. . . . His racial constitution has been fashioned to exclude any ideas of voluntary cooperation on his part. For this reason the negro, and some whites who are lacking in this virtue, will never voluntarily pay any [poll] tax." [27]

The immediate objective of all this electioneering was, of course, to persuade the other southern Democratic executive committees to adopt Thurmond and Wright as their official nominees. A number of state organizations had flirted with the States' Rights Democrats before July, and it was hoped that they would fully commit themselves after the South's defeat at Philadelphia. But, as already noted, the propensity to revolt had been limited by the degree of factional solidarity within the individual state party organizations. Dixiecrat leaders were loath to encourage a bolt if such action undermined their own authority. Thus, as the following brief survey of the Dixiecrat revolt shows, the progress of the rebellion within the states did not alter course after July—except in Louisiana.

26 McCorvey to Dixon and Horace Wilkinson, August 21, 1948, in Dixon Papers.
27 *States' Rights Information and Speakers Handbook*, 52–53.

In Alabama and Mississippi the Democratic electors had been bound to vote against Truman in the electoral college. The adoption of Thurmond and Wright, therefore, as the official nominees was only a matter of form. Similarly, in South Carolina the state Democratic executive committee voted, in accordance with resolutions passed in the state convention, to pledge its electoral votes to its governor. These were the only states where the party committees automatically endorsed the States' Rights Democrats.[28] Nowhere else in the South had the respective state organizations been obliged by earlier actions to pledge their support to the southern nominees. Although all other party committees had condemned Truman and the civil rights program, none had taken definite steps to prevent a bolt. These earlier protests had been made in the hope of blocking Truman's nomination at Philadelphia. No serious consideration had been given to the possible courses of action after the Democratic convention. Consequently, Thurmond and Wright hoped that they could persuade these uncommitted states to support electors pledged to the States' Rights candidates.

At the beginning of 1948 it had seemed that Virginia would take a lead in the movement to select unpledged electors. But Governor William Tuck's militancy had gradually declined. In July, the state convention, which was controlled by the Byrd machine, had passed a resolution authorizing the state central committee to reconvene it after the Philadelphia convention in order to give alternative instructions to Virginia's electors.[29] This meant that if no further convention were summoned, Virginia's electors would be bound to vote for the national Democratic nominee. Harry Byrd and his cohorts realized that any positive move to compel an electoral college bolt could undermine the position of the Democratic party in Virginia. Although Byrd exercised total control over the party organization, he was

28 Atlanta *Constitution*, August 4, 1948; Charleston *News and Courier*, August 8, 1948.
29 Colonel William Kemper to Hutchinson, July 5, 1948, in Box 14, Hutchinson Papers; Lynchburg *News*, July 3, 1948.

aware that the Republican party in the state might benefit considerably from a split among Democrats. So he decided to steer a neutral course between Truman and Thurmond, although a number of individual machine candidates, who faced Republican opponents in their campaigns for local office, even endorsed Truman. The States' Rights Democrats had no chance of seizing control of the party machine. They were consequently compelled to file a separate slate of electors. The regular electors, who were obliged to vote for Truman and Barkley, received no support from the state central committee. The Truman Democrats were snubbed by the state organization and deprived of $12,000 in party funds. Thus, in Virginia the Dixiecrats were thwarted by political exigency and not through lack of sympathy.[30]

There were three impending Democratic gubernatorial primaries in the South after the Philadelphia convention. In all these campaigns, candidates were pressed about their positions on the States' Rights movement. The contenders were naturally desirous to rally as much support as they could from county leaders, who were usually reluctant to associate openly with Thurmond in the wake of a state election. Local leaders were anxious not to sour relations with the Democratic party irreparably since they would need the cooperation of Washington officials on matters of patronage. In two of these states, Tennessee and Arkansas, the race question traditionally had not played a dominant role in local politics, and the majority of candidates were unwilling to exploit the issue. Sid McMath, one of the main contenders for governor in Arkansas, refused to use the Negro "as the whipping boy for the politicians' pur-

30 Robert Whitehead to G. Fred Switzer, November 24, 1948, in Box 9, Robert Whitehead Papers, Alderman Library, University of Virginia, Charlottesville; Lloyd M. Robinette to Hutchinson, July 23, 1948, Hutchinson to G. Alvin Massenburg, August 13, 1948, in Box 14, Hutchinson Papers; Hutchinson to Robinette, September 27, 1948, in Box 15, Hutchinson Papers; memo, Henry H. Fowler to McGrath, August 12, 1948, in McGrath Papers; Key, *Southern Politics*, 336–37; Frank W. Ashley, "Selected Southern Liberal Editors and the States' Rights Movement of 1948" (Ph.D. dissertation, University of South Carolina, 1959), 327, 370–74.

pose of getting votes." [31] In Tennessee, Gordon Browning, running against Jim McCord who was Edward Crump's candidate, informed Frank Dixon that he "would very much rather that the issue not be raised." [32] Both Browning and McMath won the primaries. They realized that they had nothing whatever to gain by carrying their new organizations for Thurmond and Wright.

The Dixiecrats in these two states were forced subsequently to stand without the backing of the regular Democratic organizations. In September, Tennessee's state Democratic executive committee voted to disqualify electors who refused to pledge loyalty to Truman. Tennessee's States' Rights Democrats under the leadership of Charles A. Stainback, chairman of the Democratic committee of the predominantly Negro Fayette County, consequently had to file a separate slate of electors pledged to Thurmond and Wright. One week later, the state Democratic convention in Arkansas followed suit by refusing to align the state party with the States' Rights movement. Sid McMath praised the convention for "preventing discord from disrupting our ranks." [33] Thus, supporters of the Dixiecrats in Arkansas also were compelled to appear on the ballot as a separate party.

The third state with a gubernatorial primary that summer was Georgia. Unlike in Arkansas and Tennessee, the race question remained the central issue in Georgia's primary contest—as it had been in previous ones. But the incumbent, Governor Melvin Thompson, did not control the state organization which had remained in the hands of his opponent, Herman Talmadge, the son and political successor of Eugene. Herman Talmadge based his campaign almost entirely on the civil rights program and attempted to identify Thompson as a supporter of Truman. "He is doing this in the futile hope that the Negro bloc will give him the balance of power in enough counties," explained

31 *Arkansas Gazette*, August 3, 1948.
32 Dixon to Charles A. Stainback, August 25, 1948, in Dixon Papers.
33 *Arkansas Gazette*, September 24, 25, 1948.

Talmadge.[34] Thus, when Talmadge beat Thompson resoundingly in September, it was widely believed that the state party organization would take measures to pledge the state's electors to the Dixiecrats.[35]

Contrary to expectations, the state executive committee, headed by James S. Peters, a vocal Truman critic, took no action to instruct electors for Thurmond and Wright. Although Peters and Talmadge knew there was widespread sympathy for the States' Rights movement, they felt that the Dixiecrats would not succeed in forcing the election into the House of Representatives. Talmadge was determined not to begin his career associated with a movement that seemed doomed to failure. He probably also remembered that when his father repudiated the Roosevelt administration in the early days of the New Deal, he had brought only loss of patronage and deprivation of federal funds for Georgia. He was not prepared to risk sanctions for what was apparently a lost cause.[36] However, since he did not formally dissociate himself from Thurmond, the state legislature, at the behest of Governor Thompson, passed a bill to insure that electors cast their votes for the nominees of the national Democratic party, Truman and Barkley. Georgia's Dixiecrats were somewhat stunned. "We didn't think we'd have to resort to a third party ballot," complained the chairman of Augusta's Thurmond-Wright Club.[37]

Although the Dixiecrats failed to be placed in the Democratic column in Georgia, they did succeed in Louisiana, which became the only Dixie state to reverse its previous intimations of party regularity. Earlier in the year the state central committee had resisted suggestions that it release its electors from obligations to vote for the Democratic nominee. After the Philadelphia convention, however, demands for an electoral college bolt increased. Governor Earl Long was unwilling to

34 Atlanta *Constitution*, August 29, 1948.
35 *Ibid.*, September 8, 12, 16, 1948.
36 Herman Talmadge, interview.
37 Atlanta *Constitution*, October 2, 3, 1948.

join the Dixiecrat chorus, but failed to insure that the party organization would continue to advocate regularity in the electoral college. In August, Louisiana Congressmen F. Edward Hébert, James Domengeaux, and Otto Passman announced their support of the Louisiana States' Righters, which had been formed by the veteran anti–New Dealer, John U. Barr.[38] A number of people on the state central committee were equally receptive to the idea of mobilizing the party machine behind the States' Rights Democrats. Particularly enthusiastic were William H. Talbot, Louisiana's national committeeman, and Leander Perez, one of the state's electors and a powerful member of the state committee. At a meeting of the committee on September 10, Perez successfully carried a motion which declared Thurmond and Wright the official nominees of the Democratic party of Louisiana. Perez justified the decision by insisting that Truman and Barkley headed "not the Democratic party, but the New Deal-Communistic party." [39]

The Democratic executive committee in Louisiana, as in Alabama, had acted independently of its governor. Furthermore, it seemed that Truman and Barkley would not appear on the ballot at all, since under Louisiana law independent candidacies had to be filed with the secretary of state by August 31. But unlike in Alabama, Louisiana's governor enjoyed majority support in the state committee. There was an air of mystery about the state committee's sudden decision. If it had intended from the beginning to exclude Truman altogether from the ballot, then it acted correctly in delaying an announcement until after August 31, the closing date for filing new candidacies. There was also a senatorial primary on August 31, and, no doubt, state officials did not want it to be overshadowed by other matters. But since the state committee was pro-Long, it was rather surprising that the governor had been unable to forestall or anticipate this action. Although there is no concrete

38 New Orleans *Times-Picayune*, August 1, 3, 6, 1948.
39 *Ibid.*, September 11, 1948; Baton Rouge *Morning Advocate*, September 11, 1948; Howell, interview.

evidence, there is reason to suspect that Governor Long had foreknowledge of the committee *putsch*, but was unwilling to prevent it. This theory is reinforced by Long's subsequent maneuvers, for two weeks later the governor summoned a special session of the legislature to request legislation that would permit Truman to appear on the ballot. But Long's bombshell was not this electoral proposal, but his shattering request for the repeal of Louisiana's civil service laws. Like his brother Huey, Earl Long planned to exercise personal control over all state offices. At the same time he was able to pose as the champion of democratic justice and win the approval of the Democratic National Committee in Washington.[40] Thus, Long's attitude toward Truman's electoral prospects in Louisiana was molded by his own political ambitions. He calculated that appropriate gestures to both factions would free him to pursue his own goals.

The foregoing speculation about Earl Long's possible motives should not obscure the fact that the Long family had traditionally shied away from using the race issue for political purposes.[41] Undoubtedly, Long was aware of the widespread antagonism toward Truman's policies in Louisiana but was not prepared to make battle himself on the race question. He therefore compromised by requesting legislation which would authorize Truman and Barkley to appear on the ballot under a column headed "national Democratic party," but would deny them the rooster symbol of the state party. The legislature, in fact, was not even prepared to make this concession and decreed that the Philadelphia nominees should not be privileged

---

40 New Orleans *Times-Picayune*, September 22, 23, 24, 1948; New York *Times*, September 16, 1948; Hellen Fuller, "Huey's Brother Has a Problem," *New Republic* (October 4, 1948); L. Vaughan Howard and David D. Deener, *Presidential Politics in Louisiana, 1952* (New Orleans, 1954), 53–64; L. Vaughan Howard, *Civil Service Development in Louisiana* (New Orleans, 1956), 105–11. Senator Ellender, who was in Louisiana at the time, claimed that he had been behind Long's move to persuade the legislature to enable the Philadelphia nominees to appear on the ballot. Ellender, interview.

41 T. Harry Williams, *Huey Long* (New York, 1969), 703–706; T. Harry Williams, *Romance and Realism in Southern Politics* (Louisiana Paperbacks ed.; Baton Rouge, 1966), 80–84.

with the "Democratic" nomenclature at all. Both Long and the state executive committee agreed to the bill, which also gave Truman's supporters until October 5 to file a slate of qualified electors.[42]

In the three remaining states of the South—Florida, North Carolina, and Texas—there were no further dramatic developments. In all three states the civil rights program alone had aroused insufficient popular animosity to persuade the respective state organizations to support Thurmond and Wright. Although both Florida and Texas had powerful and numerous Dixiecrat factions, they were unable to win over the respective state Democratic parties to their cause. In Florida, Frank Upchurch failed to gain control of the state executive committee, which remained in the hands of Claude Pepper's progressive faction.[43] In Texas, Governor Jester retained control of the state convention, which voted, despite heavy opposition from former Texas Regulars, to pledge the state's electors to Truman. Loyal Democrats had been determined to prevent the anti–New Deal faction from seizing control of the convention, as it had done in 1944. Sam Rayburn and Senator Tom Connally helped line up support for Truman, since they personally feared that division in the Democratic ranks could aid the Republicans.[44] And in North Carolina, interest in the States' Rights movement was minimal. Almost to a man, the state's officeholders campaigned for Truman in the realization that the race issue alone had little appeal and would help only the Republicans. The North Carolina Dixiecrats themselves faced considerable difficulties in having their names appear on the

42 The legislature also passed the Madden bill, which practically abolished the state civil service. Baton Rouge *Morning Advocate,* September 24, 25, 27, 1948; New Orleans *Times-Picayune,* September 25, 26, 1948.

43 Key, *Southern Politics,* 338; see also, Herbert J. Doherty, "Liberal and Conservative Voting Patterns in Florida," *Journal of Politics,* XIV (August, 1952), 403–17.

44 Connally to O. L. Jennings, August 17, 1948, in Box 104, Connally Papers; Rayburn to Robert L. Holliday, October 14, 1948, Rayburn to Gus Hodges, September 28, 1948, in Miscellaneous Files 1948, Rayburn Papers; Atlanta *Constitution,* September 15, 1948.

ballot and were rendered ineffective by constant quarreling among themselves.[45]

The Dixiecrats, then, faced an uphill struggle in trying to persuade the respective state Democratic parties of the South to pledge their electors to Thurmond and Wright. They realized that they were the prisoners of the very party they were trying to reconstitute. Despite their disenchantment with the national Democratic party, they still relied upon the South's adherence to the party to achieve their goals. Their success depended upon their ability to win control of extant state organizations. Yet only four states in the South felt they could support the States' Rights Democrats without dire political consequences. In three of these four states—Alabama, Mississippi, and South Carolina—the race issue had nearly always dominated the political process, and a majority of state and county leaders felt that the electorate owed more allegiance to white supremacy than to the national Democratic party. In the remaining seven states, key Democratic officials were unwilling or, less frequently, unable to carry the state party machine for the Dixiecrats. Although a number of anti–New Dealers in these other states were sympathetic to the southern cause, they could not persuade the regular Democrats to risk a party bolt. The States' Rights Democrats, therefore, had to resort to slates of independent electors. In these states any voter who cast his ballot for the Thurmond-Wright ticket in November would be legally a party renegade and could theoretically be disqualified from voting in future Democratic primaries.

Nearly all the resources of the Dixiecrats were devoted to these efforts to appear on the ballot. This, of course, required financial backing, and campaign directors sought various ways to raise funds. Unfortunately, there is no means of ascertaining

45 J. Melville Broughton to Martin, July 26, 1948, in Martin Papers; Hoey to E. M. Mayes, September 24, 1948, in Hoey Papers; Jonathan Daniels to author, June 24, 1970; Ashley, "Selected Southern Editors and the States' Rights Movement of 1948," 353–61.

exactly how much money was raised for the campaign and, more important, who, precisely, were the main contributors. Several allegations were made about the backing of oil magnates, but there is no substantive evidence for the view that they composed the backbone of the Dixiecrat movement. The southwestern oil company executives were only one of several groups and private individuals who contributed to the campaign chest. As might have been expected, the leaders of the States' Rights movement continually denied charges that the oil interests gave extensively to the cause.[46]

The national treasurer of the States' Rights party, George C. Wallace, insisted that party accounts should be kept in strict accordance with the federal Corrupt Practices Act. This meant that state treasurers could accept only donations made in a private capacity. It precluded gifts from corporations or labor unions.[47] From the scant evidence available, it seems that a considerable amount was raised from small contributions. For example, three days after the Birmingham conference, the Jackson *Clarion-Ledger* reported that the citizens of the small town of Inverness, Mississippi, had together collected $1,500 for the campaign.[48] Indeed, most contributions came from Mississippi and Alabama. A financial statement of October 21 reported that $159,000 had been collected, the largest donation being $3,500.[49] But an undated financial estimate in Frank Dixon's papers shows that the States' Rights Democrats had expended (or intended to expend—the distinction is not clear) some $450,000.[50] All that really can be concluded is that the Dixiecrats failed to reach their goal of $10,000 for every southern electoral vote. Even if they had raised these amounts, the

---

46 Thurmond, interview; Emile B. Ader, "The Dixiecrat Movement: A Study in American Politics" (Ph.D. dissertation, University of California, 1951), 145; Memphis *Commercial Appeal*, September 21, 1948.
47 George C. Wallace to all State Treasurers, States' Rights Democratic Campaign Committee, September 17, 1948, in Dixon Papers.
48 Clipping, Jackson *Clarion-Ledger*, July 20, 1948, in States' Rights Scrapbook.
49 Ader, "The Dixiecrat Movement," 145–46.
50 Unsigned memo, States' Rights Party Budget Estimates, undated, in Dixon Papers.

outcome of the election would not have been different, since the Dixiecrats relied upon infiltrating and controlling existing party structures and not upon their potential strength among the electorate at large as a third party.[51]

This strategy was paradoxical. The Dixiecrats believed that southerners should question their long-held political allegiances in order to preserve their peculiar society. Yet they were unwilling to dissociate themselves from a party label that only confused political patterns south of the Potomac. Their ultimate adherence to the one-party system had rendered their considerable efforts at popular suasion quite superfluous. They could not claim to be regular Democrats, when, in fact, they appeared on the ballot as independents in seven Dixie states. Similarly, they could not coherently boast that they were the standard-bearers of a new, or reconstituted, southern party, when in four states of the Deep South they operated under the canopy of the traditional Democratic party. Although the Dixiecrats embodied a revived southernism, they were unable to challenge consistently that foremost emblem of the South's reputed political unity, the Democratic party.

While the Dixiecrats were trying to consolidate their position in the South, Harry Truman worked to retain the metropolitan strongholds of the urban coalition. The details of the campaign have been described elsewhere by other historians and need not be recounted here.[52] It is important, however, to notice that Truman adhered to the advice of Clark Clifford and other campaign strategists to concentrate on the northern pivotal states. Consequently, the South played a less significant role

---

51 Telegram, W. W. Wright to Dixon, August 13, 1948, in Dixon Papers. The clerk of the House of Representatives holds the financial statements of the States' Rights Democratic party. Unfortunately, the clerk refused permission to examine the papers. This is rather ironical, since party political statements are anyway open to members of the public for the two years following each election.

52 The 1948 campaign is described in: Ross, *The Loneliest Campaign*; Abels, *Out of the Jaws of Victory*; Redding, *Inside the Democratic Party*; Stayer, "A History of the Presidential Campaign of 1948."

than ever before—to the point that, for the first time in campaign history, the president directly solicited the black vote in the cities.

After the Democratic convention had nominated Truman on a strong civil rights plank, the president and his advisers determined that this new development should be used to full advantage. Paradoxically, the walkout of the Alabama and Mississippi delegations had served to enhance Truman's image among Negroes, for it symbolized, even if it did not underline, the emancipation of the Democratic party from the South. Truman's strategists were also cognizant that Thomas Dewey, the Republican nominee, and Henry Wallace, who had been nominated to head the Progressive party ticket, were advocating specific legislation to protect minority groups. They knew, therefore, that Truman had to convey the impression that he was no longer bound by the South and that he was in a position to lead the movement for protective legislation.

Truman fully exploited the desertion of the South. At Philadelphia Truman stunned the convention delegates when he announced that he would summon a special session of Congress to enact his Fair Deal proposals, including those on civil rights.[53] Then, on July 26, after months of procrastination, the president issued two executive orders directly affecting the Negro. The orders established the Fair Employment Practices Board in the Civil Service Commission and the Committee on Equality of Treatment and Opportunity in the Armed Services. Truman explained afterwards that the latter was intended to terminate segregation in the armed forces. Civil rights leaders publicly hailed Truman's orders. A. Philip Randolph called off his civil disobedience campaign, which had been directed orig-

53 For the background to this decision, see unsigned memo, "Should the President Call Congress Back?" June 29, 1948, in Samuel Rosenman Papers, Harry S. Truman Library, Independence, Mo. (This memorandum was probably written by William Batt and not by Rosenman.) R. Alton Lee, "The Turnip Session of the Do-Nothing Congress: Presidential Campaign Strategy," *Southwestern Social Science Quarterly*, XLIV (December, 1963), 256–67.

inally at the administration's delay in desegregating the armed services. Ironically, the South's obstinacy and seeming intransigence had accelerated the process of a federal nondiscrimination policy.[54]

The desegregation order was the first sign of Truman's decision to cease his obvious temporizing on civil rights. He realized that there was little else that could be done to contain the revolt in the South. Most state party organizations below the Potomac had already indicated how they would act in November. Truman's campaign strategists realized that there were more volatile and more valuable votes to be won in the industrial states of the North. They advised the president to devote "the larger effort of the campaign" to the rehabilitation of the urban coalition. He could achieve this by presenting himself "as a crusader rallying the people to save the tremendous social gains made under the New Deal and carried forward by his administration in a difficult post-war period." They were confident that this was preferable to a conciliatory strategy. "The Negro votes," wrote Clifford, "in the crucial states will more than cancel out any votes the President may lose in the South." There was, therefore, no point in campaigning in Dixie. "A short side trip into the South during the fall with a speech in Birmingham or Atlanta" was considered sufficient.[55]

Truman followed this advice and concentrated nearly all his efforts in the North and West. He continually condemned the Republicans in the "Do-Nothing Congress" for their failure to enact his Fair Deal proposals and for their indifference to the welfare of the "common man." In Scranton, Pennsylvania, he

54 Executive Orders 9980, 9981, *3 CFR, 1943–1948,* pp. 720–22. Truman was well aware of the political implications of his executive orders. A few hours before he issued them, he instructed David Niles to phone Walter White to convey the news of his decision. Walter White to Clarence Mitchell, July 26, 1948, in Box 367/4, NAACP Files. See also, Berman, "The Politics of Civil Rights in the Truman Administration," 109–13; Dalfiume, "Desegregation of the United States Armed Forces," 248–81; Morgan, "The Presidential Executive Order as an Instrument for Policy-Making," 20–69.

55 Memo, William L. Batt, Jr., to Clifford, August 11, 1948, memo, Clifford to HST, August 17, 1948, in Clifford Papers.

told an audience of coal miners that the "awful and shameful" Taft-Hartley Act was "like a termite, undermining and eating away your legal protection to organize and bargain collectively." [56] Wherever he went, he reminded voters that Congress had defied his proposals on labor relations and social welfare. He insinuated that the center of power in the Republican party lay not with Dewey but with such congressional opponents of the New Deal and Fair Deal as Robert Taft. Men like Taft apparently believed "in the welfare of the top ahead of the welfare of the bottom." [57] And although Truman naturally never mentioned them, anti–New Deal southern Democrats were implicated in his tirades. After all, had Dixie Democrats supported him, his proposals would have been enacted.

These tactics began to reap their rewards. One by one, the major liberal and labor organizations began to give Truman their support. The Americans for Democratic Action, the AF of L, and the CIO joined Truman's crusade against the Eightieth Congress. The labor federations even cooperated by pooling their financial resources to aid the Democrats. [58] The ADA agreed with the CIO-PAC at the end of August that the "Democratic party carries forward the principles for which the American liberal-labor coalition stands," and, accordingly, endorsed Truman and Barkley. [59] Interestingly, only a few endorsements came from Negro newspaper editors. The Chicago *Defender* was the only major black newspaper to favor Truman. Most of the others supported Dewey, on the ground that as governor of New York he had enacted a fair employment practices program and that a Republican president would be unencumbered by southern bigots. [60] But, as will be seen, the

56 *Public Papers, 1948*, p. 831.
57 *Ibid.*, 727.
58 Philip Murray, radio address, July 29, 1948, in Clifford Papers; Arnold, "The CIO's Role in American Politics," 301–305; Abels, *Out of the Jaws of Victory*, 224–25.
59 Brock, *Americans for Democratic Action*, chap. 8.
60 Cecelia Van Auken, "The Negro Press in the 1948 Presidential Election," *Journalism Quarterly*, XXVI (December, 1949), 431–35; Pittsburgh *Courier*, October 23, 1948.

rank and file of Negroes overwhelmingly supported Truman, who in the final stage of the campaign stressed the very issues opposed by most southern Democrats.

Truman also accepted Clifford's advice to concentrate his efforts in the metropolitan North and therefore made only a very brief campaign appearance in Dixie. He toured Texas and delivered speeches in Raleigh and Miami. Florida, North Carolina, and Texas were, of course, in the loyal group of southern states. The leading politicians in these states, such as Sam Rayburn, Lyndon Johnson, Jonathan Daniels, Gregg Cherry, and Claude Pepper, all had been prominent opponents of the Dixiecrat movement and had supported the Fair Deal. Truman recognized that a token appearance in the South would be an appropriate booster to the Democratic loyalists. But Texas was the only Dixie state where he made characteristic whistle-stop speeches to crowds at railway stations. In Florida and North Carolina, Truman made only three speeches for predesignated purposes. Naturally, he avoided all mention of the civil rights program.[61] He devoted most of his time to the enunciation of his other Fair Deal proposals and clearly directed his remarks to southern liberals. He did, however, hint at his concern over the southern bolters on one occasion. At a monument dedication ceremony in Raleigh, he pointedly eulogized Andrew Jackson's courage in resisting South Carolina's nullification proclamation. The president chose his words carefully. He praised Old Hickory, who "knew that the way to correct injustice in a democracy is by reason and debate, never by walking out in a huff." [62]

One other reason why Truman limited his activities in the South should be noted. At the end of the summer, Henry Wallace toured Dixie to campaign for the Progressive ticket.

61 Jonathan Daniels to HST, July 19, 1948, telegram, Thurmond to HST, September 25, 1948, in OF 200, Truman Papers; draft of speech by Claude Pepper, October 7, 1948, in McGrath Papers; *Public Papers, 1948*, pp. 570–99.
62 *Public Papers, 1948*, p. 820.

Wherever he traveled, Wallace insisted that he would address only unsegregated audiences. Nearly all his speeches dealt with the civil rights problem. Wallace suspected Truman of insincerity and hypocrisy and contended that he himself was the only candidate prepared to take an unequivocal stand on the question of segregation. He touched upon the nerve center of southern sensibility. In Norfolk he flayed "reactionaries" who justified their own bigotry as protective devices for southern womanhood. In Memphis, defying Crump's attempt to ban his meetings, Wallace condemned segregation as "an insult to humanity" and proposed the repeal of the southern prohibition on interracial marriages. Needless to say, Wallace evoked a hostile response from whites. He was badly mobbed at a number of speaking engagements. Insults and indignity followed him everywhere he went.[63] There can be no doubt that Wallace's reception convinced Truman that an organized campaign tour in the South could only hinder his candidacy. If Truman acquiesced to segregated meetings, Negroes in the North would desert him. If he insisted on integrated meetings, he would suffer Wallace's fate and, perhaps, encourage further defections to the Dixiecrats. And, of course, Wallace served as a reminder to the South that, like Truman, he had been a heartbeat from the presidency.

Truman felt, therefore, inactivity to be the best strategy for carrying those southern states that had not adopted Thurmond and Wright as their official Democratic nominees. Although individual officeholders and the staff of the Democratic National Committee continued to work quietly for Truman south of the Potomac, the president himself concentrated on the metropolitan states. But even in the North he deliberately delayed overt discussion of the civil rights question until the final stages of the campaign. Undoubtedly, Truman hoped that his record would suffice to persuade northern Negroes to remain in the

63 MacDougall, *Gideon's Army: The Campaign and the Vote* (3 vols.; New York, 1965), III, 665–67, 708–28; Memphis *Commercial Appeal,* September 4, 19, 1948; New York *Times,* August 30, 31, September 2, 3, 5, 8, 9, 1948.

Democratic fold. He relied upon party workers and the publicity divisions of the Democratic National Committee to advertise his record. The front page of one committee handout, entitled *The Truman Record*, was dedicated entirely to the civil rights question. It insisted in its headline that "For Negro Americans Truman is the Only Choice" and warned that any vote cast against Truman was a vote for "the Negro-hating States' Rights Party." [64] But despite strong criticism from the Negro press, the president refrained from campaigning personally on the race question and left this delicate issue to his subordinates.

Truman hoped thereby to reap the electoral benefit of his civil rights policy without losing too much ground in the South. Yet he realized that a total silence on the race issue would convince black voters that Wallace's accusations of insincerity were well founded. Accordingly, he accepted the advice proffered earlier to deliver a major speech in what Harold Cruse has termed "the most strategically important community of black America," Harlem.[65] On October 29 Harlem residents listened to the first president ever to campaign in this black community. Truman reminded the sixty-five thousand Negroes in his audience that that day marked the first anniversary of the publication of *To Secure These Rights*. He pointed out that he had acted on the proposals in his special message to Congress and in his two executive orders in July. To an enthusiastic audience he proclaimed that "our determination to attain the goal of equal rights and equal opportunity must be resolute and unwavering." [66]

The Harlem speech was perhaps the most outstanding symbol of the profound change in the geographic and social balance within the Democratic party. For the first time, a Demo-

64 Democratic National Committee, *The Truman Record* (probably September, 1948), in Redding Papers.
65 Harold Cruse, *The Crisis of the Negro Intellectual* (Apollo ed.; New York, 1968), 12; memo, William L. Batt, Jr., to Clifford, August 11, 1948, in Clifford Papers.
66 *Public Papers, 1948*, pp. 923, 925; New York *Times*, October 30, 1948.

cratic candidate for the presidency had gone into the black ghettos to solicit votes. Although Truman had trodden cautiously throughout the campaign on the race issue to prevent further unnecessary disintegration in the South, he had, nevertheless, decided to climax his campaign in the very district that white supremacists had constantly attacked as the nest of black depravity. The great cities of the South—Charleston, Atlanta, New Orleans, Memphis—had been ignored by Harry Truman for the nerve center of the black community on New York's West Side.

The election of November 2, 1948, is textbook history. The result seemed a foregone conclusion. Nobody doubted that, with the Democratic party split into three parties, Dewey would emerge as the certain victor. The Chicago *Tribune* was so confident of a Republican victory that it ran off an edition with the headline "Dewey defeats Truman" before the election results had come in.[67] But to the bewilderment of the pollsters, the pundits, and the politicians, Truman defeated Dewey by 303 electoral votes to 189. Strom Thurmond carried the four southern states where he appeared as the Democratic nominee. All the other Dixie states went for Truman.

Although the distribution of electoral votes was somewhat different from that in the 1944 election, Truman preserved the urban strongholds. He carried each of the twelve largest cities, where he polled almost one and a half million votes more than Thomas Dewey. Although this represented a substantial decline from Roosevelt's metropolitan plurality in 1944, the urban vote contributed 67.6 percent of the overall gross national plurality. This compares with 63.8 percent for 1944 and 45.1 percent in 1940. Dewey won the states of Maryland, Michigan, New York, and Pennsylvania. But in the first three of these

---

67 The photograph of Harry Truman holding up this notorious newspaper headline ranks among the best known of election victory pictures. Reproductions can be found in numerous textbooks. See, for example, T. Harry Williams, Richard N. Current, and Frank Freidel, *A History of the United States Since 1865* (2nd ed.; New York, 1964), 694.

states, the Wallace vote exceeded the difference between the Republican and Democratic vote. Therefore, had Wallace not been on the ballot, these states would probably have gone to Truman.[68]

Although there are no really satisfactory ward figures, it seems certain that Negroes in the big cities voted in large numbers for the Democrats. Reports from predominantly black districts indicated that Negroes had inclined overwhelmingly for Truman. According to an NAACP survey, nearly 109,000 Negroes in Harlem voted for Truman, while only 34,000 voted for Dewey and 29,000 for Wallace.[69] Democratic Congresswoman Helen Douglas of California calculated that in the predominantly black precincts of California's Fourth Congressional District, Truman polled 61.3 percent.[70] And Philleo Nash, a White House aide, informed Truman in a postelection memorandum that in Illinois, Ohio, and California "the majorities in the Negro districts exceeded the margin by which you carried the state."[71]

In the South, Truman carried all the states where he appeared on the ballot as the Democratic nominee. Thus, on the surface it appeared that party loyalty still superseded fundamental ideological issues in the political consciousness of southerners. In Georgia, where the race issue had so dominated recent politics, Thurmond polled only 20.3 percent of the popular vote to Truman's 60.8 percent and Dewey's 18.3 percent. In North Carolina Thurmond received only 8.8 percent of the vote. Thurmond's most impressive showing was in Mississippi, where 87.2 percent of the electorate cast their votes for him. In Alabama, where Truman was not even on the ballot as an independent, the States' Rights Democrats polled 79.8 percent,

---

68 Lubell, *The Future of American Politics*, 34–35; Eldersveld, "The Influence of Metropolitan Party Pluralities in Presidential Elections Since 1920," 1189–206; U.S. Bureau of the Census, *Historical Statistics*, 606.

69 Van Auken, "The Negro Press in the 1948 Presidential Election," 433. The figures have been rounded off.

70 Helen G. Douglas to Clifford, January 13, 1949, in Clifford Papers. The figures given are averages tabulated from the letter.

71 Memo, Philleo Nash to HST, November 6, 1948, in Clifford Papers.

while Dewey polled a surprisingly high 19 percent of the vote
—although a large proportion of these votes would probably
have been cast for Truman had he been on the ballot. In South
Carolina and Louisiana, Thurmond received 72 percent and
49.1 percent, while the president won 24.1 percent and 32.7
percent of the votes respectively. Truman's strong performance
in Louisiana reflected the state's traditional avoidance of racial
politics.

However, state-by-state voting statistics did not reflect ac-
curately the vortex of political attitudes. Although, taken as a
whole, all the states opted for the official Democratic nominees,
the electorate was far more sensitive to the substantive questions that arose in the 1948 election than the bare figures would
suggest. Although, undoubtedly, voters were torn between traditional Democratic loyalty and particularist protest, they resolved these pressures with discrimination and consistency.
Thurmond drew his greatest support from areas with a large
Negro population—areas which had previously remained most
loyal to the Democratic party *because* it had never interfered
with the racial *modus vivendi*. Other studies have confirmed
that counties with a high proportion of Negroes tended to vote
more heavily for Thurmond, while those with fewer Negroes
supported Truman. For example, in South Carolina Thurmond
polled 89.4 percent of the vote in the ten counties that had a
Negro population of at least 60 percent. On the other hand,
in the nine counties with a low concentration of Negroes
(under 30 percent) Thurmond polled only 61.3 percent of the
total vote.[72]

It should not be inferred, therefore, that whites from the
Black Belt were ultimately more rational and less habitual in
their voting behavior than were their counterparts in the hills
and cities. After all, Texas, which had a comparatively low
Negro population, had produced a substantial anti–New Deal

72 William J. Keefe, "Southern Politics Revisited," *Public Opinion Quarterly*,
XX (Summer, 1956), 405–12; Heard, *A Two Party South?*, 26–27; Key,
Southern Politics, 342–44.

contingent since the mid-thirties. The nature of the affiliation to the Democratic party of voters from the "white" areas of the South was different and—notwithstanding apparently contradictory evidence in the 1948 election—less tenacious than that of the Black Belt, which was circumscribed by the racial question. There were insufficient incentives in the white regions to overturn long-held, albeit less adhesive, patterns of political allegiances. Southern conservatives continued to espouse a realignment in the party system, while the advocates of social reform were not so antagonized by the civil rights program as to forsake the benefits of one-party rule and federal paternalism. However, the white inhabitants of the predominantly Negro counties, who had formed the backbone of the Democratic party (and had eschewed political revolts in the 1890s and 1928), realized that their rationale for loyalty to the party no longer existed.

This unquestionable revival of meaningful political division in the South was not the only significant portent of the 1948 election. Equally important was that civil rights had emerged as a forceful and respectable issue in presidential politics. Racial questions would no longer be determined purely by impotent civil rights organizations and dedicated clergymen. The rights of Negroes had become as contentious an issue as economic policy and the nature of the government's custodianship over the poor and unemployed. The matter would no longer be dismissed as a problem for private individuals to solve. Both major parties had made specific and irrevocable commitments to human equality. They had agreed that if the resources of the government could be used to remedy or prevent an economic depression, then they could be legitimately employed to create an egalitarian democracy. Politicians who aspired to high office would no longer be able to circumvent with impunity the discussion of this embarrassing flaw in the American polity.[73]

73 Sitkoff, "Harry Truman and the Election of 1948," 614–16.

Indeed, the legitimization of the civil rights issue in 1948 would change the style and character of all subsequent election campaigns. Furthermore, as at the end of the nineteenth century, it would also alter the nature of political alignments. For over fifty years southerners had supported the Democratic party. The reasons for this almost unswerving allegiance differed from person to person and from decade to decade. For some southerners, the party had embodied the Jeffersonian ideals of self-sufficiency, local autonomy, and rustic pride. For others it had been a protection against the rapacious ambitions of Negroes or the insufferable hardships of unemployment and declining agricultural prices. Although the Democratic party in the South represented multifarious qualities to different men, it had served on several occasions as a reminder that despite frequent and often tragic disagreements over labor unionism, social welfare, and agricultural reform, white southerners were essentially united in a common bond that usually defied definition. However, by 1948 nearly all white southerners, be they Black Belt planters, dirt farmers, or industrial workers, realized that they were neither politically nor ideologically homogeneous. They knew that the convenient but random huddling under the Democratic umbrella could not provide them with a key to the Eden of racial harmony or societal unity. Southerners had become politicized not only intellectually but in their behavior at the polling stations. Their beloved party could no longer guarantee political advancement, racial purity, and a sustained respect for the iconographic folklore of the Lost Cause. The party had become an urban and urbane agent of social reform. It had finally, if sometimes hesitatingly, cast its lot with the impatient aspirations of liberal intellectuals, underprivileged Negroes, and ambitious industrial workers. Southern Democrats could no longer delude themselves. Their party consisted not of a grand coalition but of incompatible bedfellows.

Epilogue

W HEN POLITICAL scientists and
contemporary commentators analyzed the Dixiecrat revolt in
the years following the election of 1948, they tended to dis-
miss it as another misguided third party movement which
would rapidly fade into familiar historical oblivion.[1] However,
its assignment to the dustbin of history was premature. Analysts too readily interpreted the States' Rights Democratic
party as an impulsive gesture of racial insecurity and southern
impetuosity. They neglected to acknowledge that it was a con-
vergent political movement representing both the climax of a
decade of political discontent and the springboard for the resolution of ironical political contradictions. Admittedly, Thur-

---

[1] Emile B. Ader, "Why the Dixiecrats Failed," *Journal of Politics*, XV (August, 1953), 356–69; Emile B. Ader, *The Dixiecrat Movement: Its Role in
Third Party Politics* (Washington, D.C., 1955); Lemmon, "The Ideology of
the 'Dixiecrat' Movement," 162–71; William G. Carleton, "The Dilemma of
the Dixiecrats," *Virginia Quarterly Review*, XXIV (Summer, 1948), 336–53;
Carleton, "The Fate of Our Fourth Party," 449–59; Heard, *A Two Party
South?*, 20–33, 160–68; Dewey W. Grantham, Jr., "An American Politics for
the South," in Charles G. Sellers (ed.), *The Southerner as American* (Chapel
Hill, 1960), 165–66. Numan V. Bartley has recently suggested that the movement created a "neobourbon" consciousness that fittingly equipped southerners for their "massive resistance" to school desegregation. However, his
study does not deal with the deep-rooted causes of the movement or with
the partisan effects. See Numan V. Bartley, *The Rise of Massive Resistance:
Race and Politics in the South During the 1950's* (Baton Rouge, 1969),
passim.

mond and Wright were unsuccessful in their main purpose—
that is, to throw the election into the House of Representatives
or to force the Democratic leadership to make concessions to
the South by dropping its controversial proposals on civil rights
and concomitantly spurning the urban coalition. Yet, notwithstanding these obvious failures, their achievements were more
enduring than negligible. In the first place, they provided a
coherent and voluble vehicle for channeling the South's growing sense of political isolation. Before 1948, southerners had
eschewed organized, tactical means of conveying their fears
and apprehensions to the Democratic hierarchy in Washington.
Truman's civil rights proposals, however, released inhibitions
against political action and were largely responsible for the
creation of this concrete challenge to Democratic supremacy.
Thurmond himself recognized that his movement had per-
formed a vital political function. "We have shown the political
leaders of this Nation," he wrote after the election, "that the
South can and will be independent when a principle is involved." The South, he believed, had firmly established itself
as a separate political entity which would no longer permit itself to be taken for granted by the Democratic party.[2] The
second notable success of the States' Rights Democrats was
their demonstration that southerners would reexamine their political culture if the racial status quo, which was the basis of
that culture, was in any way threatened. Their ability to carry
the four states with the highest proportion of Negroes, together
with their formidable showing in the Black Belt of the other
Dixie states, indicated that any tampering with the racial
modus vivendi was sufficient cause to cast aside enduring and
cherished credos and modes of behavior.

Of course, Thurmond did fail in his immediate objective to
capture control of the electoral college. However, he was more
successful in his ultimate objective than his contemporaries
could have realized. He showed southerners that regional politi-

2 Thurmond to Dixon, November 11, 1948, in Dixon Papers; also, Thurmond
to W. A. Kimbel, November 15, 1948, in Box 10, Thurmond Papers.

cal organization was a feasible and viable approach for combatting those economic and social reforms deemed abhorrent. Although he worked within the traditional party framework wherever he could—in the four states he carried, he appeared as the Democratic nominee—he demonstrated that blind and unquestioning allegiance to one party was neither necessary nor beneficial. The rationale for Dixie's historical affinity for the Democrats was no longer applicable. The Republicans could no longer be stigmatized as the sinister evangelists of black rule in the South. The Democratic party, which had recently wooed Negroes in the North, had appeared as the new champion of racial equality. Southerners, especially those who lived in the onetime Black Belt fortress of Democratic rule, realized that the *raison d'être* of their party affiliation had passed. In 1948 they made a final attempt to win control of the national Democratic party in order to restore old Wilsonian concepts. They tried to do this by beginning at the state level and working upward. In this they failed. But in their failure came the realization that the South had made the first critical step toward emancipation from the one-party system in presidential elections. The southern ideologist, Charles Wallace Collins, commented after the election that "the time is ripe for new party alignments."[3] Even the opponents of the States' Rights Democrats realized that disillusionment with the Democratic party would portend a new era in southern politics.

It has been argued that the creation of the States' Rights party was the culmination of years of general discontent below the Potomac with the national Democratic party. But the Dixiecrat movement was not only an attestation of alienation and political paradox. It was also an oracular liberating force in the South's one-party system.[4] Political events since 1948 tend to underscore the view that the Dixiecrats represented not the dying gasp of

3 Charles Wallace Collins to Dixon, January 23, 1949, in Dixon Papers.
4 See Heard, *A Two Party South?*, 20–129; Bartley, *The Rise of Massive Resistance, passim;* George Brown Tindall, *The Disruption of the Solid South* (Athens, 1972), 36–72.

southern particularism but the beginning of a new, invigorated "massive resistance." The States' Rights Democrats had foreseen that the federal government would continue its quest for racial justice. Indeed, within six years of the 1948 election, their fears were further confirmed when the Supreme Court reversed the *Plessy* v. *Ferguson* decision and declared segregation in the public schools unconstitutional.[5] Southern resistance thereafter centered increasingly on the school desegregation crisis. The heightened sense of southern identity and solidarity that earlier had accompanied the white primary decision and the publication of *To Secure These Rights* seems almost trifling when compared to the reaction to the *Brown* v. *Board of Education* ruling. Yet the widespread opposition to desegregation, together with the further desertions from the Democratic party, must be seen as another chapter in the saga of the dissidence and sectionalism that had prevailed in the South during the 1940s.

Indeed, many of the protagonists in the States' Rights movement gained later fame for their opposition to the civil rights movement of the subsequent decades. J. Strom Thurmond was elected to the Senate, where he became a leading opponent of all civil rights legislation. Perhaps most symbolic of all, Thurmond disaffiliated from the Democratic party in 1964 and joined the Republican party, where he became the unofficial spokesman for southern affairs. The police commissioner of Birmingham, Eugene "Bull" Connor, who had campaigned for the selection of electors pledged to vote against Truman, acquired notoriety throughout the world when he set police dogs and high-pressure fire hoses onto peaceful marchers led by the Reverend Martin Luther King in 1963. And a young alternate from Alabama at the 1948 convention became the spiritual successor to Thurmond in 1968, when he set up his own political party, the American Independent party, which, among other things, aimed to reverse recent developments in the integration of southern schools. He was, of course, Governor George Wallace.

5 *Plessy* v. *Ferguson*, 106 U.S. 537 (1896); *Brown* v. *Board of Education of Topeka*, 347 U.S. 483 (1954).

The 1948 election was not only a rehearsal ground for the die-hard segregationists. A glance at subsequent election returns indicates that for the South the 1948 election was, in academic parlance, a critical election. V. O. Key has defined a "critical" election as one in which there is a high incidence of involvement and a subsequent realignment that seems to persist for several succeeding elections.[6] Since 1948 there has occurred a fairly dramatic shift toward the Republican party in the South. In 1952 the states of Florida, Tennessee, Texas, and Virginia gave electoral majorities to Dwight D. Eisenhower. In all other southern states the Republicans made substantial gains. Particularly staggering were the results in the Deep South, which always had been considered an impregnable Democratic fortress. In Alabama Eisenhower polled 35 percent of the vote; in Georgia, 30 percent; in Louisiana, 47 percent; in Mississippi, 40 percent; and in South Carolina, 49 percent. Indeed, Eisenhower's main strength was in counties which had a high proportion of Negroes—and had been Strom Thurmond's strongholds in 1948.[7] In the 1956 election, Eisenhower held all the Dixie states he had carried in 1952 and, in addition, won the electoral votes of Louisiana. This was the first time since 1876 that Louisiana had gone to the Republicans. Although Louisiana and Texas returned to the Democratic fold in 1960, John F. Kennedy, the Democratic candidate, failed to gain the electoral college votes of Mississippi and half of those of Alabama. The unpledged electors of these states cast their electoral votes for Harry Byrd. The trend toward the Republican party was virtually sealed in the landslide victory of 1964, when the incumbent Democratic president, Lyndon Johnson, won every state in the Union, except Arizona (which was the home state of his Republican opponent, Barry Goldwater), Mississippi, South Carolina, Georgia, Louisiana, and Alabama (where, as in 1948, the state executive committee succeeded in keeping the Democratic nominee off the ballot). By

6 V. O. Key, "A Theory of Critical Elections," *Journal of Politics*, XVII (February, 1955), 3–18.
7 U.S. Bureau of the Census, *Historical Statistics*, 686; Keefe, "Southern Politics Revisited," 405–12.

1964 the Deep South had finally cast off a political anomaly that had frustrated it since World War II.

In the 1964 election, southern disaffection with the Democratic party had reached its zenith. President Johnson, who, like President Truman was regarded by southerners as traitorous not only to his party but to his place of birth as well, had committed himself to the employment of the full resources of the federal government to destroy the remaining vestiges of Jim Crow. The South found in his opponent, Barry Goldwater, a candidate who reflected its own anxieties. States' rights became the catchphrase of Goldwater, as it had of Strom Thurmond. However, as a result of Goldwater's defeat, southerners felt that the Republican party would not nominate another states' rights conservative in the near future. They determined, therefore, to plan in advance for the next election. Long before the 1968 campaign, George Wallace emerged as the new messiah of the politically thwarted South. So, in 1968 as in 1948, party leaders in the Deep South turned to an independent in the hope that they could deadlock the election in the electoral college and force the election into the House of Representatives.

In 1968, as in 1948, they failed. But it seemed that this was to be the last failure. The new president, Richard M. Nixon, a lifelong Republican, was particularly anxious to draw the South firmly into the GOP. Both his language and his actions were tuned to the anxieties of most southerners, as, indeed, they were to conservatives throughout the nation. Especially in the field of civil rights, the Republican Nixon was desirous to tone down the missionary enthusiasm of his Democratic predecessors. He deliberately scaled down the network of federal programs created by President Johnson to improve conditions in the ghettos. He even advocated a policy of "benign neglect" toward the Negro in an attempt to remove grievances entertained by whites against the benefactors of the poverty programs. Furthermore, Nixon was unreserved in his criticism of the Supreme Court, which, he claimed, was oblivious and insensitive to the preeminent values and concerns of society at large. He thus nominated renowned practitioners of judicial restraint to the bench and castigated the Senate when it rejected the nominations of the two southerners on the grounds that the nominees were racially prejudiced. This historically ironical spectacle profoundly impressed former southern Democrats. They finally realized that the Republicans were the natural standard-bearers of retrenchment and racial conservatism. In the election of 1972 they flocked to the GOP. Mississippi, the stronghold of the Dixiecrats, delivered a massive 79 percent of the vote to Nixon—the highest vote in the nation. Alabama and Georgia cast proportionally more votes for Nixon than any other state. Seven of the eleven Dixie states gave Nixon a majority of over 70 percent. Republicanism, at least in presidential elections, had become the outstanding political hallmark of white southerners. The solid South was once again solid—solidly Republican. The Dixiecrat rebellion had reached its natural and logical conclusion.

Bibliography

PRIMARY SOURCES

Manuscripts

Ames, Jessie Daniel. Southern Historical Collection, University of North Carolina, Chapel Hill.

Ayers, Harry M. University of Alabama, Tuscaloosa.

Bailey, Josiah W. Duke University Library, Durham, North Carolina.

Ball, William Watts. Duke University Library, Durham, North Carolina.

Bankhead, John H. Alabama Department of Archives, Montgomery.

Barkley, Alben W. University of Kentucky Library, Lexington.

Bilbo, Theodore G. University of Southern Mississippi, Hattiesburg.

Burns, Gladys King. Letters from George Wallace regarding her master's thesis on the States' Rights movement in Alabama. Alabama Department of Archives, Montgomery.

Clifford, Clark M. Harry S. Truman Library, Independence, Missouri.

Connally, Tom. Manuscripts Division, Library of Congress, Washington, D.C.

Daniels, Jonathan. Southern Historical Collection, University of North Carolina, Chapel Hill.

Daniels, Jonathan. Letter to author, June 24, 1970.

Democratic National Committee, Records of. Franklin D. Roosevelt Library, Hyde Park, New York; Harry S. Truman Library, Independence, Missouri.

Dixon, Frank M. Alabama Department of Archives, Montgomery.

Doughton, Robert L. Southern Historical Collection, University of North Carolina, Chapel Hill.

Fair Employment Practices Committee, Records of. National Archives, Washington, D.C.

Green, Theodore F. Manuscripts Division, Library of Congress, Washington, D.C.

Hobbs, Samuel F. University of Alabama Library, Tuscaloosa.

Hoey, Clyde R. Duke University Library, Durham, North Carolina.

Hutchinson, Martin A. Alderman Library, University of Virginia, Charlottesville.

Jefferies, Richard M. South Caroliniana Library, Columbia, South Carolina.

Johnston, Olin D. South Carolina Department of Archives, Columbia; South Caroliniana Library, Columbia, South Carolina.

Jones, Sam. Otis P. Morgan Collection of Governor Sam Jones' Campaign Speeches, 1947–1948. Louisiana State University Library, Baton Rouge.

Labor Archives, Department of. Office Files of Secretaries Frances Perkins and Lewis B. Schwellenbach. National Archives, Washington, D.C.

Lewis, David J. Duke University Library, Durham, North Carolina.

McDuffie, John. University of Alabama, Tuscaloosa.

McGrath, J. Howard. Harry S. Truman Library, Independence, Missouri.

McKellar, Kenneth D. Memphis Public Library, Memphis, Tennessee.

McNaughton, Frank. Harry S. Truman Library, Independence, Missouri.

Martin, John Santford. Duke University Library, Durham, North Carolina.

Mason, Lucy Randolph. Duke University Library, Durham, North Carolina.

Matthews, Francis P. Harry S. Truman Library, Independence, Missouri.

Maybank, Burnet R. South Carolina Department of Archives, Columbia.

Murphree, Dennis. Mississippi Department of Archives and History, Jackson.

Murray, Philip. Catholic University, Washington, D.C.

Nash, Philleo. Harry S. Truman Library, Independence, Missouri.

National Association for the Advancement of Colored People, Files of. Manuscripts Division, Library of Congress, Washington, D.C.

Overton, John H. Louisiana State University Library, Baton Rouge.

President's Committee on Civil Rights, Records of. Harry S. Truman Library, Independence, Missouri.

Rayburn, Sam. Sam Rayburn Library, Bonham, Texas.

Redding, John M. Harry S. Truman Library, Independence, Missouri.

Roosevelt, Franklin D. Official and Personal Files. Franklin D. Roosevelt Library, Hyde Park, New York.

Rosenman, Samuel I. Franklin D. Roosevelt Library, Hyde Park, New York; Harry S. Truman Library, Independence, Missouri.

Rushton, Marion. Alabama Department of Archives, Montgomery.

Sparks, Chauncey. Alabama Department of Archives, Montgomery.

Spingarn, Stephen J. Harry S. Truman Library, Independence, Missouri.

States' Rights Scrapbook (clippings and mimeographed speeches). Mississippi Department of Archives and History, Jackson.

Thurmond, J. Strom. South Carolina Department of Archives, Columbia; South Caroliniana Library, Columbia, South Carolina.

Thurmond, J. Strom. Statement on "1948 States Rights Movement." In possession of the author.

Truman, Harry S. Official and Personal Files. Harry S. Truman Library, Independence, Missouri.

Wallace, Henry A. Manuscripts Division, Library of Congress, Washington, D.C.

Whitehead, Robert. Alderman Library, University of Virginia, Charlottesville.

Williams, Aubrey. Franklin D. Roosevelt Library, Hyde Park, New York.

Williams, Ransome J. South Carolina Department of Archives, Columbia.

Government Documents

Louisiana. *Official Journal, Proceedings of the House of Representatives.* 14th Regular Session, 1948.

———. *Official Journal, Proceedings of the Senate.* 14th Regular Session, 1948.

Mansfield, Harvey C., *et al. A Short History of OPA.* Washington, D.C., 1947.

Public Papers of the Presidents of the United States, Harry S. Truman: Containing the Public Messages, Speeches, and Statements of the President, 1945–1952. 8 vols., Washington, D.C., 1961–66.

South Carolina. *Journal of the Senate.* 84th General Assembly, 1942.

————. *Journal of the Senate*. 85th General Assembly, 1944.

Tennessee. *House Journal*. 75th General Assembly, 1947.

————. *Senate Journal*. 75th General Assembly, 1947.

U.S. Bureau of the Census. *Historical Statistics of the United States from Colonial Times to 1957*. Washington, D.C., 1960.

U.S. Congress. *Congressional Record*. 77th–80th Congresses.

————. Committees on the Judiciary. *Joint Hearings to Confirm and Establish the Titles of the States to the Tidelands*. 80th Cong., 2nd Sess.

U.S. Department of Labor. *11th Annual Report of the National Labor Relations Board*. Washington, D.C., 1946.

————. *12th Annual Report of the National Labor Relations Board*. Washington, D.C., 1947.

————. *13th Annual Report of the National Labor Relations Board*. Washington, D.C., 1948.

————. *Bulletin 898: Labor in the South*. Washington, D.C., 1947.

U.S. Fair Employment Practices Committee. *First Report*. Washington, D.C., 1945.

————. *Final Report*. Washington, D.C., 1947.

U.S. House of Representatives. Committee on Banking and Currency. *Hearings to Amend the Emergency Price Control Act*. 79th Cong., 2nd Sess.

————. Committee on the Election of the President, Vice-President, and Representatives in Congress. *Hearings to Amend the Soldiers' Voting Act*. 78th Cong., 1st Sess.

————. Committee on Expenditures in the Executive Departments. *Hearings to Establish a Full Employment Program*. 79th Cong., 1st Sess.

————. Committee on Expenditures in the Executive Departments. *Hearings to Reorganize the Executive Office of the President*. 79th Cong., 2nd Sess.

————. Subcommittee on Elections of the Committee on House Administration. *Hearings to Make Unlawful the Requirement for the Payment of a Poll Tax*. 80th Cong., 1st Sess.

————. Special Committee to Investigate Campaign Expenditures. *Hearings to Investigate Campaign Expenditures, 1944*. 78th Cong., 2nd Sess.

————. Special Committee to Investigate Campaign Expenditures. *Hearings to Investigate the Election of Members of the House of Representatives*. 79th Cong., 2nd Sess.

————. Special Committee to Investigate Executive Agencies. *Hearings to Continue a Select Committee to Investigate Acts of Executive Agencies Beyond the Scope of Their Authority* (OPA). 79th Cong., 2nd Sess.

————. Committee on the Judiciary. *Report 1778 on Confirming and Establishing the Titles of the States to Lands Beneath Navigable Waters.* 80th Cong., 2nd Sess.

————. Committee on the Judiciary. *Report 1597 on Mob Violence and Lynching.* 80th Cong., 2nd Sess.

————. Subcommittee No. 4 of the Committee on the Judiciary. *Hearings on Declaring the Date of Termination of Hostilities in the Present War.* 79th Cong., 1st Sess.

————. Subcommittee No. 4 of the Committee on the Judiciary. *Hearings to Prevent the Crime of Lynching.* 80th Cong., 2nd Sess.

————. Committee on Labor. *Hearings to Make the United States Employment Service a Federal Agency.* 79th Cong., 2nd Sess.

————. Committee on Military Affairs. *Hearings to Authorize Operation by the United States of Certain Plants in the Interests of National Defense.* 78th Cong., 1st Sess.

————. Special Committee on Un-American Activities. *Report 1311 on Investigation of Un-American Propaganda Activities in the United States.* 78th Cong., 2nd Sess.

U.S. President's Committee on Civil Rights. *To Secure These Rights.* Washington, D.C., 1947.

U.S. Senate. Committee on Banking and Currency. *Hearings to Extend the Emergency Price Control Act.* 79th Cong., 1st Sess.

————. Committee on Banking and Currency. *Hearings to Amend the Emergency Price Control Act.* 79th Cong., 2nd Sess.

————. Subcommittee of the Committee on Education and Labor. *Hearings to Establish a Fair Employment Practices Commission.* 79th Cong., 1st Sess.

————. Subcommittee of the Committee on Education and Labor. *Hearings to Provide a National System of Employment Offices.* 79th Cong., 1st Sess.

————. Subcommittee of the Committee on Education and Labor. *Hearings to Provide Additional Facilities for the Mediation of Labor Disputes.* 79th Cong., 2nd Sess.

————. Subcommittee of the Committee on Education and Labor. *Hearings to Provide a National System of Employment Offices.* 79th Cong., 2nd Sess.

————. Special Committee to Investigate Senatorial Campaign Expenditures. *Hearings on Bilbo Campaign, 1946.* 79th Cong., 2nd Sess.

————. Special Committee to Investigate Senatorial Campaign Expenditures. *Report 1 on Investigation of Senatorial Campaign Expenditures, 1946.* 80th Cong., 1st Sess.

————. Committee on the Judiciary. *Hearings to Make Unlawful the Requirement for the Payment of a Poll Tax.* 78th Cong., 1st Sess.

————. Committee on the Judiciary. *Hearings to Quiet the Titles of the States to the Tidelands.* 79th Cong., 2nd Sess.

————. Committee on the Judiciary. *Report 1592, Confirming and Establishing the Titles of the States of Land and Resources in and beneath Navigable Waters within State Boundaries.* 80th Cong., 2nd Sess.

————. Subcommittee of the Committee on the Judiciary. *Hearings to Amend the Constitution Regarding the Election of the President and Vice-President.* 80th Cong., 2nd Sess.

————. Subcommittee of the Committee on the Judiciary. *Hearings to Prevent the Crime of Lynching.* 80th Cong., 2nd Sess.

————. Subcommittee of the Committee on Labor and Public Welfare. *Hearings to Amend the Fair Labor Standards Act.* 80th Cong., 2nd Sess.

————. Subcommittee of the Committee on Labor and Public Welfare. *Hearings to Prohibit Discrimination in Employment.* 80th Cong., 1st Sess.

Newspapers

Arkansas Gazette

Atlanta *Constitution*

Baton Rouge *Morning Advocate*

Birmingham *News*

Charleston *News and Courier*

Columbia (S.C.) *Record*

Dallas *Morning News*

Detroit *News*

Houston *Post*

Jackson *Clarion-Ledger*

Lynchburg (Va.) *News*

Memphis *Commercial Appeal*

Mobile *Register*

New Orleans *Times-Picayune*

New York *Times*

Norfolk *Journal and Guide*
Pittsburgh *Courier*
Raleigh *News and Observer*
Washington *Post*

Magazines and Special Interest Newspapers

Alabama
Alabama News Digest (CIO)
CIO News
Crisis (NAACP)
Nation
New Republic
New South (Southern Regional Council)
Newswee
Southern Frontier (Commission on Interracial Cooperation)
Southern Patriot (Southern Conference for Human Welfare)
Southern Planter
Southern Weekly
Statesman (Eugene Talmadge's campaign newspaper)
States' Righter (States' Rights Democrats)
Texas Bulletin
Texas Weekly (Renamed *Texas Digest,* November, 1940)

Magazine Articles

Barr, John U. "Louisiana Can Be Proud." *Louisiana Police Jury Review,* XIII (April, 1949), 13–17.

Byrd, Harry F. "Are We Losing Our Freedom?" *American Magazine,* CXXXVI (September, 1943), 42–43, 132–34.

Cohn, David L. "How the South Feels." *Atlantic Monthly,* CLXXIII (January, 1944), 47–51.

Davis, Jimmie H. "Louisiana and the Postwar Era." *Louisiana Police Jury Review,* IX (April, 1945), 10–18.

Graves, John Temple. "The Solid South Is Cracking." *American Mercury,* LVI (April, 1943), 401–406.

Jones, Sam H. "Will Dixie Bolt the New Deal?" *Saturday Evening Post* (March 6, 1943).

Murray, Philip. "Labor's Political Aims." *American Magazine*, CXXXVII (February, 1944), 28–29, 98.

Peacock, Eugene. "Why Are the Dixiecrats?" *Christian Century*, LXV (September 22, 1948), 975–77.

Perez, Leander. "Are You a States' Righter?" *Louisiana Police Jury Review*, XIV (April, 1950), 9–12.

"The President's Program: Civil Rights, States' Rights, and the Reconstruction Background." *Staple Cotton Review*, XXVI (April, 1948).

Wright, Fielding. "Give the Government Back to the People." *American Magazine*, CXLVI (July, 1948), 36, 37, 126, 127.

Memoirs and Polemics

Arnall, Ellis G. *The Shore Dimly Seen*. Philadelphia, 1946.

———. *What the People Want*. Philadelphia, 1947.

Barkley, Alben W. *That Reminds Me*. Garden City, N.Y., 1954.

Bilbo, Theodore G. *Take Your Choice: Separation or Mongrelization*. Poplarville, Miss., 1947.

Byrnes, James F. *All in One Lifetime*. New York, 1958.

Collins, Charles Wallace. *Whither Solid South? A Study in Politics and Race Relations*. New Orleans, 1947.

Connally, Tom, and Alfred Steinberg. *My Name Is Tom Connally*. New York, 1954.

Flynn, Edward J. *You're the Boss*. New York, 1947.

Gaer, Joseph. *The First Round: The Story of the CIO Political Action Committee*. New York, 1944.

Landry, Stuart O. *The Cult of Equality: A Study of the Race Problem*. New Orleans, 1945.

Lilienthal, David E. *The Journals of David E. Lilienthal, II: The Atomic Energy Years, 1945–1950*. New York, 1964.

Mason, Lucy Randolph. *To Win These Rights*. New York, 1952.

Molyneaux, Peter. *The South's Political Plight*. Dallas, 1948.

Nelson, Donald M. *Arsenal of Democracy: The Story of American War Production*. New York, 1946.

Redding, Jack. *Inside the Democratic Party*. New York, 1958.

Roosevelt, Elliot, ed. *F.D.R.: His Personal Letters, 1928–1945*. 2 vols., New York, 1950.

Rosenman, Samuel I. *Working with Roosevelt*. London, 1952.

————, comp. *The Public Papers and Addresses of Franklin D. Roosevelt.* 13 vols., New York, 1938–50.

Truman, Harry S. *Memoirs: Years of Decision* and *Years of Trial and Hope, 1946–1952.* 2 vols., Signet ed., New York, 1965.

White, Walter. *A Man Called White.* New York, 1948.

Interviews with the Author

Senator Allen Ellender. September, 1969.

Mrs. Roland B. Howell (Democratic national committeewoman for Louisiana, 1940–48). October, 1968.

Courtney Pace (Legislative assistant to Senator James O. Eastland). September, 1969.

Boris Shiskin. October, 1969.

Senator Herman Talmadge. September, 1969.

Senator J. Strom Thurmond. October, 1969.

Miscellaneous

American Federation of Labor. *Report of the Proceedings of the 66th Convention of the American Federation of Labor.* San Francisco, 1947.

————. *Report of the Proceedings of the 67th Convention of the American Federation of Labor.* Cincinnati, 1948.

Congress of Industrial Organizations. *The Case Against "Right to Work" Laws.* N.p., n.d.

CIO Political Action Committee. *Full Employment: The Proceedings of the Conference on Full Employment, CIO-PAC.* New York, 1944.

Congressional Quarterly News Features. *Congressional Quarterly Almanac, 1945–1948.* 4 vols., Washington, D.C., 1945–48.

Democracy at Work: The Official Report of the Democratic Convention. Philadelphia, 1948.

Democratic National Committee. *Official Report of the Proceedings of the Democratic National Convention, 1936.* N.p., 1936.

————. *Official Report of the Proceedings of the Democratic National Convention, 1944.* N.p., 1944.

National States' Rights Democrats Campaign Committee. *States' Rights Information and Speakers Handbook.* Jackson, 1948.

SECONDARY SOURCES

Books

Abels, Jules. *Out of the Jaws of Victory*. New York, 1959.

Ader, Emile B. *The Dixiecrat Movement: Its Role in Third-Party Politics.* Washington, D.C., 1955.

Allen, Robert S., and William V. Shannon. *The Truman Merry-Go-Round.* New York, 1950.

Anderson, Patrick. *The President's Men*. Garden City, N.Y., 1968.

Ashmore, Harry S. *An Epitaph for Dixie*. New York, 1958.

Bailey, Stephen K. *Congress Makes a Law: The Story Behind the Employment Act of 1946*. New York, 1950.

Bartley, Ernest R. *The Tidelands Oil Controversy: A Legal and Historical Analysis.* Austin, 1953.

Bartley, Numan V. *The Rise of Massive Resistance: Race and Politics in the South during the 1950s*. Baton Rouge, 1969.

Bernd, Joseph L. *Grass Roots Politics in Georgia*. Atlanta, 1960.

Bernstein, Barton J., ed. *Towards a New Past: Dissenting Essays in American History.* New York, 1969.

Binkley, Wilfred E. *President and Congress.* 3rd rev. ed., New York, 1962.

Brock, Clifton. *Americans for Democratic Action: Its Role in National Politics.* Washington, D.C., 1962.

Buni, Andrew. *The Negro in Virginia Politics, 1902–1965*. Charlottesville, 1967.

Burner, David. *The Politics of Provincialism: The Democratic Party in Transition, 1918–1932.* New York, 1968.

Burns, James M. *The Deadlock of Democracy: Four Party Politics in America.* Englewood Cliffs, N.J., 1963.

———. *Roosevelt: The Lion and the Fox*. New York, 1956.

———. *Roosevelt: The Soldier of Freedom, 1940–1945*. New York, 1970.

Calkins, Fay. *The CIO and the Democratic Party*. Chicago, 1952.

Carr, Robert K. *Federal Protection of Civil Rights*. Ithaca, 1947.

Casdorph, Paul. *A History of the Republican Party in Texas, 1865–1965.* Austin, 1965.

Clark, Thomas D. *The Emerging South*. New York, 1961.

Conrad, David E. *The Forgotten Farmers: The Story of the Sharecroppers in the New Deal.* Urbana, 1965.

Dabbs, James M. *The Southern Heritage*. New York, 1958.

Dabney, Virginius. *Below the Potomac*. New York, 1942.

————. *Liberalism in the South*. Chapel Hill, 1932.

Daniels, Jonathan. *The Man of Independence*. New York and Philadelphia, 1950.

Davies, Richard O. *Housing Reform During the Truman Administration*. Columbia, Mo., 1966.

Derber, Milton, and Edwin Young, eds. *Labor and the New Deal*. Madison, 1957.

Donahoe, Bernard F. *Private Plans and Public Dangers: The Story of FDR's Third Nomination*. Notre Dame, 1965.

Dykeman, Wilma, and James Stokeley. *Seeds of Southern Change: The Life of Will Alexander*. Chicago, 1962.

Freidel, Frank. *F.D.R. and the South*. Baton Rouge, 1965.

Garfinkel, Herbert. *When Negroes March: The March on Washington Movement in the Organizational Politics for FEPC*. Glencoe, 1959.

Graham, Otis L. *An Encore for Reform: The Old Progressives and the New Deal*. New York, 1967.

Grantham, Jr., Dewey W. *The Democratic South*. Athens, Ga., 1963.

Graves, John Temple. *The Fighting South*. New York, 1943.

Green, A. Wigfall. *The Man Bilbo*. Baton Rouge, 1963.

Grundstein, Nathan. *Presidential Delegation of Authority in Wartime*. Pittsburgh, 1961.

Harris, Joseph P. *The Advice and Consent of the Senate*. Berkeley and Los Angeles, 1953.

Harris, Robert J. *The Quest for Equality: The Constitution, Congress, and the Supreme Court*. Baton Rouge, 1960.

Heard, Alexander. *A Two-Party South?* Chapel Hill, 1952.

————, and Donald S. Strong. *Southern Primaries and Elections*. University, Ala., 1950.

Hoover, Calvin B., and Benjamin U. Ratchford. *Economic Resources and Policies of the South*. New York, 1951.

Howard, Donald S. *The WPA and Federal Relief Policy*. New York, 1943.

Howard, L. Vaughan. *Civil Service Development in Louisiana*. New Orleans, 1956.

————, and David R. Deener. *Presidential Politics in Louisiana, 1952*. New Orleans, 1954.

Huss, John E. *Senator for the South: A Biography of Olin D. Johnston.* Garden City, N.Y., 1961.

Johnson, Charles S. *Patterns of Negro Segregation.* New York, 1943.

————, et al. *Into the Main Stream: A Survey of Best Practices in Race Relations in the South.* Chapel Hill, 1947.

————, et al. *To Stem This Tide: A Survey of Racial Tension Areas in the United States.* Boston and Chicago, 1943.

Josephson, Matthew. *Sidney Hillman: Statesman of American Labor.* New York, 1952.

Kennedy, Stetson. *Southern Exposure.* New York, 1946.

Kesselman, Louis C. *The Social Politics of FEPC: A Study in Reform Movements.* Chapel Hill, 1948.

Key, V. O. *Southern Politics in State and Nation.* New York, 1949.

Kirkendall, Richard S., ed. *The Truman Period as a Research Field.* Columbia, Mo., 1967.

Koenig, Louis W., ed. *The Truman Administration.* New York, 1956.

Konvitz, Milton R., and Theodore Leskes. *A Century of Civil Rights.* New York, 1961.

Krueger, Thomas A. *And Promises to Keep: The Southern Conference for Human Welfare, 1938–1948.* Nashville, 1967.

Lee, Alfred McClung, and Norman D. Humphrey. *Race Riot.* New York, 1943.

Lee, R. Alton. *Truman and Taft-Hartley.* Lexington, Ky., 1966.

Leuchtenburg, William E. *Franklin D. Roosevelt and the New Deal, 1932–1940.* New York, 1963.

Lewinson, Paul. *Race, Class and Party.* New York, 1932.

Lively, Robert A. *The South in Action: A Sectional Crusade Against Freight Rate Discrimination.* Chapel Hill, 1949.

Logan, Rayford W., ed. *What the Negro Wants.* Chapel Hill, 1944.

Logan, Spencer. *A Negro's Faith in America.* New York, 1946.

Lubell, Samuel. *The Future of American Politics.* London, 1952.

Lumpkin, Katherine D. *The South in Progress.* New York, 1940.

Luthin, Reinhard. *American Demagogues: Twentieth Century.* Boston, 1954.

McClure, Arthur F. *The Truman Administration and the Problems of Postwar Labor, 1945–1948.* Cranbury, N.J., 1969.

MacDougall, Curtis D. *Gideon's Army.* 3 vols., New York, 1965.

McKay, Seth S. *Texas and the Fair Deal, 1945–1952*. San Antonio, 1954.

————. *Texas Politics, 1906–1944*. Lubbock, 1952.

Marshall, F. Ray. *Labor in the South*. Cambridge, Mass., 1967.

Mezerik, Avrahm G. *The Revolt of the South and West*. New York, 1946.

Michie, Allan A., and Frank Rhylick. *Dixie Demagogues*. New York, 1939.

Miller, William D. *Mr. Crump of Memphis*. Baton Rouge, 1964.

Millis, Harry A., and Emily C. Brown. *From the Wagner Act to Taft-Hartley*. Chicago, 1950.

Moon, Henry Lee. *Balance of Power: The Negro Vote*. New York, 1949.

Moore, John R. *Senator Josiah William Bailey of North Carolina: A Political Biography*. Durham, 1968.

Murray, Florence, ed. *Negro Handbook, 1946–1947*. New York, 1947.

Myrdal, Gunnar. *An American Dilemma: The Negro Problem and Modern Democracy*. 2 vols., McGraw-Hill, New York, 1964.

Odum, Howard W. *Race and Rumors of Race*. Chapel Hill, 1943.

Ogden, Frederic D. *The Poll Tax in the South*. University, Ala., 1958.

Parmet, Herbert S., and Marle B. Hecht. *Never Again: A President Runs for a Third Term*. New York, 1968.

Patterson, James T. *Congressional Conservatism and the New Deal*. Lexington, Ky., 1967.

Phillips, Cabell. *The Truman Presidency: The History of a Triumphant Succession*. New York, 1966.

Quint, Howard H. *Profile in Black and White*. Washington, D.C., 1958.

Ross, Irwin. *The Loneliest Campaign: The Truman Victory of 1948*. New York, 1968.

Ruchames, Louis. *Race, Jobs, and Politics: The Story of the FEPC*. New York, 1953.

Schlesinger, Jr., Arthur M. *The Age of Roosevelt, II: The Coming of the New Deal*. Boston, 1959.

————. *The Age of Roosevelt, III: The Politics of Upheaval*. Boston, 1960.

Seidman, Joel. *American Labor from Defense to Reconversion*. Chicago, 1953.

Sellers, Charles G., ed. *The Southerner as American*. Chapel Hill, 1960.

Shannon, Jasper B. *Toward a New Politics in the South*. Knoxville, 1949.

Sindler, Allan P. *Huey Long's Louisiana: State Politics, 1920–1952*. Baltimore, 1956.

Somers, Herman M. *Presidential Agency: OWMR, the Office of War Mobilization and Reconversion.* Cambridge, Mass., 1950.

Steiberg, Alfred. *The Man from Missouri: The Life and Times of Harry S. Truman.* New York, 1962.

Stinnett, Ronald F. *Democrats, Dinners, and Dollars: A History of the Democratic Party, Its Dinners, Its Rituals.* Ames, 1967.

Tindall, George B. *The Disruption of the Solid South.* Athens, 1972.

————. *The Emergence of the New South, 1913–1945.* Baton Rouge, 1967.

Tugwell, Rexford G. *The Democratic Roosevelt.* New York, 1957.

Twitty, W. Bradley. *Y'All Come.* Nashville, 1962.

Vance, Rupert B., and Nicholas J. Demerath, eds. *The Urban South.* Chapel Hill, 1954.

Vandiver, Frank E., ed. *The Idea of the South: The Pursuit of a Central Theme.* Chicago, 1964.

Warne, Colston E., *et al. Labor in Postwar America.* New York, 1949.

Waskow, Arthur I. *From Race Riot to Sit-In: 1919 and the 1960s.* Garden City, N.Y., 1966.

White, Walter, and Thurgood Marshall. *What Caused the Detroit Riot?* New York, 1943.

Wilkinson, III, J. Harvie. *Harry Byrd and the Changing Face of Virginia Politics, 1945–1966.* Charlottesville, 1968.

Williams, T. Harry. *Huey Long.* New York, 1969.

Wolfskill, George. *The Revolt of the Conservatives.* Boston, 1962.

————, and John A. Hudson. *All But the People: Franklin D. Roosevelt and His Critics, 1933–1939.* New York, 1969.

Wolters, Raymond. *Negroes and the Great Depression: The Problem of Economic Recovery.* Westport, Conn., 1970.

Young, Roland. *Congressional Politics in the Second World War.* New York, 1956.

Articles

Ader, Emile B. "Why the Dixiecrats Failed." *Journal of Politics,* XV (August, 1953), 356–69.

Auken, Cecelia Van. "The Negro Press in the 1948 Presidential Election." *Journalism Quarterly,* XXVI (December, 1949), 431–35.

Barker, Lucius J. "The Supreme Court as Policy Maker: The Tidelands Oil Controversy." *Journal of Politics,* XXIV (May, 1962), 350–66.

Bernstein, Barton J. "The Truman Administration and Its Reconversion Wage Policy." *Labor History*, VI (Fall, 1965), 214–31.

————. "The Truman Administration and the Steel Strike of 1946." *Journal of American History*, LII (March, 1966), 791–803.

————. "Walter Reuther and the General Motors Strike of 1945–1946." *Michigan History*, XLIX (September, 1965), 260–77.

Bogardus, Emory S. "Public Opinion and the Presidential Election of 1948." *Social Forces*, XXVIII (October, 1949), 79–83.

Burns, Arthur F. "Some Reflections on the Employment Act." *Political Science Quarterly*, LXXXVII (December, 1962), 481–504.

Carleton, William G. "The Conservative South: A Political Myth." *Virginia Quarterly Review*, XXII (Spring, 1946), 179–92.

————. "The Dilemma of the Democrats." *Virginia Quarterly Review*, XXIV (Summer, 1948), 336–53.

————. "The Fate of Our Fourth Party." *Yale Review*, XXXVIII (March, 1949), 449–59.

————. "The Southern Politician: 1900 and 1950." *Journal of Politics*, XIII (May, 1951), 215–31.

Childs, Marquis W. "Year of Doubt." *Yale Review*, XXXVII (September, 1948), 1–10.

Christensen, Janice E. "The Constitutionality of National Anti-Poll Tax Bills." *Minnesota Law Review*, XXXIII (February, 1949), 217–54.

Collins, Charles Wallace. "Constitutional Aspects of the Truman Civil Rights Program." *Illinois Law Review of Northwestern University*, XLIV (April, 1949).

Dalfiume, Richard M. "The 'Forgotten Years' of the Negro Revolution." *Journal of American History*, LV (June, 1968), 90–106.

Dauer, Manning J. "Recent Southern Political Thought." *Journal of Politics*, X (May, 1948), 354–84.

Degler, Carl. "American Political Parties and the Rise of the City: An Interpretation." *Journal of American History*, LI (June, 1964), 41–59.

De Vyer, Frank T. "The Present Status of Labor Unions in the South, 1948." *Southern Economic Journal*, XVI (July, 1949), 1–22.

Dinnerstein, Leonard. "The Senate's Rejection of Aubrey Williams as Rural Electrification Administrator." *Alabama Review*, XXI (April, 1968), 133–43.

Doherty, Herbert J. "Liberal and Conservative Voting Patterns in Florida." *Journal of Politics*, XIV (August, 1952), 403–17.

Eldersveld, Samuel J. "The Influence of Metropolitan Party Pluralities in

Presidential Elections Since 1920: A Study of Twelve Key Cities." *American Political Science Review*, XLIII (December, 1949), 1189–206.

Ewing, Cortez A. M. "Southern Governors." *Journal of Politics*, X (May, 1948), 385–409.

Fishel, Jr., Leslie H. "The Negro in the New Deal Era." *Wisconsin Magazine of History*, XLVIII (Winter, 1964–65), 111–26.

Gordon, Rita W. "The Change in the Political Alignment of Chicago's Negroes During the New Deal." *Journal of American History*, LVI (December, 1969), 584–603.

Green, Fletcher M. "Resurgent Southern Sectionalism." *North Carolina Historical Review*, XXXIII (April, 1956), 222–40.

Hamby, Alonzo L. "The Liberals, Truman, and F.D.R. as Symbol and Myth." *Journal of American History*, LVI (March, 1970), 859–67.

Harrell, James A. "Negro Leadership in the Election Year 1936." *Journal of Southern History*, XXXIV (November, 1968), 546–64.

Heacock, Walter J. "William B. Bankhead and the New Deal." *Journal of Southern History*, XXI (August, 1955), 347–59.

Heberle, Rudolf. "The Impact of the War on Population Distribution in the South." *Papers of the Institute of Research and Training in the Social Sciences*, Vanderbilt University, VII (January, 1945), 8–27.

Hofstadter, Richard. "From Calhoun to the Dixiecrats." *Social Research*, XVI (June, 1949), 135–50.

Johnson, Charles S. "The Present Status of Race Relations in the South." *Social Forces*, XXIII (October, 1944), 27–32.

————. "Social Changes and Their Effects on Race Relations in the South." *Social Forces*, XXIII (March, 1945), 343–48.

Kallenbach, Joseph E. "Constitutional Aspects of Federal Anti-Poll Tax Legislation." *Michigan Law Review*, XLV (April, 1947), 717–32.

Keefe, William J. "Southern Politics Revisited." *Public Opinion Quarterly*, XX (Summer, 1956), 405–12.

Key, Jack B. "Henry B. Steagall: The Conservative as Reformer." *Alabama Review*, XVII (July, 1964), 198–209.

Key, V. O. "A Theory of Critical Elections." *Journal of Politics*, XVII (February, 1955), 3–18.

Lasseter, Dillard B. "The Impact of the War on the South and Implications for Postwar Developments." *Social Forces*, XXIII (October, 1944), 20–26.

Lee, R. Alton. "The Turnip Session of the Do-Nothing Congress: Presidential Campaign Strategy." *Southwestern Social Science Quarterly*, XLIV (December, 1963), 256–67.

Lemmon, Sarah M. "Governor Eugene Talmadge and the New Deal." *James Sprunt Studies in History and Political Science,* XXXIX (1957), 152–68.

————. "The Ideology of the 'Dixiecrat' Movement." *Social Forces,* XXX (December, 1951), 162–71.

Lester, Richard A. "Southern Wage Differentials: Developments, Analysis, and Implications." *Southern Economic Journal,* XIII (April, 1947), 386–94.

Maslow, Will. "FEPC: A Case History in Parliamentary Maneuver." *University of Chicago Law Review,* XIII (June, 1946), 407–44.

Moore, John R. "The Conservative Coalition in the United States Senate, 1942–1945." *Journal of Southern History,* XXXIII (August, 1967), 368–76.

————. "Senator Josiah W. Bailey and the 'Conservative Manifesto' of 1937." *Journal of Southern History,* XXXI (February, 1965), 21–39.

Muelder, Walter G. "National Unity and National Ethics." *Annals of the American Academy of Political and Social Science,* CCXLIV (1946), 10–18.

Nixon, H. Clarence. "The Politics of the Hills." *Journal of Politics,* VIII (May, 1946), 123–33.

————. "The Southern Governors' Conference as a Pressure Group." *Journal of Politics,* VI (August, 1944), 338–45.

————. "Southern Regionalism Limited." *Virginia Quarterly Review,* XXVI (Spring, 1950), 161–70.

Northrup, Herbert R. "Unions and Negro Employment." *Annals of the American Academy of Political and Social Science,* CCXLIV (1946), 42–47.

Odum, Howard W. "Social Change in the South." *Journal of Politics,* X (May, 1948), 242–58.

Overacker, Louise. "Campaign Finance in the Presidential Election of 1940." *American Political Science Review,* XXXV (August, 1941), 701–27.

————. "Campaign Funds in the Presidential Election of 1936." *American Political Science Review,* XXXI (June, 1937), 473–98.

————. "Labor's Political Contributions." *Political Science Quarterly,* LIV (March, 1939), 56–68.

————. "Presidential Campaign Funds, 1944." *American Political Science Review,* XXXIX (October, 1945), 899–925.

Patterson, James T. "A Conservative Coalition in Congress, 1933–1939." *Journal of American History,* LII (March, 1966), 757–72.

————. "The Failure of Party Realignment in the South, 1937–1939." *Journal of Politics,* XXVII (August, 1965), 602–17.

Phillips, Ulrich B. "The Central Theme of Southern History." *American Historical Review,* XXIV (October, 1928), 30–43.

Podhoretz, Norman. "Truman and the Idea of the Common Man." *Commentary,* XXI (May, 1956), 469–74.

Price, Hugh D. "The Negro and Florida Politics." *Journal of Politics,* XVII (May, 1955), 198–220.

Robinson, George W. "Alben Barkley and the 1944 Tax Veto." *Register of the Kentucky Historical Society,* LXVII (July, 1969), 197–210.

Rockwell, Landon G. "The Planning Function of the National Resources Planning Board." *Journal of Politics,* VII (May, 1945), 169–78.

Rosenfarb, Joseph. "Labor's Role in the Election." *Public Opinion Quarterly,* VIII (Fall, 1944), 376–90.

Shannon, Jasper B. "Presidential Politics in the South." *Journal of Politics,* X (August, 1948), 464–89.

Sitkoff, Harvard. "Harry Truman and the Election of 1948: The Coming of Age of Civil Rights in American Politics." *Journal of Southern History,* XXXVII (November, 1971), 597–616.

Stone, Alfred H. "A Mississippian's View of Civil Rights, States' Rights, and the Reconstruction Background." *Journal of Mississippi History,* X (July, 1948), 181–239.

Strong, Donald S. "The Rise of Negro Voting in Texas." *American Political Science Review,* XLII (June, 1948), 510–22.

Swisher, Carl B. "The Supreme Court and the South." *Journal of Politics,* X (May, 1948), 282–305.

Weeks, O. Douglas. "The White Primary, 1944–1948." *American Political Science Review,* XLII (June, 1948), 500–10.

Williams, Henry N. "The Poll Tax and Constitutional Problems Involved in Its Repeal." *University of Chicago Law Review,* XI (February, 1944), 177–83.

Zeigler, Luther H. "Senator Walter George's 1938 Campaign." *Georgia Historical Quarterly,* XLIII (December, 1959), 333–53.

Unpublished Studies

Ader, Emile B. "The Dixiecrat Movement: A Study in American Politics." Ph.D. dissertation, University of California, 1951.

Arnold, Delbert D. "The CIO's Role in American Politics." Ph.D. dissertation, University of Maryland, 1952.

Ashley, Frank W. "Selected Southern Liberal Editors and the States'

Rights Movement of 1948." Ph.D. dissertation, University of South Carolina, 1959.

Barker, Lucius J. "Offshore Oil Politics: A Study in Public Policy Making." Ph.D. dissertation, University of Illinois, 1954.

Berman, William C. "The Politics of Civil Rights in the Truman Administration." Ph.D. dissertation, Ohio State University, 1963.

Bernstein, Barton J. "The Ambiguous Legacy: The Truman Administration and Civil Rights." Paper in Harry S. Truman Library.

Burrows, Edward F. "The Commission on Interracial Cooperation." Ph.D. dissertation, University of Wisconsin, 1954.

Carneal, Thomas W. "President Truman's Leadership in the Field of Civil Rights Legislation." M.A. thesis, University of Kansas City, 1965.

Chesteen, Richard Dallas. "The 1948 States' Rights Movement in Mississippi." M.A. thesis, University of Mississippi, 1964.

Crownover, A. Blair. "Franklin D. Roosevelt and the Primary Campaigns of the 1938 Congressional Election." Senior thesis, Princeton University, 1955.

Dalfiume, Richard M. "Desegregation of the United States Armed Forces, 1939–1953." Ph.D. dissertation, University of Missouri, 1966.

Davies, Reynold J. "A Study of Federal Civil Rights Programs During the Presidency of Harry S. Truman." M.A. thesis, University of Kansas, 1959.

Hamby, Alonzo Lee. "Harry S. Truman and American Liberalism, 1945–1948." Ph.D. dissertation, University of Missouri, 1965.

Hartmann, Susan M. "President Truman and the Eightieth Congress." Ph.D. dissertation, University of Missouri, 1966.

Hilliard, Elbert Riley. "A Biography of Fielding Wright: Mississippi's Mr. States' Rights." M.A. thesis, Mississippi State University, 1959.

Hinchey, Mary H. "The Frustration of the New Deal Revival, 1944–1946." Ph.D. dissertation, University of Missouri, 1965.

Kifer, Allen F. "The Negro Under the New Deal, 1933–1941." Ph.D. dissertation, University of Wisconsin, 1961.

Kirkendall, Richard S. "Truman and the South." Paper in possession of the author.

Leary, William H. "Race Relations in Turmoil: Southern Liberals and World War II." M.A. thesis, University of Virginia, 1967.

Minton, John D. "The New Deal in Tennessee, 1932–1938." Ph.D. dissertation, Vanderbilt University, 1959.

Morgan, Ruth L. P. "The Presidential Executive Order as an Instrument for Policy-Making." Ph.D. dissertation, Louisiana State University, 1966.

Murray, William D. "The Folsom Gubernatorial Campaign of 1946." M.A. thesis, University of Alabama, 1949.

Owen, Hugh Carl. "The Rise of Negro Voting in Georgia, 1944–1950." M.A. thesis, Emory University, 1951.

Patenaude, Lionel V. "The New Deal and Texas." Ph.D. dissertation, University of Texas, 1953.

Poen, Monte. "The Truman Administration and National Health Insurance." Ph.D. dissertation, University of Missouri, 1967.

Riker, William H. "The CIO in Politics, 1936–1946." Ph.D. dissertation, Harvard University, 1948.

Ross, Hugh. "The Third Term Campaign of 1940." Ph.D. dissertation, Stanford University, 1959.

Saenger, Martha Lee. "Labor Political Action at Mid-Twentieth Century: A Case Study of the CIO-PAC Campaigns of 1944 and the Textile Workers Union of America." Ph.D. dissertation, Ohio State University, 1959.

Stayer, James M. "A History of the Presidential Campaign of 1948." M.A. thesis, University of Virginia, 1958.

Stoesen, Alexander R. "The Senatorial Career of Claude D. Pepper." Ph.D. dissertation, University of North Carolina, 1965.

Street, Kenneth W. "Harry S. Truman: His Role as Legislative Leader, 1945–1948." Ph.D. dissertation, University of Texas, 1963.

Taylor, Thomas Elkin. "A Political Biography of Ellis Arnall." M.A. thesis, Emory University, 1959.

Thiel, Robert Ellis. "Kenneth D. McKellar and the Politics of the Tennessee Valley Authority." M.A. thesis, University of Virginia, 1967.

Tolleson, William Jean. "The Rift in the Texas Democratic Party, 1944." M.A. thesis, University of Texas, 1953.

Index

Acheson, Dean, 186
Adams, Arthur, 257
Agricultural Adjustment Administration, 5, 6
Alabama, 23, 83
Alabama: 1942 elections in, 27; 1944 senatorial primary in, 105–106; Negro voting in, 173, 183–85; 1946 gubernatorial primary in, 189–90; States' Rights revolt in, 251–54, 274, 281, 293, 294, 311–12; walk-out of, in 1948 Democratic convention, 280; support for Eisenhower in, 319
Alabama Dry Dock and Shipbuilding Company, 86–87
Alexander, Will W., 78, 80
Allred, James, 109
American Civil Liberties Union, 63
American Democratic National Committee, 103
American Federation of Labor (AFL), 56, 74, 187–88
American Jewish Committee, 63
Americans for Democratic Action (ADA): formed, 227; maneuvers of, in 1948 Democratic convention, 268–70, 271, 273, 277, 278; and Truman, 306; mentioned, 264
Ames, Jessie Daniel, 26, 78
Antilynching legislation, 18
Anti–New Deal bloc: and Smith-Connally bill, 41; and election campaign of 1944, pp. 103–104, 107–13; and employment act, 147, 149–50; and

price controls, 151–53, 154; mentioned, 33–38, 55, 95, 260, 281. *See also* Southern Democrats
Anti-poll tax legislation: debated, 24–25, 42–44; and CIO-PAC, 59; and Southern Conference for Human Welfare, 80; and Truman administration, 143–44, 202, 224, 233; mentioned, 78, 127, 293
Arkansas: anti-Truman sentiment in, 242; States' Rights revolt in, 257–58, 295–96; and conference of States' Rights Democrats, 262
Arkansas Free Enterprise Association, 257, 281
Arnall, Ellis G.: in election of 1942, p. 26; on race relations in Georgia, 88; on formation of southern party, 95–96, 112; and election laws in Georgia, 174, 178, 180; and Henry Wallace, 178
Arnold, Remmie, 160, 188
Arvey, Jacob, 269
Atlanta Conference, 79
Austin, Warren, 10

Bailey, Josiah W.: on the New Deal, 2, 5, 10, 12, 17; on composition of Democratic party, 30, 77–78, 93; and wartime politics, 33; on implications of soldiers' vote bill, 47–49, 52; on *Smith* v. *Allwright*, 91; on Truman administration, 132, 146
Ball, William Watts, 102